Fiscal Policy Making in the European Union

Fiscal Policy Making in the European Union

An assessment of current practice and challenges

Edited by
Martin Larch and João Nogueira Martins

LONDON AND NEW YORK

First published 2009 by Routledge

2 Park Square, Milton Park, Abingdon, Oxfordshire OX14 4RN
52 Vanderbilt Avenue, New York, NY 10017

Routledge is an imprint of the Taylor & Francis Group, an informa business

First issued in paperback 2018

Copyright © European Communities, 2009

The information and views set out in this book are those of the authors and do not necessarily reflect those of the Commission of the European Communities

All rights reserved. No part of this book may be reprinted or reproduced or utilised in any form or by any electronic, mechanical, or other means, now known or hereafter invented, including photocopying and recording, or in any information storage or retrieval system, without permission in writing from the publishers.

Notice:
Product or corporate names may be trademarks or registered trademarks, and are used only for identification and explanation without intent to infringe.

ISBN 978-1-138-42546-0 (hbk)
ISBN 978-92-79-11451-9 (pbk)

Typeset in 10.5 on 12pt Baskerville by
Taylor & Francis Books

Contents

List of figures	ix
List of tables	xi
List of contributors	xiii

1 Introduction 1
MARTIN LARCH AND JOÃO NOGUEIRA MARTINS

PART I
Long-term sustainability 5

2 A further inquiry into the sustainability of fiscal policy in the EU 7
FERNANDO BALLABRIGA AND CARLOS MARTINEZ-MONGAY

    2.1 Introduction 7
    2.2 How to assess the sustainability of fiscal policy 9
    2.3 Government debt accounting 11
    2.4 Determinants of the fiscal primary surplus 16
    2.5 A closer look at the response of primary surplus to debt 27
    2.6 Conclusion 31
    Appendix 2.A: Complementary tables 32
    Appendix 2.B: Unit root tests 36

    Discussion, Fabrizio Balassone 43

3 Unfunded obligation measures for EU countries 45
JAGADEESH GOKHALE

    3.1 Introduction 45
    3.2 Unfunded obligation measures 46
    3.3 Evaluating unfunded obligation measures 50
    3.4 General considerations of fiscal and generational imbalance measures for EU countries 57
    3.5 Fiscal imbalance estimates for EU countries 58
    3.6 Conclusion 73

    Discussion, Per Eckefeldt 78

vi *Contents*

PART II
The measurement of the underlying budgetary position and discretionary fiscal policy 81

4   Budget balances decomposed: tracking fiscal policy in Austria 83
    PETER BRANDNER, LEOPOLD DIEBALEK AND WALPURGA KÖHLER-TÖGLHOFER

    4.1 Introduction and motivation 83
    4.2 Related literature 84
    4.3 A stylized framework 87
    4.4 Results 89
    4.5 Conclusions 95

    Discussion, Jonas Fischer 103

5   The dynamic behaviour of budget components and output: the cases of France, Germany, Portugal and Spain 106
    ANTÓNIO AFONSO AND PETER CLAEYS

    5.1 Introduction 106
    5.2 The recent fiscal imbalances in the EU 107
    5.3 A SVAR model for gauging fiscal indicators 109
    5.4 Empirical analysis 120
    5.5 Conclusion 140
    Appendix 5.A Data sources 141
    Appendix 5.B The fiscal indicator: some additional results 142
    Appendix 5.C Recursive estimates of budget elasticities 144

    Discussion, Jan in 't Veld 149

PART III
Reliability of fiscal indicators 151

6   The reliability of EMU fiscal indicators: risks and safeguards 153
    FABRIZIO BALASSONE, DANIELE FRANCO AND STEFANIA ZOTTERI

    6.1 Introduction 153
    6.2 The reconciliation account (SFA) 154
    6.3 Deficit revisions in Italy, Portugal and Greece 157
    6.4 Fiscal rules and window dressing: a simple model 160
    6.5 Conclusions 165

    Discussion, João Nogueira Martins 171

7   Uncertainty bounds for cyclically adjusted budget balances 173
    RAY BARRELL, IAN HURST AND JAMES MITCHELL

    7.1 Introduction 173
    7.2 Estimating the output gap and its uncertainty 173

7.3 Cyclically adjusting the budget deficit   179
7.4 Uncertainty in the adjustment   184
7.5 Implications and conclusions   190

Discussion, György Kopits   192

Bibliography   194
Index   201

Figures

2.1	Primary surplus, debt and output (percentage of GDP)	17
2.2	Posterior density functions for the response of the primary surplus to debt accumulation	29
2.3	Gross debt development	37
3.1	Projected total expenditure and receipts (hypothetical data)	51
3.2	Social security benefit and wage profiles by age	52
3.3	Consumption and wage profiles by age	53
3.4	Fiscal imbalances of EU countries (billions of €)	61
3.5	Imbalances of EU countries – percentage of the present value of GDP	62
3.6	Demographic components of fiscal imbalances	63
3.7	Budget allocation components of fiscal imbalances	63
3.8	Present value of GDP through 2051 (billions of inflation-adjusted €)	64
4.1	Results for the total balance	90
4.2	Decomposition of the total balance	91
4.3	Results for the primary balance	93
4.4	Decomposition of the primary balance	94
4.5	Results for the total revenues	96
4.6	Decomposition of the total revenues	97
4.7	Results for primary expenditures	98
4.8	Decomposition of primary expenditures	99
4.9	Results for the total balance	100
4.10	'Core' discretionary policy	101
4.11	Determinants of the actual budget balance	104
5.1	General government spending, revenue and deficit (percentage of GDP)	108
5.2	Output gap, cyclically adjusted net lending, spending and revenue (percentage of potential GDP)	110
5.3	Impulse responses	122
5.4	Forecast error variance decomposition	126
5.5	SVAR indicator of output gap, structural net lending, expenditure and revenues (percentage of potential GDP)	130
5.6	Sensitivity analysis: SVAR indicators of structural net lending (percentage of potential GDP)	137
6.1	Italy: net borrowing and change in debt (millions of €)	158
6.2	Portugal: net borrowing and change in debt (millions of €)	159
6.3	Greece: net borrowing and change in debt (millions of €)	160
7.1	Germany: budget deficit cyclical adjustment – real time	180

7.2	UK: budget deficit cyclical adjustment – real time	181
7.3	France: budget deficit cyclical adjustment – real time	181
7.4	Italy: budget deficit cyclical adjustment – real time	182
7.5	Spain: budget deficit cyclical adjustment – real time	182
7.6	Netherlands: budget deficit cyclical adjustment – real time	183
7.7	Belgium: budget deficit cyclical adjustment – real time	184

Tables

2.1	Gross debt developments, 1977–2005 (percentage of GDP)	12
2.2	Debt accounting, 1977–2005 and 1977–1993	15
2.3	Fiscal reaction function: econometric results for the baseline model	21
2.4	Estimates of the response of the primary surplus to debt in alternative models	23
2.5	Robustness with respect to the SFAs, baseline models	25
2.6	Refined estimates	26
2.7	Posterior distributions for δ	28
2.8	Government balances, interest payments and primary surpluses, 1977–2005	32
2.9	Implicit interest rates of gross government debt, 1977–2005	34
2.10	Debt accounting, 1994–1996, 1997–1999 and 2000–2005	34
2.11	Unit root tests for gross debt series in percentage of GDP, 1977–2005	36
2.12	Unit root tests for gross primary surplus series in percentage of GDP, 1977–2005	41
3.1	Total revenues, total expenditures, budget balances and consolidated debt levels (2004) – EU countries and EU average	59
3.2	Annual changes in fiscal imbalances: interest accruals and shifting the projection window	66
3.3	Comparing public balances and accruing fiscal imbalances in EU countries for 2005 (€ billions)	70
3.4	Long-term budget reporting	72
4.1	Estimation results	92
4.2	What do the different budget indicators capture?	104
5.1	OECD output elasticities of various budget items	114
5.2	Identification in the long and short term	118
5.3	Parameters γ and α	118
5.4	VAR break date test	121
5.5	Large fiscal expansions and contractions	134
5.6	Net lending elasticity and parameters γ and α	136
5.7	Budget elasticities from OLS on equation 5.7	139
5.8	Elasticities imposed on equation 5.5	140
6.1	Total SFA and its components (percentage of GDP) after revisions	156
6.2	Total SFA and its components (percentage of GDP) before revisions	157
6.3	Determinants of deficit- and debt-specific SFA – EU15	164
6.4	Determinants of deficit- and debt-specific SFA – euro area	164
6.5	General government net borrowing/lending, 2000–2004	166

6.6	General government debt, 2000–2004	167
6.7	General government change in debt, 2000–2004	168
7.1	Real-time and final output gaps as yearly averages	176
7.2	The unreliability of real-time output gap point estimates	177
7.3	Standard deviations of output gap estimates in selected years – full sample and recursive compared	179
7.4	Multiplier effects of a 1 per cent of GDP impulse for one year	187
7.5	Effects on budget as a percentage of GDP of a 1 per cent of GDP impulse for one year	188
7.6	Effects on budget as a percentage of GDP when GDP changes by 1 per cent as a result of shocks	188
7.7	Cyclically adjusted budget deficits	189

Contributors

António Afonso, European Central Bank; antonio.afonso@ecb.int – Technical University of Lisbon (ISEG/UTL and UECE); aafonso@iseg.utl.pt.

Fabrizio Balassone, Banca d'Italia, Research Department; fabrizio.balassone@bancaditalia.it.

Fernando Ballabriga, ESADE; fernando.ballabriga@esade.edu.

Ray Barrell, National Institute of Economic and Social Research; R.Barrell@niesr.ac.uk.

Peter Brandner, Federal Ministry of Finance, Austria; peter.brandner@bmf.gv.at.

Peter Claeys, European University Institute; Peter.Claeys@EUI.eu.

Leopold Diebalek, Oesterreichische Nationalbank; leopold.diebalek@oenb.at.

Per Eckefeldt, European Commission – Directorate General Economic and Financial Affairs; per.eckefeldt@ec.europa.eu.

Jonas Fischer, European Commission – Directorate General Economic and Financial Affairs; jonas.fischer@ec.europa.eu.

Daniele Franco, Banca d'Italia, Research Department; daniele.franco@bancaditalia.it.

Jagadeesh Gokhale, Senior Fellow at Cato Institute; jgokhale@cato.org.

Ian Hurst, National Institute of Economic and Social Research; I.Hurst@niesr.ac.uk.

Walpurga Köhler-Töglhofer, Oesterreichische Nationalbank; walpurga.koehler-toeglhofer @oenb.at.

György Kopits, National Bank of Hungary; gkopits@earthlink.net.

Martin Larch, European Commission – Directorate General Economic and Financial Affairs; martin.larch@ec.europa.eu.

Carlos Martinez-Mongay, European Commission – Directorate General Economic and Financial Affairs; carlos.martinez@ec.europa.eu.

James Mitchell, National Institute of Economic and Social Research; J.Mitchell@niesr.ac.uk.

João Nogueira Martins, European Commission – Directorate General Economic and Financial Affairs; joao.nogueiramartins@ec.europa.eu.

Jan in 't Veld, European Commission – Directorate General Economic and Financial Affairs; jan.intveld@ec.europa.eu.

Stefania Zotteri, Banca d'Italia, Research Department; stefania.zotteri@bancaditalia.it.

1 Introduction

Martin Larch and João Nogueira Martins[1]

Fiscal indicators are the backbone of effective fiscal policy making, including the coordination and surveillance of budgetary policy at the EU level. The quality and success of the EU surveillance framework, in particular the timeliness and appropriateness of any policy recommendation or decision taken in the context of the Stability and Growth Pact (SGP), crucially depend on the quality of its diagnostic instruments. The right conclusions can only be drawn if the underlying analysis is comprehensive and accurate.

Ever since its inception, the history of fiscal surveillance in the EU and of the SGP has inter alia been characterized by a continuous upgrading of the analytical toolkit, so as to be able to respond to new requirements and challenges with the ultimate goal to provide a robust, consistent and accurate assessment of fiscal policy in the Economic and Monetary Union.

The 2005 reform of the SGP has confronted us with a number of important new challenges. Key requirements of the reformed Pact are made contingent on the prevailing economic conditions in the Member States and are expressed in structural terms, net of cyclical factors and one-off and other temporary measures. As a consequence, the reform has broadened and stepped up the scope for gauging the economic and fiscal performance.

As regards the preventive arm of the reformed Pact, the adjustment process towards sustainable medium-term budgetary positions can be modulated depending on prevailing or expected cyclical conditions. In good times the annual structural adjustment should be higher than the 0.5 per cent of GDP benchmark; it can be less than that in economic bad times. The medium-term objectives (MTOs) themselves are defined in structural terms. Finally, as regards the corrective arm of the reformed Pact, the annual adjustment to be achieved by Member States with an excessive deficit is also expressed in structural terms.

Besides the increased focus on structural budget balances, there is another and more complex element in the reformed Pact with important implications for the assessment of fiscal performance, notably long-term sustainability. The EU Council agreement of March 2005, which underpins the reform of the Pact, while confirming the key role of the 3 per cent and 60 per cent of GDP thresholds of the government deficit and debt, puts additional emphasis on the public finance developments over the long term. It specifically identifies the surveillance of debt and sustainability as one of the main areas where improvements can be made to revive the provisions of the SGP.

The increased prominence of both the structural budget balance and the long-term sustainability in the EU fiscal surveillance framework raises a number of straightforward yet taxing questions related to the measurement of economic and fiscal performance. Is the current toolkit sufficiently appropriate with respect to the provisions of the reformed SGP? How accurate are the available estimates of the cyclical position and the structural budget balance? What are the major caveats and how can they be overcome? Besides the available standard indicators, what are the viable alternatives to the assessment of the long-term sustainability of public finances?

These and a number of other issues were the focus of the workshop on Fiscal Indicators in the EU Budgetary Surveillance organized by the Directorate General for Economic and Affairs on 22 September 2006 in Brussels. This volume collects the papers presented at the workshop together with the respective discussions. The three sessions of the workshop mirror the main challenges outlined above, notably (i) long-term sustainability, (ii) the measurement of the underlying budgetary position and discretionary fiscal policy and (iii) the reliability of fiscal indicators.

Reflecting the increasing relevance of long-term issues, the first part of this volume covers two chapters which discuss alternative avenues to assess the long-term sustainability of public finance. The work by F. Ballabriga and C. Martinez-Mongay discusses various tests and rules based on the recent literature on fiscal-reaction functions. They test for a positive response of the primary surplus to accumulated debt in the data and check for robustness considering alternative specifications, estimation techniques and structural breaks. One of their interesting policy conclusions is that stricter conditions do not necessarily ensure sustainability; what matters is enforcement. They conclude that the response to debt has fluctuated over the sample 1977–2005, but sustainability has been prevalent in EU15: most governments have tended to apply a fluctuating but generally positive primary surplus adjustment in response to debt accumulation.

The chapter by J. Gokhale uses long-term economic and fiscal projections to determine if and to what extent current and future expenditure trends, in particular taking into account ageing population, give rise to fiscal imbalances. The results show relatively large gaps which will have to be tackled in the coming years. He proposes the adoption of an extended framework of budget accounting and reporting within the context of the SGP's long-term fiscal policy surveillance requirement. Gokhale argues that traditional debt and deficit measures can be potentially misleading as measures of a nation's fiscal stance and suggests adopting fiscal and generational imbalance measures, as these indicators incorporate comprehensive information about future fiscal prospects under current policies. He also provides estimates which show large fiscal imbalances for most EU countries until 2051. The author acknowledges that different underlying assumptions may generate wide variations in estimates of fiscal and generational imbalances and in their ratios to GDP or tax bases. Yet, rather than an argument against adopting such measures, this implies a need to supplement those estimates with measures of the associated uncertainty.

The second part of this volume is devoted to the measurement of the underlying budgetary position and discretionary fiscal policy. The empirical results in Chapters 4 and 5 highlight a tendency of running pro-cyclical policies, especially in economic 'good' times. P. Brandner, L. Diebalek and W. Köhler-Töglhofer estimate an unobserved components model while A. Afonso and P. Claeys apply structural VAR analysis. These two chapters identify a recurring pattern according to which estimated changes in the headline deficit net of cyclical factors were not consistent with the policy objective of stabilizing cyclical swings of aggregate output. More in particular, Brandner and co-authors track fiscal policy behaviour over time by decomposing the observed budget balance into four unobserved components: a core balance, an automatic or built-in fiscal stabilizer component, a component reflecting discretionary fiscal policy responses to the business cycle, and, finally, a component reflecting all other transitory shocks to the fiscal position. Their results for Austria highlight that the revenue side seems to be prone to pro-cyclical responses whereas the expenditure side shows opposite behaviour. Moreover, during economic downturns, the overall impact of fiscal policy seems to be countercyclical, whereas in periods of economic upturn the impact of automatic stabilizers is nearly neutralized.

Afonso and Claeys' focus is on the relation between the cyclical components of total revenues and expenditures and the budget balance in France, Germany, Portugal and Spain. A disaggregate analysis of fiscal policy in a structural VAR that mixes long- and short-term constraints allows them to look into the transmission channels of fiscal policy and to derive a model-based indicator of structural balance. Their main conclusions are that fiscal slippages are mainly due to reversals in tax policies, which are unmatched by expenditure adjustments. As a consequence, deficits rise when economic conditions worsen but cause a 'ratcheting up' in the size of government in economic booms. The Pact has not eradicated these pro-cyclical policies. Bad policies in economic 'good' times also contribute to aggregate macroeconomic instability.

The result of both teams heralded concerns about the conduct of fiscal policy in recent years. During the expansion preceding the post-2007 global financial and economic crisis, a number of EU Member States did not take fully advantage of the favourable economic conditions to make progress towards their medium-term budgetary objectives (MTOs). Following old habits, they reduced taxes and increased spending in the wake of revenue windfalls just to find out a little later that additional revenues should have been saved for 'bad' times.

The third part of these proceedings calls attention to the reliability of fiscal indicators; the two respective chapters recall and illustrate the margins of uncertainty involved in the available set of fiscal indicators. A critical view of the reliability of the underlying fiscal statistics is offered in Chapter 6 by F. Balassone, D. Franco and S. Zotteri on the basis of episodes of large-scale upward revision in government deficits. They discuss the causes of such revisions and raise attention to the potential for opportunistic accounting, or 'fiscal window dressing' in their own words. A permanent and detailed cross-checking of available data – starting with, but going deeper than, the simple comparisons of deficit and changes in debt – should reduce the scope for exploiting existing loop-holes in the reporting of budgetary positions.

In Chapter 7, R. Barrell, I. Hurst and J. Mitchell provide estimates of the degree of uncertainty attached to the output gap. Uncertainty about the cyclically adjusted budget deficit is further compounded by uncertainty on the link between the gap and the government accounts. They advocate estimates the measurement of fiscal stance should make explicit the bounds around the available estimates on the cyclically adjusted deficit. Yet those in charge of fiscal surveillance cannot waive the responsibility of taking action, even if taking decisions in real time implies taking into account a certain, and in some cases a high, degree of uncertainty.

Note

1 The views expressed in this chapter are those of the authors and are not attributable to the European Commission. Assistance by Fabio Balboni and Stig Malmedal is gratefully acknowledged.

Part I
Long-term sustainability

2 A further inquiry into the sustainability of fiscal policy in the EU

Fernando Ballabriga and Carlos Martinez-Mongay[1]

2.1 Introduction

The Stability and Growth Pact (SGP) is one of the main pillars of the Economic and Monetary Union (EMU). It was agreed with the aim of setting a proper balance between fiscal discipline and the macroeconomic stabilization role of fiscal policy. It was conceived as a discipline device which should ensure budgetary balances close to balance or in surplus, while keeping gross debt at low levels in terms of GDP.

Since the very moment of its conception the Pact has been the subject of numerous criticisms, which would suggest more or less drastic reforms of the institutional framework of the EU Member States (see, among many others, Brunila and Martinez-Mongay 2002; Buti et al. 2003, 2005). The debate on the drawbacks, challenges and possible reforms of the Pact significantly gathered momentum in 2002, when budgetary developments in some Member States, especially in Germany and France, put the Pact under serious stress. The final trigger for reform took place in November 2003 when the ECOFIN Council refused to adopt the recommendations by the European Commission to step up the excessive deficit procedure for France and Germany (see, for instance, Buti 2007).

In a communication adopted in September 2004 the European Commission put forward a series of proposals to introduce changes in the Pact (European Commission 2004). These mainly aimed at avoiding pro-cyclical policies, better defining the medium-term objective (MTO) of fiscal policy, giving greater prominence to the debt criterion, considering economic circumstances in the implementation of the excessive deficit procedure (EDP) and improving governance and enforcement. Taking the Commission communication as a starting point, the ECOFIN Council of March 2005 reached an agreement to introduce changes in the Pact. Where necessary, legislative changes were proposed in both its preventive (surveillance and coordination of economic policies basically through the assessment of convergence and stability programmes) and corrective (excessive deficit procedure) arms (Council of the European Union 2005). The legislative process ended in July 2005.

One of the most recurrent critical issues on the Pact was based on an apparently excessive focus on short-term objectives for the budget deficit, which might not only create incentives for creative accounting and the recourse to one-off deficit-reducing measures, but also lead to almost fully disregarding debt developments, and so to an inadequate handling of long-term sustainability issues.

Disregard of the issue of public debt was considered as a clear limitation of the original SGP (Buti et al. 2005). Consequently, taking public debt and long-term sustainability more into consideration when assessing budgetary positions was broadly shared by policy makers as one of the lines along which the Pact should be reformed. The agreement reached at the

ECOFIN Council in March 2005 gave a more prominent role to debt in the preventive arm by differentiating medium-term budgetary objectives across Member States on the basis of their potential growth and debt levels. Also, structural reforms with positive effects on long-term fiscal sustainability have to be taken into consideration when assessing the adjustment path towards the medium-term objective, when considering deviations from the target, and when evaluating the deficits exceeding the 3 per cent of GDP limit.

The Council also called for giving a stronger weight to public debt in the implementation of the Pact, but was not able to agree on, for instance, a minimum debt reduction for countries with very high debt ratios (Buti et al. 2005). In terms of the role of debt and sustainability, the reform of the Pact also appears limited when compared with some proposals made during the long debate on the Pact, such as the permanent balance rule by Buiter and Grafe (2003) and the debt sustainability pact by Coeuré and Pisani-Ferry (2003). The permanent budget balance is given by the difference between the constant long-run average future values of tax revenue and government spending. The rule proposed by Buiter and Grafe (2003) was to keep the permanent budget adjusted for inflation and real growth in balance or surplus. For countries with debt levels below 50 per cent of GDP, Coeuré and Pisani-Ferry (2003) proposed giving them the choice of opting out of the corrective arm (the excessive deficit procedure) and adopting a so-called debt sustainability pact, according to which countries should submit a five-year budgetary programme with a debt ratio target for the period.

However, if the concern is government solvency such debt criteria impose unnecessary constraints on fiscal policy on the basis of debt ceilings (as the Pact also does) or relationships between the components of the budget and ad hoc discount factors. Where government solvency is concerned, this chapter emphasizes that sufficient conditions for solvency are rather weak, while, as general rule, it does not appear that sustainability has been in danger during the last 30 years in Europe.

Specifically, this chapter analyses sustainability within the framework of the recent literature on fiscal reaction functions, which provides a convenient framework to assess fiscal sustainability. This literature investigates the type of fiscal flow reaction (namely the primary surplus) to public debt accumulation that would guarantee fiscal sustainability. Bohn (1998) and Canzoneri et al. (2001) have developed and applied this approach for the US case. Ballabriga and Martinez-Mongay (2003, 2005) have estimated the reaction of the primary surplus to debt levels for the EU Member States. In the line of Canzoneri et al. (2001), Ballabriga and Martinez-Mongay (2003) focused on the fiscal dominance versus monetary dominance debate. They estimated fiscal and monetary policy reaction functions and found supportive evidence of a monetary dominance regime in the EU Member States. Our paper of 2005 put the emphasis on fiscal sustainability and, in this sense, is closer to Bohn (1998). By fine-tuning the estimation of the fiscal reaction functions reported in 2003, the paper provided evidence of the existence of a structural policy shift in the run-up to the euro (after 1995), which enhanced sustainability.

On theory grounds, Ballabriga and Martinez-Mongay (2005) have been criticized for seemingly discarding the distinction between ad hoc sustainability and model-based sustainability as discussed in Bohn (2005a). On empirical grounds, the availability of additional sample evidence allows one to compare the existence of the sustainability-enhancing impulse associated to the run-up to the euro with a potential post-EMU fatigue, which would have shown up after 1999. Furthermore, the ad hoc dummy-modelling approach for the 'euro impulse' can be complemented with an endogenous mechanism for structural shift detection.

Within this framework, the objective of this chapter is to develop further the assessment of the sustainability of EU public finances. Alternative theoretical and empirical approaches in the literature to assess the sustainability of public finances are discussed in Section 2.2. Section 2.3 takes a first descriptive look at the evolution of gross debt series in 14 Member States (EU15 except Luxembourg), the US and Japan over the period 1977–2005. Section 2.4 presents alternative estimates of the reaction of the primary surplus to debt levels and concludes that a positive reaction of the former to the latter is rather ubiquitous both across countries and over time. This section also presents evidence of a series of structural breaks in such a response, which can be associated to the adoption of the Maastricht Treaty and the convergence criteria after 1992, to the launching of the euro after 1995, and to the adoption of the euro after 1999. Moreover, a positive response of the primary surplus to debt levels is robust with respect to alternative specifications and estimation methods. Comparing the posterior distributions generated by the pre-Maastricht, Maastricht and EMU sub-sample periods, Section 2.5 considers Bayesian modelling as a systematic endogenous mechanism to explore potential structural breaks in the response of the primary surplus to debt levels. Section 2.6 concludes the chapter.

2.2 How to assess the sustainability of fiscal policy

Definition of sustainability

In line with standard practice in dynamic optimization models, we term fiscal policy as sustainable when government debt issuing policy does not use Ponzi financing schemes, i.e. financing strategies consisting in rolling over a given initial level of debt that would never be repaid. The absence of Ponzi schemes in debt policy is a general equilibrium condition required by rational private sector agents in order to be willing to lend to the government. A no-Ponzi scheme condition guarantees that the government intertemporal budget constraint (IBC) is satisfied, so that its outstanding debt is backed by future primary surpluses.

Formally, a no-Ponzi scheme condition takes the form of a transversality condition (TC) whereby the discounted value of debt issued infinitely far in the future is zero. In stochastic economies, IBCs and TCs take the algebraic form of expectations of products of the discount factor and the components of the government budget equation. As we discuss below, this fact turns out to be relevant to distinguishing between existing approaches in the literature to assess the sustainability of fiscal policy.

To make explicit the IBC and TC expressions we start out from the budget equation for period t:

$$d_{t-1} = (s_t + d_t)\beta_t \tag{2.1}$$

where d is the stock of debt at the end of the period, s is the primary surplus, both as a percentage of GDP, and β is the discount factor. Forwarding equation (2.1) one period, iterating forward T periods and taking expectations conditional on information at time $t(E_t)$ gives:

$$d_t = E_t \sum_{j=1}^{T}(\alpha_{tj} s_{t+j}) + E_t(\alpha_{tT} d_{t+T}) \qquad \text{with } \alpha_{tj} = \prod_{j\geq 1} \beta_{t+j} \tag{2.2}$$

Taking finally the iteration to the limit and given convergence of the discounted sum we get:

$$d_t = E_t \sum_{j=1}^{\infty} \left(\alpha_{tj} s_{t+j}\right) + \lim_{T \to \infty} E_t(\alpha_{tT} d_{t+T}) \qquad (2.3)$$

which shows that:

$$d_t = E_t \sum_{j=1}^{\infty} \left(\alpha_{tj} s_{t+j}\right) \Leftrightarrow \lim_{T \to \infty} E_t(\alpha_{tT} d_{t+T}) = 0 \qquad (2.4)$$

The right-hand side term in (2.4) is the TC that excludes Ponzi schemes, so that the discounted value of debt issued infinitely far in the future is zero, and the left term is the government IBC, which states that outstanding debt is backed by future primary surpluses. Bohn (1995) has shown that conditions of type (2.4) apply to a wide range of general equilibrium stochastic models, providing therefore a rather general test for fiscal sustainability.

A key characteristic of (2.4) is that, in a general equilibrium stochastic setting, the discount rate α depends on the risky rate of return, which in turn depends on the intertemporal marginal rate of substitution of consumers (Bohn, 1995). This means that we should expect, in general, a non-zero correlation[2] between α and fiscal variables s and d, and implies therefore that the factorization of expression (2.4) as discounted values of expected fiscal terms is generally incorrect. This complicates the empirical testing of fiscal sustainability.

Testing sustainability

The most common empirical approach in the literature to test fiscal policy sustainability is based on the analysis of the time series properties of fiscal data. Influential papers in this stream of the literature are Hamilton and Flavin (1986), Trehan and Walsh (1988, 1991) and Quintos (1995).

This approach rewrites (2.4) in the form:

$$d_t = \sum_{j=1}^{\infty} (1+r)^{-j} E_t(s_{t+j}) \Leftrightarrow \lim_{T \to \infty} (1+r)^{-T} E_t(d_{t+T}) = 0 \qquad (2.5)$$

where r is usually interpreted as the difference between the expected return on government debt and the growth rate of GDP. Then unit roots and cointegration conditions on fiscal debt and deficit guaranteeing that this version of the government IBC holds are derived and tested.

But versions of (2.5) are problematic. A first problem is that (2.5) factorizes the product of the discount rate and fiscal variables, ignoring that the discount factor may be correlated with the primary surplus and debt, as we have just mentioned. The choice of this discount factor is a second controversial feature of this empirical approach, since, as we have also mentioned, the proper discount factor in a stochastic setting is the risky rate of return (i.e. the return of state-contingent claims), not the rate of safe assets. The arbitrariness of both the factorization and the choice of the discount factor have motivated the distinction (Bohn 2005a) between ad hoc sustainability, based on (2.5), and model-based sustainability, based on (2.4).

The third characterizing feature of this approach is that it tests (2.5) by testing for unit roots and cointegration among debt and the components of the budget deficit. However, the order of integration of debt seems to be irrelevant, as any debt series that are stationary after any finite number of differencing operation would satisfy (2.5) (Bohn, 2005b), rendering the order of integration of government debt uninformative for fiscal policy sustainability.

A more recent and promising alternative empirical approach to sustainability testing is provided by the literature on fiscal reaction functions. This literature investigates the type of flow reaction to government debt accumulation that would guarantee that (2.4) is satisfied. Its main result (Bohn 1998; Canzoneri et al. 2001) is that a positive response of the primary surplus to debt accumulation is a sufficient condition for sustainability. More precisely, assume that the primary surplus can be written as:

$$s_t = \delta_t d_{t-1} + \varphi_t \tag{2.6}$$

where δ is a bounded component and $\delta_t \geq 0 \ \forall t$ with $\delta_t > 0$ applying infinitely often. Then it can be shown that fiscal policy satisfies the general condition (2.4).

The intuition of this result is that by adjusting the primary surplus in response to debt developments the government reduces the exponential growth of debt by a factor δ relative to the discount rate, which is sufficient to satisfy the TC in (2.4).

2.3 Government debt accounting

The evolution of government debt is the bottom-line reference for the sustainability of fiscal policy. In this section we take a look at debt developments in the EU15 Member States, excluding Luxembourg, during the sample period 1977–2005, with the US and Japan as background references. A debt accounting exercise is also performed, which provides an illustrative first contact with fiscal data.

Fiscal developments

While in 1977 debt levels measured in terms of GDP were close to or well below the 60 per cent Maastricht reference value, 15 years later, in the aftermath of the adoption of the Maastricht Treaty, seven European countries, as well as the US and Japan, were recording debt levels above such a reference value (Table 2.1). In three of them (Belgium, Greece and Italy), government gross debt had jumped above 100 per cent of GDP, while in Ireland the figure was higher than 90 per cent of GDP. In the rest of the countries debt had also increased, and it was approaching the 60 per cent ratio in the cases of Spain and Portugal. Until the first half of the 1990s, just after the formal launching of the euro, the upward trend continued in most of the countries in the sample. Only Ireland, Finland and, to a lesser extent, Belgium and the Netherlands had managed to curb rising debt levels. As a result, all the countries in the sample, except the UK, were recording debt levels close to or well above the 60 per cent reference value by the middle of the past decade.

The mid-1990s marked a turning point in debt developments in most EU countries, as well as in the US. Only in Germany, Greece and France were the debt ratios still on an increasing path. Between 1996 and 1999, the debt had decreased by around 8 percentage points of GDP per year in Ireland, by 4.5 in Belgium and by between 3 and 4 points in the Netherlands, Portugal, Finland, Denmark and Sweden. Debt reduction was also sizeable in

Table 2.1 Gross debt developments, 1977–2005 (percentage of GDP)

	1977	1978–93*	1993	1994–96*	1996	1997–99*	1999	2000–05*	2005
Belgium	58.7	4.5	130.5	−1.2	126.9	−4.4	113.6	−3.4	93.3
Germany	26.8	1.2	45.8	4.2	58.4	0.6	60.2	1.3	67.7
Greece	20.1	5.6	110.1	0.4	111.3	0.3	112.3	−0.8	107.5
Spain	12.9	2.8	56.9	3.3	66.7	−1.7	61.6	−3.1	43.2
France	19.1	1.5	43.7	4.6	57.6	0.2	58.3	1.5	67.2
Italy	54.7	3.8	114.9	1.9	120.6	−2.3	113.7	−1.2	106.4
Ireland	58.5	2.1	92.6	−6.7	72.4	−8.1	48.1	−3.4	27.6
Netherlands	37.8	2.3	74.8	−0.9	72.1	−3.9	60.5	−1.3	52.9
Austria	28.5	2.0	60.4	2.4	67.6	−0.4	66.5	−0.6	62.9
Portugal	30.3	1.7	58.2	0.6	59.9	−2.9	51.4	2.1	63.9
Finland	7.8	3.0	56.1	0.2	56.7	−3.6	46.0	−0.9	40.5
Denmark	13.8	4.0	77.0	−2.6	69.2	−3.9	57.4	−3.6	35.9
Sweden	26.7	2.7	70.6	0.8	73.0	−3.6	62.2	−2.0	50.3
UK	60.8	−0.8	47.5	1.6	52.2	−2.4	44.9	−0.2	43.5
US	46.9	1.8	75.4	−0.7	73.4	−3.1	64.1	0.4	66.4
Japan	34.9	2.5	74.9	6.3	93.9	10.6	125.7	5.9	161.1

Source: European Commission for EU15 and OECD for US and Japan

Note:
* Average of the annual changes in percent of GDP over the period. Including the extremes of the interval.

Spain, Italy and the UK. Similar debt-decreasing trends seem to be still in motion in the current decade, albeit at a slower pace. However, debt has continued to increase in Germany and France, while the downward trends have been reversed in Portugal and the US. In Japan, debt levels have not ceased to increase, especially since the early 1990s on the back of a strong expansionary fiscal policy.

Such debt developments are associated to soaring deficits and interest expenditure, and resulted in a perverse feedback between higher deficits, higher debt levels, higher interest expenditure and back to higher deficits, while primary surpluses plummeted (Table 2.8 in Appendix 2.A).

Already in the second half of the 1970s, the sizes of the general government deficits in percentage of GDP were high by international standards in a few EU countries. This was the case of Belgium, Italy, Ireland and Portugal, which, as shown above, recorded debt increases until the early 1990s. However, in a majority of countries, budget balances were below the 3 per cent of GDP threshold and in some cases they were close to balance or in surplus. Deficits soared during the 1980s, and in 1993, in the aftermath of the economic crisis, only Ireland and Denmark were recording deficits below 3 per cent of GDP. High deficits were also predominant until the mid-1990s, and it was only after the launching of the euro that countries were able to rein in deficits. Leaving aside Greece (and Japan) no country recorded a government deficit above 3 per cent of GDP in 1999. In EMU and underlying the slowdown in debt reduction, deficits have risen again, especially in Germany, Greece, France, Italy, Portugal and the UK, although up to lower levels than in the past, especially than in the first half of the 1990s.

A steadily rising debt, combined with high interest rates,[3] put pressure on interest expenditures. In 1977, interest expenditure represented less than 5 per cent of GDP. Only in Belgium, Italy, Ireland and the UK, countries with debt levels above 50 per cent of

GDP, did interest expenditure represent more than 3.5 per cent of GDP. In countries like Spain or Finland, interest expenditure was almost negligible (less than 1 per cent). However, 15 years later, in no European country, except in the UK, was interest expenditure below 3 per cent of GDP, and in the high-debt ones interest expenditure was above (Greece, Italy) or very close to 10 per cent of GDP (Belgium). Since then, the ratio to GDP of interest expenditure has been on a steady downward path. This appears unambiguously linked to the stability-oriented economic policy framework already largely set up in the second stage of EMU (until the late 1990s), characterized by a better control of inflation, which significantly lowered interest rates in many countries, and a fiscal tightening prompted by the Maastricht criteria and further enhanced by the SGP, which reduced debt levels. In the most recent years, interest expenditure has attained levels well below those corresponding to the early 1990s and, in some cases, of the magnitude observed in the late 1970s.[4]

In a majority of countries, primary deficits were contributing to debt accumulation in the late 1970s. Only in France, the Netherlands, the Nordic countries and the UK did revenues overweigh primary spending. However, in the early 1990s, when both deficits and interest expenditures were at their peak, a positive reaction of the primary surplus to debt accumulation seems to be predominant. Only in Spain and France and the US did primary surpluses deteriorate while debt was rising.[5] With the exception of Portugal in the second half of the 1990s, and Japan, a general improvement of primary balances over the 1990s helped to put debt levels on a downward path. However, in parallel with the reduction of debt levels, primary surpluses have actually worsened during the current decade. This is the case for all the EU countries except Spain, Austria and Denmark, where primary surpluses did not deteriorate while debt fell.

All in all, periods of rising debt appear broadly coincidental with an improvement in primary balances, while primary balances have tended to worsen in parallel with the reduction of debt. Therefore, Tables 2.1 and 2.8 (the latter in Appendix 2.A) seem to suggest that fiscal behaviour in the EU (and probably in the US, but less evident in Japan) has overall been sensitive to debt developments.

Debt accounting

Further insights about government debt developments during our sample period are obtained by performing a simple accounting exercise of the sources of debt growth. The exercise highlights the importance of the growth dividend compared to that of the so-called stock-flow adjustment (SFA) as determinants of debt growth.

Expressing the fiscal variables in percent of GDP, the flow government budget identity for period t can be written as:

$$d_t = -s_t + \left(\frac{1+i_t}{1+\lambda_t}\right)d_{t-1} \qquad (2.7)$$

where i is the nominal interest charge on government debt and λ is the nominal GDP growth rate. Subtracting then d_{t-1} on both sides of expression (2.7) and rearranging terms, we obtain the equivalent expression:

$$d_t - d_{t-1} = def_t - \left(\frac{\lambda_t}{1+\lambda_t}\right)d_{t-1} \qquad (2.8)$$

according to which the change in the debt-to-GDP ratio in year t is equal to the budget deficit inclusive of interest expenditure, $def_t = -s_t + i_t d_{t-1}$, minus the growth dividend, the second term in the right-hand side.

In the real world, equations (2.7)–(2.8) do not generally hold. The reason is that the principles according to which the government deficit and debt are compiled are different. As a result, once it is corrected from the effect of nominal growth, the change in the outstanding stock of debt can be larger or smaller than the deficit (European Commission 2005: 108–115). One of the main reasons for this comes from the differences in the gross and net recording of transactions with financial assets.[6] Specifically, the government balance is the difference between expenditures and revenues, excluding financial transactions. However, government debt is compiled in gross terms, and it changes when the financial assets of the government change, thus generating flows of payments and receipts that do not enter the deficit. When the government accumulates financial assets, debt increases above the right-hand side of equation (2.8), while the opposite applies for a reduction of financial assets. Such a residual is known as the stock-flow adjustment (SFA). Taking it into account, equation (2.8) becomes:

$$d_t - d_{t-1} = def_t - \left(\frac{\lambda_t}{1+\lambda_t}\right) d_{t-1} + sfa_t \tag{2.9}$$

where sfa is the stock-flow adjustment in percentage of GDP.

Averaging over the sample period both sides of expression (2.9) it is possible to obtain the average contribution of each of the right-hand side components to the average debt growth, all in terms of GDP. The result is shown in Table 2.2 for the whole sample period, 1977–2005, and for the first half of it, 1977–1993. Table 2.10 in Appendix 2.A presents the results of the same exercise for different sub-periods between 1994 and 2005.

Considering the whole sample period, the most striking feature in Table 2.2 is that, as a general rule, the growth dividend has fully offset pervasive budget deficits. The exceptions appear to be Germany, where annual deficits have been around a quarter of a percentage point of GDP higher than the growth dividend, France, with a difference slightly above half a percentage point of GDP, and Italy (and Japan), where the difference is around 1 percentage point of GDP. The table also reveals that SFAs have been important for debt dynamics in an ample majority of the 16 countries in the sample.[7]

The picture changes slightly if one looks at the first part of the period. Until 1993, the number of countries in which the growth dividend did not compensate for the deficit includes not only France and Italy (and Japan), but also Belgium, Greece, Spain and the Netherlands. On the other hand, the contribution of the SFA is even greater than in the whole sample period.

Interestingly, both over the full sample and until 1993, the number of countries that managed to maintain primary surpluses is not negligible, although the surpluses were in many cases relatively small. As a matter of fact, primary deficits appear to be the characteristic of only some catching-up countries, such as Greece, Spain and Portugal, where the growth dividend was relatively high.

A drastic reduction of budget deficits below the average growth dividend, which is unambiguously associated to the reduction of debt levels recorded after 1996, is the most salient characteristic of debt dynamics in most EU countries after 1993, and in particular after 1996 (see Table 2.10 in Appendix 2.A), once the effects of the 1992–1993 economic crisis had faded out, and the enhanced budgetary surveillance and fiscal discipline

Table 2.2 Debt accounting, 1977–2005 and 1977–1993

	Debt	Deficit	Interest burden	Primary balance	Nominal GDP growth	Inflation	Real GDP growth	Stock-flow adjustment
	(1)	*(2)*	*(3)*	*(4)*	*(5)*	*(6)*	*(7)*	*(8)*
				1977–2005				
Belgium	1.23	5.07	7.79	−2.72	−5.09	−2.95	−2.14	1.26
Germany	1.46	2.44	2.81	−0.37	−2.22	−1.25	−0.97	1.24
Greece	3.12	7.73	6.84	0.89	−8.66	−6.82	−1.85	4.05
Spain	1.08	3.14	2.77	0.28	−3.52	−2.31	−1.22	1.46
France	1.72	2.59	2.65	−0.05	−1.95	−1.13	−0.82	1.07
Italy	1.84	7.52	7.58	−0.05	−6.83	−5.26	−1.57	1.15
Ireland	−1.10	3.94	5.36	−1.42	−7.09	−3.80	−3.29	2.04
Netherlands	0.54	2.86	4.56	−1.70	−2.78	−1.37	−1.40	0.46
Austria	1.23	2.54	3.34	−0.79	−2.47	−1.29	−1.18	1.16
Portugal	1.20	5.15	4.61	0.54	−6.11	−4.80	−1.31	2.16
Finland	1.17	−1.47	2.25	−3.72	−1.71	−0.85	−0.86	4.34
Denmark	0.79	0.76	5.32	−4.62	−2.99	−1.92	−1.07	3.02
Sweden	0.84	1.32	4.90	−3.58	−3.46	−2.30	−1.16	2.98
UK	−0.62	2.54	3.58	−1.04	−3.60	−2.51	−1.09	0.45
US	0.70	3.09	2.67	0.41	−2.82	−0.97	−1.85	0.43
Japan	4.51	3.12	1.45	1.67	−2.16	−0.28	−1.88	3.55
				1977–1993				
Belgium	4.48	7.75	8.45	−0.70	−5.74	−3.83	−1.91	2.34
Germany	1.19	2.30	2.56	−0.26	−2.91	−1.85	−1.06	1.80
Greece	5.63	8.89	5.56	3.33	−8.17	−7.70	−0.47	4.51
Spain	2.75	3.84	2.22	1.47	−3.23	−2.51	−0.71	2.08
France	1.54	2.14	2.32	−0.17	−1.94	−1.37	−0.56	1.25
Italy	3.76	9.95	7.63	2.32	−8.23	−6.69	−1.54	1.85
Ireland	2.13	7.31	7.21	0.10	−8.05	−5.23	−2.81	2.84
Netherlands	2.31	3.95	4.98	−1.03	−2.56	−1.30	−1.26	0.72
Austria	1.99	2.74	0.00	−0.46	−2.62	−1.61	−1.02	1.84
Portugal	1.74	6.02	5.26	0.76	−8.30	−6.94	−1.36	3.88
Finland	3.02	−1.89	1.62	−3.51	−1.05	−0.83	−0.22	5.74
Denmark	3.95	2.02	6.17	−4.24	−3.28	−2.52	−0.77	5.22
Sweden	2.74	1.95	5.30	−3.35	−3.96	−3.26	−0.70	4.53
UK	−0.83	2.88	4.12	−1.23	−4.54	−3.59	−0.95	0.85
US	1.78	3.86	2.69	1.16	−3.75	−2.18	−1.56	1.56
Japan	2.50	1.11	1.47	−0.36	−3.57	−1.42	−2.14	5.06

Source: European Commission for EU15 and OECD for US and Japan

Notes:
(1) Annual average change in the debt-to-GDP ratio (%)
(2) Annual average change in the deficit-to-GDP ratio (%)
(3) Annual average change in interest expenditure (% of GDP)
(4) Annual average change in the primary balance-to-GDP ratio (%) (4) = (2) − (3)
(5) Annual average effect of nominal GDP growth
(6) Annual average effect of inflation
(7) Annual average effect of real GDP growth (7) = (5) − (6)
(8) Annual average stock-flow adjustment (8) = (1) − (2) − (5)

framework was in place. Still, favourable developments in the SFA, in many cases reflecting the allocation of privatizations proceeds to redeem debt, had a significant impact on debt dynamics, especially in the second half of the 1990s. During most of the last decade, primary surpluses have been ubiquitous.

Although informative about debt developments and the contribution of different budget components to debt accumulation, data in Tables 2.1 and 2.2 convey scarce information about the sustainability of fiscal policy. For example, one might be tempted to interpret the fact that budget deficits have been the norm in our sample as indicative of underlying Ponzi games. However, sustainability conditions impose very weak constraints on the behaviour of deficits. As a matter of fact, sustainability is compatible with permanent budget deficits as long as they induce a debt growth rate lower than the discount rate.[8] Similarly, a declining debt-to-GDP ratio might be seen as indicative of fiscal sustainability, but it is actually compatible with Ponzi schemes whereby the government rolls over a given level of debt when the interest rate on government debt is lower than the GDP growth rate. This analysis above suggests in fact that commonly used fiscal indicators may be misleading as signals of sustainability and that more formal approaches are needed in order to establish whether a given fiscal policy is sustainable.

2.4 Determinants of the fiscal primary surplus

Baseline model

In accordance with the fiscal reaction function approach to sustainability discussed in Section 2.2, we start with the following basic specification of the determinants of the primary surplus:

$$s_t = c + \delta d_{t-1} + \gamma x_t + \rho s_{t-1} + \varepsilon_t \tag{2.10}$$

The motivation for equation (2.10) is to capture the potential response of the primary surplus to debt, while trying to avoid omitted variable bias. To that end we include two components considered important in government fiscal behaviour: on the one hand, the response to the cyclical conditions of the economy, as represented by the output gap x; on the other hand, the inertial process typically associated with fiscal policy that is captured by the primary surplus lag. Finally, equation (2.10) incorporates a random term representing other potential factors affecting the evolution of the primary surplus, as for example non-systematic discretionary policy actions.

Figure 2.1 plots the three series involved in equation (2.10) for each one of the 16 countries in the sample. As already pointed out in Section 2.3, there seems to be in a number of countries a positive correlation between the primary surplus and the stock of debt at the end of the previous period. Interestingly, although one would have expected a strong positive correlation between primary surpluses and output gaps, so primary balances would improve in times of positive output gaps, Figure 2.1 seems to suggest that in a number of countries such an automatic counter-cyclical behaviour of the primary balances has been offset by pro-cyclical discretionary fiscal policies.

Table 2.3 presents summary statistics related to the estimation of model (2.10) by ordinary least squares (OLS). A positive and statistically significant (at 5 per cent at least) response is observed in Belgium, Spain, Italy, the Netherlands, Portugal, Denmark, Sweden, the UK and the US. In the rest of the countries, except in Japan, the reaction of the primary

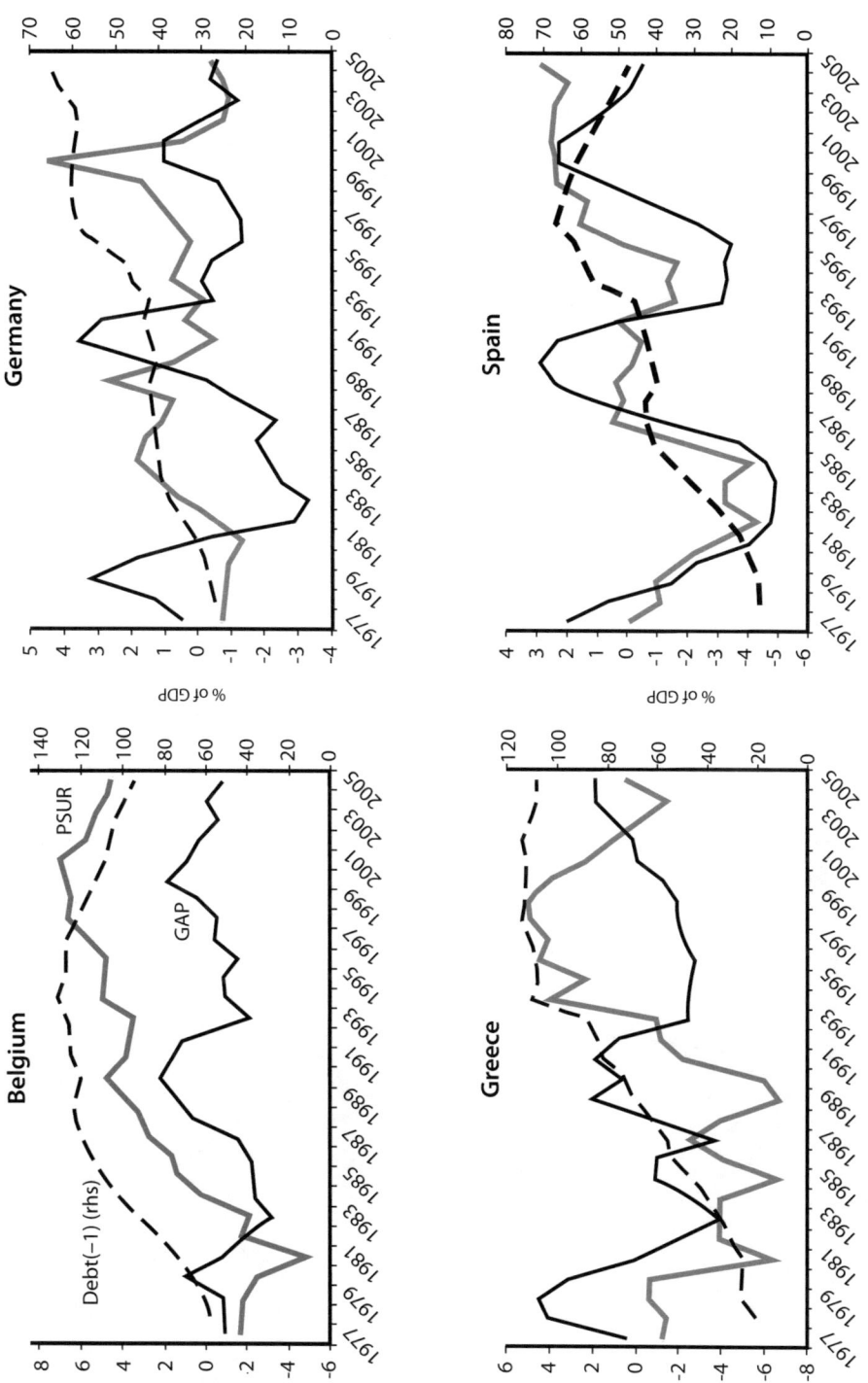

Figure 2.1 Primary surplus, debt and output (percentage of GDP).

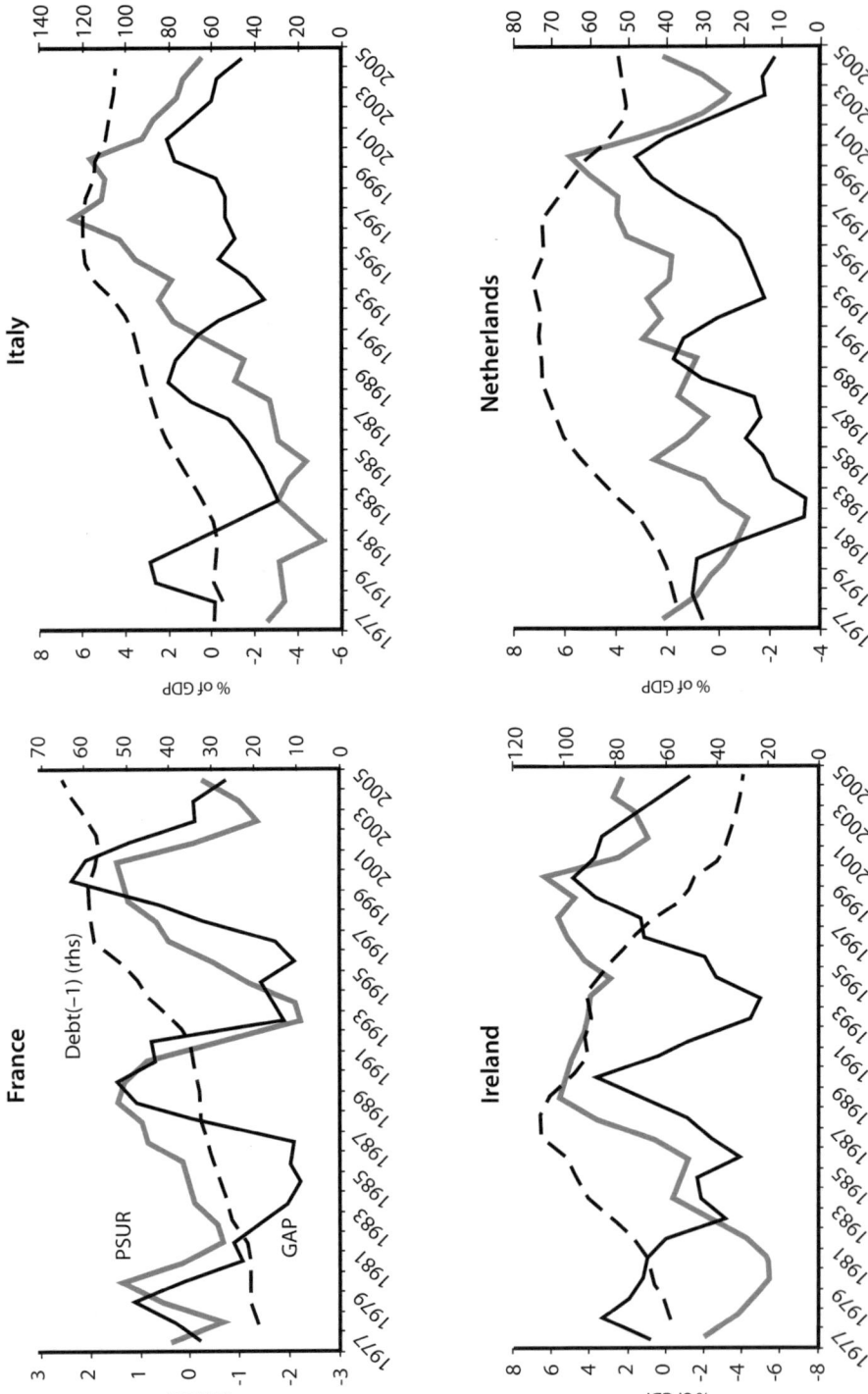

Figure 2.1 continued

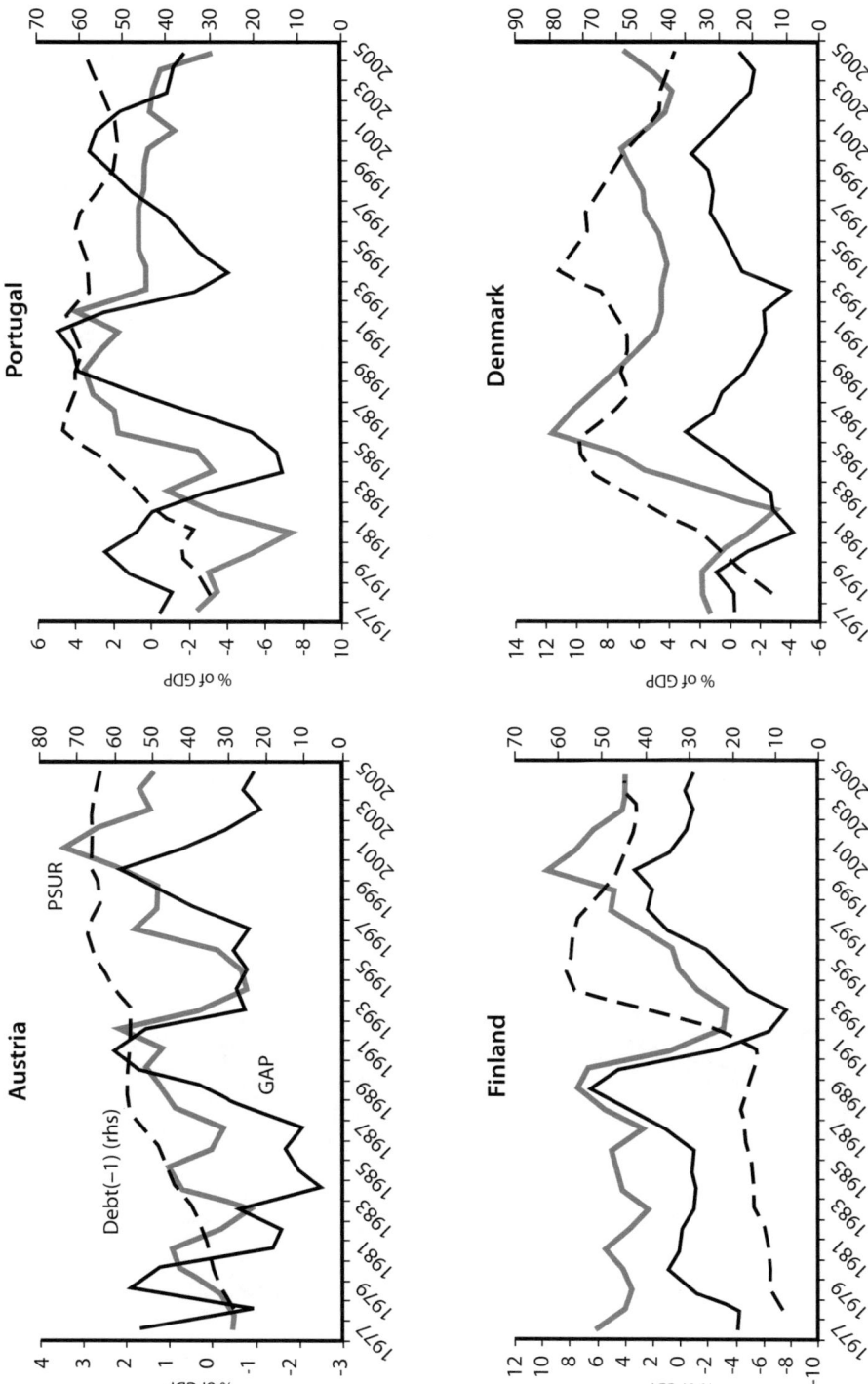

Figure 2.1 continued

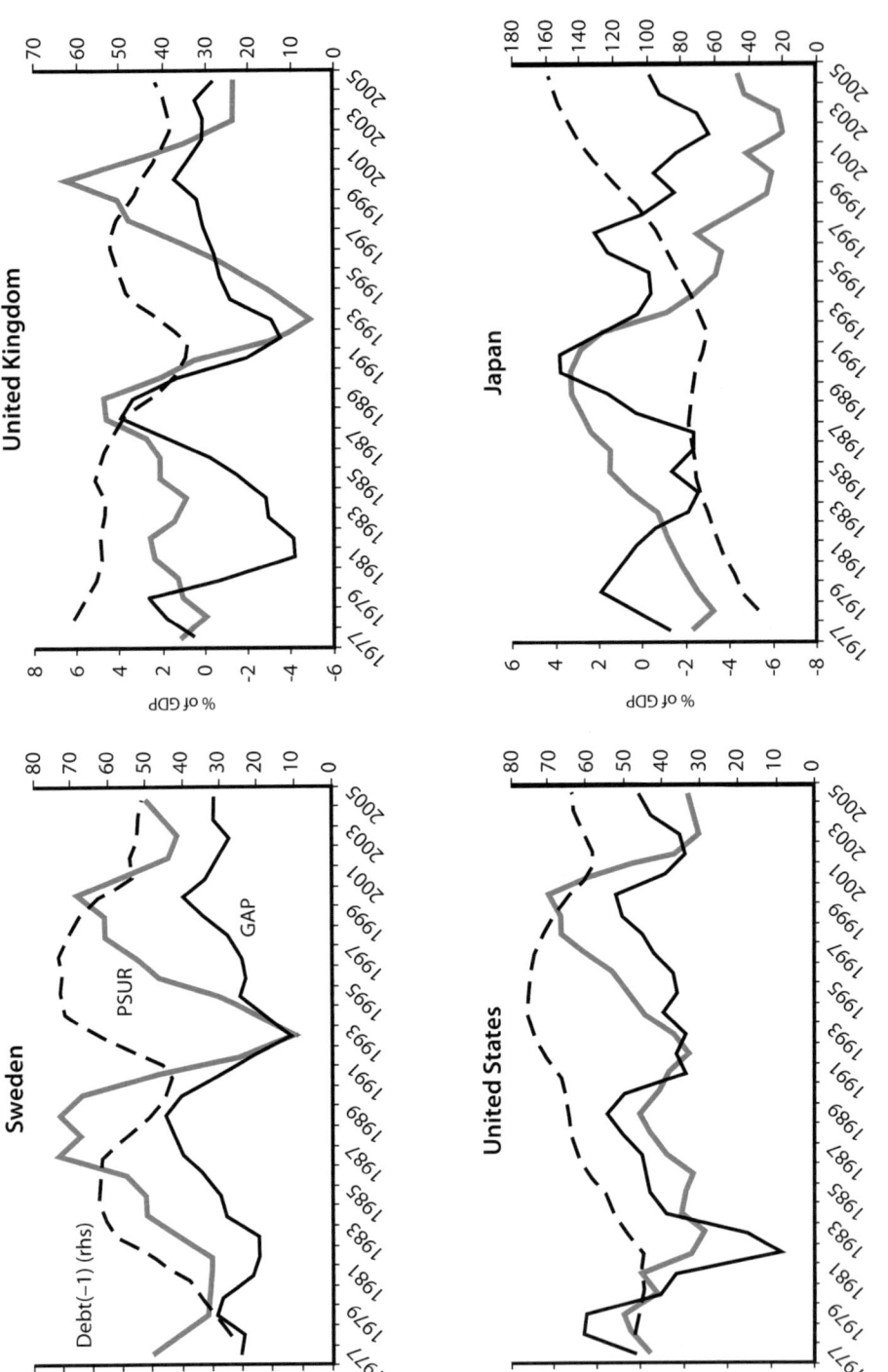

Figure 2.1 continued

balance to debt stocks is either significant at 10 per cent (Ireland and Austria) or non-significant, although the estimate is positive. Only in Japan is the estimate negative but non-significant. When significant, the reaction of the primary surplus to the output gap is positive, thus pointing to counter-cyclical fiscal policies. This seems to be the case in most EU Member States not in the euro area, as well as in Finland, Austria and, to a much lesser extent, Portugal. In Belgium, Germany, Greece and Ireland the correlation between the primary balance and the output gap is negative albeit non-significant. Finally, in all the countries, except in Portugal, the inertia is statistically significant, positive indeed and in some cases relatively strong. In countries like Ireland, Japan and, to a lesser extent, Belgium, the UK and the US it appears pretty close to 1.

Table 2.3 Fiscal reaction function: econometric results for the baseline model

	Intercept	DEBT	GAP	$PSUR_{-1}$	R^2	h-Durbin
Belgium	−2.64	0.03	−0.01	0.78	0.95	−1.73
	0.82***	0.01***	0.13	0.09***		
Germany	−0.11	0.01	−0.14	0.49	0.33	−0.54
	0.69	0.02	0.10	0.24**		
Greece	−2.48	0.03	−0.08	0.65	0.74	0.01
	1.38*	0.02	0.16	0.13***		
Spain	−1.50	0.04	0.19	0.57	0.82	0.001
	0.42**	0.01***	0.12	0.18***		
France	0.04	0.00	0.11	0.59	0.48	6.06
	0.55	0.01	0.16	0.19***		
Italy	−4.93	0.06	0.01	0.61	0.92	0.09
	1.59***	0.02***	0.11	0.10***		
Ireland	−1.12	0.02*	−0.05	0.91	0.88	0.76
	0.98	0.01	0.11	0.06***		
Netherlands	−1.51	0.04	0.26	0.44	0.57	0.98
	−1.01	0.02**	0.21	0.21**		
Austria	−0.63	0.02*	0.20	0.45	0.48	0.68
	0.61	0.01	0.10**	0.16***		
Portugal	−8.37	0.15	0.18	0.27	0.72	2.00
	−2.80***	0.05***	0.10*	0.16		
Finland	1.71	0.01	0.51	0.51	0.78	1.34
	0.55***	0.01	0.12***	0.10***		
Denmark	−0.15	0.04	0.51	0.62	0.84	2.57
	0.62	0.02**	0.16***	0.10***		
Sweden	−0.82	0.07	1.12	0.42	0.84	2.41
	1.68	0.03***	0.31***	0.14***		
UK	−5.48	0.12	0.25	0.77	0.78	1.34
	1.61***	0.03***	0.12**	0.09***		
US	−2.08	0.04	0.33	0.74	0.79	2.68
	0.98**	0.02**	0.07***	0.10***		
Japan	0.03	−0.00	0.02	0.93	0.86	1.78
	0.47	0.01	0.11	0.08***		

Source: European Commission for EU15 and OECD for US and Japan

Notes: The sample period is 1997–2005
Models estimated by OLSQ with heteroskedastic-consistent standard errors
*** significant at 1%;
** significant at 5%;
* significant at 10%

In general, and given its simplicity, the explanatory power of the model is relatively good. In any case, it is comparable to or better than other estimates in the literature, such as Ballabriga and Martinez-Mongay (2003) or Bohn (2005a). The explanatory power is high in Belgium, Greece, Spain, Italy, Ireland, Finland, Denmark, Sweden, the UK, the US and Japan, where 75 per cent or more of the variability of the primary surplus within the sample period is explained by the stock of debt, the output gap and the inertia. However, in some cases, such as Germany, France and Austria, the explanatory power of the model is lower. In addition, although in many countries the model passes the usual specification tests, in others, such as Belgium, France, Portugal, Denmark, Sweden, the US and Japan, the h-Durbin statistic suggests a clear departure from the white noise hypothesis for the residuals.

Robustness checks

Taken at face value, Table 2.3 raises some doubts about the sustainability of fiscal policies in Germany, Greece, France, Ireland, Austria, Finland and, indeed, Japan, where a positive and significant reaction of the primary balance to the stock of debt has not been estimated. However, according to Section 2.2, the reaction of the primary surplus to debt levels does not need to be positive all the time, while the descriptive analysis carried out in Section 2.3 suggests that fiscal policy has changed over the sample period, in particular after 1993 once the convergence criteria entered into force. Therefore, there is a case for exploring possible structural breaks, as well as non-linearity (Bohn 2005a), in the response of the primary balance to the stock of debt. In addition, the fact that the fiscal policy stance may have an impact on the cycle would imply that output gaps may be partially determined by the primary surplus, thus leading to simultaneity biases (Ballabriga and Martinez-Mongay 2003), which might put into question the estimation method and advocate for instrumental variable methods. Alternatively, it might also call for the substitution of the contemporaneous output gap by the lagged one in order to avoid simultaneity. Finally, the parameters in specification (2.10) can be seen as a linearization of the parameters in a partial adjustment non-linear model, in which the actual responses of the primary balance to the debt and the output gap are the estimates in (2.10) divided by the complement of the inertia (Ballabriga and Martinez-Mongay 2005). This would ask for a non-linear estimation of (2.10). Alternatively, one could consider a linear specification in which the inertia is absent.

Table 2.4 contains the result of the analysis of robustness of the estimates of the primary surplus reaction to debt against the above alternative specifications of the reaction function. In all cases, the table shows the estimate of the coefficient of debt and its heteroskedastic-consistent standard error.[9] The first column reproduces the results for the baseline model (2.10) in Table 2.3. The second column presents the baseline model estimated by instrumental variable methods. Following Ballabriga and Martinez-Mongay (2003), the instrument for the contemporaneous output gap for each country is a sort of country-specific international gap estimated on the basis of the bilateral trade-weighted average of the output gaps of the rest of the OECD countries. Overall, the potential simultaneity bias seems to be negligible. France, where the estimate shifts from positive to negative but remains non-significant; the Netherlands, where it decreases; and Portugal, where it increases but remains positive and significant, are the only differences with respect to the OLSQ estimation. Similarly, dealing with potential simultaneity bias by substituting the contemporaneous gap with the lagged one (third column) leaves results basically unaffected, with just a reduction in the size and significance (10 per cent) of the coefficient in Portugal.

Table 2.4 Estimates of the response of the primary surplus to debt in alternative models

	Baseline OLSQ	Baseline IV	OLSQ GaP_{-1}	OLSQ static	Baseline non-linear	Baseline NL2SLS (IV)	DEBT2	DUM93	DUM96	DUM01	DUM93 DUM01	DUM96 DUM01
Belgium	0.03	0.03	0.03	0.11	0.15	0.14	0.03	0.04	0.05	0.04	0.05	0.05
	0.01***	0.01***	0.01***	0.01***	0.04***	0.04***	0.01**	0.01***	0.01***	0.01***	0.01***	0.02***
Germany	0.01	0.01	0.01	0.02	0.01	0.02	0.01	0.05	0.04	0.06	0.10	0.06
	0.02	0.02	0.02	0.02	0.04	0.04	0.02	0.03	0.03	0.03	0.03***	0.03**
Greece	0.03	0.03	0.03	0.07	0.08	0.08	0.06	0.01	0.03	0.03**	0.00	0.04
	0.02	0.02*	0.01**	0.01***	0.03***	0.03***	0.02	0.03	0.03	0.04	0.03	0.02
Spain	0.04	0.04	0.04	0.06	0.09	0.10	0.04	0.03	0.02	0.04	0.03	0.02
	0.01***	0.01***	0.01***	0.01***	0.03***	0.04***	0.01***	0.02	0.01*	0.01***	0.02	0.01**
France	0.00	-0.01	0.01	-0.01	0.00	-0.02	-0.00	0.05	-0.02	0.01	0.06	-0.02
	0.01	0.01	0.01	0.01	0.03	0.01	0.01	0.04	0.03	0.01	0.05	0.03
Italy	0.06	0.06	0.06	0.14	0.14	0.14	0.09	0.06	0.06	0.05	0.05	0.06
	0.02***	0.02***	0.02***	0.01***	0.02***	0.02***	0.02***	0.02***	0.02***	0.02***	0.02***	0.02***
Ireland	0.02	0.02	0.01	0.03	0.22	0.24	0.03	0.02	0.03	0.01	0.02	0.04
	0.01*	0.02	0.01	0.02	0.17	0.17	0.01**	0.02	0.01**	0.02	0.03	0.02
Netherlands	0.04	0.03	0.04	0.06	0.08	0.10	0.04	0.04	0.05	0.04	0.03	0.04
	0.02**	0.02*	0.02**	0.02***	0.03***	0.05***	0.02**	0.02**	0.02***	0.02*	0.02	0.02*
Austria	0.02	0.02	0.03	0.04	0.04	0.04	0.03	0.03	0.01	0.02	0.04	0.01
	0.01*	0.01*	0.01*	0.01***	0.02**	0.02**	0.02	0.02**	0.01	0.01	0.01***	0.02
Portugal	0.15	0.19	0.03	0.04	0.20	0.21	0.23	0.16	0.17	0.16	0.16	0.17
	0.05***	0.06***	0.01*	0.01***	0.05***	0.04***	0.04***	0.05***	0.05***	0.05***	0.05***	0.05***
Finland	0.01	0.01	0.02	-0.02	0.02	0.02	0.01	-0.26	0.00	0.01	-0.26	0.00
	0.01	0.01	0.02	0.02	0.03	0.02	0.02	0.09***	0.02	0.02	0.09***	0.03
Denmark	0.04	0.04	0.05	0.08	0.11	0.15	0.05	0.05	0.05	0.05	0.07	0.05
	0.02***	0.02***	0.02***	0.02***	0.03***	0.05***	0.02*	0.02***	0.02*	0.02***	0.02***	0.02***
Sweden	0.07	0.07	0.09	0.05	0.12	0.13	0.09	0.09	0.06	0.07	0.07	0.04
	0.02***	0.02***	0.02***	0.02***	0.05***	0.07**	0.03***	0.03**	0.03*	0.03**	0.04*	0.03
UK	0.12	0.12	0.13	0.08	0.53	0.50	0.10	0.15	0.14	0.10	0.12	0.10
	0.03***	0.03***	0.04***	0.05	0.21***	0.19***	0.03***	0.03***	0.03***	0.05**	0.04***	0.04**
US	0.04	0.04	0.04	0.05	0.14	0.17	0.05	0.02	0.04	0.04	-0.02	0.01
	0.02**	0.02**	0.02**	0.03**	0.07**	0.10*	0.01***	0.02	0.02**	0.01**	0.02	0.02
Japan	-0.00	-0.00	-0.00	-0.04	-0.03	-0.02	-0.00	0.05	0.02	-0.01	0.05	0.01
	0.00	0.00	0.00	0.01***	0.07	0.07	0.01	0.01***	0.02	0.01	0.01***	0.03

Source: European Commission for EU15 and OECD for US and Japan

Note: *** significant at 1%; ** significant at 5%; * significant at 10%

The fourth column considers the effects of dropping inertia in (2.10). As a general rule, the reaction of the primary surplus to debt becomes larger in many countries, and significant in Greece and Austria. However, it decreases in Portugal and becomes non-significant in Sweden and the UK. Moreover, usual tests indicate the presence of significant misspecification errors. The estimation of the baseline model by non-linear methods (fifth column) does not change the conclusions of the baseline model either, since the non-linear estimates are very close to the linear ones in the first column of Table 2.4 after being divided by $(1-\rho)$ with ρ as estimated in the fourth column of Table 2.3. Similarly, estimation of the model by non-linear two-stage least squares (instrumental variables with the international output gap as the instrument for the contemporaneous output gap, sixth column) gives debt reactions which are equal to those in the second column of Table 2.4 when divided by $(1-\rho)$.

Columns 7 to 12 deal with possible specification biases linked to non-linearities and structural breaks in the response to debt. Only Greece, Ireland and Denmark (and the US) appear sensitive to the inclusion of the square of the deviation of the debt with respect to its sample average (column DEBT2). The consideration of dummies that take value 1 from 1993 onwards (DUM93), from 1996 (DUM96) or from 2001 (DUM01), individually or combined, has significant effects on the estimates of the reaction to debt in several countries, with interesting implications about the effects on fiscal behaviour of economic integration in the EU. This seems to be the case in at least Germany, Greece, Spain, Ireland, Austria and Finland. As shown below, in most euro area countries, the introduction of structural breaks leads to an increase of the reaction to debt after 1993 and/or 1996, while in some cases the response falls after 2001. Also, the consideration of structural breaks has significant impacts in the US and Japan.

To assess the impact of the large and relatively omnipresent and persistent SFAs showed in Section 2.3, the baseline model has been re-estimated by including a sort of 'gross primary surplus' obtained by subtracting the SFAs, calculated for each year in the debt accounting exercise (see Table 2.2) to the recorded primary surplus. The result is the primary surplus that would have been compiled if positive SFAs had been considered as primary expenditures, while negative SFAs had been accounted as revenues. The results of re-estimating (2.10) with this gross primary balance are presented in Table 2.5 in the rows labelled 'GPSUR'.

Alternatively, model (2.10) has been re-estimated by re-calculating the stock of debt net of SFAs to obtain the stock of debt that would have prevailed had the SFAs been zero. The results are shown in Table 2.5 in the rows labelled NDEBT. Leaving aside the fact that the reactions of the 'gross primary surplus' to gross debt tend to be higher than that of the standard primary surplus, be it to gross or 'net' debt, the main conclusions of Table 2.3 remain unaltered.

Finally, the main conclusions of Table 2.3 also remain when a country-specific selection model is carried out, so that for each country the model with the best adjustment power and the least misspecification error is chosen, as shown in Table 2.6.[10]

If the whole period is considered (see column DEBT in Table 2.6) there is no country for which a negative and statistically significant reaction to debt has been estimated. Moreover, in some euro area countries such as Belgium, Greece, Spain, Ireland, the Netherlands and Austria, the reaction of the primary balance to the stock of debt was increased either after 1993, thus linked to the adoption of the Maastricht Treaty and the convergence criteria, or after 1996, thus in the aftermath of the formal launching of the euro at the end of 1995. As a result, a non-significant reaction in Greece and Austria became significant during the 1990s, thus fulfilling the sustainability condition (2.6). In the case of Spain, a relatively weak

Table 2.5 Robustness with respect to the SFAs, baseline models

	Model	Intercept	DEBT	GAP	$PSUR_{-1}$	R^2	h-Durbin
Belgium	GPSUR	−7.77**	0.08**	−0.18	0.73***	0.85	−2.42
	NDEBT	−3.52***	0.04***	−0.00	0.75***	0.92	−1.62
Germany	GPSUR	−4.49***	0.08***	−0.14	0.13	0.24	−0.20
	NDEBT	−0.03	0.01	−0.14	0.50	0.29	−0.48
Greece	GPSUR	−9.33**	0.07*	0.35	0.13	0.29	−0.31
	NDEBT	−2.89	0.03	−0.15	0.62***	0.74	−0.22
Spain	GPSUR	−4.44***	0.09***	0.53**	0.24	0.70	1.06
	NDEBT	−1.65***	0.04***	0.17	0.55***	0.85	0.16
France	GPSUR	−0.81	0.58	0.38**	0.20	0.26	2.06
	NDEBT	0.30	−0.01	0.16	0.55***	0.51	6.38
Italy	GPSUR	−9.16***	0.10***	0.34**	0.47***	0.91	0.18
	NDEBT	−5.76***	0.06***	0.01	0.57***	0.92	0.13
Ireland	GPSUR	−3.28	0.05*	0.24	0.66***	0.50	−2.65
	NDEBT	−0.98	0.02	−0.03	0.90***	0.87	0.73
Netherlands	GPSUR	−4.20***	0.09***	0.34	0.38**	0.69	−0.28
	NDEBT	−1.95**	0.05**	0.20	0.49**	0.66	1.08
Austria	GPSUR	−5.68***	0.10***	0.07	0.20	0.47	1.57
	NDEBT	−0.54	0.02	0.19*	0.46***	0.48	0.80
Portugal	GPSUR	−13.6***	0.23**	0.35	0.44***	0.59	−0.82
	NDEBT	−7.59**	0.14**	0.13	0.38	0.65	1.98
Finland	GPSUR	−3.18***	0.10***	0.82**	0.21	0.66	2.93
	NDEBT	1.94***	0.02	0.63***	0.39***	0.82	1.14
Denmark	GPSUR	−4.37*	0.12***	1.31***	0.45***	0.79	0.41
	NDEBT	−0.35	0.05***	0.47***	0.61***	0.83	2.88
Sweden	GPSUR	−15.4***	0.32***	1.81***	0.00	0.88	−0.71
	NDEBT	−1.50	0.09***	1.25***	0.37***	0.88	2.36
UK	GPSUR	−6.59***	0.15***	0.39*	0.67***	0.72	0.47
	NDEBT	−7.63***	0.17***	0.28***	0.79***	0.85	0.37
US	GPSUR	−7.97***	0.13***	0.24	0.51***	0.62	0.06
	NDEBT	−2.36**	0.04**	0.29***	0.75***	0.81	2.40
Japan	GPSUR	−1.48	0.00	−0.01	0.67***	0.55	−0.71
	NDEBT	0.27	−0.01	0.02	0.90***	0.88	1.95

Source: European Commission for EU15 and OECD for US and Japan

Notes:
*** significant at 1%;
** significant at 5%;
* significant at 10%

response became much stronger after 1996. In France, the positive and relatively large response of the primary balance to debt was halved after 1993, but still leaving it with a size comparable to that estimated for other countries (around 0.05). In Japan, the change in fiscal policy that occurred after the crisis of the early 1990s has totally offset the secular positive reaction of the primary surplus to debt.

Interestingly, in a number of countries, namely Germany, Greece, France and Italy, there is some evidence of a sort of EMU fatigue, which has lowered the reaction of the primary surplus to debt during the 2000s. The reduction appears sizeable in Germany, as well as in France, where it added to that taking place after 1993. The reduction has also been important

Table 2.6 Refined estimates

	Intercept	DEBT	GAP	PSUR$_{-1}$	Maastricht	Launching of the euro	EMU	Adj. R^2	DW/h-Durbin
Belgium (1a)	−3.73 1.06***	0.04 0.01***	0.13 0.12	0.57 0.14***		0.01 0.004***		0.93	−1.74
Germany (1b)	−2.25 1.00**	0.07 0.03**	−0.10 0.08	0.34 0.09***			−0.04 0.01***	0.55	−0.66
Greece	−2.85 1.23**	0.02 0.01	0.18 0.17	0.44 0.15***	0.03 0.01*** (2)			0.77	−1.38
Spain	−1.20 0.34***	0.02 0.01*	0.32 0.09***	0.26 0.14*		0.03 0.01***		0.87	0.69
France (1a)	−2.44 0.89***	0.11 0.03***	0.26 0.12**	0.18 0.15	−0.06 −0.02***		−0.02 0.01***	0.70	1.96
Italy (1a)	−4.69 1.57***	0.06 0.02***	0.01 0.10	0.67 0.11***			−0.01 0.003***	0.93	−1.16
Ireland	−2.63 1.17**	0.03 0.01**	−0.06 0.10	0.82 0.06***		0.03 0.01***		0.88	1.04
Netherlands	−1.96 0.98**	0.05 0.02***	0.30 0.19	0.22 0.19		0.02 0.006***		0.64	1.49
Austria	−0.32 0.57	0.01 0.01	0.17 0.09*	0.32 0.15**		0.01 0.006*		0.57	−0.70
Portugal (1c)	−13.0 2.52***	0.23 0.04***	0.20 0.08**	0.22 0.15				0.72	1.45
Finland (1d)	2.17 0.52***	0.00 0.01	0.45 0.09***	0.52 0.07***				0.82	−1.20
Denmark	−0.15 0.62	0.04 0.02***	0.51 0.16***	0.62 0.10***				0.82	2.93
Sweden (1d)	−0.94 1.52	0.07 0.02***	0.95 0.29***	0.54 0.14***				0.85	1.52
UK (1c)	−4.03 1.74**	0.10 0.03***	0.23 0.09***	0.78 0.09***				0.83	−0.84
US (1c)	−3.37 0.98***	0.05 0.01***	0.40 0.08***	0.72 0.09***				0.83	1.25
Japan	−2.87 0.52***	0.05 0.01***	0.16 0.09*	0.60 0.05***	−0.04 0.004***			0.95	−0.09

Source: European Commission for EU15 and OECD for US and Japan

Notes:
(1a) The model includes an intervention in 1993 to correct for the effect of large statistical revisions of debt levels that took place in such a year;
(1b) the model includes an intervention in 1995 when the debt rose by almost 8 percentage points ¾ of which was explained by stock-flow adjustment;
(1c) the model includes a non-linear term: positive in the cases of Portugal and the US and negative in the UK;
(1d) the model includes a dummy taking value 1 between 1990 and 1992, the coefficient of which is negative and significant at 1% (-0.15) in Finland and at 5% (−0.05) in Sweden;
(2) the dummy takes value 1 between 1993 and 2000.

Standard errors are shown below the parameter estimate.
*** significant at 1%;
** significant at 5%;
* significant at 10%

in Greece, where the positive reaction of 0.03 that prevailed during the 1990s gave way to the behaviour already observed in the 1970s and the 1980s.

All in all, after controlling for breaks in the baseline model (Table 2.3), Table 2.6 confirms that the fulfilment of the sustainability condition given by (2.6) has been general across the sample.[11] Greece and Finland seem to be the only outstanding exceptions. However, in the latter case, one should bear in mind that the events of the period 1990–1992, when the collapse of the former USSR and the 1992 crisis overlapped prompting a dramatic increase of debt levels (see Section 2.3), made the estimation of reaction function for this country very difficult. In addition, the primary surplus has started to fall only recently while its debt has been on a downward path since 1993, which does not point precisely to an unsustainable fiscal behaviour. On the other hand, we should not forget that our requirement for sustainability is a sufficient but not a necessary condition.

2.5 A closer look at the response of primary surplus to debt

The analysis in Section 2.4 provides robust evidence supporting the conclusion that most EU countries can be characterized as having a positive response of the primary surplus to debt accumulation over the full sample period. It also allows the identification of some significant shifts in the response of some countries as the economic and monetary integration process in Europe has evolved, indicating the existence of some degree of time variation in that response.

However, the analysis of the last section does not allow tracing with some precision within that degree of time variation. This is so because it cannot provide relatively precise estimates of the value of the response in small sub-samples, due to the lack of degrees of freedom. It provides estimates of the average response for the overall sample period, which is then permanently corrected with ad hoc dummy effects after specific sample events. But it does not provide a systematic updating mechanism to obtain explicit probability distributions of the primary surplus response to debt for different (small) sub-sample periods. Explicit characterization of these distributions would be helpful for a systematic investigation of the statistical evolution of time variation over the sample.

This section goes a step into this direction by specifying and estimating a Bayesian version of our basic model (2.10), which avoids ad hoc permanent corrections of the response to debt accumulation. A Bayesian updating scheme is a sensible approach in our small sample setting, where low degrees of freedom and difficulties in applying asymptotic results or establishing long-run statistical properties of time series make questionable the application of classical econometric methods.

Model (2.10) has a vector autoregressive form with government debt and output gap as exogenous variables. This allows a straight application of the Bayesian Vector Autoregressive (BVAR) methodology.[12] BVAR models are well designed to handle the trade-off between over- and under-parameterization in contexts of limited size samples, providing an objective scheme for the updating of prior estimates.

The specification of prior beliefs is in fact the critical point once we move to a Bayesian framework. With long samples, the prior effect on posterior estimates is negligible because sample information ends up shaping the final results. However, with small samples, the prior might be the determinant factor (arguably leading to ad hoc final results when prior information is ad hoc). This will be the case if the specified prior is so tight (very small variance) that final results are unaffected by sample observations. On the other extreme, a too loose (large variance) prior could lead to very volatile posterior estimates, largely affected by new sample observations, as it is the typical case in a context of scarce degrees of freedom.

Ideally we want a not too loose/not too tight prior, a prior that deals with the degrees of freedom problem but is at the same time sensitive to new sample observations that call for its modification. This is one of the underlying principles in BVAR models. A second principle is that the prior odds are tilted towards own lags, which have a higher prior variance.

With these principles in mind our prior specification treats the parameter vector in (2.10), $\beta = (\rho, \delta, \gamma, c)$, as a multivariate normal with independent components and the following mean vector and covariance matrix:

$$\bar{\beta}\begin{pmatrix} \hat{\rho} \\ \hat{\delta} \\ 0 \\ 0 \end{pmatrix}; \quad cov(\beta) = diag[0.5\hat{\sigma}_\varepsilon \quad 0.01(0.5\hat{\sigma}_\varepsilon) \quad 0.01(0.5\hat{\sigma}_\varepsilon) \quad 40(0.5\hat{\sigma}_\varepsilon)] \quad (2.11)$$

where $\hat{\rho}$ and $\hat{\delta}$ are the least square estimates in Table 2.6 and $\hat{\sigma}_\varepsilon$ is the least square estimate of the error term variance in an autoregressive regression of the primary surplus with one lag, a scaling factor helpful to control for the units of measurement of variables.

In line with BVAR models, the covariance in (2.11) gives more weight to the own lag coefficient (50 per cent of the error term variance) than to the coefficients of other variables (1 per cent of the own lag coefficient variance), and specifies a flat prior for the constant term. As for the prior mean vector, a common practice in the BVAR literature is to specify a prior mean equal to one for the own first lag and equal to zero for the rest of the coefficients in the equation. The vector in (2.11) incorporates a slight deviation from this practice by taking as useful prior information the estimates in Table 2.6 for the inertia component and, our focus of attention, the reaction to debt accumulation.

Our objective is to compare the posterior distribution of the primary surplus response to debt across different sub-samples. To that end, we combine according to the Bayes rule the prior information in (2.11) with each of the following three sub-sample periods: 1977–1991,

Table 2.7 Posterior distributions for δ

	1977–1991		1992–1999		2000–2005	
	Mean	Standard deviation	Mean	Standard deviation	Mean	Standard deviation
Belgium	0.05	0.022	0.02	0.019	0.04	0.027
Germany	0.07	0.043	0.04	0.023	0.02	0.010
Greece	−0.02	0.035	0.07	0.049	0.00	0.032
Spain	0.04	0.025	0.04	0.043	0.02	0.015
France	0.07	0.028	0.07	0.032	0.04	0.042
Italy	0.04	0.020	0.03	0.032	0.02	0.014
Ireland	0.06	0.027	0.00	0.020	0.10	0.041
Netherlands	0.04	0.020	0.01	0.033	0.05	0.057
Austria	0.03	0.018	0.01	0.040	0.02	0.044
Portugal	0.15	0.058	0.11	0.008	0.10	0.070
Finland	0.05	0.105	0.06	0.046	0.11	0.031
Denmark	0.08	0.038	0.01	0.015	0.05	0.075
Sweden	0.10	0.051	0.10	0.097	0.09	0.056
UK	0.05	0.039	0.16	0.053	0.10	0.029
US	0.01	0.026	0.03	0.016	0.03	0.045
Japan	0.05	0.017	−0.02	0.028	−0.02	0.030

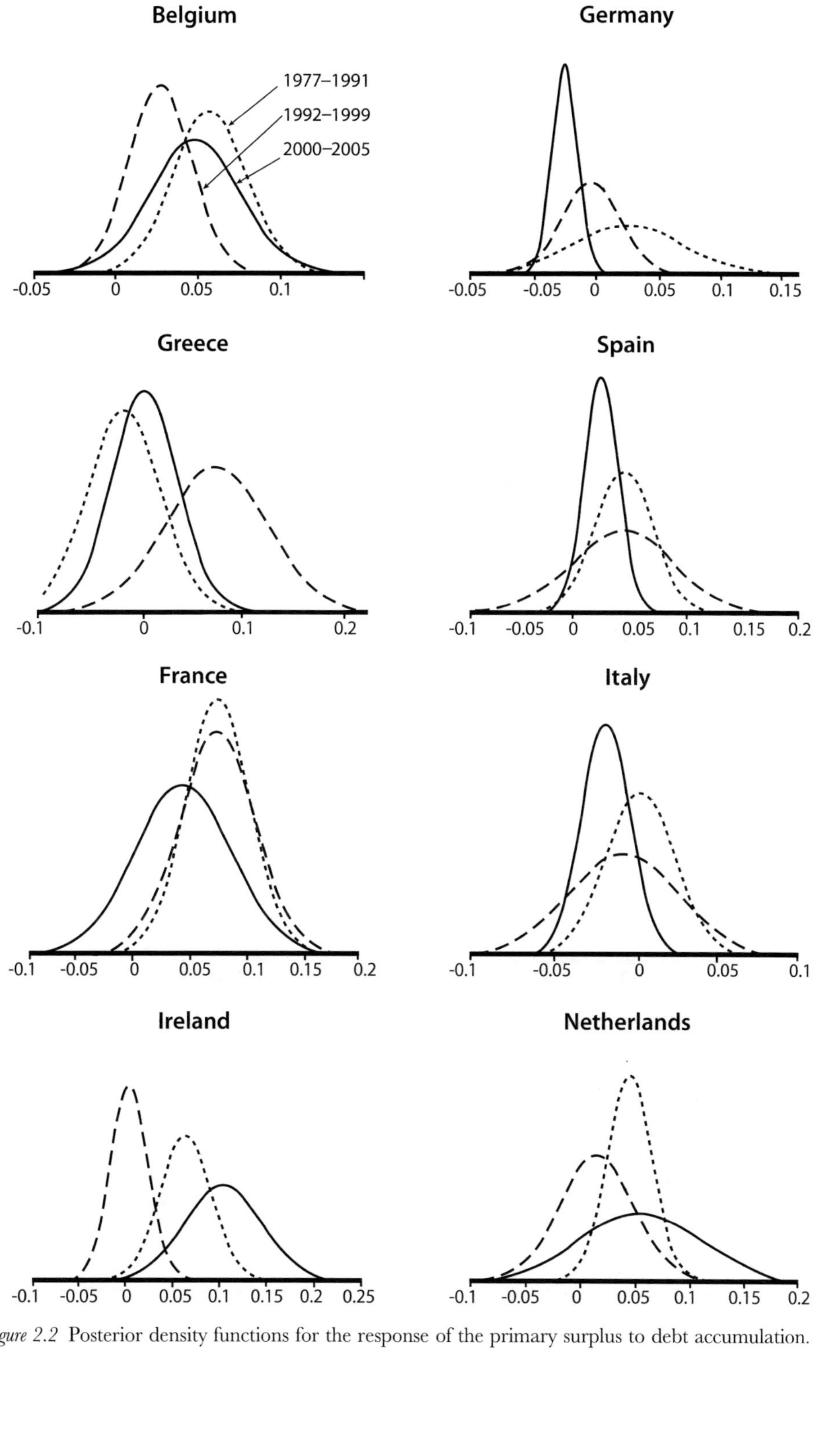

Figure 2.2 Posterior density functions for the response of the primary surplus to debt accumulation.

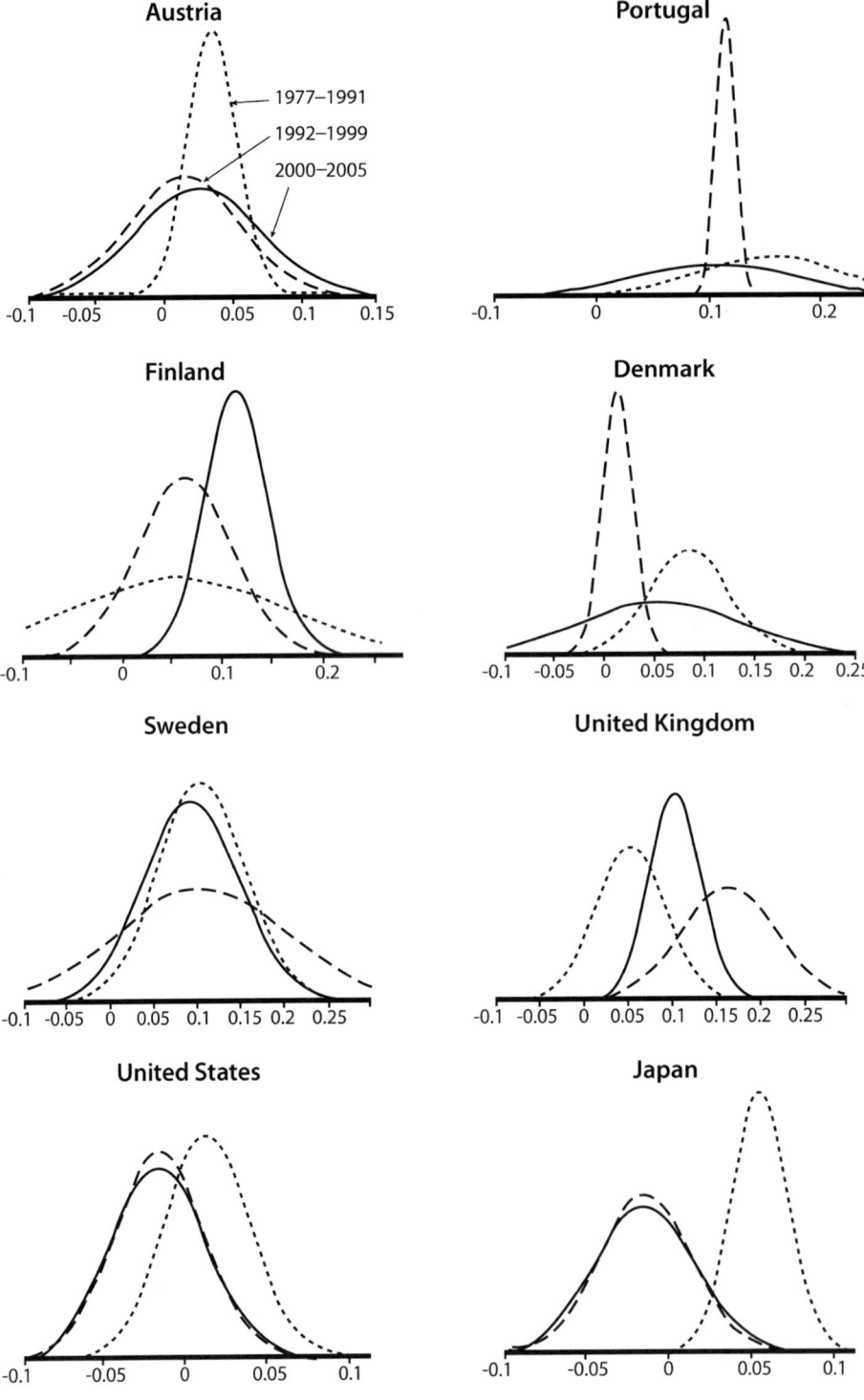

Figure 2.2 continued

1992–1999, 2000–2005. Doing this, we can assess the extent to which the information in each of these sub-periods is compatible with the estimates for the overall sample response in Table 2.6. The resulting posterior densities are reported in Table 2.7, with the corresponding graphical representation in Figure 2.2.

A general feature of the information in Table 2.7 is that it conveys evidence of time variation in the response to debt accumulation in most countries. More specifically, we detect a rather clear shift across sub-periods of the posterior distribution in the cases of Belgium, Germany, Greece, France, Ireland, the Netherlands, Finland, Denmark, the UK and Japan. The rest of the countries in the panel seem to display more stability. On the other hand, in most euro area countries the shift in the posterior may be associated with the economic and monetary integration effects modelled as dummy effects in Table 2.6. Only in the cases of Spain and Austria are the integration effects identified in Table 2.6 not visible in Table 2.7.

Looking at particular countries, some interesting features are noteworthy. First, the results for Germany and France nicely reflect the progressive deterioration of fiscal discipline across sub-periods, especially in the case of Germany. Second, the posterior is centred on a non-positive mean in the cases of Greece (except in 1992–1999) and Japan (except in 1977–1991). Third, Finland now displays a progressive and significant improvement in terms of the sustainability of its fiscal policy. The difficulties visible during the period 1977–1991 are overcome in the following two sub-periods, ending with a sound fiscal position. This is in sharp contrast with the overall conclusion in Table 2.6.

Overall, Table 2.7 conveys a similar qualitative message as Table 2.6: the response of the primary surplus to accumulated debt has been generally positive across countries and sub-sample periods, except in Greece and Japan. This result reinforces the robustness of the conclusion that fiscal policy has been sustainable in EU15 countries during the last 30 years.

2.6 Conclusion

This chapter analyses the sustainability of EU15 public finances in line with the recent literature on fiscal reaction functions. According to this approach a positive response of the primary surplus to debt accumulation is sufficient for sustainability in a wide range of dynamic stochastic general equilibrium models, thus providing a rather general condition for testing the sustainability of fiscal policy.

Our baseline fiscal reaction function specification assumes that the primary surplus responds to debt accumulation and to the output gap, and also incorporates the lagged surplus to capture fiscal inertia. The estimation of this baseline model for the sample period 1977–2005 suggests that a positive response to debt accumulation is quite widespread, thus indicating that fiscal policy is sustainable in most countries.

A main concern of the chapter is the robustness of this result. Therefore, we consider several alternatives to our baseline in order to investigate the potential existence of simultaneity bias, the effect of including and excluding different explanatory variables, and the effect of specifying a non-linear fiscal reaction function. The qualitative baseline result is robust to these changes. We also explore the existence of structural breaks in the response to debt through the inclusion of ad hoc dummy effects associated with specific events along the process of economic and monetary integration in the European Union. This analysis does not change the qualitative baseline result, but reveals the existence of a Maastricht/ euro-launching positive correction in the response to debt in many countries, and the existence of a 'Maastricht fatigue' in some of them, indicating time variation in the response of governments to debt accumulation.

Another main concern of this chapter is to provide an alternative to ad hoc dummies in order to investigate this time variation in the response to debt accumulation from a more systematic perspective. In this respect, we argue that a Bayesian approach provides a sensible endogenous updating scheme in our small sample context, and we estimate a Bayesian version of the baseline model for three different sub-samples: 1977–1991, 1992–1999, 2000–2005. We find that the posterior distribution has tended to shift across sub-samples in most countries, which supports the hypothesis of a time varying response to debt. The comparison of posteriors provides an explicit characterization of this time variation, and indicates that a positive posterior mean for the response to debt accumulation is pervasive. This enhances the robustness of our results.

From a policy perspective, we see two messages from our analysis. First, if sustainability is the issue, there is no clear reason for concern. The evidence for last 30 years suggests that, with the exception of Greece, EU15 governments have tended to apply a fluctuating but generally positive primary surplus adjustment in response to debt accumulation. This is sufficient to guarantee the sustainability of fiscal policy.[13] Second, the posterior distribution from our Bayesian analysis provides a sensible, easy-to-update indicator for the evolution of the sustainability position of countries. A country with a posterior centred on a non-positive response for a given number of periods could be asked for a fiscal correction on sustainability grounds.

Finally, a comment on follow-up research. A natural direction for further work in the issue of sustainability is to try to specify and estimate a model with time varying coefficients. This may require longer samples. A successful attempt, though, would generate time series for the response of the primary surplus to debt accumulation, thus providing the raw material that would allow moving from the objective of testing sustainability, the focus of this chapter, to the objective of identifying its potential determinants.

Appendix 2.A Complementary tables

Table 2.8 Government balances, interest payments and primary surpluses, 1977–2005

	Government balances (net lending in % of GDP)*								
	1977	1977–93**	1993	1993–96**	1996	1996–99**	1999	1999–05**	2005
Belgium	−5.6	−7.8	−7.0	−4.8	−3.8	−1.8	−0.5	0.0	−0.1
Germany	−2.4	−2.3	−3.4	−3.1	−3.3	−2.4	−1.5	−2.5	−3.3
Greece	−2.5	−8.9	−13.6	−10.3	−7.4	−5.4	−3.5	−4.9	−4.4
Spain	−0.6	−3.8	−6.6	−6.1	−4.9	−3.0	−1.2	−0.3	1.1
France	−0.8	−2.1	−5.6	−5.0	−4.1	−2.8	−1.7	−2.7	−2.9
Italy	−6.9	−10.0	−9.1	−8.1	−6.9	−3.7	−1.7	−2.8	−4.3
Ireland	−6.9	−7.3	−2.3	−1.5	−0.1	1.5	2.4	1.4	1.0
Netherlands	−0.8	−4.0	−3.0	−3.0	−1.7	−0.7	0.6	−0.7	−0.3
Austria	−2.2	−2.7	−4.1	−4.4	−4.0	−2.6	−2.3	−1.3	−1.6
Portugal	−3.8	−6.0	−5.6	−5.3	−4.5	−3.4	−2.7	−3.6	−6.0
Finland	5.4	1.9	−7.8	−5.6	−3.5	−0.4	1.6	3.5	2.4
Denmark	−0.6	−2.0	−2.8	−2.1	−1.1	0.6	2.2	2.4	4.7
Sweden	1.6	−2.0	−11.4	−7.7	−2.8	0.1	2.3	1.9	2.7
UK	−3.2	−2.9	−7.7	−6.0	−4.2	−1.3	1.1	−0.9	−3.5
US	−2.1	−3.9	−4.9	−3.5	−2.2	−0.4	0.9	−2.1	−4.1
Japan	−2.8	−1.1	−2.4	−4.0	−5.1	−5.4	−7.2	−6.9	−6.1

Table continued on next page.

Table 2.8 (continued)

	Interest expenditure (% of GDP)							
	1977	1977–93***	1993	1993–96***	1996	1996–99***	1999	1999–05***	2005
Belgium	3.8	8.4	10.3	9.3	8.5	7.6	6.9	5.8	4.5
Germany	1.7	2.6	3.1	3.4	3.5	3.3	3.1	3.0	2.8
Greece	1.2	5.6	12.6	12.8	12.0	10.1	8.4	6.5	4.8
Spain	0.3	2.2	4.9	5.0	5.2	4.4	3.5	2.7	1.8
France	1.1	2.3	3.3	3.5	3.6	3.3	3.0	2.9	2.7
Italy	4.3	7.6	11.7	11.1	11.3	8.9	6.7	5.7	4.7
Ireland	4.9	7.2	6.2	5.3	4.5	3.5	2.4	1.5	1.2
Netherlands	2.9	5.0	5.8	5.5	5.3	4.8	4.3	3.1	2.4
Austria	1.8	3.2	4.2	4.1	3.9	3.7	3.5	3.3	2.9
Portugal	1.4	5.3	5.7	5.6	5.1	3.9	3.0	2.9	2.7
Finland	0.8	1.6	4.5	4.7	4.2	3.7	3.0	2.3	1.6
Denmark	1.7	6.2	7.2	6.4	5.7	4.8	4.1	3.1	2.1
Sweden	2.4	5.3	5.8	6.3	6.5	5.7	4.7	3.0	1.9
UK	4.3	4.1	2.8	3.3	3.7	3.5	2.9	2.3	2.2
US	1.6	2.7	3.4	3.4	3.4	3.1	2.7	2.1	1.8
Japan	0.5	1.5	1.2	1.3	1.3	1.4	1.5	1.5	1.6

	Primary surpluses (% of GDP)*							
	1977	1977–93****	1993	1993–96****	1996	1996–99****	1999	1999–05****	2005
Belgium	−1.7	0.7	3.4	4.5	4.7	5.8	6.4	5.8	4.5
Germany	−0.7	0.3	−0.2	0.2	0.2	0.9	1.7	0.5	−0.5
Greece	−1.3	−3.3	−1.0	2.5	4.6	4.6	4.9	1.6	0.5
Spain	−0.1	−1.5	−1.7	−1.1	0.4	1.4	2.3	2.4	2.9
France	0.3	0.2	−2.3	−1.5	−0.4	0.5	1.2	0.2	−0.2
Italy	−2.6	−2.3	2.5	3.0	4.3	5.2	4.9	2.8	0.4
Ireland	−2.0	−0.1	3.9	3.8	4.4	5.0	4.8	2.9	2.2
Netherlands	2.1	1.0	2.8	2.5	3.6	4.1	4.9	2.4	2.2
Austria	−0.5	0.5	0.1	−0.4	−0.1	1.1	1.2	2.0	1.2
Portugal	−2.4	−0.8	0.1	0.4	0.6	0.4	0.3	−0.7	−3.3
Finland	6.1	3.5	−3.3	−0.9	0.6	3.3	4.6	5.8	4.1
Denmark	1.2	4.2	4.4	4.3	4.6	5.5	6.3	5.4	6.8
Sweden	4.0	3.3	−5.6	−1.5	3.7	5.8	7.0	5.0	4.6
UK	1.1	1.2	−4.9	−2.7	−0.5	2.1	4.1	1.5	−1.3
US	−0.6	−1.2	−1.5	0.0	1.2	2.7	3.6	0.0	−2.3
Japan	−2.3	0.4	−1.2	−2.7	−3.7	−4.0	−5.8	−5.5	−4.4

Source: European Commission for EU15 and OECD for US and Japan

Notes:
* A minus sign represents a deficit
** Averages of the balances recorded during the period including the two extreme years of the time interval
*** Averages of the interest expenditure recorded during the period including the two extreme years of the time interval
**** Averages of the balances recorded during the period including the two extreme years of the time interval

Table 2.9 Implicit interest rates of gross government debt, 1977–2005

	1977	1977–93*	1993	1993–96*	1996	1996–99*	1999	1999–05*	2005
Belgium	6.5	8.1	7.9	7.2	6.7	6.3	6.0	5.6	4.8
Germany	6.2	6.7	6.9	6.5	6.0	5.6	5.2	4.8	4.2
Greece	6.1	9.4	11.5	11.7	10.8	9.0	7.5	5.9	4.5
Spain	2.2	5.6	8.7	8.2	7.9	6.8	5.6	5.0	4.2
France	6.0	8.0	7.5	7.0	6.3	5.7	5.1	4.7	4.0
Italy	7.8	9.6	10.2	9.4	9.3	7.6	5.9	5.3	4.4
Ireland	8.3	8.4	6.7	6.4	6.2	5.9	5.0	4.3	4.2
Netherlands	7.7	8.3	7.7	7.6	7.4	7.3	7.1	5.8	4.6
Austria	6.2	6.8	6.9	6.3	5.8	5.6	5.3	5.0	4.5
Portugal	4.5	9.7	9.9	9.4	8.5	7.0	5.9	5.2	4.2
Finland	9.8	9.2	8.0	8.3	7.4	7.2	6.5	5.2	4.1
Denmark	12.5	11.5	9.3	9.0	8.2	7.6	7.1	6.5	6.0
Sweden	9.0	10.4	8.2	8.7	8.9	8.3	7.5	5.6	3.9
UK	7.1	8.3	5.9	6.5	7.0	7.1	6.5	5.7	5.0
US	3.4	4.6	4.5	4.6	4.6	4.5	4.2	3.5	2.7
Japan	1.4	2.2	1.6	1.5	1.4	1.3	1.2	1.0	1.0

Source: European Commission for EU15 and OECD for US and Japan

Notes: * Averages of the ratio of the interest expenditure to debt recorded during the period including the two extreme years of the time interval

Table 2.10 Debt accounting, 1994–96, 1997–99 and 2000–05

	Debt	Deficit	Interest burden	Primary balance	Nominal GDP growth	Inflation	Real GDP growth	Stock-flow adjustment
	(1)	(2)	(3)	(4)	(5)	(6)	(7)	(8)
				1994–1996				
Belgium	−1.19	4.08	8.89	−4.81	−4.44	−1.65	−2.79	−0.83
Germany	4.20	3.04	3.44	−0.40	−1.60	−0.74	−0.86	2.76
Greece	0.40	9.26	12.89	−3.63	−11.49	−9.39	−2.10	2.63
Spain	3.27	5.91	5.01	0.90	−3.73	−2.33	−1.40	1.08
France	4.63	4.80	3.57	1.23	−1.48	−0.68	−0.80	1.31
Italy	1.89	7.74	10.93	−3.20	−7.29	−5.19	−2.10	1.45
Ireland	−6.73	1.24	4.98	−3.75	−8.02	−1.89	−6.13	0.05
Netherlands	−0.88	2.97	5.41	−2.44	−3.49	−1.34	−2.15	−0.35
Austria	2.42	4.57	0.00	0.54	−2.60	−1.14	−1.46	0.45
Portugal	0.60	5.14	5.58	−0.44	−4.13	−2.48	−1.65	−0.41
Finland	0.21	4.84	4.76	0.09	−3.09	−1.09	−2.00	−1.54
Denmark	−2.62	1.93	6.20	−4.27	−3.79	−1.14	−2.65	−0.76
Sweden	0.78	6.49	6.43	0.06	−3.75	−1.69	−2.06	−1.96
UK	1.56	5.43	3.41	2.02	−2.79	−1.25	−1.54	−1.08
US	−0.65	2.96	3.44	−0.48	−1.86	0.66	−2.51	−1.76
Japan	6.34	4.51	1.28	3.23	−1.02	0.48	−1.50	2.85

Table continued on next page.

Table 2.10 (continued)

	Debt	Deficit	Interest burden	Primary balance	Nominal GDP growth	Inflation	Real GDP growth	Stock-flow adjustment
	(1)	(2)	(3)	(4)	(5)	(6)	(7)	(8)
1997–1999								
Belgium	−4.45	1.12	7.31	−6.19	−4.78	−1.52	−3.26	−0.79
Germany	0.58	2.09	3.29	−1.20	−1.37	−0.24	−1.13	−0.15
Greece	0.33	4.78	9.43	−4.65	−8.95	−5.35	−3.60	4.50
Spain	−1.72	2.41	4.10	−1.69	−4.23	−1.58	−2.65	0.10
France	0.22	2.45	3.24	−0.79	−2.04	−0.37	−1.67	−0.19
Italy	−2.29	2.55	8.08	−5.52	−4.48	−2.49	−1.99	−0.37
Ireland	−8.10	−2.03	3.19	−5.23	−8.47	−2.83	−5.64	2.40
Netherlands	−3.88	0.39	4.64	−4.25	−4.14	−1.41	−2.73	−0.13
Austria	−0.38	2.18	0.00	−1.44	−2.02	−0.20	−1.82	−0.54
Portugal	−2.86	3.05	3.45	−0.40	−4.19	−1.96	−2.23	−1.72
Finland	−3.58	−0.69	3.56	−4.25	−3.66	−1.15	−2.51	0.77
Denmark	−3.93	−1.19	4.54	−5.74	−2.69	−1.04	−1.65	−0.04
Sweden	−3.60	−1.07	5.39	−6.47	−3.10	−0.77	−2.33	0.58
UK	−2.44	0.34	3.38	−3.04	−2.77	−1.28	−1.49	−0.01
US	−3.12	−0.16	3.02	−3.19	−1.81	1.23	−3.04	−1.14
Japan	10.59	5.52	1.40	4.11	0.61	0.36	0.26	4.46
2000–2005								
Belgium	−3.38	−0.08	5.61	−5.69	−3.83	−1.95	−1.88	0.53
Germany	1.26	2.70	2.96	−0.26	−1.12	−0.42	−0.69	−0.32
Greece	−0.80	5.17	6.16	−0.99	−8.41	−3.90	−4.51	2.44
Spain	−3.07	0.14	2.54	−2.40	−3.87	−2.11	−1.76	0.66
France	1.49	2.84	2.84	0.01	−2.18	−1.08	−1.09	0.82
Italy	−1.23	3.02	5.51	−2.48	−4.05	−2.86	−1.19	−0.20
Ireland	−3.41	−1.27	1.36	−2.63	−3.37	−1.40	−1.96	1.22
Netherlands	−1.26	0.94	2.89	−1.95	−2.32	−1.56	−0.76	0.12
Austria	−0.59	1.16	0.00	−2.08	−2.23	−1.09	−1.14	0.47
Portugal	2.09	3.72	2.85	0.87	−2.21	−1.64	−0.57	0.57
Finland	−0.92	−3.81	2.14	−5.94	−1.80	−0.63	−1.17	4.69
Denmark	−3.59	−2.42	2.88	−5.30	−1.96	−1.16	−0.80	0.79
Sweden	−1.97	−1.87	2.75	−4.62	−2.16	−0.80	−1.36	2.06
UK	−0.23	1.21	2.25	−1.04	−1.92	−0.89	−1.03	0.48
US	0.39	2.59	2.05	0.54	−1.34	0.34	−1.68	−0.86
Japan	5.91	6.90	1.49	5.41	−0.37	2.06	−2.43	−0.61

Source: European Commission for EU15 and OECD for US and Japan

Notes:
(1) Annual average change in the debt-to-GDP ratio (%)
(2) Annual average change in the deficit-to-GDP ratio (%)
(3) Annual average change in interest expenditure (% of GDP)
(4) Annual average change in the primary balance-to-GDP ratio (%) (4) = (2) - (3)
(5) Annual average effect of nominal GDP growth
(6) Annual average effect of inflation
(7) Annual average effect of real GDP growth (7) = (5) - (6)
(8) Annual average stock-flow adjustment (8) = (1) - (2) - (5)

Appendix 2.B Unit root tests

The comparison of developments in government gross debt over the last ten years (see Figure 2.3) reveals that debt growth has been entirely nominal in Belgium, Spain, Ireland, Italy, the Netherlands, Finland and Sweden, and has been real in Germany, Greece, France, Austria, Portugal, the UK, the US and Japan. When measured in both nominal and real terms, government gross debt appears to behave as integrated series in a majority of countries. As a matter of fact the usual unit root tests are not able to reject the null hypothesis of unit root for both nominal and real debt.[14]

When debt levels are scaled by GDP a somewhat different picture emerges. After being on a rising path, the debt-to-GDP ratio attained a maximum in most countries around the mid-1990s and has been on a descendent path since then. The clearest exceptions appear to be Germany and France (and Japan). Yet, as shown in Table 2.11, the usual unit root tests, including that by Kwaitkowski et al. (1992), where the null hypothesis is mean or trend stationary when the residuals are assumed to be AR(1),[15] fail to present unambiguous statistical evidence against the existence of a unit root in the debt-to-GDP ratios. (See Figure 2.3.)

Table 2.12 reports unit root test results for the primary surplus scaled by GDP with only marginally more consistent results across alternative tests.

Table 2.11 Unit root tests for gross debt series in percentage of GDP, 1977–2005

	η_μ (1)	η_τ (2)	W-S (3)	ADF (4)	PP (5)
Belgium	0.60	0.37	−1.71	−2.88	−0.86
Germany	1.46	0.10*	−2.04	−2.83	−8.77
Greece	1.44	0.30	−0.63	0.25	0.64
Spain	1.15	0.28	−1.27	−1.44	0.74
France	1.50	0.14*	−1.46	−3.14°	−8.18
Italy	1.28	0.32	−0.67	−1.39	−0.93
Ireland	0.79	0.36	−1.33	−2.81	−2.53
Netherlands	0.44*	0.37	−2.86	−3.18°°	−1.74
Austria	1.36	0.33	−0.25	−0.64	−0.86
Portugal	0.62	0.29	−1.65	−3.74°°	−4.74
Finland	1.15	0.15*	−2.02	−2.21	−5.38
Denmark	0.35*	0.29	−1.08	−2.35	−3.66
Sweden	0.46*	0.19	−2.15	−2.70	−5.91
UK	0.75	0.13*	−2.63	−3.08	−8.44
US	0.83	0.33	−2.18	−2.29	−2.94
Japan	1.32	0.31	−1.32	−3.25	−2.24

Notes:
(1) Test of Kwaitkowski et al. (null hypothesis mean-stationary): critical value at 5%: 0.46
(2) Test of Kwaitkowski et al. (null hypothesis trend-stationary): critical value at 5%: 0.15
(3) Weighted-symmetric (null hypothesis unit root)
(4) Augmented Dickey–Fuller (null hypothesis unit root)
(5) Phillips–Perron (null hypothesis unit root)
* The null of mean/trend-stationary can be accepted at 5%
°°° The null unit root can be rejected at 1% (°° 5%, ° 10%)

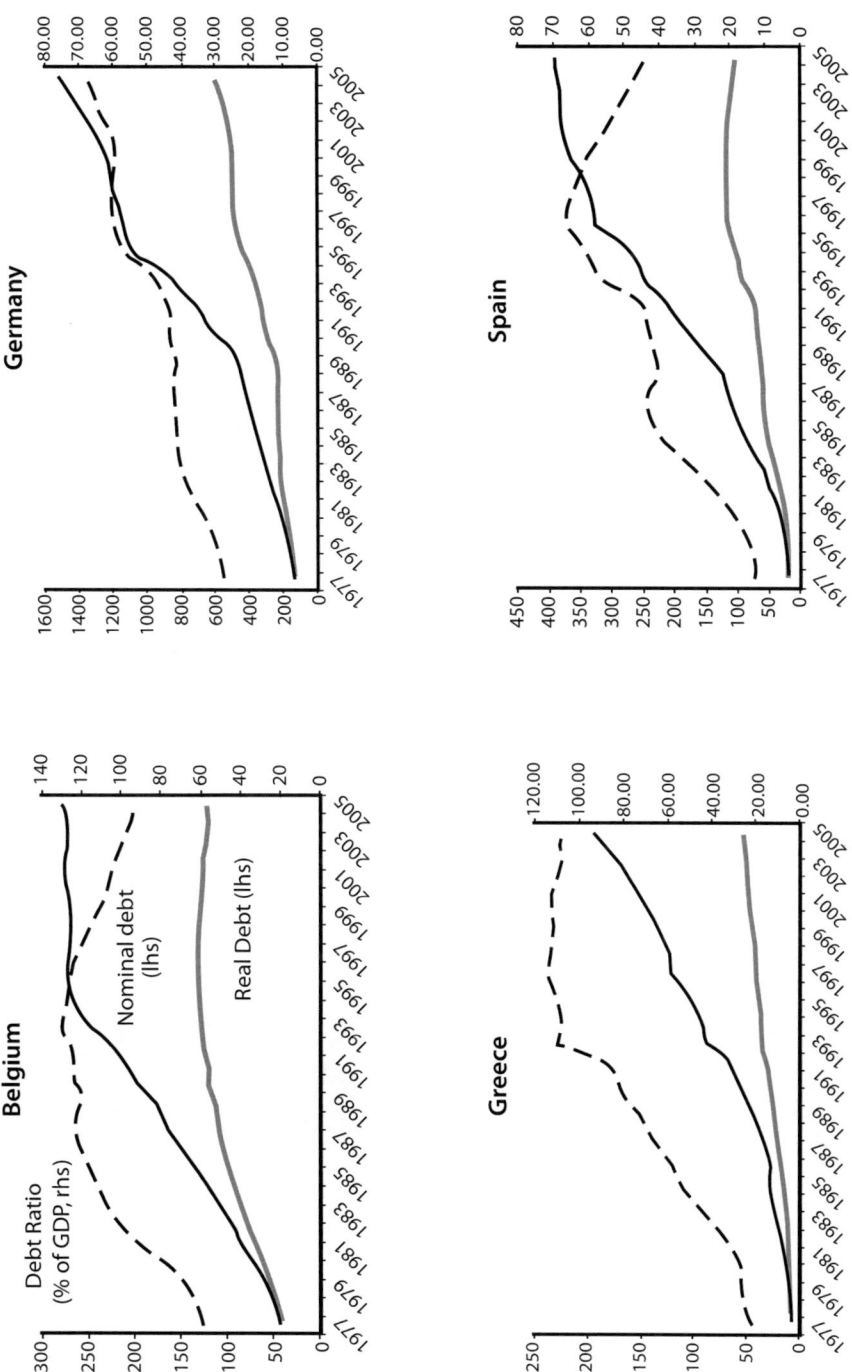

Figure 2.3 Gross debt development.

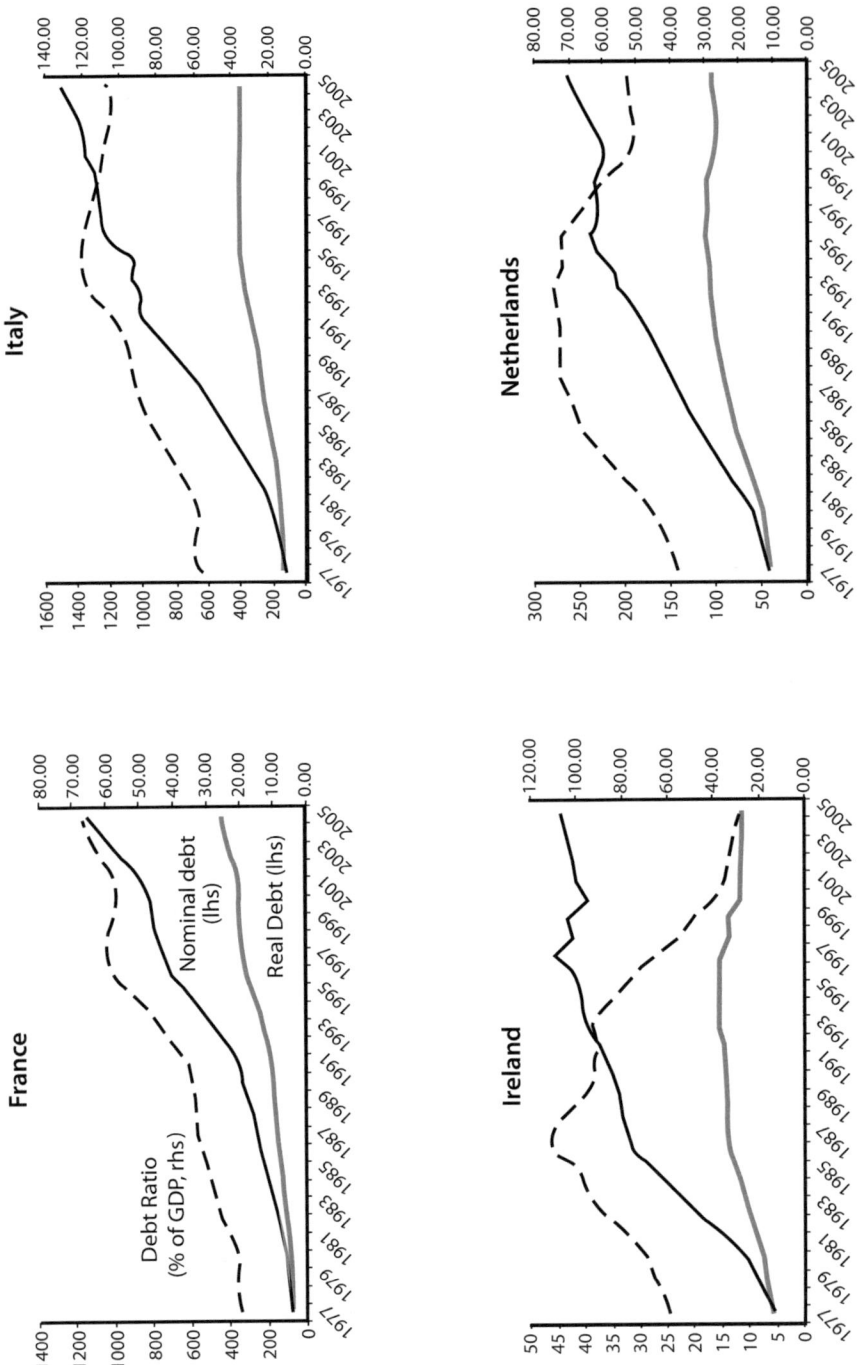

Figure 2.3 continued

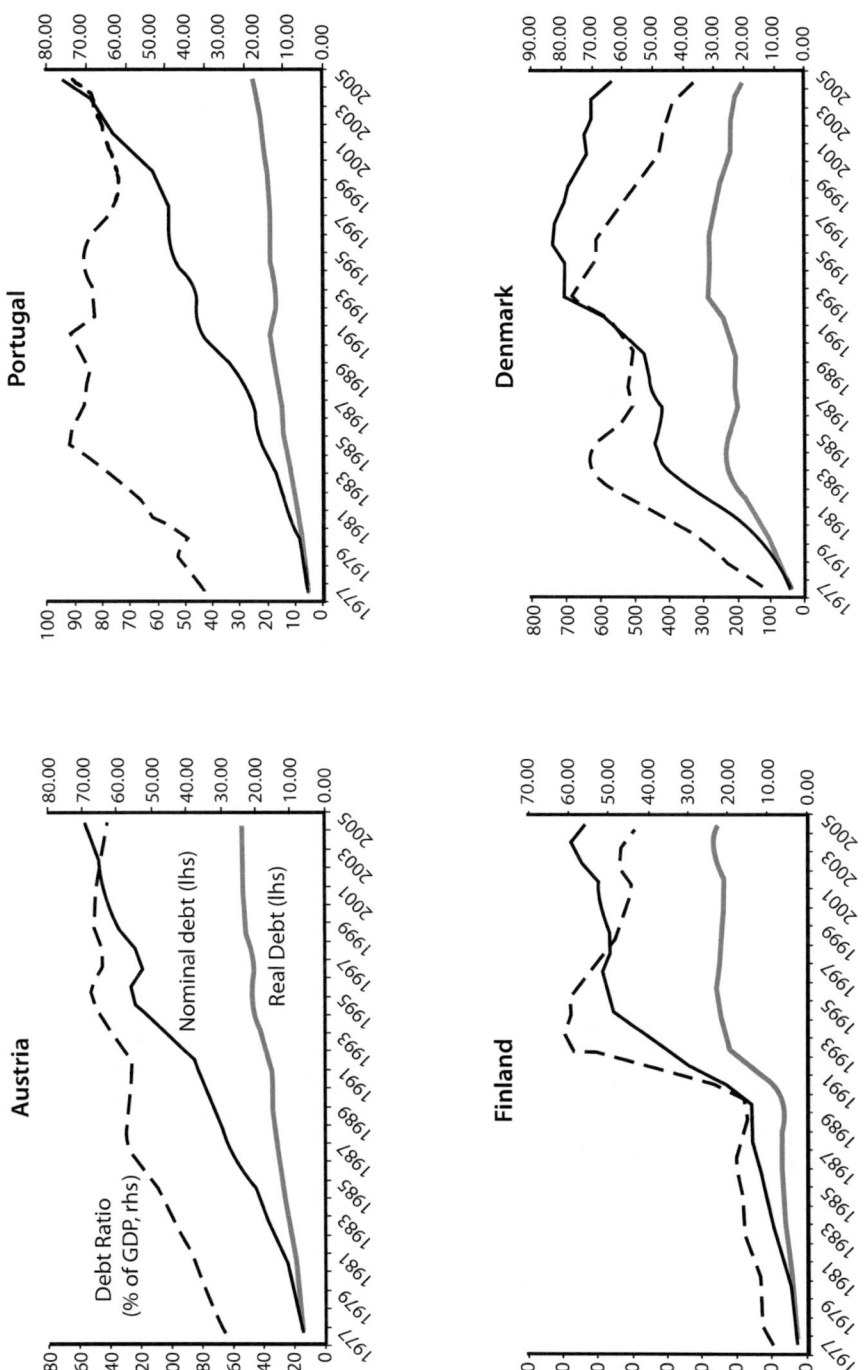

Figure 2.3 continued

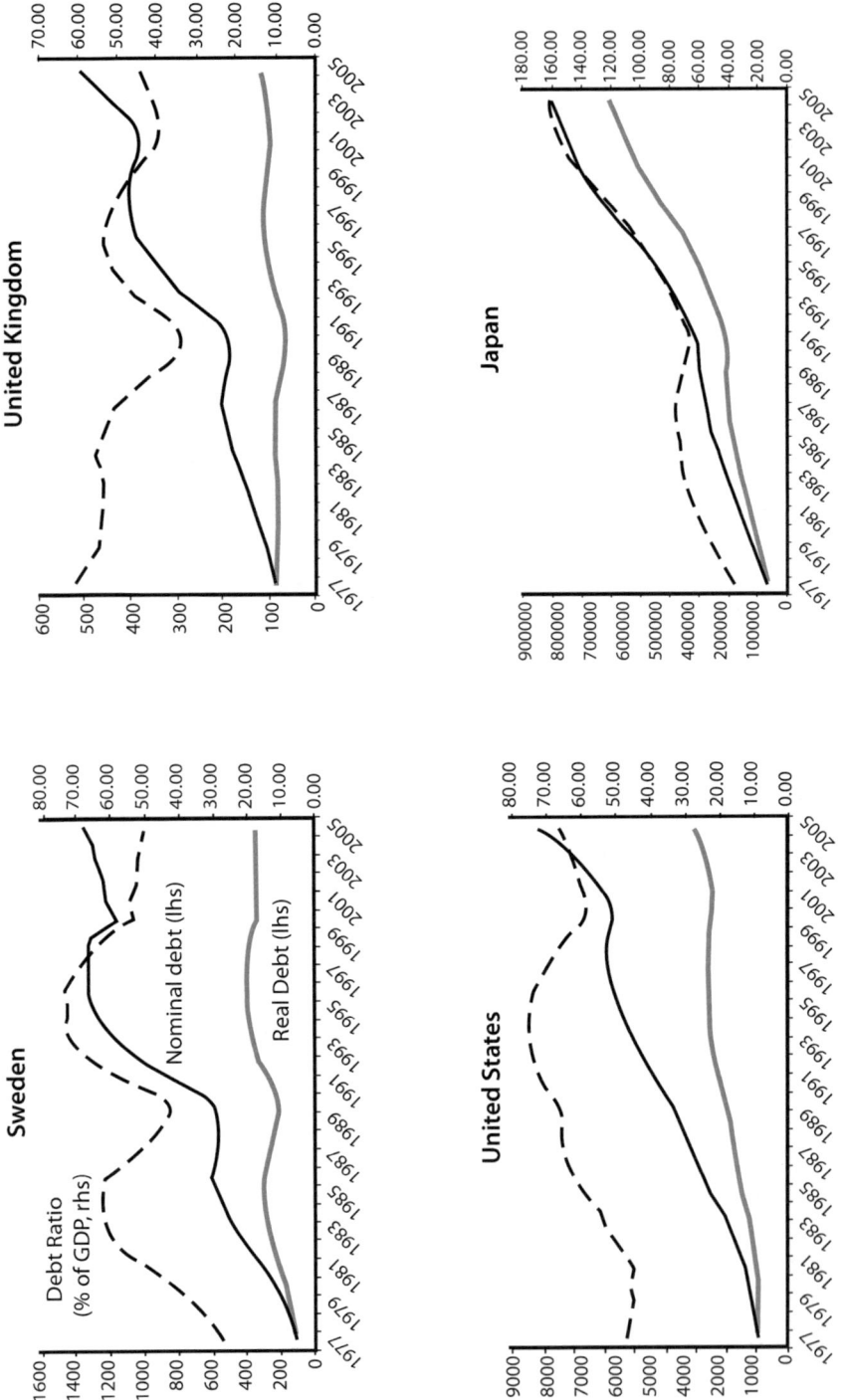

Figure 2.3 continued

Table 2.12 Unit root tests for gross primary surplus series in percentage of GDP, 1977–2005

	η_μ (1)	η_τ (2)	W-S (3)	ADF (4)	PP (5)
Belgium	1.30	0.23	−1.70	−1.20	−4.92
Germany	0.19*	0.14*	−2.48	−2.19	−12.6
Greece	0.77	0.17	−1.74	−1.97	−6.95
Spain	1.03	0.12*	−2.19	−3.94°°	−10.1
France	0.08*	0.06*	−3.73°°°	−3.73°°	−10.5
Italy	1.18	0.19	−1.10	−0.71	−3.02
Ireland	0.94	0.28	−1.49	−1.30	−4.60
Netherlands	0.54	0.12*	−3.11°°	−3.08	−11.1
Austria	0.64	0.06*	−2.77	−2.47	−12.7
Portugal	0.48	0.28	−1.30	−0.75	−4.76
Finland	0.14*	0.14*	−2.13	−1.92	−8.76
Denmark	0.34*	0.16	−2.47	−2.48	−7.83
Sweden	0.11*	0.08*	−3.56°°	−3.22°	9.69
UK	0.11*	0.07*	−3.76°°°	−3.37°°	−9.22
US	0.24*	0.12*	−3.36	−3.22°°	−7.07°
Japan	0.70	0.30	−2.02	−2.35	−3.84

Notes:
(1) Test of Kwaitkowski et al. (null hypothesis mean-stationary). Critical value at 5%: 0.46
(2) Test of Kwaitkowski et al. (null hypothesis trend-stationary). Critical value at 5%: 0.15
(3) Weighted-symmetric (null hypothesis unit root)
(4) Augmented Dickey–Fuller (null hypothesis unit root)
(5) Phillips–Perron (null hypothesis unit root)
* The null of mean/trend-stationary can be accepted at 5%
°°° The null unit root can be rejected at 1% (°° 5%, ° 10%)

Notes

1 The views expressed in this paper are those of the authors and are not attributable to the European Commission.
2 In particular, all three may depend on aggregate output.
3 For instance, between 1977 and 1993 the implicit interest rate on government debt (the ratio of interest expenditure to the stock of debt) had increased from 6.5 to 8 per cent in Belgium, from 6 to 11.5 per cent in Greece, from 2 to 9 per cent in Spain, from 6 to 7.5 per cent in France, from 8 to 10 per cent in Italy, and from 4.5 to 10 per cent in Portugal (see Table 2.8 in Appendix 2.A).
4 In addition, the implicit interest rates on government debt are well below not only those recorded in the early 1990s, but also those recorded at the beginning of the sample period (1977). As a matter of fact, the implicit interest rates have converged across euro-area Member States to around 4.5 per cent in 2005 (see Table 2.8 in Appendix 2.A).
5 Note that a stronger deterioration was recorded in Finland and Sweden. However, the timing in Tables 2.1 and 2.8 may not be the most appropriate for these two countries. The bulk of the increase in debt levels in Finland took place suddenly in the early 1990s, when after the fall of the Soviet regime the concomitant drastic reduction of Finnish exports plunged the country into a recession, the result of which was that the surplus of 5 per cent of GDP recorded in 1990 turned into a deficit of 8 per cent of GDP in 1993. In parallel, debt levels rose from 14 per cent of GDP in 1990 to 56 per cent of GDP in 1993. Similarly, in Sweden the surplus of 4 per cent of GDP recorded in 1990 turned into a deficit of 11 per cent of GDP in 1993, with debt going up from 42 to 71 per cent of GDP. Also note that the deterioration of the primary surplus in the UK in the late 1980s/early 1990s is associated to a reduction of debt levels from 61 per cent of GDP in 1977 to 48 per cent of GDP in 1993.
6 This is not the only reason (European Commission 2005). The fact that deficits are compiled in accrual terms, while debt is a cash concept, also leads to differences between the changes in

debt and the deficit in any given year. Additional differences arise from other adjustments and valuation effects.

7 As noted in European Commission (2005) large SFAs are a source of concern, especially in high-debt countries in deficit. On the one hand, by excessively focusing on deficits, budgetary surveillance may create incentives to shift budget items from deficit ('above the line') to SFAs ('below the line'). On the other hand, large SFAs may be indicative of inconsistent and low-quality budgetary statistics. However, large SFAs may not always be the result of bad fiscal behaviour. It appears that countries with low debt levels and in surplus (see the cases of Finland, Denmark or Sweden in Table 2.1) would prefer to invest in financial assets rather than to reduce the already low debt.

8 Sustainability is even compatible with policies that may generate primary deficits on average, as for example fiscal policies that target debt/output stabilization require a surplus or a deficit depending on output fluctuations.

9 Detailed estimates are available upon request from the authors.

10 Notice that some models (Belgium, France, Italy, see Table 2.6) include an intervention in 1993 (i.e. a variable that takes value 1 in that year, 0 elsewhere) with no significant impacts as regards the reaction of the primary surplus to debt levels. This intervention tries to deal with a large increase in debt levels observed in many countries in 1993, which appears to be associated to the application of the statistical regulations adopted in connection with the fiscal Maastricht criteria with a view to providing rigorous criteria to compile deficit and debt levels in the Member States. As shown by the large SFAs recorded that year, such debt increases were not associated to increases in the deficit and/or the reduction of the growth dividend. In the case of Germany the intervention takes place in 1995, when the new Erblastentilgungsfonds (administered by the federal level) took over the debt from the Treuhandanstalt, which privatized the assets of the former East Germany and accumulated debt in order to make the companies fit for privatization (or to cover the social payments if companies were liquidated). The new fund also took over a debt stock of about 7 per cent of GDP. While they do not have a significant impact on the estimates of debt reaction, the inclusion of such interventions improves the adjustment and the specification tests.

11 Implicit in our analysis is the assumption that debt and primary surplus have the same order of integration. Appendix 2.B reports unit root test results which fail to display unambiguous statistical evidence in this sense. However, our sample size is too small for this matter and we take this as inconclusive evidence.

12 For a description of the methodology see e.g. Doan et al. (1984) and Ballabriga (1997).

13 Although the size of response is also relevant in order to exclude explosive debt-to-GDP ratios.

14 Results available on request from the authors.

15 The Barlett window, $1 - s/(l + 1)$, in the test is calculated for $l = 1$ (then $s = 1$).

Discussion

Fabrizio Balassone

Chapter 2 estimates fiscal reaction functions for EU member countries over 1977–2005 to assess the sustainability of fiscal policy. Specifically, the chapter tests the consistency of fiscal policy with solvency as defined by the 'no-Ponzi game' condition. The authors find that a sufficient condition for solvency – i.e. that the primary balance improve in response to an increase in the debt-to-GDP ratio – is met in most countries (the more so after Maastricht). From this they derive strong policy implications. They argue that 'if the concern is government solvency [debt ceilings] impose unnecessary constraint on fiscal policy' and 'if sustainability is the issue, there is no clear reason for concern [in the EU]'.

The chapter clearly defines the analytical issues. The econometric analysis is accurate. The results appear to be robust. However, some caution is warranted in deriving the policy implications.

The no-Ponzi game condition is a weak requirement. It requires that the debt-to-GDP ratio grows at a rate lower than the difference between the interest rate and the growth rate (McCallum 1984). It is consistent with an ever growing debt ratio, a situation that most analysts would not regard as sustainable.

Moreover, while the chapter finds that the response of the primary balance to the debt ratio was positive in most EU countries over 1977–2005, this does not allow a straightforward extrapolation of this behaviour in the future. A growing debt ratio calls for a growing primary surplus, but what is the maximum sustainable primary surplus? Whether a given fiscal policy is or is not sustainable ultimately depends on its effects on macro parameters such as the rate of interest and the rate of growth. '[T]he issue is how interest service will affect the economy' (Musgrave and Musgrave 1984, p. 689), and 'the problem of the debt burden is a problem of an expanding national income' (Domar 1944, p. 166).

Policy implications aside, the reading of econometric results in the chapter would benefit from further discussion of some issues: for instance, those concerning the 'power' of the tests conducted in the chapter, and the role of the cyclicality of fiscal policy in determining debt dynamics.

The solvency test conducted in the chapter cannot identify policies that are inconsistent with solvency. A positive response of the primary balance to the debt ratio is a sufficient condition for solvency, but it is not necessary. A policy characterized by a negligible or even negative response of the primary balance to the debt ratio could still be consistent with solvency (and sustainability). This may explain, for instance, why a country like Finland, whose debt-to-GDP ratio has never exceeded 57 per cent over the sample period, fails to pass the solvency test in Section 2.4.

The estimated fiscal reaction functions indicate a very low sensitivity of the primary surplus to cyclical conditions (as measured by the output gap). As noted by the authors, this suggests that pro-cyclical discretionary policy is offsetting the operation of automatic stabilizers. There is evidence that such offsetting is asymmetric – i.e. that it mainly occurs during upturns – thereby introducing a ratchet-effect on debt dynamics, with significant implications for sustainability (Balassone and Francese 2004).

3 Unfunded obligation measures for EU countries

Jagadeesh Gokhale[1]

3.1 Introduction

Europe is undergoing two major transitions – demographic and economic. First, the populations of many European countries are ageing rapidly as their baby-boom generations approach and enter retirement, human longevity continues to increase, and fertility rates remain well below replacement. Second, 16 European countries have joined in a monetary union (EMU) by adopting the euro as a common currency, and more countries are to join the EMU during the next few years. The objective of monetary union is to eliminate exchange rate risks and streamline product pricing and price comparisons of similar goods and services across member nations to induce greater competitive efficiencies. Entering a monetary union implies surrendering control over monetary policymaking, but all current and prospective EMU nations would largely retain sovereignty in setting fiscal policies – except for the loose overall constraints set under the latest Maastricht agreement.

Both transitions will place tremendous but conflicting pressures on Member States' domestic national budgets. Decision makers will face growing demands to increase public expenditures and fulfil promises of retirement and health care benefits to retirees precisely when growth in labour forces and tax bases slows. That points towards larger future fiscal deficits and growing debt levels. At the same time, policymakers will face growing pressures from the 'EMU club' to maintain low deficits, prevent increases in interest rates, and maintain European investment levels. Exercising proper economic stewardship during these twin transitions will become more difficult if policymakers remain poorly informed about the likely consequences of making alternative policy choices.

To streamline the process of monetary union, prospective EMU member countries adopted the Stability and Growth Pact in 1997 (SGP-97). Along with the Treaty of the European Union, SGP-97 provided the framework of rules for coordinating fiscal policies across EMU members – both current and prospective ones. It was generally accepted that without such coordination, Member States would have stronger incentives to follow 'short-sighted' fiscal policies causing chronic budget deficits and higher debt-to-GDP ratios. If carried too far, such policies would erode the European Central Bank's ability to maintain the euro's purchasing power. If high deficits ultimately cause faster inflation, it would only neutralize the advantages of establishing a monetary union.

Beginning in 2002, however, the SGP-97's deficit and debt constraints and its preventive and corrective mechanisms proved unacceptable.[2] SGP-97 called for corrective fiscal policies to be adopted if a breach of deficits or debt limits appeared imminent regardless of the Member State's position in the business cycle and potential for GDP growth. A revised Stability and Growth Pact has now been in effect since March 2005 (SGP-05). It incorporates constraints and objectives (time paths of future deficits and debt) tailored to each member country's economic conditions.

The revised agreement introduces greater flexibility in implementing the SGP's constraints and allows implementation of preventive and corrective mechanisms to be deferred in case a member country faces temporary economic difficulties. Some observers claim, however, that although SGP-05 continues to define constraints in terms of traditional deficit and debt-to-GDP levels, it really represents an abandonment of the original objectives underlying those constraints (Feldstein 2005; Wierts et al. 2006) of preventing excessive discretion in fiscal policies. If correct, this would constitute good news. This chapter's thesis is that traditional fiscal measures – annual deficits and debt-to-GDP levels – are both potentially misleading indicators of a country's fiscal stance.

The SGP-05 also calls for the development of long-term fiscal indicators for policy surveillance of Member States. This effort should consider recently developed fiscal measures that are theoretically sound and policy relevant. They would better inform EU policy-makers of the condition of each Member State's current fiscal stance and provide a basis for an apples-to-apples comparison of the policy options and trade-offs that each country faces. The bad news is that many member countries and EMU policymaking bodies appear to be a long way from developing appropriate long-term fiscal accounting measures and from developing a consensus on whether they should be part of formal preventive mechanisms.

This chapter first addresses issues relating to the proper accounting and reporting of the government's net prospective payment obligations. It compares alternative long-term measures of a country's fiscal stance and discusses their theoretical soundness, applicability to budget reporting, and ability to reveal information about the true economic choices that policymakers face. Four types of measures are considered – traditional deficit and debt measures, accrual accounting measures and two measures based on actuarial accounting. The latter include generational accounting and fiscal and generational imbalance measures.

The chapter argues for the adoption of fiscal and generational imbalance measures by integrating these measures into existing country budget reports. It provides brief examples of how fiscal and generational imbalance measures could help policymakers to define the feasible set of policy choices and the trade-offs involved in selecting from among them.

This chapter also attempts to quantify the size of the long-term fiscal challenges confronting EU countries by reporting estimates of fiscal imbalances (FI) for 23 EU countries. The FI estimates suggest sizable gaps between the fiscal shortfalls reported under traditional backward-looking debt and deficit measures and those implied by forward-looking fiscal imbalance measures.

The chapter concludes by suggesting that European countries need to undertake a third transition – to step back from the current broad provision of social insurance programmes and allow greater scope for individual determination and private provision of these services. Introducing this important element in structural reforms by encouraging significant reductions in public spending commitments appears to be the only economically feasible way of addressing future fiscal challenges. The alternative of increasing taxes and imposing additional regulatory restrictions on member countries to preserve the status quo in social protection programmes is likely to prove counterproductive.

3.2 Unfunded obligation measures

Concern about fiscal sustainability arising out of the current demographic structure in developed countries has spurred interest in developing forward-looking measures of fiscal policy. Several alternatives exist for depicting the future course of federal budget balances. The first and most obvious measure is a projection of future total government revenues, expenditures and the annual gaps between the two. Although future projections of this type are reported in the official budgets of many countries, the projections are usually limited to the next five or ten years. For example, the annual budget reports of the UK Treasury (HM Treasury 2006) adopt a five-year time horizon – with the horizon advancing by one year every year. The same is true of the official budget reports of many other EU countries.[3]

Given the obvious inadequacy of such short-term budget projections for designing long-term policy reforms, several measures have been proposed by budget practitioners and academic economists. They include (i) simply extending the time horizon of traditional deficit and debt measures, (ii) accrual accounting, (iii) generational accounting, and (iv) fiscal and generational imbalances. This section provides a discussion of their strengths and weaknesses.

Traditional measures – government deficits and debt

Traditional short-term deficit and debt measures of the national fiscal stance are grounded in Keynesian macroeconomic theory that considers the gap between revenues and expenditures as providing a fiscal impulse that could be calibrated for macroeconomic stabilization over business cycle time horizons. Given the need for greater spending on welfare programmes during economic downturns and the wide prevalence of progressive income taxation, annual budget deficits naturally move counter-cyclically. Discretionary elements of revenues and expenditures could be used, however, to enhance these counter-cyclical movements to yield even larger macroeconomic impulses to dampen business cycles and stabilize the pace of economic activity and growth. A large and growing literature has attempted to measure the economic impulses from discretionary fiscal policy using annual deficits as the key measure of fiscal impulses provided by government policies (Galí and Perotti 2003; Alesina and Perotti 1995).

Fiscal policymakers and budget practitioners have an abiding interest in maintaining these definitions and tools for exercising short-term operational control over government budgets. Hence, if short-horizon fiscal measures prove inadequate for analysing long-term fiscal sustainability and structural reform issues, the simplest solution is to extend the time horizon over which traditional deficits and debt are projected. One proposal is to project and report government revenues, expenditures and surpluses/deficits over the next 50 or 75 years under alternative economic and demographic assumptions. These measures can be calculated for both the general government as a whole and for sub-programmes that are financed out of dedicated revenues – such as retirement and health programmes.

Accrual accounting measures

For most EU countries, future outlay increases on retirement and health benefits are already built into fiscal systems, and they imply growing annual deficits. Hence, the evaluation of a country's fiscal stance should explicitly recognize those costs as additional debt owed by the government. One way of doing so is to adopt accrual accounting, which would include a summary measure of future payment obligations net of assets accrued from past transactions – called 'unfunded accrued obligations'. Accrual accounting considers the government's financial obligations and assets that have been 'earned' or 'booked' based on events that have occurred through the current period, whether or not the funds associated with those events have been paid or received as yet.

In the context of government finances, there could be considerable uncertainty and controversy about what constitutes an obligation-triggering event. A common example is that of public pension programmes that link benefits payable in the future to current or past labour force participation, earnings or tax payments. However, when social transfers scheduled under today's laws may be altered by changing those laws, it remains unclear whether past employment, tax payments or other such events are by themselves sufficient to trigger future benefits and, therefore, whether those events justify inclusion in 'unfunded accrued obligations' on a par with contractual (deeded) debt owed by the government.

This problem could be resolved by distinguishing the information provision role of budget measures from the liability recognition function that is usually associated with budget accounting and reporting. Fulfilling the former need not imply the latter, and this difference should be made transparent. The objective under the former is to characterize the stance of current fiscal policy without implying any additional recognition of liabilities that are on a par with outstanding explicit debt.

Hence, as a 'budget measure', the inclusion of accrued obligations in accounting for the government's financial condition would reflect the future implications of existing policies. Under this assumption, if maintaining current policies would result in future transfers based on past triggering events, those accruals should be included in measuring the government's total financial obligations under current laws. Similarly, events that would trigger larger future government receipts under today's policies would increase the government's total accrued assets.

The liabilities created by some government programmes may already be evaluated under accrual accounting – for example, the budget costs of loans and loan guarantees, insurance and underwriting costs, and so on. Several developed countries have adopted accrual accounting for their government budgets although only a couple of them have adopted such accounting comprehensively (New Zealand and Sweden).[4] Accrual accounting could be broadly applied to public pension and other programmes that imply future government net payment obligations but are excluded from traditional debt and deficit measures.

Generational accounting

Generational accounting reorganizes government budget information and implements actuarial estimates of the lifetime fiscal treatment of current and future generations (Auerbach et al. 1991, 1994). Each generation's resources include those it earns, inherits and receives from the government as transfer payments net of taxes. Generational accounting calculates the last of these three elements on a prospective basis for each living generation. It also calculates the generational account for future generations based on the government's overall budget constraint – which specifies that the government must pay for all the public goods and services it provides. As such, generational accounting helps to assess the government's net financial commitments to current generations under current fiscal policies and, by implication, the net fiscal burden those policies would place on future generations.[5]

Generational accounting employs an ex post perspective in analysing the long-term sustainability of current fiscal policy. Allowing PV_P_c to represent the present value of total government purchases of future public goods under current policies (subscript c), PV_L_c to represent the total present value of prospective lifetime net tax payments (tax payments minus transfer receipts) by living generations under current policies, PV_F_h to represent the total lifetime net taxes of future-born generations under a hypothetical policy (subscript h)

for achieving budget balance, and NW_c to represent the government's current financial net wealth, the government's ex post intertemporal budget constraint could be specified as

$$PV\_P_c \equiv NW_c + PV\_L_c + PV\_F_h \tag{3.1}$$

Equation (3.1) says that given future net payments by current generations under current policies and assuming that the government's intertemporal budget constraint is balanced – as it must be ex post – reveals, by construction, the hypothetical net payments required from future generations. Note that the objective of this exercise is to discover the total hypothetical payment that must be imposed on future generations as a whole to deliver ex post budget balance.[6]

Imposing existing fiscal policies on current newborns throughout their lifetimes yields their generational account. Its ratio to the present value of their lifetime earnings, where earnings are projected using an assumed rate of productivity growth, yields a lifetime net tax rate for current newborns. Imposing the (hypothetical) residual unfunded obligation, PV_F_h, exclusively on future generations (assuming an equal productivity-growth-adjusted distribution per capita of the total hypothetical burden across all future generations) implies a hypothetical lifetime net tax rate on those generations – again under the assumed rate of labour productivity growth and labour earnings.

Current fiscal policy is considered to be balanced and sustainable if, given (i) government spending commitment, PV_P_c, (ii) government net financial assets, NW_c, and (iii) lifetime net tax rates estimated under current fiscal policies for today's newborns (based on their net payments under current policies), the hypothetical total payment from future generations, PV_F_h (that balances the government's intertemporal budget constraint specified in equation 3.1) implies the same lifetime net tax rate for future generations.[7]

Fiscal and generational imbalances

Fiscal and generational imbalance measures are an offshoot of generational accounting. They are designed to parsimoniously capture the most important elements of generational accounting with an eye towards simplicity and policy relevance. The fiscal imbalance measure is the present value of government financial shortfalls projected to occur throughout the future under the assumption that current policies remain unchanged. However, unlike generational accounting's distinction between the fiscal treatment of living and future generations, the *FI* measure projects all (including future) generations' net payments under current policies. In other words, it views the government's intertemporal budget constraint from a 'current policy' (ex ante) perspective. Although the government's budget (equation (3.1)) would remain unbalanced under such a fiscal treatment of future generations, that is precisely the point of the calculation – to measure the size of the total imbalance built into current fiscal policies.

The *FI* measure equals the present value of prospective lifetime net payments (taxes minus transfers) to living and future generations plus the present value of projected government purchases and minus the government's current net financial assets. Thus,

$$FI = PV\_P_c - PV\_L_c - PV\_F_c - NW_c \tag{3.2}$$

Because it is the government's budget choices that are being evaluated, present values are calculated using the government's opportunity cost of funds – the interest rate expected to prevail on the longest-term government bonds.

FI measures can also be calculated for government sub-programmes that exclusively provide transfers to private individuals (old-age retirement benefits, for example) and are financed out of dedicated revenues (a payroll tax, for example). The revenues and expenditures of such programmes are attributable to particular generations.

$$FI_s = PV\_L_{s,c} - PV\_F_{s,c} - NW_{s,c} \tag{3.3}$$

Here, the subscript s indicates a generic 'social security' programme that conforms to the financing conditions described above.

Generational imbalance (*GI*) measures the contribution of past and living generations to *FI*. The motivation for the *GI* measure is the same as that for generational accounting – to analyse the intergenerational redistribution of resources that current fiscal policies would bring about if they were maintained throughout the lifetimes of current generations. *GI* represents the simplest decomposition of *FI*. It is alternatively called the 'closed-group unfunded obligation' where the term 'closed-group' refers to past and living generations. That is, *GI* is derived by subtracting the government's total unfunded obligations under current policies on account of future generations from *FI*.[8] However, whereas *FI* can be calculated for the entire government and for sub-programmes having the features described earlier, the *GI* measure can be easily calculated only for such sub-programmes.[9]

The significance and policy relevance of *GI* measures are not well appreciated, even among budget practitioners. Many believe that *GI* is similar to the unfunded accrued obligation concept and is relevant only to 'fully funded' pension programmes – such as those offered by private employers.[10] However, the *GI* measure is also relevant and useful within the context of a 'pay-as-you-go' public pension system. It indicates the amount of total outstanding obligations arising under current policies on account of past and living generations. Obligations arising from past generations' transactions with the government and from the past transactions of living generations are incorporated in the government's accumulated net financial assets. Also included in *GI* are future net payment obligations under current policies triggered by past transactions involving living generations and future payment obligations that would be triggered under current policies by future events involving living generations.

The size of *GI* reveals the amount of benefits living generations may, under current policies, expect to receive from a government programme in excess of their past and future expected taxes or contributions towards funding them. This measure remains policy-relevant because it represents a net (expected) wealth gain for living generations. Not only are such fiscal-policy-induced wealth gains directly policy-relevant, they also hold the potential to influence those generations' economic choices – their consumption and labour force participation. Hence, analysing the potential economic implications of the current fiscal stance requires a measure of the public provision of net benefits to living generations. Note that this measure is also forward-looking – and fundamentally different from the traditional backward-looking debt and deficit measures.

3.3 Evaluating unfunded obligation measures

Long-term projections of revenues, expenditures and annual deficits

Time series of annual budget cash flow projections – revenues, expenditures, deficits and debt – have some advantages but also have a few shortcomings: Their advantage lies in clearly exhibiting the time profile of future revenue shortfalls given projected discretionary and ageing-related spending. Such projections are useful for showing how quickly large financial shortfalls are likely to emerge under current policies. For example, Figure 3.1 shows a nominal revenue time series and two alternative nominal expenditure time series. Under the Expenditures-I alternative, moderate deficits accrue during the first decade and then rise rapidly as a result of ageing-related expenses. Under the Expenditure-II alternative, however, the gap between revenues and expenditures is very small during the first ten years, but it expands more rapidly thereafter compared to the Expenditure-I alternative. The difference in the timing and accrual rates of ageing-related deficits constitutes useful and policy-relevant information.

One obvious shortcoming of such time profiles of nominal revenues, expenditures, and deficits is that they do not place current and future dollars on a level playing field. Although future nominal deficits appear to be larger, their real values may not be as large if projected inflation plus real interest rates are high.

Second, nominal deficits and debt levels do not appear to hold significant and stable relationships with other economic variables of interest – namely, interest rates, currency values, inflation, productivity growth, etc. Hence, strict fiscal rules based on deficits and debt may not be sufficient to ensure fiscal stability and long-term sustainability. Third, some countries could follow policies that maintain or even reduce explicit deficits and debt levels while simultaneously increasing prospective deficits (the so-called 'one-off' measures). Such policies would alter the timing of deficit accruals but are unlikely to be associated with any measurable regularity in real fiscal impulses.

The reason for drawing such a conclusion is that a particular time series of government net cash flows may be associated with myriad ways of arranging the sizes and timing of different taxes and expenditures – each of which may generate different expectations among the public about whether they are temporary or permanent, and each of which could be associated with different distributions of fiscal burdens among private agents situated differently in their life-cycle stages. Hence, a particular time series of deficits and debt may be associated with wildly different real underlying fiscal policies – that is, a given time series may be associated with different real flows and distributions of consumption, saving, investment and output, and different levels of real interest rates, inflation and exchange rates. These differences in real economic outcomes would emerge primarily because each distinct policy would exert differential effects on different sub-groups of individuals – distinguished, especially, with regard to their life-cycle stage.[11]

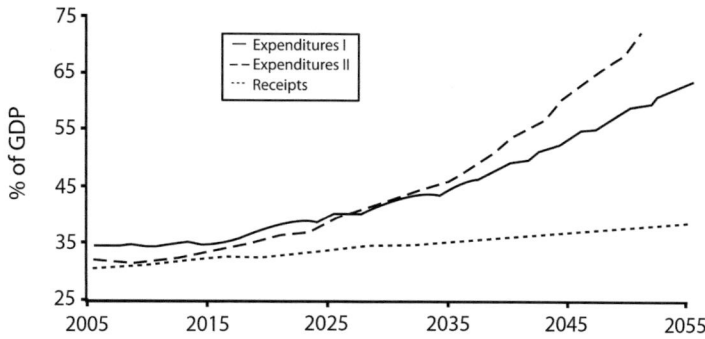

Figure 3.1 Projected total expenditure and receipts (hypothetical data).

To provide a simple example, consider a strictly pay-as-you-go expansion of a public pension programme. Retiree benefits are increased immediately and permanently by €X each year and those increases are financed by additional receipts of €X each year sourced from workers' payrolls. Figure 3.2 shows stylized profiles of public pension benefits and wage earnings by age. Those profiles show that the policy of pay-as-you-go pension increases would benefit older generations and the payroll tax increases would impose additional financial burdens on younger workers. By construction, however, there would be no change in the time series of the projected difference between total annual receipts and outlays as a result of this policy change.

One could argue that showing the government's future funding shortfall in terms of total receipt and outlay time series would capture such a policy change as an upward shift in both series. However, other policies could be implemented that would maintain both the projected levels of revenues and expenditures and the gap between them (annual deficits), yet exert real economic effects by redistributing resources across generations. Consider Figure 3.3, which shows stylized profiles by age of payroll tax and consumption tax payments. Because the consumption tax profile is flatter and extends across older individuals, a permanent pay-as-you-go structural tax change – that is, an annually-revenue-neutral switch from consumption to labour income taxes – would accomplish a sizable redistribution of tax burdens and wealth across generations.

As in the case of the pay-as-you-go expansion of public pensions, this policy also provides a windfall benefit to current older generations but reduces the lifetime resources of younger and future generations.[12] However, such a policy change would be invisible to Figure 3.1's fiscal measure – the time series of projected revenues, expenditures and deficits. If propensities to consume out of resources of older generations are different (say, higher) than those of younger generations, permanent redistributive policy changes of this type would very likely exert real economic effects – affecting saving, capital formation, interest rates, and eventually inflation and exchange rates.

The above discussion suggests that when policymakers enact diverse fiscal changes designed to alter the time profiles of expenditures and revenues to reduce short-term deficits, only some of those policies may be reflected in traditional cash-flow measures such as deficit and debt levels, or time series of total expenditure and revenue levels as shown in Figure 3.1. The net result of such policies may be larger or smaller deficits and debt levels

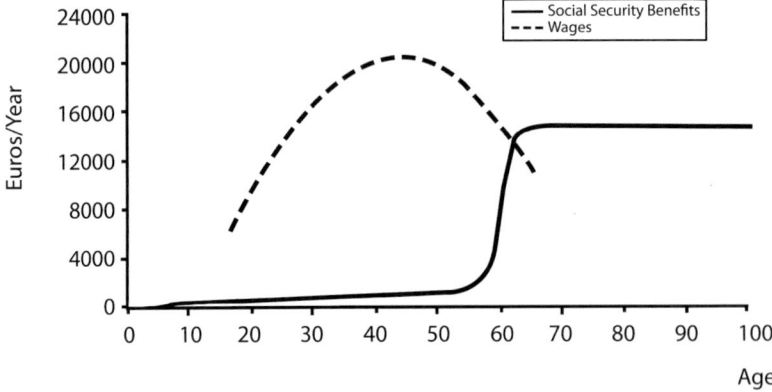

Figure 3.2 Social security benefit and wage profiles by age.

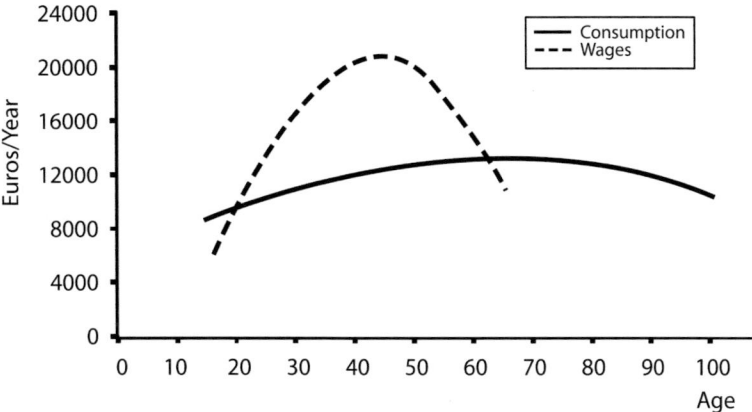

Figure 3.3 Consumption and wage profiles by age.

over time, but also erosions or increases in national saving and capital formation independent of the impact on short- and long-term deficits and debt levels. Because Figure 3.1 does not fully reflect the impact of all policy changes, it remains a poor guide for decision makers and should be complemented with additional information. In the words of Auerbach and Kotlikoff, 'conventional deficit measures may cause alarm when alarm is not warranted and, conversely, may calm observers when alarm is most appropriate'.[13]

Accrual accounting

As mentioned earlier, accrual accounting 'books' obligations and assets based on triggering events through the current period. Since the objective of accrual accounting for the budget would be to characterize current policy, future benefits based on past births, labour force participation, earnings and tax payments (as is common in the case of public pensions) should be counted among government obligations. Even in the case of health care benefits, future payments based on projected cost growth may be included to get a fuller estimate of the government's financial obligations under current policies.

Proposals to adopt accrual accounting for measuring the government's intertemporal budget balance are generally motivated by the attractive symmetry of applying the same accounting rules to the government as are applied to private companies when evaluating their pension and other obligations. However, the government as an economic entity is sufficiently different from private entities to warrant a different accounting standard. In particular, private entities can potentially fail and terminate at any time, whereas the government is infinitely lived, at least in principle. Moreover, unlike private entities, governments possess the sovereign power to levy taxes.

The purpose of accrual accounting for private firms is to reveal the amount of funds that must be set aside to meet contractual deferred liabilities – pensions and health coverage for retired employees, etc. Most such liabilities are created from past employee performance and are measurable because they are determined by applying explicit benefit formulae. In contrast, the objective of long-term government budget accounting is to evaluate the sustainability of current tax and spending rules – not to evaluate total liabilities if the 'government fails'. Given its power to levy taxes, the government need not necessarily set funds aside each time it enacts laws that create additional future payment obligations. Applying accrual accounting to government liabilities could, therefore, create the impression that the government's future obligations to pay pension, health and welfare benefits somehow are contractual obligations – or liabilities – that can never be reduced.[14]

Moreover, accrual accounting measures are also (partially) backward-looking because they include only those future fiscal flows (taxes and transfers) that would result from past triggering events. Given that governments are infinitely lived in principle, however, it does not appear legitimate to ignore future obligation-triggering events – labour force participation, earnings, tax payments, etc. – if current policies are continued.[15] Indeed, if accrued net obligations are positive but continuing current fiscal policies would generate net future receipts, reporting accrued net obligations would indicate a large positive net liability position even though current policies may be sustainable.

Generational accounting

Generational accounting's actuarial (as opposed to accrual) approach includes an evaluation of future government obligations and resources triggered by future obligating events. This method provides a comprehensive perspective for evaluating current fiscal policy. However, its ex post perspective on the government intertemporal budget constraint (equation 3.1) implies that concepts associated with generational accounting such as 'generational balance' (equation 3.1) involve subtle thought experiments that are difficult to communicate. Those experiments involve hypothetical and non-implementable policies – of treating all future-born generations differently compared to the treatment of living generations under existing fiscal policies. In addition, generational accounts are calculated from the perspective of private individuals rather than of the government's financial constraint. That makes generational accounts difficult to integrate with existing budget reports, which usually include short-term projected annual aggregate cash flows (revenues, expenditures and budget deficits) and total outstanding net debt.

Generational accounts are calculated and used as complementary indicators of fiscal policy in several countries. They are reported in considerable detail in most generational accounting studies – for individual age–sex cohorts (Auerbach et al. 1999). Generational accounting also reports the generational lifetime fiscal burdens that would prevail under policy adjustments for achieving a sustainable fiscal policy. Alternatively, it reports the 'menu of pain' – policy changes that would be required to restore sustainability. However, the key information about the sustainability of current policies often becomes obscured by the focus (and often confusion) associated with the multiplicity of numbers included in most generational accounting reports.[16]

Fiscal and generational imbalances

Fiscal imbalance. The *FI* measure assumes continuation of current policy (including scheduled future changes in current laws) throughout the future. Thus it involves no complicated thought experiments or hypothetical future policies. It provides a summary measure of total budget shortfalls – the sum of accrued shortfalls to date and prospective shortfalls under current policy evaluated without a time limit. It is a comprehensive measure of the government's fiscal position because it spans the entire future without limit and includes the totality of government's operations. The *FI* measure is also easy to communicate: It is the amount of additional resources that the government must have on hand today, invested at interest, in order to continue current policies indefinitely. Alternatively, *FI* equals the additional amount of net receipts or cost savings that the government must obtain through future policy adjustments.[17]

Many practitioners express doubts about calculating and reporting fiscal imbalances through the infinite future. Their main objection is that future projections are uncertain and the degree of uncertainty increases the further forward budget projections are carried. Hence, most agencies that report *FI* base them on projections truncated after 25, 50 or 75 years into the future.[18] Although these objections appear valid, arguments favouring infinite-horizon calculations seem to be stronger. First, setting any specific limit on the projection horizon involves the implicit assumption that the government budget is in balance beyond that horizon. However, if current policies would result in large imbalances persisting beyond the projection horizon, truncating the horizon would be equivalent to ignoring future uncertainty – exactly the opposite of most recommendations about how to deal with future uncertainty. A better approach would be to report those imbalances under the best available economic assumptions and projections in addition to the imbalances calculated under a truncated projection horizon.

Second, truncating the horizon usually leads to the 'rolling-window' problem. Reforms implemented to achieve budget balance through a predetermined time horizon would be thrown off balance by the mere passage of time, and relatively quickly.[19] If future imbalances are large and growing – as is likely to be the case in countries with rapidly ageing populations – it would necessitate repeated reforms to pull the government's finances back into balance to avoid escalating fiscal deficits.

The most important but often least appreciated reason for adopting infinite-horizon calculations is that truncated budget projections would introduce a bias in policymaking. The bias can be described using a simple example of a reform proposal to establish 'social security' personal accounts. Suppose such accounts were created by diverting a portion of existing wage taxes (assumed to be dedicated to the programme) for investment in private securities. In exchange for allowing individuals to invest a part of their payroll taxes in personal accounts, they would have to agree to actuarially fair reductions in their future social security benefits. 'Actuarially fair' means that for every euro of payroll taxes deposited in personal accounts, future benefits worth one euro in present value would be surrendered, where present values would be calculated using the government's long-term borrowing rate and average mortality factors.

Under such a reform, the government's financial position is clearly unchanged – the loss in tax revenues is exactly matched in present value by a reduction in future benefit commitments. However, if a truncated estimate of government's fiscal imbalance were used, it would show a worsening in the government's financial position: Revenue losses during the short term would be counted when evaluating the government's position, but reductions in benefit payments accruing beyond the truncated horizon would be excluded. Hence, a truncated calculation of fiscal imbalance would bias policymakers towards rejecting a personal accounts reform of public pensions even though it would leave the government's true financial position unchanged.

This example could be carried one step further. If the public pension system is initially financially unsustainable, it could be improved through the reform described earlier: The government could offer a personal accounts reform wherein future benefits are reduced by more than euro-for-euro in present value. Some individuals may agree to the exchange of smaller future benefits for personal accounts that they would own and control. Implementing such an exchange would imply a larger reduction in future government outlay commitments compared to the immediate reduction in wage tax receipts. However, again, the reduced revenues in the short term would be included under a truncated projection horizon, but the larger decline in future obligations would be excluded. Thus, focusing exclusively on a truncated *FI* measure would bias policymakers to reject a reform that could potentially improve the government's financial condition.

This example also provides the final rationale for adopting an infinite-horizon fiscal imbalance measure in preference to truncated-horizon measures. The *FI* measure facilitates an apples-to-apples comparison of different policy options. If two budget reform options are financially equivalent in present value terms but one (option A) involves higher costs in the short term compared to the other (option B), policymaking would be biased in favour of option B if the evaluation were based on a truncated projection horizon. Alternatively, reform option A might be financially sounder than option B, but the latter might involve larger short-term financial gains and larger long-term costs. If the long-term costs remain hidden under a truncated projection horizon, policymakers may be biased in favour of option B. These considerations are likely to be quite important in the EU and EMU context because of the many differences in member countries' endowments, fiscal policies and demographic profiles. Hence, long-term fiscal surveillance should be based on comprehensive and policy-neutral fiscal measures, and evaluations of fiscal options should use metrics that allow apples-to-apples comparisons among available choices.

Generational imbalance. In general, the generational imbalance measure can be calculated only for programmes not involving pure public goods and that are fully or partially financed out of dedicated government receipts. Provided that it can be implemented, the generational imbalance measure shows the amount of transfers that past and living generations may expect to receive under current policies in excess of their past and future tax payments towards funding them. Thus, excluding the contribution of future generations to the fiscal imbalance yields the generational imbalance measure (see Gokhale and Smetters 2003 for details).

Most European countries have pension and health care programmes that are partly financed out of dedicated taxes. Excess outlays over dedicated revenues are financed out of transfers from the general budget account. Although such programmes are usually considered to be 'in balance' by definition, the fiscal imbalance measure can be used to show the extent to which the general government is obligated to cover future financial shortfalls in dedicated revenues compared to benefit payments under current fiscal policies. In such cases, *GI* calculated using just dedicated taxes would indicate the extent to which past and living generations' net benefits are responsible for creating general government obligations for financing the programme.[20]

GI calculations provide information that is complementary to *FI*. The *FI* measure tells us how much additional resources must be raised to restore a sustainable fiscal policy. But *FI* cannot indicate which among the myriad ways of raising the necessary resources might be preferable. However, because *GI* provides information about how a given policy would change the net benefits of living and future generations, it can help in selecting from alternative policies.

Essentially, *GI* would inform policymakers about the trade-offs involved in raising resources from current versus future generations for achieving fiscal sustainability. For example, suppose *FI* = €2,000 billion and *GI* = €1,600 billion. This implies that past and living generations account for €1,600 of the total *FI* of €2,000, and future generations account for €400 billion.[21] Policymakers could choose to enact tax and benefit changes that reduce *GI* to €600 billion and reduce future generations' contribution to *FI* to −€600 billion. Such a policy would reduce $FI = GI + (FI - GI)$ to zero. Or policymakers could adopt an alternative combination of taxes and benefits that imposed a larger additional burden on living generations and a smaller additional burden on future generations – for example, by reducing *GI* to €400 billion and (*FI* − *GI*) to −€400 billion.

Hence, adopting the combination of *FI* and *GI* as indicators of the overall financial condition and generational stance, respectively, of current fiscal policies would provide a powerful tool for evaluating the available policy alternatives based on their impact on today's versus future generations.

3.4 General considerations of fiscal and generational imbalance measures for EU countries

Adoption of measures such as *FI* and *GI* need not imply that those amounts are immutable liabilities of the government.[22] Instead, they should be viewed as policy guideposts, designed to help in implementing appropriate changes to future fiscal policies – including future taxes, pensions and other government outlays – with the aim of restoring a sustainable fiscal outlook.[23]

Second, it is obvious that *FI* and *GI* are static measures. Adopting *FI* and *GI* for estimating country fiscal positions is only the first step in policy formulation within the EMU context. Obviously, static country-specific estimates are insufficient in the context of a monetary union among countries that are currently undergoing economic transitions and are, by definition, in disequilibrium. Even without any policy changes – were that possible – demographic transitions at differential rates would engender inter-EU-country and international capital flows and labour migrations. Those flows and future policy adjustments may invalidate the economic and demographic assumptions on which *FI* and *GI* calculations are based. Nevertheless, the static *FI* and *GI* estimates constitute useful information in the formulation of future policies because they indicate the extent of pressure generated by the current fiscal stance that would induce private sector adjustments. If maintained and allowed to grow, large fiscal and generational imbalances may imply larger future taxes and higher interest rates and may cause larger private sector adjustments in capital and labour flows.

FI and *GI* numbers presented in terms of billions (or trillions) of euros are not easily comprehensible. To provide a reference for comparison, it is useful to calculate them as ratios of GDP or the wage tax base out of which they would have to be financed. Since *FI* and *GI* refer to present values of future fiscal flows, it is appropriate to use the present values of GDP or the present value of the wage tax base when forming such ratios. These ratios would show the additional percentage of future GDP or wages that must be devoted to restore a balanced fiscal policy. Using alternative taxes or expenditures as a reference base – such as total public plus private consumption, personal plus corporate income, social transfers, etc. – would show the size of the fiscal adjustment required for achieving a balanced policy in terms of those economic flows. Such measures would provide broader understanding of the trade-offs involved under alternative combinations of future fiscal adjustments.

An important characteristic of *FI* is that, like a corpus of outstanding debt, it grows larger over time because of accruing interest costs. Hence, a non-zero *FI* represents fiscal disequilibrium and would necessitate future policy adjustments (see Gokhale and Smetters 2003 for details). In addition, fiscal policies that imply $FI \neq 0$ are unsustainable because the ratio of *FI* to the present value of GDP (or some other income or tax base) also grows larger over time.[24]

Finally, *FI* and *GI* could be decomposed according to the contributions of alternative rates of population ageing and alternative fiscal structures adopted by EU member countries. The motivation for this lies in past experience: The SGP – focused on short- and medium-term objectives – was revised in 2005 to take account of country-specific economic features. The same need is likely to arise if and when the current constraints force further consideration of longer-term structural adjustments to facilitate convergence towards a balanced fiscal stance across EU countries. Reporting the contributions of demographics and country-specific fiscal structures to long-term fiscal imbalances would reveal the feasibility and desirability of adopting differential adjustments by different EU member nations.

Although it was argued earlier that the *FI* measure would be comprehensive only if calculated over the infinite horizon, doing so in the European context proved impossible given the limited amount of data available at the time of preparing the estimates. That is because low fertility in EU countries and low net external immigration cause projected populations to implode over time for several EU countries. Hence, the *FI* measures reported in Section 3.5 below are calculated over a finite horizon – through the terminal year of population projections available from Eurostat, 2051.[25]

3.5 Fiscal imbalance estimates for EU countries

Overall fiscal imbalance and its decomposition by sources – demographics and budget policy

This section presents *FI* estimates for 23 EU countries calculated using data available at the time of writing.[26] These estimates should be regarded as provisional because there remains considerable scope for improving the underlying inputs. They are used here mainly to complement the accounting and reporting framework being proposed. Supplementing existing budget reports with *FI* and *GI* indicators would reveal the long-term implications of current EU members' policies and the sources of differences among them. Notwithstanding the scope for improving the estimates, however, the numbers reported here are based on detailed country-specific data and capture underlying inter-country demographic and fiscal policy differences.

To reveal those differences, *FI* is first calculated for the average EU economy defined with reference to four dimensions: demographics, productivity, budget allocations and generational policy. An 'EU demographic benchmark' is constructed by averaging all countries' projected populations – separately by year, age (16 and older) and gender – between 2004 and 2051.[27] The EU demographic benchmark contains about 16 million people in 2004.[28]

The EU productivity benchmark is constructed by calculating a population-weighted geometric mean of annual labour productivity growth rates (output per hour worked) across EU countries. Country-specific labour productivity growth rates are calculated by using annual geometric average growth rates during the recent past – between 1996 and 2004.

Similarly, harmonized general government taxes and expenditures are averaged to derive the 'EU budget allocation benchmark'. This benchmark consists of population-weighted averages of harmonized taxes and spending per capita.[29] Table 3.1 shows general government revenues, expenditures, surpluses/deficits, and debt figures for the base year of the calculation (2004) for the 23 EU countries included in the calculations and shows the corresponding averages across those countries. The totals are calculated using data on detailed revenue and expenditure categories taken from the Eurostat database.

It should be noted that the total revenues column in Table 3.1 includes 'imputed social contributions', which represent unfunded obligations on account of social transfer guarantees provided by some countries – guarantees that are not supported by explicit transactions for funding them. The motivation for including those imputed revenue items was to avoid

Table 3.1 Total revenues, total expenditures, budget balances and consolidated debt levels (2004) – EU countries and EU average

Country	Millions of euros					Percent of GDP			
	Total revenues	Total outlays	Surplus(+)/ deficit(-)	General govt debt	GDP	Total revenues	Total outlays	Surplus(+)/ deficit(-)	General govt debt
Belgium	134,843	140,417	-5,574	272,874	288,089	46.8	48.7	-1.9	94.7
Denmark	97,996	108,077	-10,080	84,000	197,222	49.7	54.8	-5.1	42.6
Germany	880,780	1,038,040	-157,260	1,451,000	2,215,650	39.8	46.9	-7.1	65.5
Greece	62,703	83,270	-20,567	182,702	168,417	37.2	49.4	-12.2	108.5
Spain	293,926	325,095	-31,169	388,495	837,316	35.1	38.8	-3.7	46.4
France	743,826	880,553	-136,727	1,069,165	1,659,020	44.8	53.1	-8.2	64.4
Ireland	45,282	50,072	-4,791	43,743	147,569	30.7	33.9	-3.2	29.6
Italy	564,912	657,167	-92,255	1,441,879	1,388,870	40.7	47.3	-6.6	103.8
Luxembourg	10,461	11,696	-1,235	1,782	27,056	38.7	43.2	-4.6	6.6
Netherlands	187,204	227,535	-40,331	256,924	488,642	38.3	46.6	-8.3	52.6
Austria	104,181	118,255	-14,074	150,649	235,819	44.2	50.1	-6.0	63.9
Portugal	37,945	65,668	-27,722	83,781	143,029	26.5	45.9	-19.4	58.6
Finland	66,082	76,505	-10,423	67,270	151,935	43.5	50.4	-6.9	44.3
Sweden	143,857	159,814	-15,957	144,066	282,014	51.0	56.7	-5.7	51.1
United Kingdom	640,281	750,629	-110,348	684,776	1,733,603	36.9	43.3	-6.4	39.5
Cyprus									
Czech Republic	31,608	38,468	-6,860	28,069	87,205	36.2	44.1	-7.9	32.2
Estonia	2,936	3,292	-357	486	9,043	32.5	36.4	-3.9	5.4
Hungary									
Lithuania	5,163	6,007	-844	3,522	18,083	28.6	33.2	-4.7	19.5
Latvia	3,185	3,997	-812	1,547	11,157	28.5	35.8	-7.3	13.9
Malta	1,558	2,084	-526	3,211	4,316	36.1	48.3	-12.2	74.4
Poland	65,908	85,907	-19,998	94,578	203,711	32.4	42.2	-9.8	46.4
Slovakia	8,315	13,434	-5,119	14,560	33,863	24.6	39.7	-15.1	43.0
Slovenia	10,408	12,396	-1,988	7,697	26,146	39.8	47.4	-7.6	29.4
EU benchmark*	180,146	211,234	-31,088	281,599	450,338	40.0	46.9	-6.9	62.5

Source: Author's calculations based on data from Eurostat

Note:
* Population-weighted per capita values multiplied by EU benchmark population (= total EU population divided by 23)

over-representing current fiscal deficits and retain comparability of fiscal cash flows across EU countries.

Finally, profiles by age and gender of various harmonized taxes and transfer payments per capita are averaged across all EU countries using age- and gender-specific population weights. Unfortunately, data on tax and transfer profiles are not available for all EU countries. Hence, the estimates reported below are based on available partial data used to construct the 'EU cohort-distributive benchmark'.[30]

Putting all four dimensions together yields an EU benchmark economy. As shown below, this construct enables a decomposition of country-specific fiscal imbalances into their demographic, productivity and fiscal policy (budget allocation and cohort-distribution) components. Replacing the EU benchmark value of one of the components – either one of demographic, productivity growth, budget allocation or cohort-distribution profiles – with its value for a specific country and recalculating FI would show that component's contribution to the FI of the country in question. Replacing all of a particular country's features (and rescaling to match the country's population size) would show the overall contribution of all components.

The purpose of such a set-up is to enable a detailed surveillance of country-specific differences in fiscal imbalances by distinguishing between those arising from demographic and fiscal policy differences. Knowledge of these differences is likely to prove useful when judging and negotiating long-term fiscal reforms. Agreement on an EU benchmark construct would provide a common reference point against which to evaluate each country's fiscal stance and the sources of difference. It would provide a common metric, permitting an apples-to-apples comparison of each country's fiscal position.

Fiscal imbalance estimates and components for EU countries

The EU benchmark FI is calculated by using the methodology and data described earlier. The population projections used for distributing 2004 budget aggregates by age and gender, as described above are based on projections taken from Eurostat through the year 2051. Future taxes, transfers and general government spending on public goods are estimated for the EU benchmark by applying an average labour productivity growth factor of 0.24 per cent per year. This average is calculated by taking a population-weighted geometric mean of average growth in output per hour worked for each of the 23 EU members between 1996 and 2004. The calculations use data on output per hour worked as reported by Eurostat.

A fixed and constant real rate of discount is used for discounting projected fiscal flows back to the year 2004. The inflation-adjusted discount rate is calculated as the interest rate on long-term government bonds minus average expected inflation. Long-term budget transactions spanning 50 or more years should be discounted using the government's opportunity cost of funds over a similar term. However, the longest-term interest rates available are on ten-year government bonds. The geometric mean of annual rates calculated over the period 1996–2005 and across all 23 EU countries (using data available from Eurostat at the time of writing this chapter) equals 5.39 per cent per year. Average expected inflation is calculated as the geometric mean of inflation rates across all EU countries from 1997 through 2005 (according to data availability). The resulting rate (3.01 per cent) is subtracted from the nominal interest rate on government bonds to obtain a real discount rate of 2.38 per cent.[31]

Figure 3.4 shows FI estimates for 23 EU countries and for the EU benchmark case calculated for the base year – 2004.[32] The EU-benchmark economy's overall Fiscal Imbalance

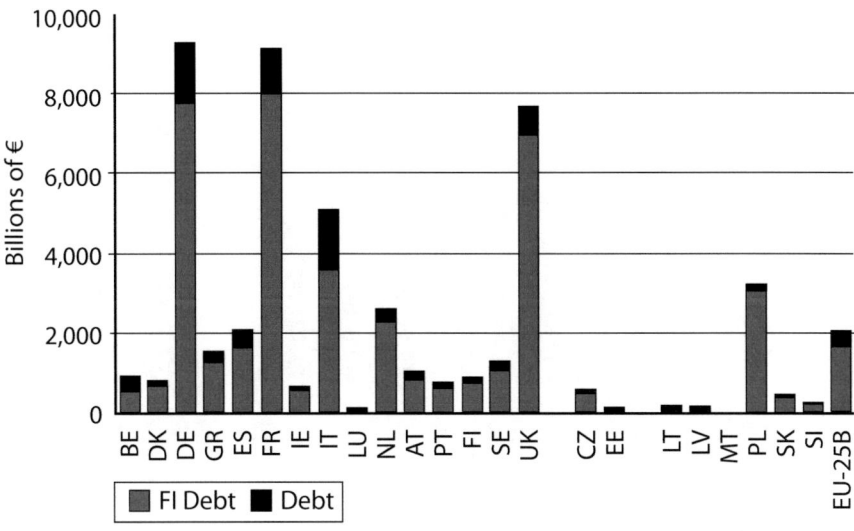

	Total FI	Debt	FI-debt		Total FI	Debt	FI-debt
Belgium	854	273	581	Sweden	1,215	144	1071
Denmark	754	84	670	UK	7,666	685	6,981
Germany	9,263	1,451	7,812	Cyprus			
Greece	1,470	183	1,288	Czech Rep.	514	28	486
Spain	2,045	389	1,656	Estonia	41	1	41
France	9,111	1,069	8,042	Hungary			
Ireland	600	44	556	Lithuania	90	4	86
Italy	5,054	1,442	3,612	Latvia	68	2	67
Luxembourg	102	2	100	Malta	19	3	16
Netherlands	2,556	257	2,299	Poland	3,163	95	3,068
Austria	967	151	817	Slovakia	391	15	376
Portugal	703	84	620	Slovenia	197	8	190
Finland	820	67	752	EU bench'k	1,971	282	1,690

Figure 3.4 Fiscal imbalances of EU countries (billions of €).
Source: Author's calculations

is estimated at €1,971 billion. Of this, outstanding debt amounts to €282 billion, and the present value of prospective fiscal shortfalls equals €1,690 billion. Note that the EU benchmark economy constructed is only one twenty-third as large as the sum total of the 23 EU economies included in the calculations. Figure 3.5 shows that *FI* for the EU benchmark equals 8.3 per cent of the present value of GDP projected through the year 2051.

Figure 3.4 also shows that, in euro terms, Germany (€9,263), France (€9,111), Italy (€5,054) and the United Kingdom (€7,666) contribute the largest fiscal imbalances. However, relative to the present value of GDP, the largest imbalance ratios prevail for Malta (12.8 per cent of GDP, although Malta has the smallest fiscal imbalance in euro terms) and Greece (10.9 per cent of GDP). Estonia (3.2 per cent of GDP), Ireland (3.4 per cent of GDP), Lithuania (3.8 per cent of GDP) and Latvia (4.9 per cent of GDP) are among those with the smallest fiscal imbalances as a percentage of the present value of their respective GDPs. The present discounted values of EU member nations' projected GDPs are shown in Figure 3.6.

62 *Jagadeesh Gokhale*

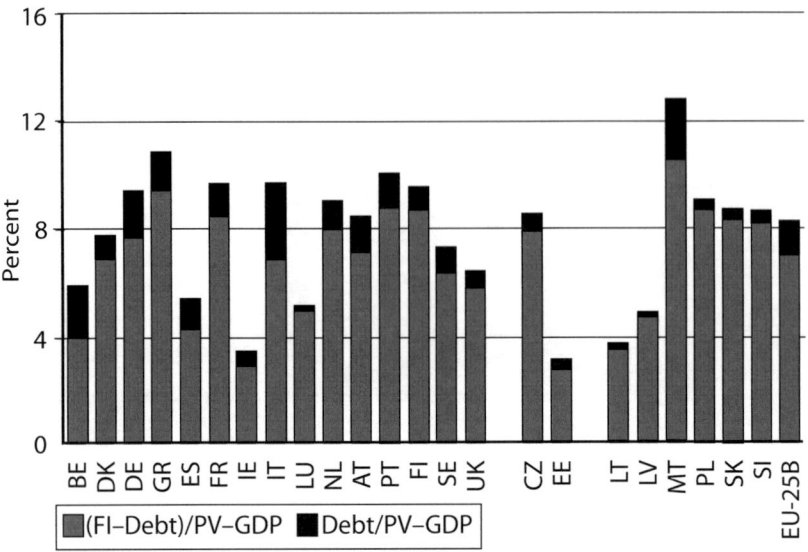

Figure 3.5 Imbalances of EU countries – percentage of the present value of GDP.
Source: Author's calculations

	Total FI	Debt	FI-debt		Total FI	Debt	FI-debt
Belgium	5.9	1.9	4.0	Sweden	7.3	0.9	6.4
Denmark	7.8	0.9	6.9	UK	6.4	0.6	5.9
Germany	9.2	1.4	7.7	Cyprus			
Greece	10.9	1.4	9.5	Czech Rep.	8.6	0.5	8.1
Spain	5.4	1.0	4.4	Estonia	3.2	0.0	3.1
France	9.7	1.1	8.5	Hungary			
Ireland	3.4	0.3	3.2	Lithuania	3.8	0.1	3.6
Italy	9.7	2.8	7.0	Latvia	4.9	0.1	4.8
Luxembourg	5.1	0.1	5.0	Malta	12.8	2.2	10.6
Netherlands	9.0	0.9	8.1	Poland	9.0	0.3	8.8
Austria	8.5	1.3	7.2	Slovakia	8.7	0.3	8.4
Portugal	10.1	1.2	8.9	Slovenia	8.7	0.3	8.3
Finland	9.6	0.8	8.8	EU bench'k	8.3	1.2	7.1

Figure 3.7 shows the demographic component of *FI*. It shows the excess imbalance resulting from using a particular country's demographic structure in place of the EU benchmark demographic structure. The figure reports this excess as a percentage of the *FI* estimated for the EU benchmark case. Thus, positive numbers indicate demographic features that increase budget shortfalls under current (EU benchmark) fiscal policies – either population ageing that is more rapid due to increases in longevity, or a larger than average baby-boom generation approaching retirement, or a baby-boom generation that is closer to retirement than under the EU benchmark case, or a recent relatively more rapid decline in fertility that reduces the number of tax-paying workers.

Figure 3.7 suggests that despite their large *FI* estimates – in both absolute euro terms and as percentages of the present value of GDP – population ageing is not more rapid than average in the case of Germany, Italy and the United Kingdom. This result may appear

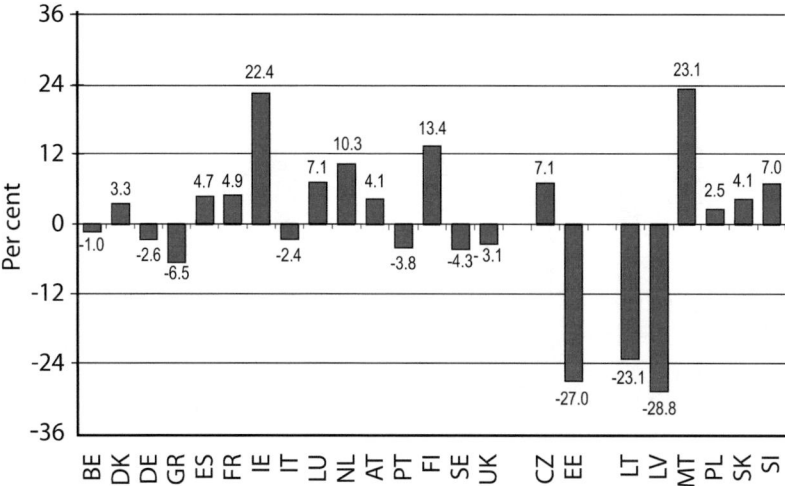

Figure 3.6 Demographic components of fiscal imbalences

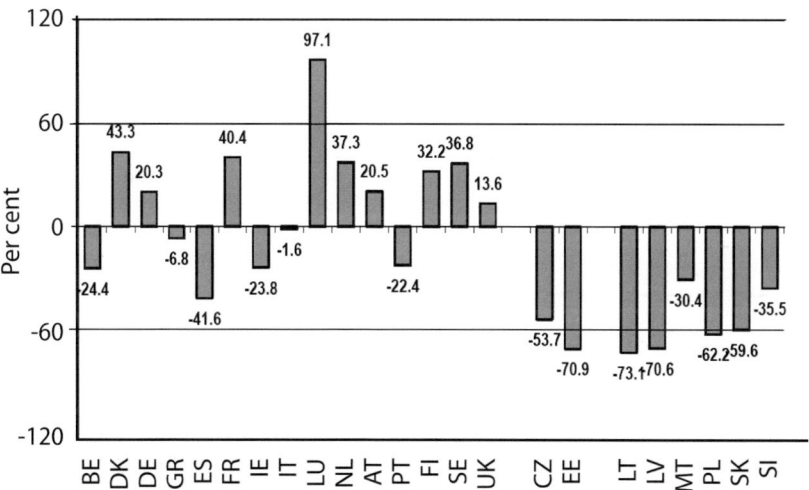

Figure 3.7 Budget allocation components of fiscal imbalances.

surprising, but it must be noted that these large countries contribute significantly to the 'average' demographics of the EU benchmark. On the other hand, France's demographics cause a 5 per cent increase in *FI* relative to the EU benchmark *FI*. The largest *FI*-increasing influence of demographics appears in the cases of Ireland and Malta, whereas Estonia, Lithuania and Latvia appear to have younger projected populations or slower population ageing through 2051.

Figure 3.8 shows the budget allocation components of *FI* for EU Member States. As mentioned earlier, this experiment replaces a particular country's harmonized tax, transfer and spending components with those of the EU benchmark case. Figure 3.8 shows that the budget allocations of Germany, France and the United Kingdom contribute significantly towards high *FI* values. However, Denmark and Luxembourg appear to be following 'budget

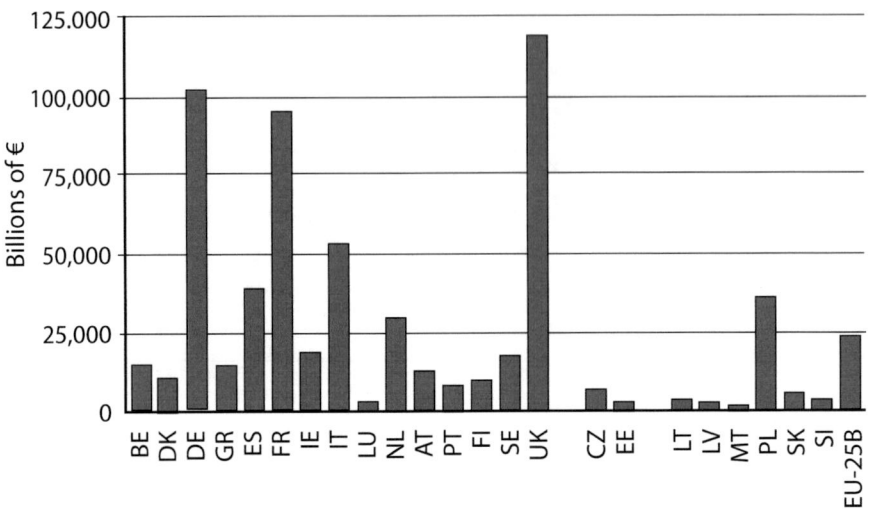

	PV_GDP (€ billions)		PV_GDP (€ billions)		PV_GDP (€ billions)
Belgium	14,435	Netherlands	28,326	Hungary	
Denmark	9,653	Austria	11,401	Lithuania	2,375
Germany	101,130	Portugal	6,985	Latvia	1,387
Greece	13,530	Finland	8,580	Malta	146
Spain	37,851	Sweden	16,682	Poland	34,970
France	94,327	UK	118,870	Slovakia	4,470
Ireland	17,435	Cyprus		Slovenia	2,271
Italy	51,949	Czech Rep.	5,987		
Luxembourg	1,982	Estonia	1,292	EU bench'k	23,891

Figure 3.8 Present value of GDP through 2051 (billions of inflation adjusted €)

allocation' policies with the largest prospective fiscal impact in terms of generating high *FI* values. Most of the new entrants into the EU appear to be following budget allocation policies consistent with reducing fiscal imbalances.

Similar experiments are not implemented here for the productivity and cohort-distribution components because the required data are unavailable. In the case of productivity, a straightforward replacement of a member country's productivity growth rate would not be appropriate because a higher productivity rate would generally reduce the projected levels of future means-tested social transfer programmes and may be associated with higher revenues in a nonlinear manner. Implementing this experiment requires careful calibration of the response of welfare expenditures to changes in productivity growth – that is not feasible given data availability.[33]

Adequate information is also not available for estimating the impact of country-specific cohort-distribution policies. However, the experiments described earlier of isolating the demographic and budget allocation components provide the basic framework for isolating these components as well. Finally, estimating *GI* measures is also not feasible given that institutional details about financing arrangements for various sub-programmes are not available (to the author).[34]

The impact of delaying fiscal adjustments

It is easy to show that *FI* grows larger over time if the initial *FI* value is positive (see Appendix A in Gokhale and Smetters 2003). That is because of accruing interest on the current *FI* – similar to that on a corpus of outstanding debt. When *FI* is calculated over a finite projection horizon, the addition of another year's budget surplus or shortfall at the end of the horizon also influences next year's *FI* estimate. Table 3.2 shows estimates of *FI* for EU countries through the year 2010. Each estimate covers a rolling period of 47 years – 2004 through 2051 for the *FI* reported under '2004', 2005 through 2052 for the *FI* reported under '2005', and so on. These calculations are based on extending each EU member nation's demographic projections for a few additional years beyond 2051.

Table 3.2 shows that *FI* (calculated over a 47-year horizon) for the EU benchmark case grows from €1,971 billion in 2004 to €2,489 billion by 2010 if current policies and long-term projections remain unchanged through that year. The increase in *FI* from one year to the next generally implies an increase in the cost of future fiscal adjustments because the resources available to pay for the shortfalls, the present value of GDP, generally grow at a slower rate.

Table 3.2 shows that with each passing year about one-third of the increase in *FI* arises from advancing the terminal year of the projection horizon by an additional year. The remainder of the increase in *FI* arises from accruing interest. This indicates the shortcoming of adopting a finite projection horizon for capturing the cost of postponing fiscal adjustments. Were policymakers to adopt fiscal adjustments to reduce fiscal imbalances as measured under a limited time horizon, a positive fiscal imbalance would re-emerge in the very next year and grow larger over time.[35]

Take the case of France. The French government reported a deficit of 2.9 per cent of GDP – that is, €49.6 billion – in 2005.[36] According to Table 3.2, however, the change in the French *FI* for 2005 equals €368.2 billion – an order of magnitude larger than the reported fiscal deficit for 2005. Similar remarks apply to current reporting on many other EU countries' fiscal stance based on traditional deficit and debt measures. Table 3.3 compares the reported annual public balances (Eurostat) with *FI* accruals for 2005 taken from Table 3.2. In the case of some EU countries, a surplus public balance indicates an improving fiscal condition, but the *FI* accrual is positive pointing to the opposite conclusion. Thus, depending on backward-looking fiscal measures such as deficits and debt would cause policymakers to draw incorrect conclusions about their country's evolving fiscal condition.

A proposal for integrated reporting of short- and long-term budgetary conditions

Even after taking account of the new SGP's constraints, each EU country retains considerable sovereignty over its fiscal policies. For sure, each EU member country retains full control over the accounting and reporting of national budget information. Nevertheless, when it comes to fulfilling SGP-related budget reporting for long-term fiscal policy surveillance, the budget reports of all countries would benefit from the introduction of a few additional features.

Both short-term budget projections and the long-term implications of current fiscal policies should be included in the reports. The *FI* measure appears to be the easiest to integrate into most existing budget-reporting frameworks because it is essentially a 'budget measure' and comprehensively incorporates forward-looking fiscal information (as discussed earlier).

Table 3.2 Annual changes in fiscal imbalances: interest accruals and shifting the projection window

Country	Measure	2004	2005	2006	2007	2008	2009	2010	2004	2005	2006	2007	2008	2009	2010
		€ billions							FI as percent of PV_GDP and annual change and components as percent of annual GDP						
EU benchmark	Fiscal imbalance	1,971.1	2,050.9	2,133.2	2,218.1	2,305.6	2,395.8	2,488.6	8.3	8.6	8.9	9.3	9.6	10.0	10.4
	Annual change	—	79.8	82.3	84.9	87.5	90.2	92.8	—	17.6	18.0	18.4	18.8	19.3	19.8
	Interest accrual	—	46.9	48.8	50.8	52.8	54.9	57.0	—	10.3	10.7	11.0	11.4	11.7	12.1
	Shift in projection window	—	32.9	33.5	34.1	34.7	35.3	35.8	—	7.3	7.3	7.4	7.5	7.5	7.6
Belgium	Fiscal imbalance	853.8	886.5	920.1	954.7	990.2	1,026.9	1,064.6	5.9	6.1	6.3	6.6	6.8	7.0	7.3
	Annual change	—	32.6	33.6	34.6	35.6	36.6	37.7	—	11.3	11.6	11.9	12.2	12.5	12.8
	Interest accrual	—	20.3	21.1	21.9	22.7	23.6	24.4	—	7.0	7.3	7.5	7.8	8.0	8.3
	Shift in projection window	—	12.3	12.5	12.7	12.9	13.1	13.2	—	4.3	4.3	4.4	4.4	4.5	4.5
Denmark	Fiscal imbalance	753.5	781.6	810.6	840.5	871.3	903.2	936.0	7.8	8.1	8.4	8.7	9.0	9.3	9.6
	Annual change	—	28.1	29.0	29.9	30.8	31.8	32.9	—	14.2	14.6	15.1	15.5	16.0	16.4
	Interest accrual	—	17.9	18.6	19.3	20.0	20.7	21.5	—	9.1	9.4	9.7	10.1	10.4	10.8
	Shift in projection window	—	10.2	10.4	10.6	10.8	11.1	11.4	—	5.2	5.2	5.3	5.5	5.6	5.7
Germany	Fiscal imbalance	9,263.4	9,605.9	9,957.5	10,318.2	10,688.3	11,067.8	11,456.9	9.2	9.5	9.9	10.2	10.6	11.0	11.4
	Annual change	—	342.5	351.5	360.7	370.1	379.5	389.1	—	15.4	15.8	16.2	16.6	17.0	17.5
	Interest accrual	—	220.5	228.6	237.0	245.6	254.4	263.4	—	9.9	10.3	10.6	11.0	11.4	11.8
	Shift in projection window	—	122.1	122.9	123.7	124.5	125.1	125.7	—	5.5	5.5	5.6	5.6	5.6	5.6
Greece	Fiscal imbalance	1,470.4	1,539.2	1,610.7	1,685.0	1,762.3	1,842.5	1,925.8	10.9	11.4	11.9	12.5	13.1	13.7	14.3
	Annual change	—	68.8	71.5	74.3	77.2	80.2	83.3	—	39.8	40.5	41.1	41.7	42.3	43.0
	Interest accrual	—	35.0	36.6	38.3	40.1	41.9	43.9	—	20.3	20.7	21.2	21.6	22.1	22.6
	Shift in projection window	—	33.8	34.9	36.0	37.1	38.3	39.4	—	19.6	19.7	19.9	20.1	20.2	20.3
Spain	Fiscal imbalance	2,044.7	2,129.9	2,217.0	2,306.1	2,397.1	2,490.1	2,585.1	5.4	5.6	5.8	6.1	6.3	6.5	6.8
	Annual change	—	85.2	87.1	89.1	91.0	93.0	95.0	—	10.1	10.3	10.4	10.7	10.9	11.2
	Interest accrual	—	48.7	50.7	52.8	54.9	57.1	59.3	—	5.8	6.0	6.2	6.4	6.7	7.0
	Shift in projection window	—	36.5	36.4	36.3	36.1	35.9	35.7	—	4.3	4.3	4.3	4.2	4.2	4.2

Table 3.2 (continued)

Country	Measure	2004	2005	2006	2007	2008	2009	2010	2004	2005	2006	2007	2008	2009	2010
		€ billions							FI as percent of PV_GDP and annual change and components as percent of annual GDP						
France	Fiscal imbalance	9,111.0	9,479.2	9,858.9	10,250.6	10,654.6	11,071.1	11,500.5	9.7	10.0	10.4	10.8	11.2	11.6	12.0
	Annual change	—	368.2	379.7	391.7	404.0	416.5	429.3	—	22.0	22.5	23.0	23.5	24.0	24.6
	Interest accrual	—	216.8	225.6	234.6	244.0	253.6	263.5	—	13.0	13.4	13.8	14.2	14.6	15.1
	Shift in projection window	—	151.4	154.1	157.1	160.0	162.9	165.9	—	9.0	9.1	9.2	9.3	9.4	9.5
Ireland	Fiscal imbalance	599.7	639.3	681.1	725.2	771.6	820.4	871.6	3.4	3.6	3.9	4.1	4.3	4.5	4.8
	Annual change	—	39.6	41.8	44.1	46.4	48.8	51.2	—	25.9	26.3	26.7	27.1	27.5	27.9
	Interest accrual	—	14.3	15.2	16.2	17.3	18.4	19.5	—	9.3	9.6	9.8	10.1	10.4	10.6
	Shift in projection window	—	25.4	26.6	27.9	29.1	30.4	31.7	—	16.6	16.7	16.9	17.0	17.2	17.3
Italy	Fiscal imbalance	5,054.0	5,224.2	5,398.2	5,576.0	5,757.7	5,943.5	6,133.4	9.7	10.1	10.4	10.8	11.1	11.5	11.9
	Annual change	—	170.2	173.9	177.8	181.8	185.8	189.9	—	12.3	12.7	13.1	13.5	13.9	14.4
	Interest accrual	—	120.3	124.3	128.5	132.7	137.0	141.5	—	8.7	9.1	9.5	9.9	10.3	10.7
	Shift in projection window	—	50.0	49.6	49.3	49.0	48.7	48.4	—	3.6	3.6	3.6	3.6	3.7	3.7
Luxembourg	Fiscal imbalance	101.7	106.6	111.6	116.8	122.1	127.7	133.4	5.1	5.3	5.5	5.7	5.9	6.2	6.4
	Annual change	—	4.8	5.0	5.2	5.4	5.6	5.8	—	17.5	17.8	18.1	18.4	18.7	19.0
	Interest accrual	—	2.4	2.5	2.7	2.8	2.9	3.0	—	8.8	9.0	9.3	9.5	9.8	10.0
	Shift in projection window	—	2.4	2.5	2.5	2.6	2.7	2.7	—	8.8	8.8	8.8	8.9	8.9	9.0
Netherlands	Fiscal imbalance	2,556.3	2,655.2	2,757.3	2,863.1	2,972.4	3,085.5	3,202.4	9.0	9.4	9.7	10.0	10.4	10.8	11.1
	Annual change	—	98.8	102.2	105.7	109.3	113.1	116.9	—	20.0	20.5	21.0	21.5	22.0	22.5
	Interest accrual	—	60.8	63.2	65.6	68.1	70.7	73.4	—	12.3	12.7	13.0	13.4	13.8	14.2
	Shift in projection window	—	38.0	39.0	40.1	41.2	42.3	43.5	—	7.7	7.8	8.0	8.1	8.2	8.4
Austria	Fiscal imbalance	967.1	1,005.1	1,044.2	1,084.3	1,125.5	1,167.8	1,211.2	8.5	8.8	9.1	9.5	9.8	10.1	10.5
	Annual change	—	38.1	39.1	40.1	41.2	42.3	43.4	—	16.1	16.5	16.9	17.2	17.6	18.0
	Interest accrual	—	23.0	23.9	24.9	25.8	26.8	27.8	—	9.7	10.1	10.4	10.8	11.2	11.6
	Shift in projection window	—	15.0	15.2	15.3	15.4	15.5	15.6	—	6.4	6.4	6.4	6.4	6.5	6.5

Table continued on next page.

Table 3.2 (continued)

Country	Measure	2004	2005	2006	2007	2008	2009	2010	2004	2005	2006	2007	2008	2009	2010
		€ billions							FI as percent of PV_GDP and annual change and components as percent of annual GDP						
Portugal	Fiscal imbalance	703.4	730.1	757.7	785.9	814.9	844.7	875.3	10.1	10.5	10.9	11.3	11.7	12.1	12.6
	Annual change	—	26.8	27.5	28.3	29.0	29.8	30.6	—	18.6	19.1	19.5	20.0	20.4	21.0
	Interest accrual	—	16.7	17.4	18.0	18.7	19.4	20.1	—	11.6	12.0	12.4	12.9	13.3	13.8
	Shift in projection window	—	10.0	10.1	10.2	10.3	10.4	10.5	—	7.0	7.0	7.1	7.1	7.1	7.2
Sweden	Fiscal imbalance	819.7	852.2	885.8	920.6	956.5	993.6	1,031.9	9.6	9.9	10.3	10.7	11.1	11.5	12.0
	Annual change	—	32.5	33.6	34.7	35.9	37.1	38.3	—	21.2	21.7	22.2	22.8	23.3	23.8
	Interest accrual	—	19.5	20.3	21.1	21.9	22.8	23.6	—	12.7	13.1	13.5	13.9	14.3	14.7
	Shift in projection window	—	13.0	13.3	13.7	14.0	14.3	14.6	—	8.5	8.6	8.7	8.9	9.0	9.1
Finland	Fiscal imbalance	1,214.6	1,264.1	1,315.5	1,369.1	1,424.7	1,482.5	1,542.6	7.3	7.6	7.8	8.1	8.4	8.7	9.1
	Annual change	—	49.5	51.5	53.5	55.6	57.8	60.0	—	17.4	17.9	18.3	18.8	19.4	19.9
	Interest accrual	—	28.9	30.1	31.3	32.6	33.9	35.3	—	10.1	10.4	10.7	11.0	11.4	11.7
	Shift in projection window	—	20.6	21.4	22.2	23.1	23.9	24.7	—	7.2	7.4	7.6	7.8	8.0	8.2
United Kingdom	Fiscal imbalance	7,666.1	8,009.6	8,366.4	8,736.9	9,121.6	9,520.7	9,934.5	6.4	6.7	7.0	7.3	7.6	7.9	8.2
	Annual change	—	343.5	356.7	370.5	384.7	399.1	413.8	—	19.5	19.9	20.3	20.7	21.1	21.6
	Interest accrual	—	182.5	190.6	199.1	207.9	217.1	226.6	—	10.3	10.6	10.9	11.2	11.5	11.8
	Shift in projection window	—	161.1	166.1	171.4	176.7	182.0	187.2	—	9.1	9.3	9.4	9.5	9.6	9.8
Cyprus	Fiscal imbalance	0.0	0.0	0.0	0.0	0.0	0.0	0.0	0.00	0.00	0.00	0.00	0.00	0.00	0.00
	Annual change	—	0.0	0.0	0.0	0.0	0.0	0.0	—	0.00	0.00	0.00	0.00	0.00	0.00
	Interest accrual	—	0.0	0.0	0.0	0.0	0.0	0.0	—	0.00	0.00	0.00	0.00	0.00	0.00
	Shift in projection window	—	0.0	0.0	0.0	0.0	0.0	0.0	—	0.00	0.00	0.00	0.00	0.00	0.00
Czech Republic	Fiscal imbalance	514.0	538.6	564.1	590.5	618.0	646.5	675.9	8.6	9.0	9.5	9.9	10.4	10.9	11.4
	Annual change	—	24.6	25.5	26.5	27.5	28.5	29.5	—	27.6	28.2	28.7	29.3	29.8	30.3
	Interest accrual	—	12.2	12.8	13.4	14.1	14.7	15.4	—	13.8	14.2	14.6	15.0	15.4	15.8
	Shift in projection window	—	12.3	12.7	13.1	13.4	13.7	14.1	—	13.9	14.0	14.2	14.3	14.4	14.5

Table 3.2 (continued)

Country	Measure	2004	2005	2006	2007	2008	2009	2010	2004	2005	2006	2007	2008	2009	2010
		€ billions							FI as percent of PV_GDP and annual change and components as percent of annual GDP						
Estonia	Fiscal imbalance	41.0	43.9	47.1	50.5	54.1	58.0	62.2	3.2	3.4	3.7	3.9	4.2	4.6	4.9
	Annual change	—	3.0	3.2	3.4	3.6	3.9	4.2	—	31.1	31.9	32.9	33.8	34.6	35.5
	Interest accrual	—	1.0	1.0	1.1	1.2	1.3	1.4	—	10.3	10.5	10.8	11.1	11.5	11.8
	Shift in projection window	—	2.0	2.1	2.3	2.4	2.6	2.8	—	20.8	21.4	22.0	22.6	23.2	23.7
Hungary	Fiscal imbalance	0.0	0.0	0.0	0.0	0.0	0.0	0.0	0.0	0.0	0.0	0.0	0.0	0.0	0.0
	Annual change	—	0.0	0.0	0.0	0.0	0.0	0.0	—	0.0	0.0	0.0	0.0	0.0	0.0
	Interest accrual	—	0.0	0.0	0.0	0.0	0.0	0.0	—	0.0	0.0	0.0	0.0	0.0	0.0
	Shift in projection window	—	0.0	0.0	0.0	0.0	0.0	0.0	—	0.0	0.0	0.0	0.0	0.0	0.0
Lithuania	Fiscal imbalance	89.5	95.4	101.7	108.5	115.7	123.4	131.5	3.8	4.0	4.3	4.6	4.9	5.3	5.6
	Annual change	—	5.9	6.3	7.2	7.2	7.7	8.1	—	31.5	32.2	33.0	33.7	34.5	35.2
	Interest accrual	—	2.1	2.3	2.4	2.6	2.8	2.9	—	11.3	11.5	11.8	12.1	12.4	12.7
	Shift in projection window	—	3.8	4.1	4.3	4.6	4.9	5.2	—	20.2	20.7	21.2	21.7	22.1	22.5
Latvia	Fiscal imbalance	68.1	72.3	76.8	81.6	86.7	92.0	97.7	4.9	5.2	5.6	6.0	6.3	6.8	7.2
	Annual change	—	4.2	4.5	4.8	5.1	5.4	5.6	—	36.5	37.2	38.0	38.7	39.4	40.1
	Interest accrual	—	1.6	1.7	1.8	1.9	2.1	2.2	—	13.9	14.2	14.5	14.8	15.2	15.6
	Shift in projection window	—	2.6	2.8	3.0	3.1	3.3	3.5	—	22.6	23.0	23.4	23.8	24.2	24.6
Malta	Fiscal imbalance	18.7	19.3	19.9	20.5	21.1	21.7	22.4	12.8	13.1	13.4	13.7	14.0	14.4	14.7
	Annual change	—	0.6	0.6	0.6	0.6	0.6	0.7	—	13.5	14.0	14.4	14.9	15.5	16.0
	Interest accrual	—	0.4	0.5	0.5	0.5	0.5	0.5	—	10.4	10.8	11.3	11.7	12.2	12.7
	Shift in projection window	—	0.1	0.1	0.1	0.1	0.1	0.1	—	3.1	3.2	3.2	3.2	3.2	3.3
Poland	Fiscal imbalance	3,162.9	3,386.9	3,626.6	3,882.8	4,156.1	4,447.3	4,757.0	9.0	9.7	10.4	11.2	12.0	12.9	13.8
	Annual change	—	224.0	239.7	256.2	273.3	291.2	309.7	—	104.4	106.1	107.7	109.3	110.8	112.2
	Interest accrual	—	75.3	80.6	86.3	92.4	98.9	105.8	—	35.1	35.7	36.3	36.9	37.6	38.4
	Shift in projection window	—	148.7	159.1	169.9	180.9	192.3	203.8	—	69.3	70.4	71.4	72.3	73.1	73.9

Table continued on next page.

Table 3.2 (continued)

Country	Measure	2004	2005	2006	2007	2008	2009	2010	2004	2005	2006	2007	2008	2009	2010
		€ billions							FI as percent of PV_GDP and annual change and components as percent of annual GDP						
Slovakia	Fiscal imbalance	390.7	415.7	442.3	470.5	500.4	531.9	565.1	8.7	9.3	9.9	10.6	11.3	12.0	12.8
	Annual change	–	25.1	26.6	28.2	29.8	31.5	33.3	–	70.9	72.0	73.1	74.2	75.2	76.1
	Interest accrual	–	9.3	9.9	10.5	11.2	11.9	12.7	–	26.3	26.8	27.3	27.8	28.4	29.0
	Shift in projection window	–	15.8	16.7	17.7	18.6	19.6	20.6	–	44.6	45.2	45.8	46.3	46.8	47.2
Slovenia	Fiscal imbalance	197.2	207.7	218.7	230.1	242.0	254.4	267.3	8.7	9.2	9.6	10.2	10.7	11.2	11.8
	Annual change	–	10.5	11.0	11.4	11.9	12.4	12.9	–	39.1	39.7	40.3	40.8	41.4	41.9
	Interest accrual	–	4.7	4.9	5.2	5.5	5.8	6.1	–	17.4	17.9	18.3	18.8	19.2	19.7
	Shift in projection window	–	5.8	6.0	6.2	6.4	6.6	6.8	–	21.7	21.8	22.0	22.1	22.1	22.2

Table 3.3 Comparing public balances and accruing fiscal imbalances in EU countries for 2005 (€ billions)

	Public deficit	FI accrual		Public deficit	FI accrual		Public deficit	FI accrual
Belgium	−0.3	32.6	Luxembourg	0.6	4.8	Estonia	−0.2	3.0
Denmark	−10.2	28.1	Netherlands	1.5	98.8	Lithuania	5.4	5.9
Germany	74.0	342.5	Austria	3.7	38.1	Latvia	0.1	4.2
Greece	8.2	68.8	Portugal	8.8	26.8	Malta	0.0	0.6
Spain	−10.0	85.2	Finland	−4.1	32.5	Poland	0.2	224.0
France	49.6	368.2	Sweden	−8.4	49.5	Slovakia	6.1	25.1
Ireland	−1.6	39.6	UK	64.5	343.5	Slovenia	1.1	10.5
Italy	58.1	170.2	Czech Rep.	2.6	24.6	EU benchmark	10.6	79.8

For social transfer (and possibly other) programmes with independent and dedicated financial resources, it is also easy to integrate presentations of both fiscal and generational imbalance measures into existing budget reports.

Many existing short-term budget reports divide the overall budget summary table into 'current' and 'capital' accounts. Table 3.4, for example, shows a prototype budget report containing 'current' and 'capital' accounts followed by additional information on long-term sustainability measures – that is, the implications of continuing current policies through the long-term projection horizon of several decades (if not through the infinite time horizon).

The *FI* figures for each year beyond the base year show *FI* as of the corresponding future year. As discussed earlier, if the initial *FI* is positive, future years' *FI* figures will grow larger over time. In addition, *FI* grows larger even as a percentage of the present value of GDP. The components of each year's change in *FI* could also be included. In the case of finite-horizon estimates, the total change in *FI* across years would include those arising from accruing interest and the addition of another year at the end of the projection horizon. As discussed earlier, such information would be useful for policymakers to appreciate the cost of postponing fiscal reforms.

This could be followed by reports of the financial implications of current policies for independently financed sub-programmes, and a final sub-section could include *FI* and its revenue and expenditure components for the rest-of-government sector. This sub-section would 'close' the account by reporting intra-government liabilities and net liabilities to the public (net outstanding debt). Supplementary tables could break out the overall fiscal imbalance into its demographic, budget allocation and cohort-distribution components – as described in earlier sections.

Comparison with sustainability measures proposed by the Ageing Working Group

The Working Group on Ageing Populations (AWG) recommends a two-stage approach to assessing the sustainability of long-term finances (Economic Policy Committee 2001). Its assessment of sustainable public finances takes the SGP's fiscal constraints as a starting point. The objective is to evaluate prospects for compliance with EMU requirements – avoiding excessive deficits and keeping debt levels below 60 per cent of GDP. The SGP requires that EU Member States maintain a 'close to balance or surplus' position over the medium term (three to five years) but not over a longer term. If followed, this would result in de facto sustainability in a simple and transparent manner (Balassone and Franco 2000).

The arguments provided in this chapter, however, suggest that such an approach would be inadequate. The problem is that a short-term and 'short-sighted' view of the implications of current policy – over the next three to five years – does not provide sufficient and relevant information to policymakers. One can envision a situation where policies are enacted to ensure compliance with the SGP's constraints, only to soon discover that the job is not yet finished – indeed, the problem may have grown larger as the budget window moves forward and the opportunity to save resources in the meanwhile with a more vigorous adjustment is lost.

Defining sustainability as a non-violation of predetermined levels of deficits and debt is simply not useful because (as discussed earlier) those indicators alone do not fully reveal the budget and real economic implications of alternative ways of achieving fiscal sustainability and economic convergence. The simple projections of future debt and deficit levels also do

Table 3.4 Long-term budget reporting

	2006	2007	2008	2009	2010
(a) Budget report – country X (€ billion)					
Current budget					
Total current receipts					
Total current outlays					
Current surplus(+)/deficit(-)					
Capital budget					
Net investment					
Net borrowing					
Public sector net debt – end of year					
(b) Future implications of current policies					
Fiscal Imbalance (Open-group obligations through year …)					
Annual change					
Interest accrual					
Shift in projection window					
Programme 1 (e.g. public pensions)					
Fiscal imbalance					
Generational imbalance					
Present value: current generations' future net benefits					
Assets (claims on rest of government)					
Present value of future generations' net benefits					
Programme 2 (e.g. unemployment insurance)					
Fiscal imbalance					
Generational imbalance					
Present value: current generations' future net benefits					
Assets (claims on rest of government)					
Present value of future generations' net benefits					
Rest of government					
Fiscal imbalance					
Net debt outstanding (from section (a) above)					
Present value of excess future outlays over revenues					
Present value of future outlays					
Present value of future revenues					
Liability to Programme 1					
Liability to Programme 2					
…					
…					

Notes:
average values over 1994–2004, data before revisions occurred since 2002
EU15 – 1994–2004 – 2SLS fixed effects estimation (1)

not comprehensively reveal the sources of economically meaningful imbalances – not just in overall budgets, but also in terms of net payments to different sub-groups, such as young, old and future generations. The traditional fiscal metrics do not permit answers to several important questions such as: How do decision makers rank alternative policies that result in the same – say, slightly lower – debt and deficit trajectories? Who benefits and who loses under each alternative, and what is the likely impact on the economy? Obviously, policymakers should be provided ways for answering such questions but traditional measures and a short-horizon focus would be insufficient. There appears to be no short cut to specifying sustainability in terms of comprehensive forward-looking measures as described earlier. More work is needed to complement existing theoretical developments with empirical information in order to improve the quality of long-term sustainability estimates.

Another issue concerns the incorporation of future policy changes that have already been enacted. The calculations reported in this chapter are based on current (2005) levels of taxes, transfers and government purchases. However, if cuts in pension benefits or revenue-increasing measures are already scheduled in the laws – information that is unavailable to the author at the time of writing – those policies should be incorporated into *FI* and *GI* calculations because they are consistent with the definition of 'current policy'. A note of caution needs to be registered, however, that not all scheduled policies may be politically or economically feasible and some may be very unlikely. In addition, future policies may be incompletely specified – say, scheduled to terminate at a certain date with no indication of what would occur thereafter. Such policy environments make it difficult to implement long-range calculations of *FI* and *GI* measures. In such cases, providing ranges of *FI* and *GI* estimates under alternative policy projections would be more appropriate – and still better than fiscal reporting exclusively on the basis of traditional short-horizon measures.

3.6 Conclusion

This chapter began by observing that EU countries are undergoing twin transitions: a demographic transition wherein the populations of most EU countries are ageing and an economic transition resulting from the adoption of a single currency and associated adjustments in fiscal constraints and agreements. These processes are likely to impose severe and conflicting pressures on policymakers, on the one hand to increase deficit spending to support expanding retiree cohorts, and on the other to limit deficits and debt in order to continue expanding a heretofore successful process of monetary unification.

This chapter proposes the adoption of an extended framework of budget accounting and reporting within the context of the SGP's long-term fiscal policy surveillance requirement. Among the several available fiscal measures, this chapter argues for adopting fiscal and generational imbalance measures because they can potentially incorporate comprehensive and policy-relevant information about the future implications of continuing current policies. The baseline *FI* and *GI* estimates can be supplemented with their demographic, budget allocation, productivity growth and cohort-distribution policy components. The advantage of doing so is to present policymakers with tools for comparing inter-country differences in fiscal stances and for evaluating the feasibility and likely economic effects of alternative policy options.

This chapter argues in detail why traditional debt and deficit measures can be potentially misleading as measures of a government's fiscal stance. It also argues that accrual accounting approaches, although already adopted by several countries, are less appropriate for government entities than for private ones. Among generational accounting and fiscal and generational imbalances, the two latter measures appear simpler to communicate and can be more easily integrated into existing budget reports – as demonstrated through a prototype reporting template described in this chapter.

This chapter also provides provisional estimates of fiscal imbalances for 23 EU countries and for the EU benchmark case under a projection horizon extending from 2004 through 2051. Although they are based on provisional and incomplete data, they are likely to be reasonably accurate estimates of prevailing fiscal imbalances in EU member countries and of the sources of inter-country differences. The estimated fiscal imbalances are quite large for many EU countries. On average, EU countries face a FI of 8.3 per cent of the present value of GDP projected through 2051. That implies a considerable shortfall of resources to pay for social transfers and other general government expenditures during the next four or five decades.

The estimates show considerable differences in underlying demographics and budget allocations that generate the country-specific *FI* values. In addition, the results show a much higher rate of accruing fiscal costs compared to public balances reported under traditional and backward-looking budget measures. Those accruals suggest the need to adopt fiscal adjustments to resolve outstanding EU fiscal imbalances sooner rather than later.

Future fiscal adjustments would involve combinations of tax increases or reductions in social and other expenditures. On balance, it appears that EU countries need to undergo a third transition in order to facilitate a resolution of outstanding fiscal imbalances – one that results in a retrenchment in the existing system of social protections – if only because the current protections appear to be unaffordable. Attempting to redress existing fiscal imbalances through yet higher taxes would exacerbate the already high tax rates that EU citizens are facing – 40 per cent for the EU benchmark economy.

Finally, one response to the fiscal measures proposed in this chapter is that different underlying assumptions may generate wide variations in estimates of fiscal and generational imbalances and in their ratios to GDP or tax bases. However, that does not constitute an argument against adopting such measures; instead, it suggests a reason to supplement them with estimates of the associated uncertainty. The usual response to uncertainty is to be 'cautious' about embracing long-term measures. However, under rapid population ageing and prospects of steep increases in the costs of social insurance programmes, a policy of 'wait and see' may be just as dangerous as it could deprive policymakers of key information on policy trade-offs and cause more delays in adopting fiscal reforms. Indeed, large changes in fiscal imbalances due to small changes in underlying economic assumptions (discount and growth rates, etc.) are more likely if the underlying long-term future fiscal shortfalls are larger rather than smaller. But if that is the case, it indicates the need for haste rather than caution in adopting the fiscal measures suggested herein.

Notes

1 The author thanks Alan Auerbach, Martin Larch, João Nogueira Martins, William Niskanen and Peter Vandoren for helpful discussions during the preparation of this manuscript and Joanne Fung for excellent research assistance. Use of data from Eurostat and the UK's Economic and Social Data Service is hereby acknowledged. All opinions expressed herein are those of the author and not necessarily those of the Cato Institute.
2 The deficit constraint requires each Member State to maintain annual deficits at 3 per cent of GDP or less. Each Member State is also required to maintain a total debt-to-GDP ratio of 60 per cent or less. These constraints were specified in the original Maastricht Treaty of the European Union.
3 See federal budget reports, for example, of Denmark National Bank (Danmarks Nationalbank 2005), General Administration of the Treasury, Kingdom of Belgium (2005), Ministry of Finance of Sweden (2005), and several other EU countries.

4 For example, New Zealand applies accrual accounting to its budget process and fiscal management, adhering to the standard principles of generally accepted accounting practice (Richardson 1996); Canadian provincial governments shifted from cash to accrual accounting methods during the 1980s (Hillier 1996); Germany's Länder have instituted pilot programmes to explore new budget accounting conventions including accrual based budgeting (Lüder 2002); Sweden has introduced accrual accounting and reporting without extending the same to its appropriations process (Swedish National Financial Authority 2001); the United Kingdom adopts accrual accounting for government agencies and is extending such accounting to broader government operations in stages (International Federation of Accountants 1995). Recent changes introduced by the Government Accounting Standards Board (GASB) require state governments in the United States to report 'other post-employment benefits' (which include health care benefits) under accrual accounting.
5 Ricardian motives that effectively extend the time horizon beyond one's own lifetime are found to be empirically inoperative – at least in the case of the United States.
6 Present values are calculated by using an interest rate reflecting private agents' (average) opportunity cost of investment.
7 Technical details about generational accounting methods are available in Gokhale et al. (1997).
8 The *FI* and *GI* concepts correspond to the accounting concepts of open-group and closed-group unfunded obligations, respectively. The open-group unfunded obligation refers to government obligations to all individuals regardless of their cohort affiliation (that is, their birth dates), whether in the past or in the (infinite) future. Limited-horizon open-group obligations are also calculated by excluding the net obligations arising after a specific (future) date. Closed-group obligation measures include the net obligations to a subset of individuals – for example, those born before a certain date. However, all past net payments and future net obligations to such individuals are included in the calculation
9 Calculating *GI* for the entire government would require making strong assumptions about the intergenerational distribution of benefits from government public goods and services provision – such as defence, international diplomacy, domestic security, judicial services, and so on.
10 Private sector firms that offer pension benefits to employees may be subject to regulations about funding adequacy. That requires measurement of existing funding levels for comparison with regulated thresholds, and accrual accounting is normally used to provide the benchmark for 100 per cent funding.
11 For a related discussion see Gokhale (2004).
12 Generally, a reduction of consumption taxes would make all existing assets more valuable because the consumption financed through their sale would now face a lower tax rate. Much of the immediate increase in asset values arising from this policy would benefit existing older generations who hold most of the country's wealth.
13 See Auerbach and Kotlikoff (1987: 103). They make the case that deficits and national debt are not theoretically well-grounded fiscal concepts and that their values over time reflect little more than the particular accounting conventions used for labelling different government transactions as taxes and transfers versus loans and repayments of principal plus interest. These arguments are amplified in Kotlikoff (1989).
14 Discussions about federal financial reporting standards in the United States go into great detail about precisely defining liability recognition criteria and the nature of events that trigger a recognizable federal liability. Such discussions are obviously driven by concerns that if the reporting standards were to adopt broader definitions of triggering events and liability recognition criteria, the public might come to view those liabilities as contractual and immutable rather than simply legal – that is, based on the laws prevailing when the payment comes due (which may be different in the future relative to current laws). For example, see Federal Accounting Standards Advisory Board (2004).
15 Including the obligations from future triggering events would convert the accrued obligation measure into the 'closed-group unfunded obligation' measure. See Gokhale and Smetters (2003) for details.
16 For example, generational accounts are supposed to represent each cohort's lifetime net fiscal burden under current policies. However, when the meta-message is that current policies are not sustainable, the value of focusing on the accounts as reported becomes diluted. Generational accounts have been subject to several other criticisms in the fiscal policy literature. See Cutler (1993), Diamond (1996), and Haveman (1994).

17 Finally, unlike traditional measures of deficits and debt, this measure is not subject to change because of the way certain government receipts and outlays are labelled – as taxes and transfers, respectively, or borrowing and repayment of principal with interest, respectively.
18 However, both the Social Security and Medicare Trustees in the United States have been reporting infinite-horizon measures of those programmes' financial shortfalls – precisely the 'fiscal imbalance' measure. They also report 'generational imbalances' for both programmes. The 2003 Technical Advisory Panel that makes recommendations to the Trustees of Social Security and Medicare has endorsed both measures as providing useful additional information.
19 This is a well-recognized phenomenon in the context of the US Social Security programme which was reformed in 1983 to achieve balance through 2058. Now, however, the programme faces a sizable 75-year shortfall because the new horizon includes financial shortfalls between 1959 and 2080.
20 Alternatively, both FI and GI could be calculated by allocating both dedicated and general taxes according to the generations that pay those taxes. This calculation would reveal the part of (zero-valued) FI that past and living generations contribute and the part future generations would contribute under current policies. Note that even if $FI = 0$, by definition because of funding from general revenues, GI (and FI - GI) need not also equal zero.
21 Note that if $FI < GI$, current policies would award living generations net benefits that exceed the total fiscal imbalance, implying that future generations would pay taxes on net.
22 Concern that the public would view the adoption of such measures as recognition that they stand on a par with outstanding government debt – as immutable government liabilities – appears to be a chief reason cited by those opposing their adoption.
23 It is implicit in this discussion that establishing a sustainable fiscal outlook is desirable because it would boost the performance of the private sector by reducing expectations of future benefits, thereby increasing private saving and work efforts.
24 This result is due to the normal condition of a dynamically efficient economy where the interest rate exceeds the growth rate. For the US context, see Abel et al. (1989). See Gokhale and Smetters (2006) for more details.
25 As noted earlier, truncating the projection horizon at 2051 implies that a fully apples-to-apples comparison of policy options would not be feasible because cost and benefits of alternative policies beyond 2051 would be excluded from the calculations. However, adopting such long horizon measures is still better than truncating the horizon after just five or ten years.
26 Cyprus and Hungary are excluded because data on their annual labour productivity growth are not available.
27 Although the terminology employed is 'EU benchmark', it should be understood that the calculations include just 23 countries. See the previous footnote.
28 Calculations regarding the construction of the 'EU benchmark' and other calculations described below are available from the author upon request.
29 An alternative method would be to use simple averages across countries of their per capita taxes and transfers. That would imply placing equal weight on each sovereign nation's budget allocation. However, the resulting allocation would not correspond to a 'representative' EU budget allocation. Implementing the alternative allocation results in a slightly smaller estimate of the 'EU benchmark' economy's Fiscal Imbalance because countries with the largest individual FI values receive smaller weights.
30 This terminology is adopted for lack of a better one. Obviously, generational policy is also influenced by changing budget allocations – and not just by changing the age–gender distributions of particular taxes and transfers. Additional information is available from the author upon request.
31 FI estimates under country-specific long-term interest rate differences are not calculated because capital mobility over time may be expected to erase existing interest rate differentials on long-term government debts. Any residual differences would reflect country-specific government default risks, which are likely to be minor. The calculation's details are available from the author upon request.
32 The estimates shown in Figure 3.4 use only one year's revenues and expenditures for making future projections. Since 2004 was neither a recession year nor a year of particularly strong growth, the estimates are unlikely to be influenced by extreme cyclical variability of fiscal cash flows. If projections of short-run budget forecasts had been available, the resulting FI estimates would have been more accurate because such projections usually incorporate expected changes in future fiscal flows due to policy changes that have already been enacted.

33 This observation may cast doubt on the validity of constructing the EU productivity benchmark as described in the text. However, that appears to be the best, if not the only, alternative.
34 However, see Gokhale and Smetters (2006) for examples based on calculations for US Social Security and Medicare programmes.
35 These calculations were made after extending the official (Eurostat) population projections beyond 2051. Details regarding the methods used are available from the author upon request.
36 Indicateurs de progrès de l'économie française (2006).

Discussion

Per Eckefeldt[1]

The excellent chapter by Jagadeesh Gokhale tries to answer the crucial question on how the EU countries should cope with ageing populations in the euro area characterized by centralized monetary policy and decentralized fiscal (economic) policies. The author draws on his extensive research in the area of intertemporal allocation of resources and its implications for the design of sustainable pension policies.

This issue is highly topical in the face of population ageing in the coming decades worldwide and especially in Europe. In particular, the reform of the EU's fiscal framework, the Stability and Growth Pact (SGP) underscores the importance of appropriately catering for long-term sustainability concerns also in the medium-term budgetary policy-making process. In more practical terms, the chapter focuses on fiscal imbalances measures. A similar measure, though with some differences, is regularly used in the EU's analysis of long-term fiscal sustainability (called the S2 sustainability gap indicator; see European Commission 2006).

With regard to the results in the chapter, it should be noted that the chapter's estimated fiscal imbalance of some 8 per cent of GDP (about 7 percentage points due to implicit debt and about 1 point due to explicit debt) is considerably higher than the Commission's estimate of 3.5 per cent of GDP (according to the so-called S2 sustainability gap indicator consistent with respecting the intertemporal budget constraint of the government over an infinite horizon). An important source of difference could be the assumption of 'current policies'. Gokhale appears to assume that the tax/benefit structure of age and gender remains unchanged over time (a preliminary assumption that may need to be modified). The Commission's data allow splitting the projected increase in the pension expenditure ratio in the EU. While the old-age dependency effect is very strong, reflecting the projected strong increase in the old-age dependency ratio (doubling in the period to 2050), this is to a considerable degree offset by a notable decrease in the benefit ratio (i.e. average pensions in relation to GDP per worker) and also to some extent by lower take-up ratio (see again European Commission 2006).

This results from the fact that the EU's long-term budgetary projections explicitly model the institutional settings in each Member State with respect to pensions. In many cases, this implies that public spending on pensions on average will rise slower than average income in the future, due to pension system reforms aimed at exactly containing spending pressures arising from an increased number of older people.

The impact of reforms is very important in the EU fiscal surveillance. In particular, with the reform of the SGP, the medium-term objectives (MTOs) for the government budgetary position should fulfil a triple aim: (i) provide a safety margin with respect to the 3 per cent of GDP deficit limit; (ii) ensure rapid progress towards sustainability; and, (iii) taking account of the first two, allow room for budgetary manoeuvre and in particular public investment. The MTOs should furthermore be revised when major reforms that improve fiscal sustainability have been undertaken, or at least every four years. It would be an advantage if fiscal indicators reflected the long-term budgetary impact of major reforms and the design of fiscal imbalance indicators therefore was made in such a way that they displayed this desirable property.

The fiscal imbalance measure proposed in the chapter could actually underestimate the sustainability challenge. Indeed, if there is a fiscal imbalance after the last year (i.e. 2051), or if there is an ageing impact also beyond that year, this would not be captured by the measure. This would, as for example in the mainstream US Congressional Budget Office (CBO) calculations, give rise to the 'rolling window' problem; when the horizon is extended, an additional imbalance is added. Fiscal indicators for assessing the long-term sustainability of public finances should gainfully reflect the size of the fiscal challenge, or imbalance over the long term. The design of fiscal imbalance indicators could therefore be made in such a way that they avoid possible underestimation of the size of the challenge by opting for an infinite horizon rather than an ad hoc cut-off point, as indeed highlighted in the chapter.

Note

1 The views expressed in this chapter are those of the author and are not attributable to the European Commission.

Part II
The measurement of the underlying budgetary position and discretionary fiscal policy

4 Budget balances decomposed
Tracking fiscal policy in Austria

Peter Brandner, Leopold Diebalek and
Walpurga Köhler-Töglhofer[1]

4.1 Introduction and motivation

The Maastricht Treaty and the Stability and Growth Pact (SGP) stipulate that budget balances in EU countries should be balanced over the business cycle, since this would allow automatic stabilizers to work properly in cushioning cyclical fluctuations and create some room for discretionary policy. Hence, in order to act in accordance with the intention of the SGP, governments should avoid pro-cyclical policies in recessions and strive for budgetary consolidation during economic booms; in other words, governments should behave counter-cyclically and react symmetrically to output fluctuations. This 'ideal' notwithstanding, there is evidence that fiscal policy behaved more pro-cyclically than counter-cyclically in the past decades. Thus the question arises to what extent a fiscal policy regime change is or would have been necessary in order for governments to comply with the spirit of the European fiscal rules.

In order to analyse this issue for a country – as we do for Austria in this chapter – one has to assess whether discretionary fiscal policy has actually offset or reinforced the operation of automatic fiscal stabilizers, whether there have been significant transitory variations in the fiscal position unrelated to business cycle fluctuations, and what the behaviour of the underlying ('core') fiscal position over time has been. The variability of the latter reflects discretionary measures not related to the cycle, such as permanent consolidation measures, measures aiming at distributional and allocative/structural goals or effects of macroeconomic shocks, demographic changes, etc.

Correcting budget balances for the effects of the business cycle in general gives a better measure of the policy-related part of the budget and reduces the simultaneity bias that may arise as budgets and economic growth interact. The conventional approach relies on adjusting the budget balance for the impact of the automatic stabilizers, i.e. decomposing the budget balance into two components: the cyclically adjusted balance and the automatic stabilizer component (or cyclical component). Adjusting the budget balance for the impact of the automatic stabilizers is only appropriate, for example, for predicting the room for discretionary stabilization policy measures in an economic slowdown, given a threshold for the general government deficit (since in this case the cyclical component should indeed be limited to effects of the automatic stabilizers). If, however, the aim is to analyse the policy behaviour related to macroeconomic developments, the adjustment should also include discretionary fiscal measures that have been a normal feature of a country's stabilization policy (Boije 2004).

On closer inspection, however, the cyclically adjusted budget balance contains several components that capture different dimensions of fiscal policy, such as a core balance describing the underlying fiscal position; a component reflecting discretionary fiscal policy responses to the business cycle that can move either pro- or counter-cyclically with the output gap; and a residual component capturing all remaining shocks to the fiscal position, reflecting transitory changes in the fiscal position due to non-stabilization-oriented discretionary policy and/or macroeconomic shocks.[2] Disregarding these latter aspects could provide an explanation for the sometimes quite substantial variations of cyclically adjusted balances during the cycle.

Following an approach suggested by Jaeger (1998) and expanded by Brandner and Diebalek (2000), we track fiscal policy behaviour over time by decomposing the observed budget balance (as a percentage of GDP) into four unobserved components: (i) a core balance, (ii) an automatic or built-in fiscal stabilizer component, (iii) a component reflecting discretionary fiscal policy responses to the business cycle, and (iv) a component reflecting all other transitory shocks to the fiscal position.

By means of an unobserved components (UC) model, we provide an estimate of a core balance for Austria. For this purpose we analyse the relationship between the budget balance and the cyclical development of the Austrian economy by looking at the impact of both automatic stabilizers and discretionary policies aimed at output stabilization – with particular attention to the latter.[3] By doing this, we can assess whether fiscal policy in a broader sense was pro- or counter-cyclical or reacted asymmetrically in up- or downturns. Moreover, by looking at disaggregated data, we can answer the question whether the pro-cyclicality/counter-cyclicality was related primarily to the expenditure or the revenue side.

In Section 4.2 we discuss some related literature before we move on to explain the methodology chosen in Section 4.3. Section 4.4 is devoted to the discussion of the main results of our study; in Section 4.5 we draw some conclusions.

4.2 Related literature

The behaviour of fiscal policy over the business cycle has received increasing attention from researchers in recent years. The conventional wisdom is that fiscal policy should be counter-cyclical, stabilizing economic growth around potential. In a recession, this would call for higher deficits, while in a boom a contractionary budget would help dampen cyclical upswings and prevent the economy from overheating. This 'ideal' notwithstanding, evidence of pro-cyclicality in fiscal policy has been uncovered in a number of studies.

Galí and Perotti (2003) show that EMU countries' fiscal policies seem to have been significantly pro-cyclical in the pre-Maastricht period. In the post-Maastricht period, however, EMU countries' fiscal policies appear to be more counter-cyclical. According to Galí and Perotti, the behaviour of discretionary fiscal policy during recessions turned from being somewhat pro-cyclical to becoming counter-cyclical. EMU countries seem to have been lagging behind non-EMU countries since they pursued largely pro-cyclical policies during the recession of the early 1990s and changed their behaviour only in the early 2000s. Galí and Perotti base their study on both a panel estimate and individual country regressions. With respect to Austria, interestingly, they find a mildly counter-cyclical fiscal policy before Maastricht (a feature that is in contrast to all other EMU countries) and a stronger counter-cyclicality in the post-Maastricht period.

Hallerberg and Strauch (2002) find pro-cyclical policies for the last three decades, at least for the EU. According to Hallerberg and Strauch, discretionary measures have tended to undermine automatic stabilizers while taxes have fluctuated counter-cyclically in a conventional manner. On the expenditure side, they find that public investment displays a consistent pro-cyclical pattern. The latter was also found by Alberola et al. (2003).

Buti et al. (1997), too, state that contractionary fiscal policies prevailed during recessions and that fiscal discipline was lacking during the expansionary periods as deficits persisted during mild phases of expansions and only abated at the peaks. They conclude that the deterioration during expansions was much more marked than the strengthening of fiscal discipline during recessions, as the debt ratio grew sharply in the 1980s and the first half of the 1990s.

Pro-cyclicality of fiscal behaviour in the EMU countries has also been observed by the IMF (2004). Based on a method very similar to Galí and Perotti (2003), the study shows that the degree of pro-cyclicality reflects, inter alia, country-specific budgetary institutions, structural characteristics, such as the sensitivity to real disturbances, and inherited fiscal positions. According to this IMF study, pro-cyclical fiscal impulses turn out to be more pronounced in good times (loosening) than in bad times (tightening), which points to the difficulty of resisting pressures to increase spending or cut taxes in the face of revenue windfalls. The study, however, also finds that the European fiscal framework appears to have led to some reduction in pro-cyclical fiscal behaviour in the EMU, owing to a more counter-cyclical policy stance in bad times that was not balanced out by sufficient deficit reduction in good times.

Also the European Commission (2001) comes to the conclusion that between 1970 and 2000 the deficits of EU countries did not fall during favourable cyclical periods, i.e. that the effects of the automatic built-in stabilizers were offset by countries' discretionary fiscal policies, namely by tax cuts and, in particular, by expenditure increases, which necessitated a tightening during economic downturns.

Gavin and Perotti (1997) detect that in Latin American countries – in sharp contrast to the industrial economies – fiscal policies have been pro-cyclical, and particularly so in recessions. For industrial countries they find asymmetries insofar as budget surpluses increase during good times; during bad times, however, the fiscal response to changes in output growth is much larger. In their view, for industrial countries this is consistent with the idea that recessions are economically and/or politically more costly than output booms, and that the fiscal policy response to them is accordingly stronger. But it is also consistent with the idea that some elements of the fiscal structure, such as unemployment compensation, are relatively insensitive to the business cycle at high levels of economic activity, but become larger in deep recessions.

As pro-cyclicality contrasts with the stabilization function of fiscal policy, a number of explanations are offered for these results, including conflicting policy goals, information problems (real-time data problems), complexity of decision-making and implementation lags. Talvi and Vegh (2000) offer a model rationalizing pro-cyclical fiscal policies primarily in developing countries but also in the industrialized world – for countries with a large variability of the tax base in general. If the latter is the case, tax smoothing would require large deficits to be run in economic downturns, and high surpluses in upswings. But finance ministers may be tempted to avoid large surpluses knowing that they will nurture political pressures to spend public money, and prefer to run a pro-cyclical policy. Tornell and Lane (1999), on the other hand, argue that the degree of political competition increases during upswings. After all, each group or power block competing for public resources knows that governments will not run surpluses during economic expansions, but that other groups will increase their appropriate share by an even greater amount. Therefore, they will compete more intensely for resources during expansions, and less so during recessions. As a consequence, fiscal policy becomes more pro-cyclical the more fragmented and open governments are to such pressures.

Yet a range of literature also points to possible asymmetries in fiscal responses to recessions and upturns. Mayes and Virén (2004) find strong evidence of asymmetric cyclical behaviour of government deficits, with these asymmetries mainly relating to the cyclically adjusted deficit. Structural deficits increase when output shrinks, but structural deficits (structural surpluses) also tend to increase (decrease) when output expands. According to Mayes and Virén, the different cyclical effects show up in both revenues and expenditures. Revenues seem to be more sensitive to output growth in depressions than in booms. Thus, in booms, the revenue/trend output ratio remains more or less constant, while in depressions it decreases quite markedly. Expenditures seem to increase in depressions and decrease in booms. They conclude that from the viewpoint of counter-cyclical fiscal policy, the main problem appears to be behaviour in 'good times' when discretionary action does not seem to help smooth the output growth path.

Also the OECD (2003) concludes – on the basis of a panel estimate – that, overall, countries conducted pro-cyclical fiscal policies in cyclical upturns and counter-cyclical policies in downturns. However, sustainability problems associated with indebtedness seem to be a key determinant of whether the fiscal stance is pro-cyclical during downturns.

Forni and Momigliano (2004), using real time data, find that fiscal policy was generally counter-cyclical during adverse economic periods. They conclude that fiscal policy was more counter-cyclical at the beginning of the 1990s than during the recent downturns.

Balassone and Francese (2004), too, highlight that fiscal policies in OECD countries have been counter-cyclical mainly in downturns. While automatic stabilizers are left free to operate during downturns, during expansions their effect is compensated by discretionary loosening, which implies that budgetary balances are not improving in upturns. Moreover, they show that overall elasticities (including the discretionary actions) are asymmetric with respect to upturns and downturns.

Tujula and Wolswijk (2004) show that fiscal policies have not operated symmetrically over the business cycle as governments have been more prone to stimulate economies in downswings via expanding budgets than to restrict economic growth in upswings via tightening budget balances.

In contrast to the above mentioned studies, Mélitz (2000) highlights that fiscal policy responds in a stabilizing manner to the cycle; the automatic stabilization through fiscal policy is, however, much weaker than generally perceived.[4] Moreover, while expansion raises tax receipts, it also raises government expenditures. Net stabilization therefore only occurs because of a larger reaction of taxes than expenditures. His findings are in principle in line with Wyplosz (1999), who also shows the 'same mildness' of the stabilizing response to the cycle. According to Wyplosz's estimates an extra per cent of output above potential raises the primary budget surplus by 0.18 (Mélitz's estimate, in contrast, amounts to about 0.10). This actually means weak automatic stabilization in contrast to what is usually estimated (see van den Noord 2000; Girouard and André 2005). Lane (2003) finds that current government spending tends to be mildly counter-cyclical; however, the government consumption component of current spending, in particular wage government spending, is pro-cyclical. Hence, he concludes that the counter-cyclical behaviour of current government spending emanates from the behaviour of government transfers (automatic stabilizers) and/or debt interest payments. The most pro-cyclical component of government spending is government investment.[5] Hercowitz and Strawczynski (2004) – similar to Lane (2003) – find the deficit/GDP ratio to be counter-cyclical. According to their finding, this is mostly due to recessions, whereas in expansions the deficit/GDP ratio is essentially a-cyclical.

In checking for the cycle dependency of cyclically adjusted figures of the European Commission (EC), Alberola et al. (2003) by means of a panel estimate conclude that the cyclical component seems to be overestimated, which means that the cyclically adjusted balances tend to be overestimated during downturns and underestimated during expansions. According to their findings, the overall impact seems, however, to be counter-cyclical in general. In their opinion this result might signal a problem with the computation of elasticities, which turn out to be too high; at the same time, the results could capture a systematic discretionary reaction of governments to developments in economic activity. But, as they state, it does not appear to be easy to disentangle the two possibilities from each other.

The approaches taken for investigating the cyclical-related impact of fiscal policies (from built-in stabilizers as well as from deliberate policy decision) are quite heterogenous. Some studies analyse overall changes in the budget balance (primary or total), without distinguishing between discretionary actions and automatic stabilizers (e.g. Mélitz 2000; Balassone and Francese 2004; Tujula and Wolswijk 2004; Lane 2003; Mayes and Virén 2004; Fatás and Mihov 2001) whereas others analyse changes in the cyclically adjusted balances (e.g. Alberola et al. 2003; OECD 2003; Forni and Momigliano 2004) or the impact on the level of cyclically adjusted primary balances (e.g. Galí and Perotti 2003).

4.3 A stylized framework

Several techniques have been developed to estimate the variations of budget aggregates arising from the economic cycle.[6] The conventional approach to correct budget balances for fluctuations in economic activity starts from a notional decomposition of the observed budget balance b_t into two (unobserved) components: the cyclically adjusted budget balance bs_t, often called structural balance, and a cyclical component ba_t aimed at capturing the built-in stabilizers. To adequately estimate the cyclical component ba_t, various methods have been developed by international institutions such as the EC, the OECD, the IMF and the ECB. Within these approaches, the structural balance bs_t is defined as the difference between the observed and the cyclical balance, $bs_t = b_t - ba_t$. Obviously, any other dimension of fiscal policy, even if it is related with the cycle, shows up in the structural component.

However, if the focus is on the development of the underlying fiscal position (adjusted for all temporary impacts irrespective of whether they are 'economy dependent or policy dependent'[7] (Braconier and Forsfält 2004)) a direct calculation of the structural balance as a 'long-run component' via specific filtering techniques (see Brandner et al. 1998) may be more appropriate. If so, the effects of the built-in stabilizers as well as cyclically related discretionary measures are captured in the resulting 'cyclical' component $ba_t = b_t - bs_t$.

To analyse the issues raised, we set up a framework that allows distinguishing between several dimensions of fiscal policy, short-run vs long-run, and active vs passive. We start with a quite general decomposition

$$b_t = \mu_t + ba_t + bd_t + \varepsilon_t \tag{4.1}$$

of the actual/observed balance b_t into the core balance μ_t, two cyclically related components – namely ba_t capturing the impact of the automatic stabilizers, and bd_t capturing the discretionary policy in response to the cycle – and a residual component ε_t reflecting all remaining (temporary) effects ('fiscal noise'). To be more precise, we specify

$$ba_t = \alpha_t \cdot I_t^a \tag{4.2.1}$$

$$bd_t = \gamma_t \cdot I_t^d \tag{4.2.2}$$

I_t^a and I_t^d are indicators for the cyclical developments which will be specified later on, and α_t and γ_t are the corresponding sensitivities/elasticities. The use of different indicators of the cyclical development is motivated by the fact that in general policy makers do not necessarily respond to variables economists have in mind.

Inserting (4.2.1) and (4.2.2) in (4.1) constitutes our unobserved component model specification, naturally cast as a state–space system. The measurement/signal equation

$$b_t = \mu_t + \alpha_t \cdot I_t^a + \gamma_t \cdot I_t^d + \varepsilon_t \tag{4.3.1}$$

links the observed balance to its components, while the state/transition equations

$$\mu_{t+1} = \mu_t + \eta_{t+1} \qquad \eta_t \sim iid\ \mathcal{N}(0, \sigma_\eta) \tag{4.3.2}$$

$$\alpha_{t+1} = \alpha_t + \psi_{t+1} \qquad \psi_t \sim iid\ \mathcal{N}(0, \sigma_\psi) \tag{4.3.3}$$

$$\gamma_{t+1} = \gamma_t + \zeta_{t+1} \qquad \zeta_t \sim iid\ \mathcal{N}(0, \sigma_\zeta) \tag{4.3.4}$$

describe the dynamics of the states. In the estimation, the log-likelihood is constructed using the Kalman filter.[8]

Equation (4.3.2) specifies the core balance as a random walk, the innovations η_t capturing fiscal shocks that have a permanent or enduring impact on the level of the budget balance. Similarly, equations (4.3.3) and (4.3.4) set up the automatic sensitivity of the budget balance α_t and the policy response γ_t as random walks. While a positive (negative) sign of γ_t typically indicates a counter-cyclical (pro-cyclical) reaction of discretionary fiscal policy, the sign is interpreted just the other way round in the case of expenditure variables. In principle, all three state equations could be generalized to include exogenous variables. We take (4.3.1)–(4.3.4) as a transparent, easy-to-use device to decompose budget balances.

In the general representation (4.3.2)–(4.3.4) the states – and hence budget components – are assumed to move stochastically. If the estimation yields very small variances, this is an indication that the corresponding component is rather deterministic. In such a case, the model can be simplified by setting disturbances to zero (the states would then enter (4.3.1) as recursive coefficients).

Since the focus of our interest lies primarily on the impact of the policy response to cyclical developments (rather than on the automatic stabilizers), we can estimate a smaller, 'reduced model' for the structural balance bs_t consisting of the measurement equation

$$bs_t = \mu_t + \gamma_t \cdot I_t^d + \varepsilon_t \tag{4.4}$$

and state equations (4.3.2) and (4.3.4).

By taking the cyclically adjusted (primary) budget balance $bs_t = b_t - ba_t$ as calculated by the European Commission as dependent variables,[9] we refrain from estimating the cyclical component, which is thus $ba_t = \alpha_t \cdot I_t^a = \alpha \cdot GAP_t$.

If, however, the discretionary policy response component and the automatic stabilizer component respond to the same cyclical indicator I^c, general equation (4.3.1) is reduced to

$$b_t = \mu_t + (\alpha + \gamma)_t \cdot I_t^c + \varepsilon_t \qquad (4.5.1)$$

state equation (4.3.2) and

$$(\alpha + \gamma)_{t+1} = (\alpha + \gamma)_t + \zeta_{t+1} \qquad \zeta_t \sim iid\ \mathcal{N}(0, \sigma_\zeta) \qquad (4.5.2)$$

Whereas the actual budget balance is expressed as a ratio of nominal GDP, the core balance and the cyclically adjusted balances are expressed as ratios of nominal potential GDP (since cyclically adjusted balances should be interpreted as values of the deficits (surpluses) that would be observed if output were at some reference potential level). However, one should be aware of the fact that policy makers, the public and international institutions such as the EC generally monitor the development of public finances relative to nominal GDP. Actual and cyclically adjusted budget balance figures as well as revenue and expenditure figures are taken from the AMECO database of the European Commission.

The indicator I_t^a is always specified as the output gap. However, at the current stage of our research, the indicator I_t^d is specified as the output gap on the one hand and split up into I_t^{d+} and I_t^{d-} on the other hand in order to capture upturns and downturns.[10]

4.4 Results

Estimating the impact of the discretionary policy response to the cycle only (equation 4.4), i.e. taking the cyclically adjusted total balance in percent of potential GDP as dependent variable and the output gap as explanatory variable, gives a negative parameter value for γ of a size of about -0.35 (see Figure 4.1, Figure 4.2 and Table 4.1). A negative value of this coefficient reveals a pro-cyclical impact of discretionary policy responses on cyclical developments.

The comparison of this coefficient with the size of the overall budget sensitivity as estimated by the OECD and used by the EC (+0.47) leads to the conclusion that the overall impact of fiscal policy (summing up the automatic and discretionary components) was slightly counter-cyclical in Austria in the past.[11] Taking into account the fact that the overall budget sensitivity for Austria as estimated by the OECD was lower in earlier publications, this could indicate a slightly stronger counter-cyclicality of overall fiscal policy for recent years.

Figure 4.1 also reveals that the core balance is slightly smoother than the cyclically adjusted budget balance. The driving forces of the core balance were major structural problems of the Austrian economy in the early 1980s; consolidation measures in the second half of the 1980s; a major income tax reform which came into effect in 1990; the implementation of long-term care benefits in 1993; the fiscal impact of EU membership in the mid-1990s; the implementation of further consolidation packages between 1995 and 1997 in order to fulfil the Maastricht fiscal criteria in 1997; and another consolidation package in 2000/2001 to reach a balanced budget.

The first result is confirmed when we use the alternative specification (4.5.1) and look for the 'overall' budget sensitivity to the output gap, i.e. estimating the automatic and the

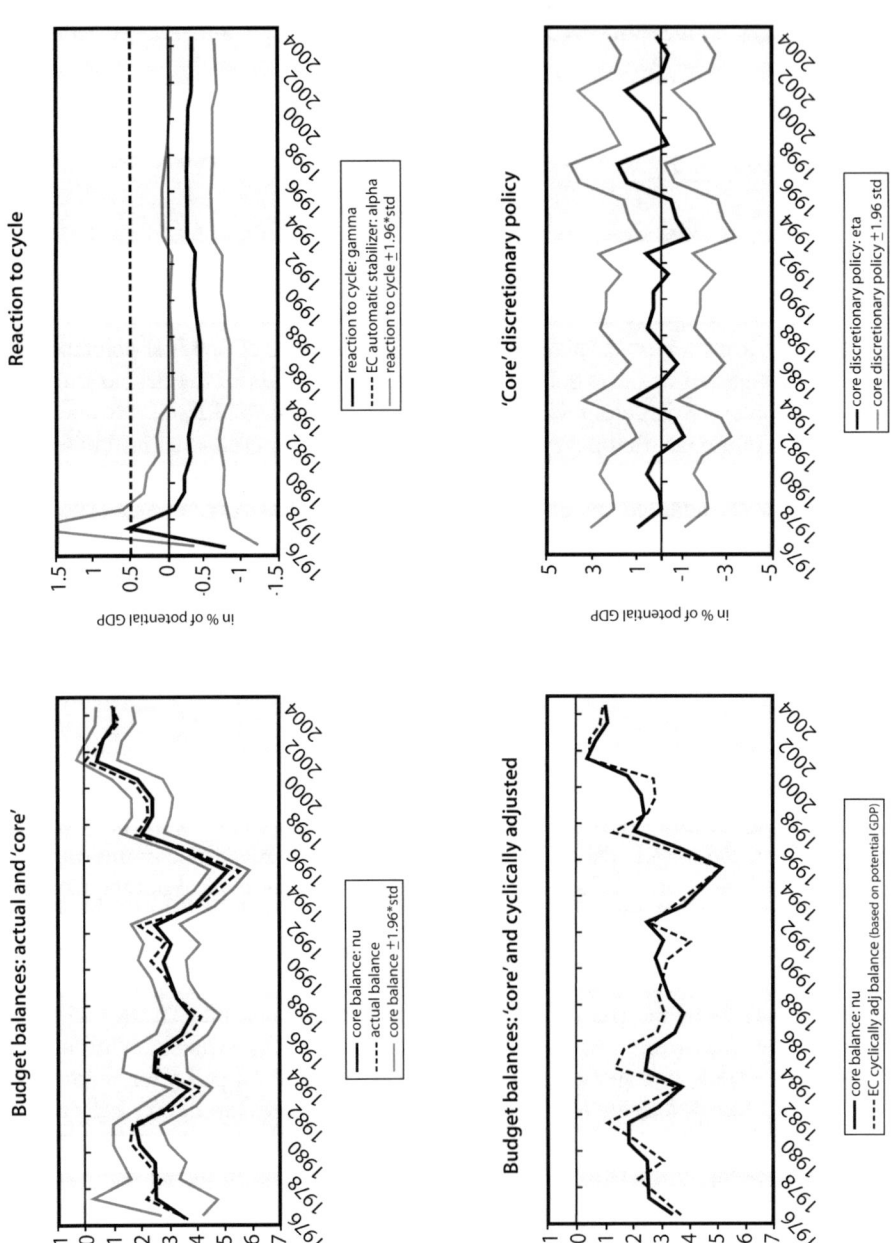

Figure 4.1 Results for the total balance.

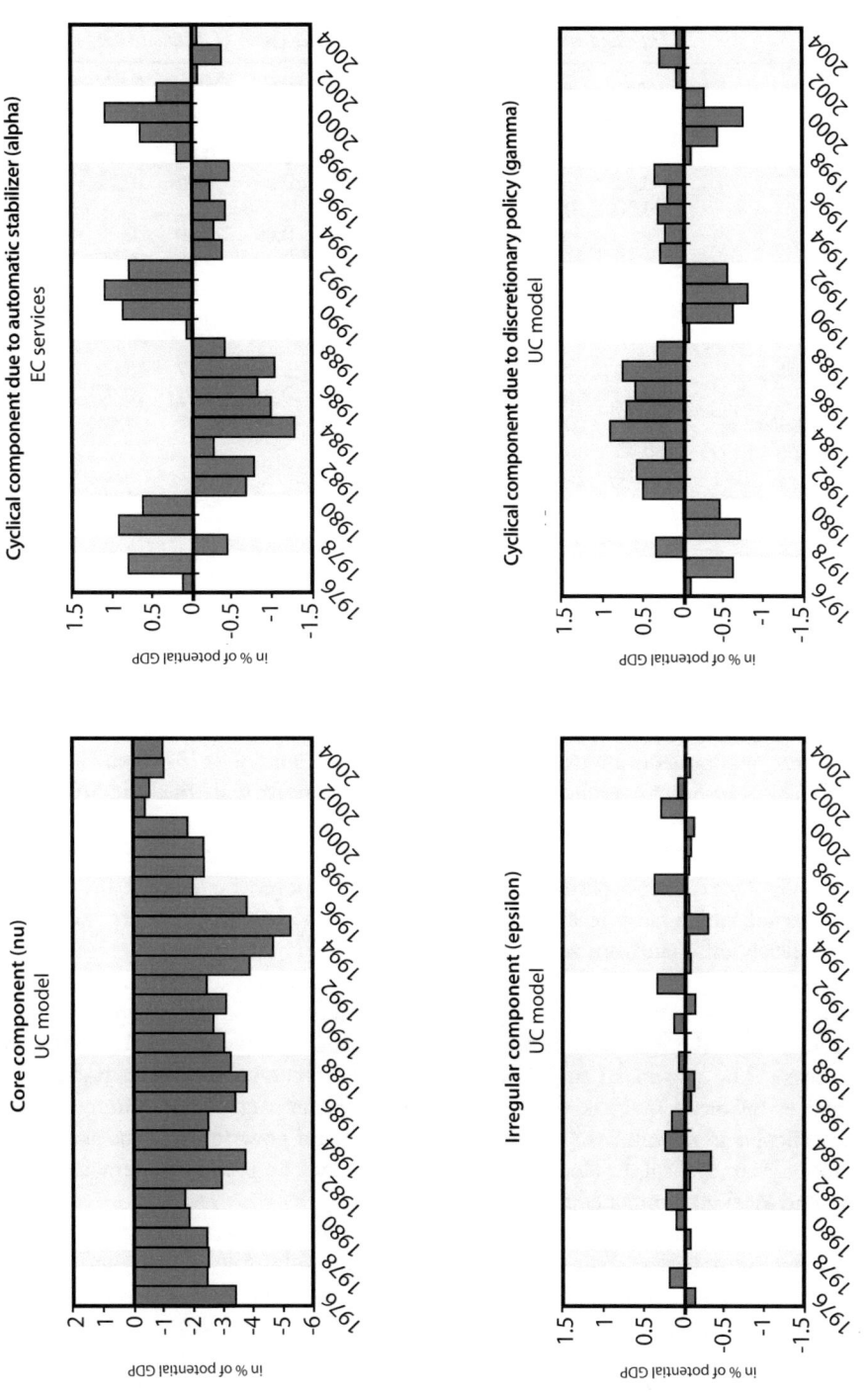

Figure 4.2 Decomposition of the total balance.

Table 4.1 Estimation results

Parameter	Total balance	Primary balance	Total revenues	Primary expenditure	Total balance	Primary balance	Total revenues	Primary expenditure
Dependent variable: cyclically adjusted balances (in % of potential GDP)								
$\text{var}(\varepsilon)$	0.14	0.00	0.00	0.00	0.04	0.00	0.00	0.00
$\text{var}(\eta)$	0.86	1.15	0.79	0.84	0.95	1.04	0.74	0.85
$\text{var}(\xi)$	0.00	0.00	0.00	0.00	.	.	.	.
$\text{var}(\xi^+)$	.	.	.	.	0.00	0.00	0.00	0.00
$\text{var}(\xi^-)$	.	.	.	.	0.02	0.02	0.00	0.00
Final states:								
Core balance (μ_T)	−1.06	1.88	48.72	46.84	−1.06	1.87	48.69	46.83
	(−0.35)	(−0.04)	(0.03)	(0.03)	(0.21)	(0.04)	(0.04)	(0.04)
Automatic stabilizer α^{*}	0.47	0.47	0.43	−0.04	0.47	0.47	0.43	−0.04
Discretionary policy (γ_T)	−0.35	−0.37	−0.30	0.07	.	.	.	.
	(0.16)	(0.16)	(0.13)	(0.14)				
in upturns (γ_T^+)	.	.	.	.	−0.42	−0.40	−0.43	0.00
					(0.19)	(0.19)	(0.16)	(0.17)
in downturns (γ_T^-)	.	.	.	.	−0.04	0.04	−0.11	0.12
					(0.42)	(0.44)	(0.23)	(0.15)

Notes:
Sample period: 1976–2004; standard deviations in parenthesis
*' Estimated by the OECD and used by the European Commission

policy response components in one go. A positive coefficient of 0.15 signals a slightly counter-cyclical behaviour overall.[12] Repeating the estimations with the primary budget balance gives nearly identical coefficients (see Figures 4.3 and 4.4).

This finding contrasts with Galí and Perotti's (2003) results. In their country estimates they find a slightly counter-cyclical discretionary fiscal response for Austria for the pre-Maastricht period, which became stronger in the after-Maastricht period (but the coefficients are not statistically different from zero).

A 'pro-cyclical fiscal policy response' of the general government is, however, not much of a surprise; on the one hand it can be explained by the federal structure of government in Austria, consisting of the federal government, the nine provinces and the local governments (municipalities). The provincial and local governments' fiscal policies have traditionally been aimed at balanced budgets – thus undermining the impact of the automatic stabilizers, in particular in downturns.[13] Thus, even if the federal government aims at counter-cyclical responses to cyclical developments, this ambition may be partly counteracted by the provincial and local governments' fiscal strategy.

Moreover, from the late 1970s to the end of the 1980s the federal government's strategy was influenced by a budget rule termed the 'Seidel formula' (see Katterl and Köhler-Töglhofer 2005), which set a threshold for the cash deficit of the federal government at a level of 2.5 per cent of GDP.

In a next step we ask whether cyclically adjusted spending and revenues (as a share of nominal potential GDP) react in a specific pro- or counter-cyclical manner. Our estimation results indicate a relatively strong pro-cyclical discretionary response of the cyclically adjusted revenues to the cycle (see Figure 4.5 and 4.6).

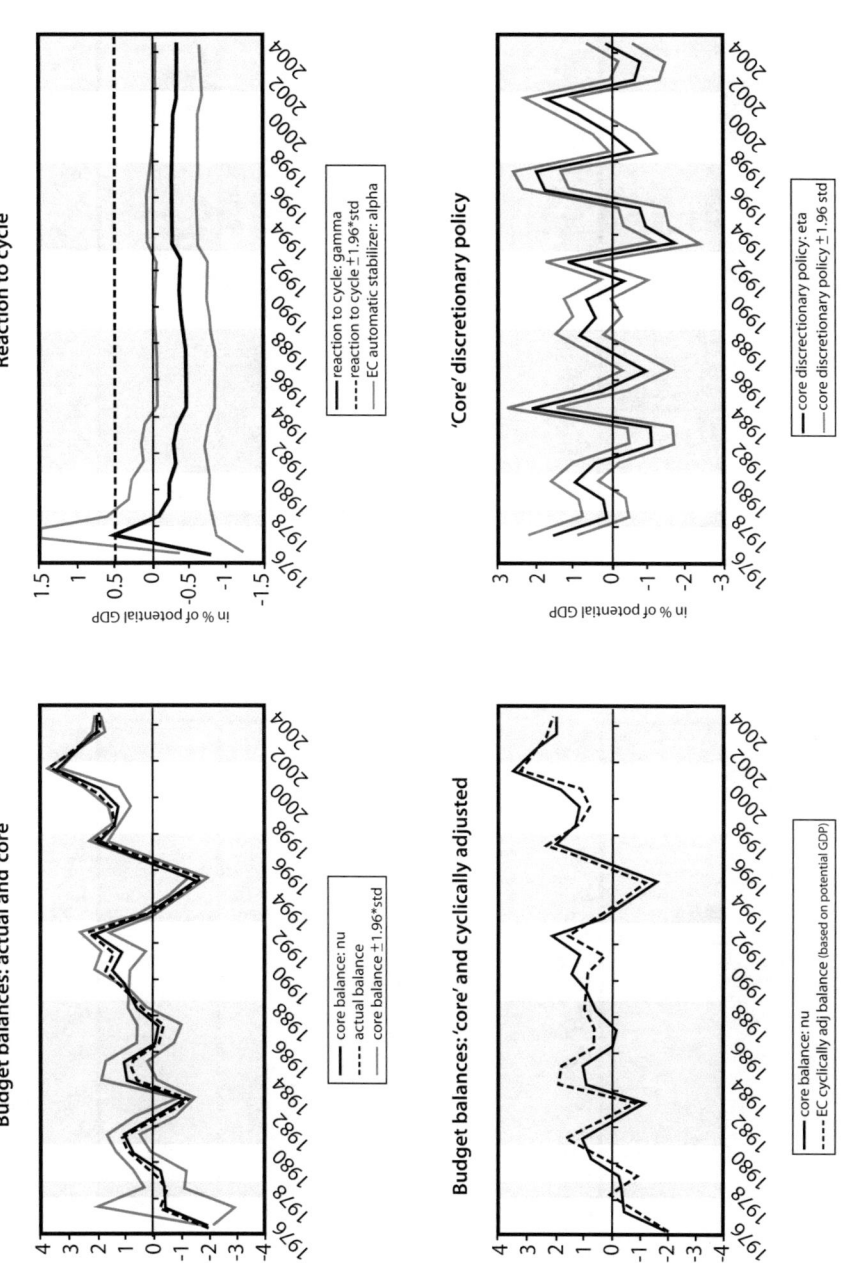

Figure 4.3 Results for the primary balance.

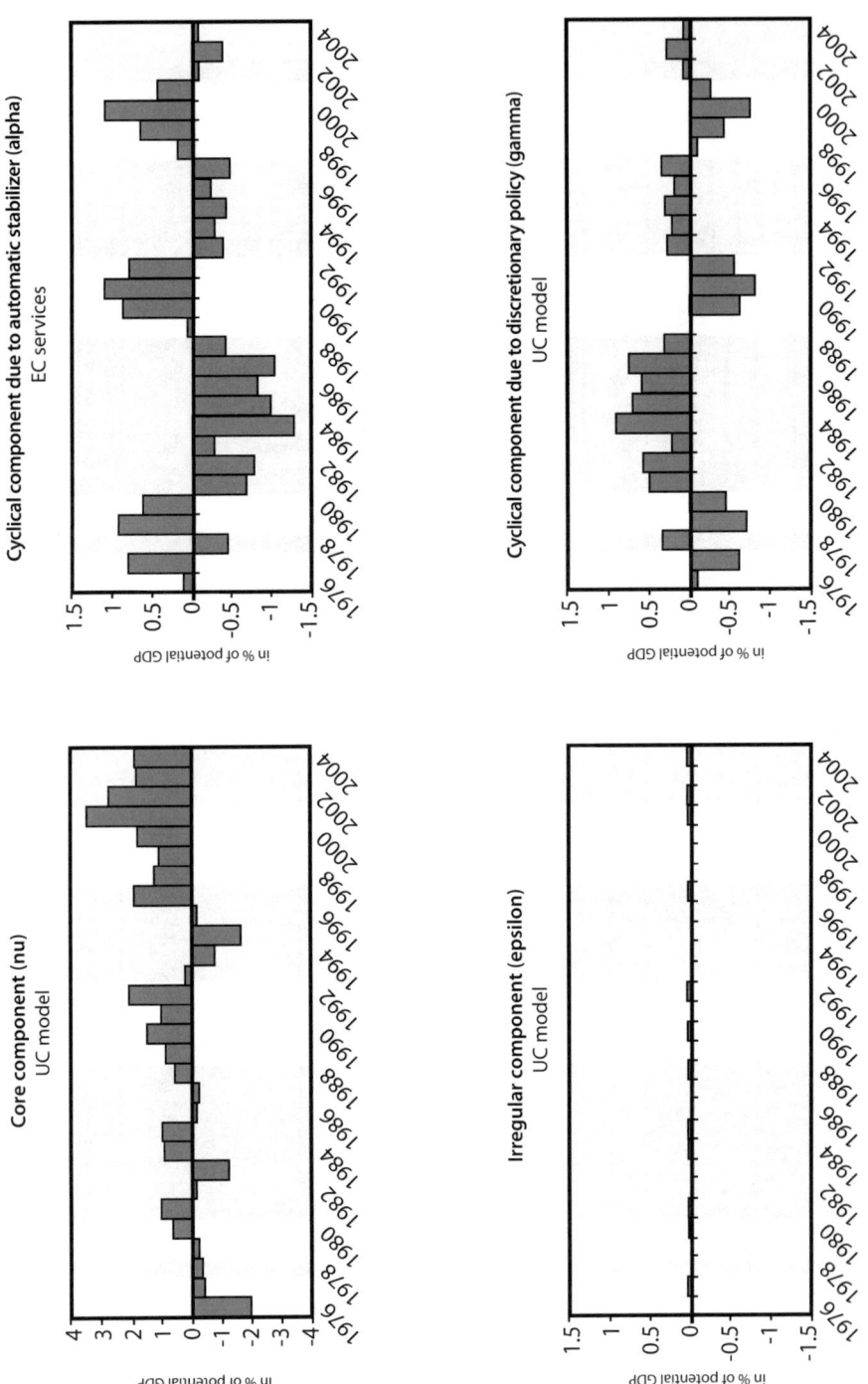

Figure 4.4 Decomposition of the primary balance.

On the expenditure side, the relatively minor impact of the automatic stabilizers related to the unemployment transfers seems to be completely neutralized[14] (see Figures 4.7 and 4.8).

Next we check for an asymmetric cyclical behaviour in downturns and upturns, i.e. taking the cyclically adjusted (primary) budget balance as dependent variable and looking for the discretionary fiscal policy impact in upturns (periods in which the real growth rate is above the potential growth rate) and downturns (periods in which the real growth rate is below the potential growth rate). It appears that in upturns a strong pro-cyclical discretionary policy impact dominates (however, the γ coefficient is slightly smaller than the overall budget sensitivity estimated by the OECD for Austria),[15] whereas the pro-cyclical impact in downturns turns out to be negligible. Hence, we can conclude that in Austria overall fiscal policy in downturns is counter-cyclical, whereas in upturns the working of automatic stabilizers is neutralized (see Figure 4.9). This is in principle in line with general findings based on panel regressions for OECD countries (such as those by OECD 2003, Balassone and Francese 2004; or Forni and Momigliano 2004; these papers provide evidence for counter-cyclical behaviour in downturns and – at least the first two studies – pro-cyclicality in upturns).

Finally we focus on the evolution of the core balances. Compared to the cyclically adjusted budget balances the core balances exhibit slightly less variability.

As mentioned in the introduction, the variability of these reflect discretionary measures not related to the cycle, such as permanent consolidation measures, measures aiming at distributional and allocative/structural goals or effects of macroeconomic shocks, demographic changes, etc. Thus Figure 4.10 depicts major episodes of fiscal consolidation on the one hand and the introduction of expenditure measures aiming at further improving the Austrian welfare state on the other hand, as well as the impact of structural changes in the Austrian economy.

For example, in 1984 Austria implemented a sizeable consolidation package, including the increase of the VAT rate and other indirect taxes as well as the contribution rate of the unemployment insurance scheme. Another big consolidation package was implemented in 1996–1997 in order to fulfil the fiscal Maastricht criteria. A further comparatively huge consolidation package was launched in 2000–2001 with the goal of bringing the general government budget to a close to balance position. While these events resulted in an improvement of the core primary balances, they also show up in the core revenue or core expenditure ratio, respectively, or in both, depending on the composition of the consolidation packages.

The tremendous structural crisis that Austria faced at the beginning of the 1980s is also reflected in the development of the core primary balance. The worsening of the primary balance at the beginning of the 1990s was, however, caused by the implementation of social policy measures, i.e. by extending the entitlement period for maternity leave payments from one to two years and in addition by implementing long-term care benefits without adequate financing measures.

4.5 Conclusions

Our estimation results highlight that, first of all, the overall effect of fiscal policy (the automatic stabilizer and discretionary policy component) in Austria has been slightly counter-cyclical. However, our estimates also indicate that discretionary policy in response to the business cycle has been pro-cyclical. Given the federal structure enabling the provincial and local governments to implement conflicting fiscal strategies, and given the fact that the

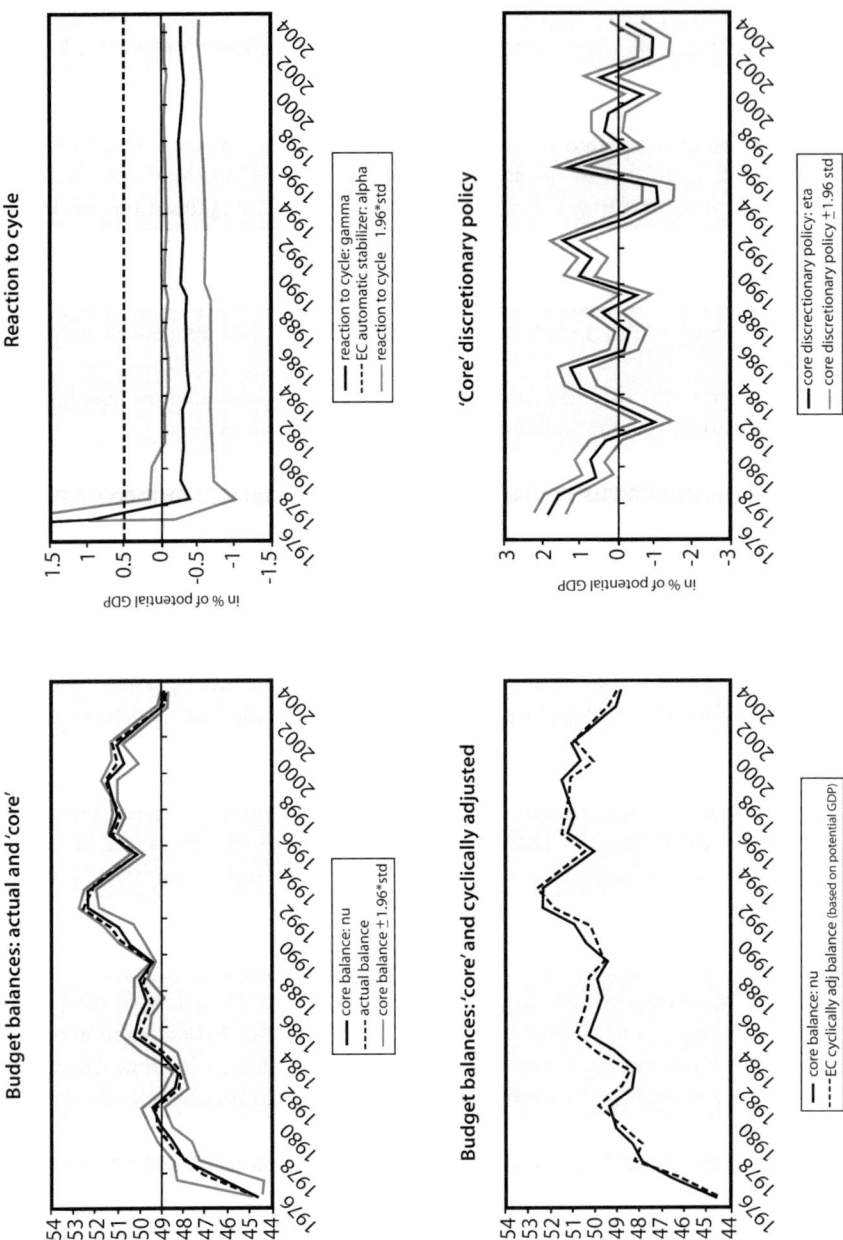

Figure 4.5 Results for the total revenues.

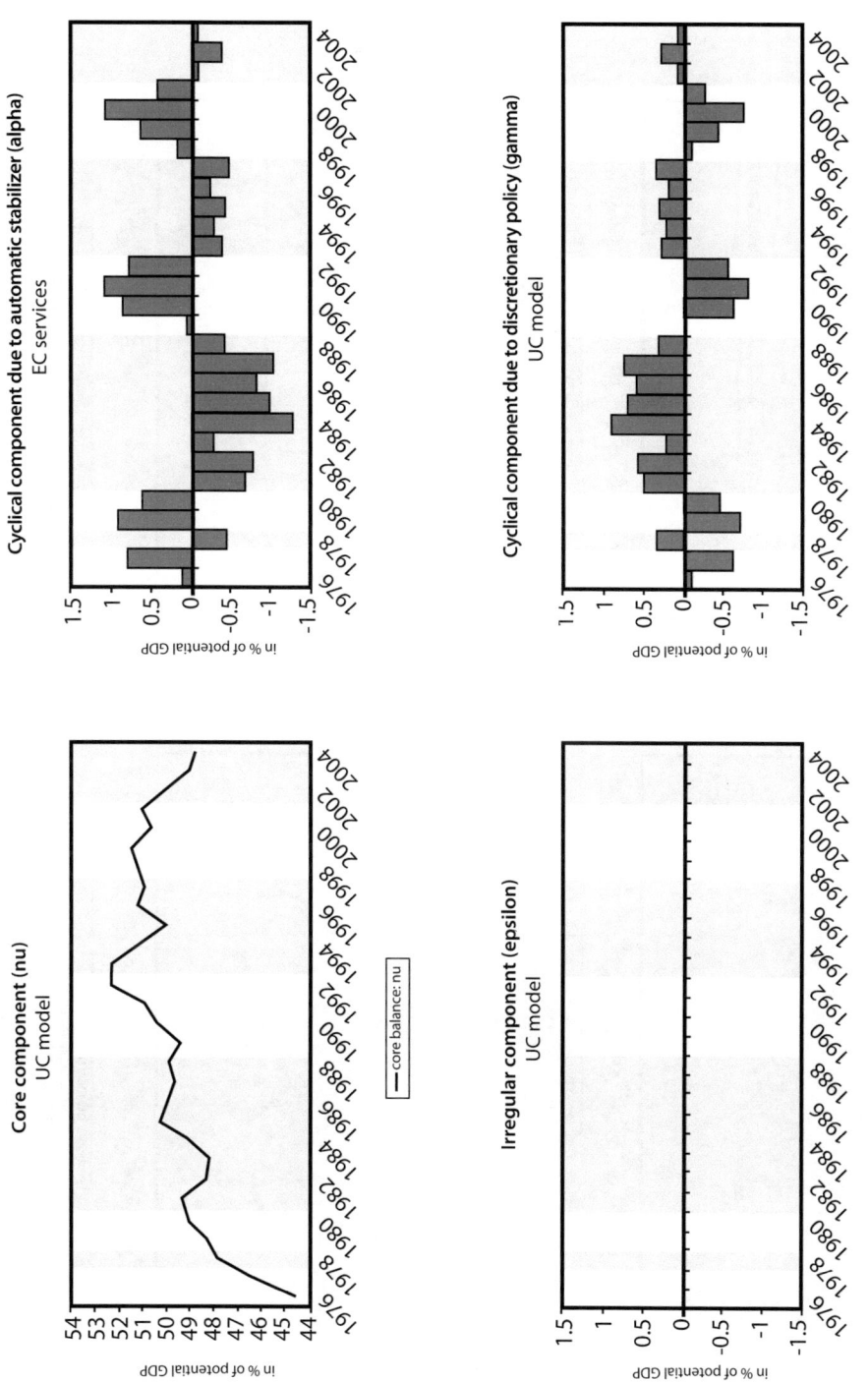

Figure 4.6 Decomposition of total revenues.

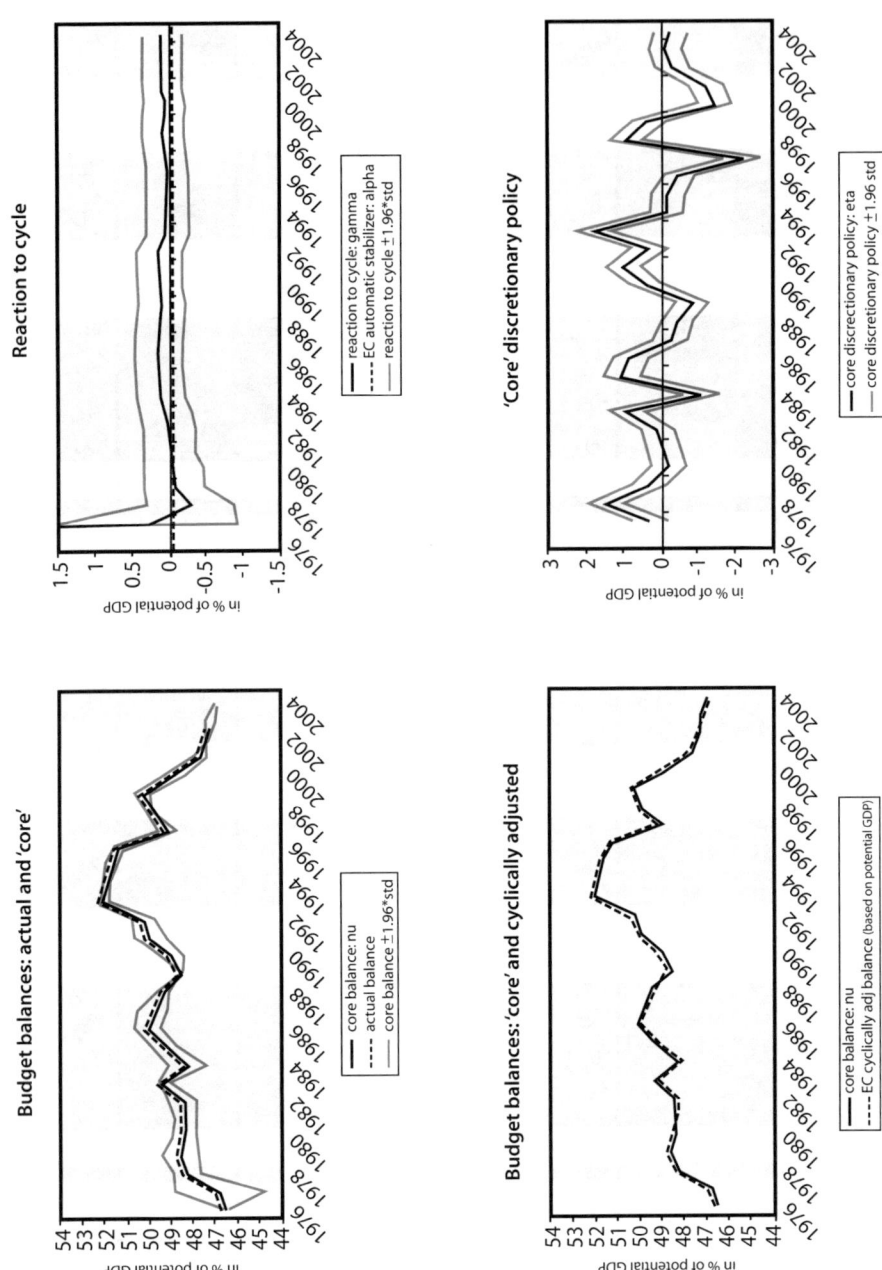

Figure 4.7 Results for primary expenditures.

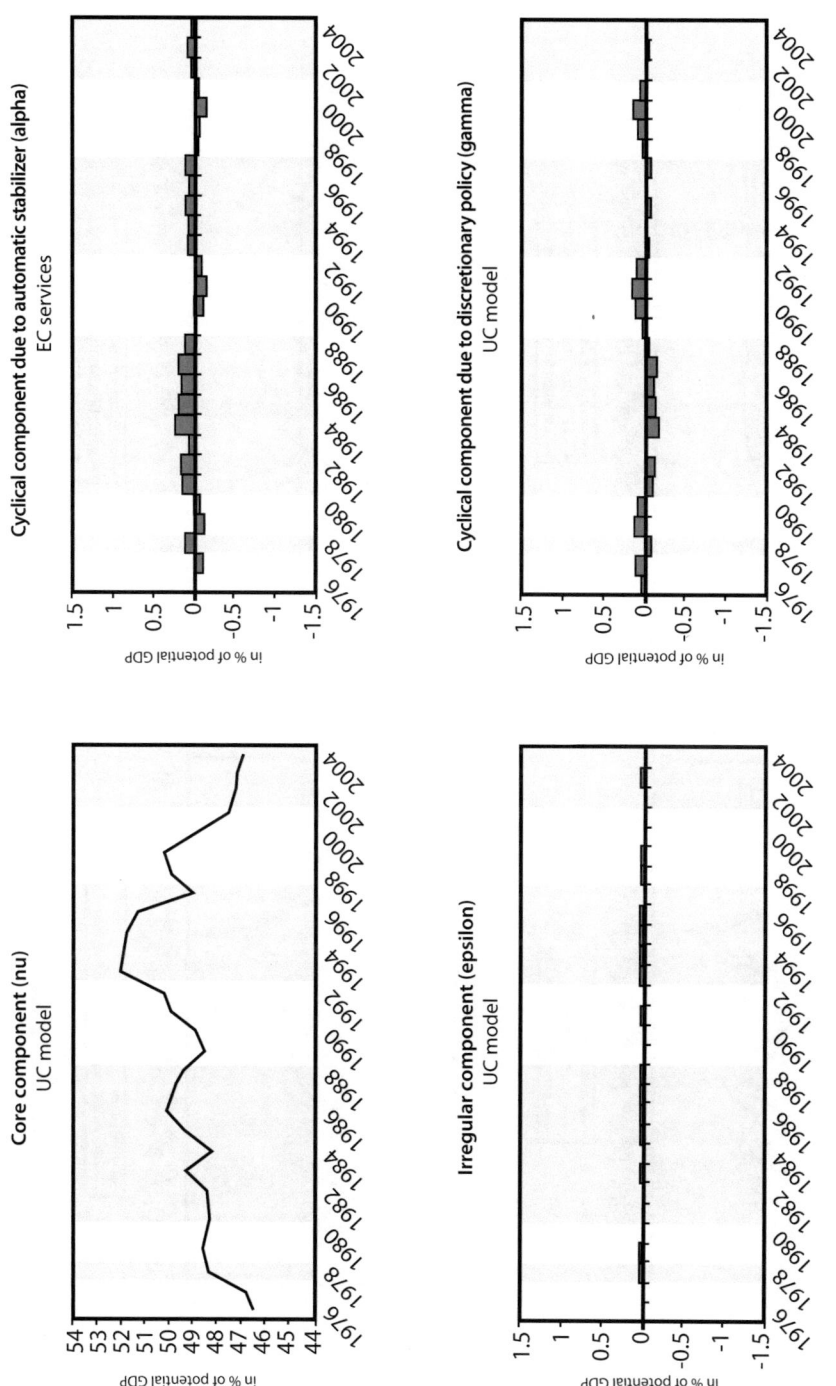

Figure 4.8 Decomposition of the primary expenditures.

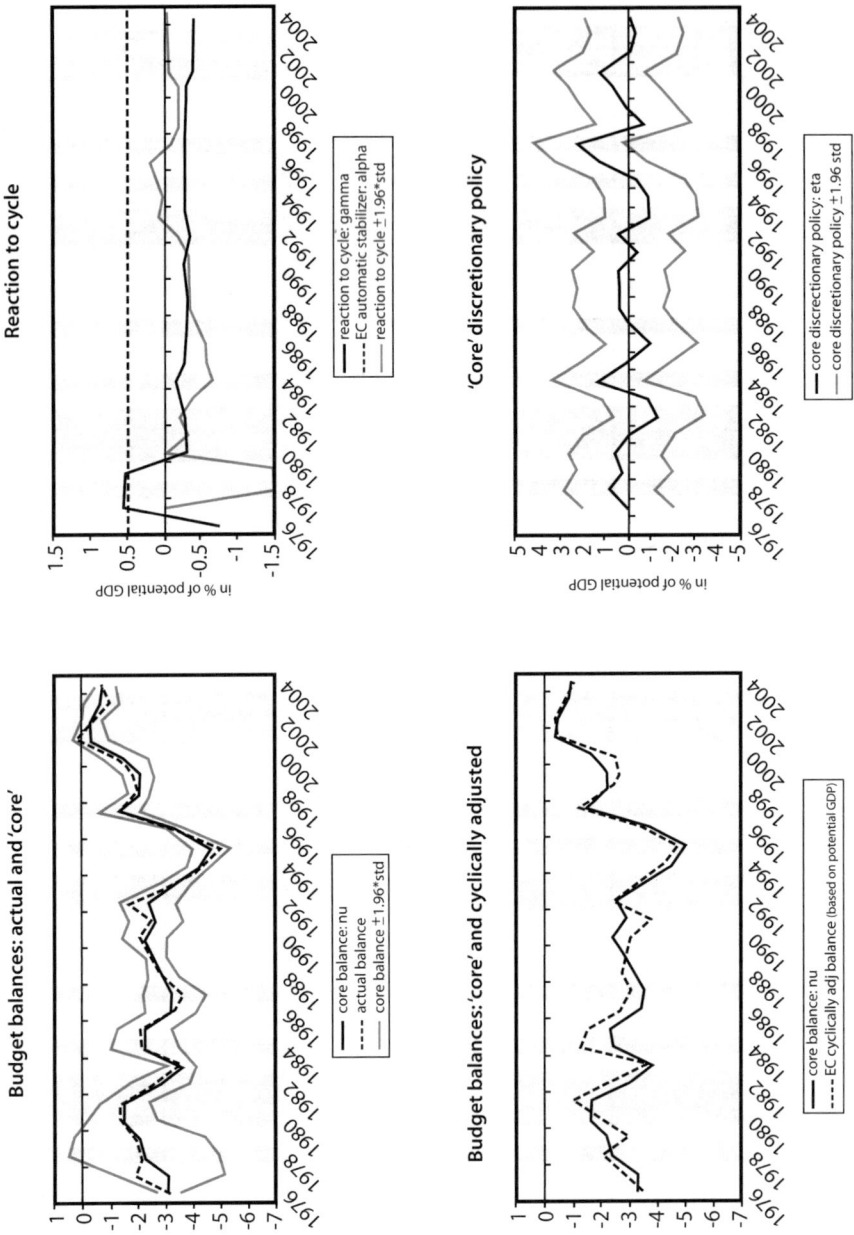

Figure 4.9 Results for the total balance.

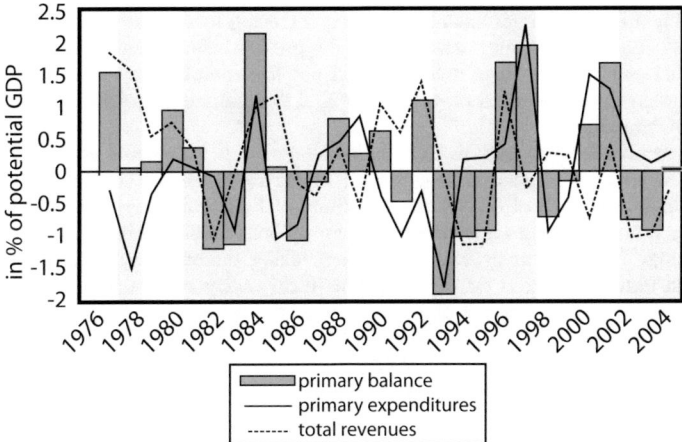

Figure 4.10 'Core' discretionary policy.

central government budget was influenced (at least on average) by the rule that the cash deficit should not exceed the threshold of 2.5 per cent of GDP, this result does not really come as a great surprise. Second, and more interestingly, there is the fact that in particular the revenue side seems to be prone to pro-cyclical responses whereas the relatively minor impact of the automatic stabilizers on the expenditure side seems to be completely neutralized. Finally – and this finding is generally in line with other studies – our estimates imply that during economic downturns the overall impact of fiscal policy seems to be countercyclical, whereas in periods of economic upturn the impact of automatic stabilizers is nearly neutralized.

Notes

1 The views expressed herein are those of the authors and should not be attributed to the Federal Ministry of Finance, Austria, and the Oesterreichische Nationalbank. We are grateful to Jonas Fischer for helpful comments.
2 Galí and Perotti (2003) conceptually split the cyclically adjusted budget balance into a 'systematic' or 'endogenous' component (a component that reflects changes in structural spending or revenues in a systematic way in response to changes in the actual or expected cyclical conditions of the economy; corresponding to γ in Section 4.3) and a 'non-systematic' or 'exogenous' component (that captures changes in the budget variables that do not correspond to systematic responses in cyclical conditions, but are instead the consequence of exogenous political processes of extraordinary non-economic circumstances; corresponding to what we name core balance in this paper).
3 Further research will focus on the analysis of the 'driving forces' of the core balance.
4 According to Wyplosz (2002) this mildly stabilizing response (coefficients of 0.1–0.2 instead of around 0.5) could be an effect of the extension of the sample period to include the 1990s, an atypical period of low growth and closing down of the deficit to meet the Maastricht convergence criteria. It may also reflect the combination of the counter-cyclical automatic stabilizers, with an elasticity of 0.5, with discretionary pro-cyclical actions.
5 Also Alberola et al. (2003) confirm this result.
6 However, all these techniques are subject to a number of methodological problems, notably defining trend/potential output – a shortcoming that unfortunately is also valid for our approach.
7 I.e. pro- or counter-cyclical discretionary policy measures such as a temporary increase in the volume of labour-market programmes due to political decisions.
8 Estimations have been carried out with RATS v6.

9 The cyclically adjusted budget balance has been corrected for an estimated output gap (compositional effects are not taken into account), i.e. the budget balance figures are adjusted for (a) the difference between actual output and estimated potential output (the output gap) and (b) the difference between the actual unemployment rate and the estimated equilibrium unemployment rate (the unemployment gap).

10 We intend to broaden the analysis to include the period $t-1$ expected real GDP growth rate of period t on which the respective budget draft in Austria is based. This projection is part of the regular economic outlook of the Austrian Institute of Economic Research (WIFO). Even though growth does not represent an adequate proxy for cyclical conditions one has to bear in mind that politicians may just look at growth rates when taking discretionary decisions. Using real-time growth data moves the focus on the intentions fiscal policy makers had, when deciding discretionary measures, whereas the use of ex post output gap allows the assessment of the actual (or ex post) counter-/pro-cyclicality of fiscal policies (Forni and Momigliano 2004).

11 However, as stated by Alberola et al. (2003) (by means of a panel regression) such a result could also signal problems with the estimation of the budget elasticity. They actually find a negative and significant correlation between the output gap and the structural balance which they interpret as an overestimation of the cyclical component. Consequently, in downturns structural balances tend to be overestimated while they are underestimated in expansions.

12 In order to filter out the effect of the interest expenditures we estimate the equations also with the cyclically adjusted and unadjusted primary balance as dependent variables.

13 The resources of the provincial and local governments stem mainly from an elaborate tax-sharing system and from federal transfers. The sub-levels mainly participate in cyclically sensitive tax revenues. Own sources of revenues are of less importance for the provincial governments, but of slightly more relevance for the local governments. Without any room for manoeuvre on the revenue side, the provincial and local governments in principle have to adjust their expenditures to the predetermined revenues (see Diebalek et al. 2005).

14 However, if the dependent variables are taken as ratios of the nominal GDP instead of potential nominal GDP we get a pronounced pro-cyclicality of the cyclically adjusted revenues and a pronounced counter-cyclicality of the cyclically adjusted expenditures.

15 However, the coefficient is of the same size as the overall budget sensitivity calculated by the OeNB. Taking the OeNB's value of the overall budget sensitivity would lead to the conclusion that the impact of the automatic stabilizers is completely neutralized in upturns.

Discussion

Jonas Fischer[1]

The chapter by Peter Brandner, Leopold Diebalek and Walpurga Köhler-Töglhofer presents an unobserved component model that decomposes the budget balance into different components, namely a 'core', an 'automatic stabilizer', a 'discretionary stabilization' and a 'residual' component. The method has been, for illustrative purposes, applied to Austrian budget data but the model is easily applicable to any country as the necessary budgetary data are readily available across countries. Indeed, the easy applicability is one of the key advantages of the approach.

In terms of the results for Austria, they mainly confirm 'conventional wisdom', in particular in that they indicate that discretionary fiscal policy has been pro-cyclical off-setting some of the impact of the automatic stabilizers, especially in up-turns. Below I will concentrate my comments in this area and the implication of decomposing the cyclical part of the budget balance into a component related to the 'automatic stabilizers' and a part related to 'discretionary stabilization'. This decomposition allows the study of whether budget policies have been counter- or pro-cyclical over and beyond what can be ascribed to the automatic stabilizers. If pro-cyclical budget behaviour is observed, it may be of particular interest to know whether this 'bad outcome' is due to active government policies or whether it is events outside its control that are to blame. This distinction is important in the context of the application of the revised Stability and Growth Pact where the government's intent carries more weight than before the reform. Equally, it is an important distinction to make when assessing failures/accomplishments of the past budget behaviour with a view to drawing conclusions on how to improve budget rules and institutions for the future.

In this context I would like to make some comparisons between the authors' decomposition and the most common alternative indicator used for the same purposes, namely the cyclically adjusted budget balance: the CAB.[2] The CAB is the nominal budget balance adjusted with the (unobservable) estimated budget impact from the cycle. Several international institutions estimate CABs, notably the Commission, the ECB, the OECD and the IMF. Methods vary and the results differ on the margin across compilers but the basic approach is the same. I will first comment on what the authors' decomposition and the CAB implies in relation to commonly used budget terms such as the 'fiscal stance', the 'structural' budget balance, the 'discretionary' policy component and the 'fiscal impulse'. These budget concepts are useful to discuss various fiscal policy issues. However, lacking alternatives, the concepts are often captured by using the CAB across the board.

As a starting point, Figure 4.11 provides a two-dimensional decomposition of the budget balance. Vertically, the budget balance is decomposed into factors which are economy-induced and those which are policy-induced. Horizontally, a distinction is made between factors with a temporary impact on the budget as opposed to those which have a permanent impact.

104 *Jonas Fischer*

Square A would thus include factors related to the temporary state of the economy at given tax and expenditure rules. An example would be unemployment benefit expenditures and temporary higher/lower tax revenues due to tax bases being temporarily higher/lower than their trend values or tax elasticities being temporarily higher/lower than normal. Square B includes, for example, temporary higher expenditures due to discretionary stabilization policy measures. Square C would capture, for example, how potential GDP and demographic trends affect the budget balance permanently, while square D includes the impact on the budget from permanent changes to tax and expenditure rules.[3]

On this basis a comparison of the coverage of the authors' decomposition can be made to the coverage of the CAB in relation to the different budget concepts. This is done in Table 4.2.

Let me go through the concepts in turn. First, if the aim is to capture the permanent budget trend all temporary influences should be taken out. This would correspond to the concept of a 'structural budget balance' (C+D). The core component in the authors' model would then seem most suitable to capture this. When the CAB on the other hand is used for this purpose, policy-induced temporary factors (box B) are not netted out. In fact, this distinction is increasingly recognized and for example the Commission now regularly nets out 'one-off budget measures' from the CAB and labels this as the 'structural budget balance'.

Second, the 'fiscal stance' relates to whether the budget balance, over and beyond the impact of the automatic stabilizers, does or does not contribute to smoothing the cycle. This would imply netting out the cyclical economy-induced component and looking at boxes B+C+D. Using the authors' model the 'discretionary component' would probably be used to assess the fiscal stance. However, the change in the CAB would be better designed for this purpose. While it is straightforward that boxes B and D should be included in a measure of the fiscal stance it may be less clear with box C, which takes into account economy-induced permanent changes. Ultimately it depends on the precise question to be analysed.

	Temporary	Permanent
Economy	A	C
Policy	B	D

Figure 4.11 Determinants of the actual budget balance.

Table 4.2 What do the different budget indicators capture?

Budget concept	Determinants of budget balance in Figure 4.11	Corresponding best to which component in authors' decomposition:	Use of CAB (or primary CAB)
Structural budget balance (level)	C+D	Core component	CAB (B+C+D)
Fiscal stance (change)	B+C+D	Discretionary component (B)	Change CAB (B+C+D)
Discretionary policy (change)	B+D	Discretionary component (B)	Change CAB (B+C+D)
Fiscal impulse (change)	A+B+C+D	(n.a. change nominal balance)	(n.a. change nominal balance)

Last, if the interest is to identify the impact of discretionary policy decisions, then temporary and permanent economy-induced budget components should not be taken into account (thus look at B+D). Here it is worth noting that if the CAB is used for this purpose it would also include economy-induced permanent changes (box C) while the discretionary component in the authors' model would not capture policy-induced permanent changes (box D). The overall point here is that it is important to be precise in what is the objective of the analysis and what the indicator used actually captures. Conceptually at least, the authors' 'core component' would be better than the CAB when assessing the structural budget balance, while the change in the CAB would be best designed to capture the 'fiscal stance' as understood here. To study the 'discretionary policy' response of the government the model looks better designed from a conceptual perspective than the change in the CAB.

It is also worth looking a bit closer at some aspects related to what is actually meant by 'discretionary policy' when using budget indicators.[4] One issue relates to budget rules across layers of government. For example, say that a local government (where most of government consumption takes place) runs deficits to cover for higher expenditures, although they are forbidden to borrow, but that they are bailed out by the central level through additional grants. This could be regarded as a discretionary measure by the government (box B above), given that a separate decision was taken to this end, but it could also be regarded as 'semi-automatic' if it is common practice (box A above). Clearly, how it is counted may make a difference in the policy assessment. Another issue relates to the benchmark used for what is 'neutral policy' and then in particular the indexation of expenditures. CAB calculations based on trend GDP estimates use as an implicit benchmark that expenditures develop in line with potential GDP. If some expenditures, such as welfare expenditures, are instead indexed to nominal GDP the difference between the two growth rates would not be included in the 'cyclical part' and would thus be counted as non-cyclical. In fact, to the extent that expenditures are actually indexed, to – say – inflation, these items could be labelled 'automatic destabilizers'! Overall, it is the non-indexation of expenditures which provides most of the cyclical stabilization from the budget.

My last comment relates to the budget balance itself: observable and the base for most budget indicators. Further work to decompose the nominal balance in sub-components allowing better analysis of different budget behaviour is of course very useful to make assessments better. Nevertheless, in a setting where the objective is to give short-term policy advice based on the latest figures, it should be remembered that the large volatility and uncertainty lies with the revisions to the nominal balance, from the initial estimated to the final outcomes some years later,[5] and that this uncertainty by far outweighs any difference from using alternative approaches to estimate the cycle or the cyclical component of the budget. However, looking at longer historical time series the issue is quite different, and the authors' approach will hopefully soon be tested and used also for additional countries.

Notes

1 The views expressed in this chapter are those of the author and are not attributable to the European Commission.
2 The CAB is usually estimated as: CAB = nominal budget balance to GDP – budget sensitivity to the output gap * output gap.
3 See also Braconier and Forsfält (2004).
4 See also Boije and Fischer (2006).
5 See for example Gordo Mora and Nogueira Martins (2007).

5 The dynamic behaviour of budget components and output

The cases of France, Germany, Portugal and Spain

António Afonso and Peter Claeys[1]

5.1 Introduction

In recent years, we have witnessed a worldwide swing towards fiscal profligacy. In the European Union, this has come somewhat as a surprise as the Maastricht Treaty and afterwards the Stability and Growth Pact seemed to have put in place a set of fiscal rules that guarantee the sustainability of public finances. The difficulty in applying the Pact, first to Portugal and later on to France and Germany, has been followed by a more widespread breach of the 3 per cent deficit limit in several EU countries. A revised version of the Pact was adopted in March 2005; it takes a more flexible approach in terms of curbing excessive deficits over a longer period of time, and pays more attention to sustainability of public finances. As part of the Lisbon Strategy, considerably more attention is given to the composition of budget adjustments with a view to promoting economic growth.

A variety of political and economic factors probably underlie the observed rise in public deficit and debt ratios. We try to uncover any underlying past trends behind the development of public finances that may contribute to explaining the recent budgetary outlook in France, Germany, Portugal and Spain. While the first three countries were subject to several steps of the Excessive Deficit Procedure, Spain on the other hand could be seen as an example of more vigorous fiscal management. We are particularly interested in the underlying causes of the breach of the Pact's rules by looking into adjustments in various budget components. At the same time, we look into how these adjustments contribute to the long-term growth prospects and outlook for the sustainability of public finances.

To that end, we construct a model-based indicator of structural balance by combining insights from the growing empirical literature on the effects of fiscal policy – modelled with structural VARs – with statistical methods for cyclically adjusting fiscal balances. Our approach innovates on existing evidence in using a mixture of short- and long-term restrictions to identify economic and fiscal shocks in a small-scale empirical model in economic growth and fiscal variables. This allows for permanent shocks to determine trending behaviour of output and fiscal variables à la Blanchard and Quah (1989). Discretionary fiscal adjustments are captured by filtering out the fiscal balance for cyclical reactions of budget items, following Blanchard and Perotti (2002).

The quantitative indicator that we obtain is best seen in the light of the growing theoretical literature on the qualitative effects of fiscal policy. Dynamic stochastic general equilibrium models with nominal rigidities search for a rationale for fiscal stabilization policies. At the same time, these New Keynesian models attribute quite some importance to both supply- and demand-side effects of fiscal policy adjustments. Our indicator is consistent with such a distinction. We take a first step by restricting attention to overall expenditure and revenues, but more elaborate models might incorporate refinements in the compositional adjustments of budget balance. In contrast to statistical models for adjusting fiscal balance, our economic indicator of structural balance has some attractive practical properties. Uncertainty is explicitly quantified, and theoretical assumptions can be explicitly tested. Also, the end-of-sample problem is reduced. The model is not necessarily more demanding in terms of data availability.

The main result of our study is that both pre-EMU consolidations and expansions in recent years are mainly based on revenue changes. The derailing of public finances comes from tax reductions being implemented in good economic times. As total revenues apparently remain constant, spending cuts are not implemented. As a consequence, deficits show up again when economic boom turns into bust. The easy way out of deficits is to reverse previous tax cuts, leading to a 'ratcheting up' of spending over the next economic cycle. This pro-cyclical bias in fiscal policies has not been eliminated with the Stability and Growth Pact. Governments still implement bad policies in good times. These policy reversals have negative economic effects. We find fiscal policy to have minor supply but large demand effects. Pro-cyclical policies unnecessarily induce macroeconomic fluctuations.

The remainder of the chapter is organized as follows. In Section 5.2, we briefly review some recent fiscal developments in the EU, notably for the cases of France, Germany, Portugal and Spain. Our structural VAR approach towards disentangling these developments, and the derivation of the fiscal indicator, is discussed in Section 5.3. Section 5.4 reports our empirical results, and Section 5.5 concludes the chapter.

5.2 The recent fiscal imbalances in the EU

The fiscal framework of EMU has been considered a means for implementing fiscal consolidation. However, recent developments in several Euro area countries raise the question as to whether fiscal sustainability is endangered, in view of rising deficits and debts at a moment when the effects of ageing populations will have a further burdening effect. In 2005, Excessive Deficit Procedures (EDP) have been carried out for both France and Germany, while yet another EDP was launched for Portugal. There were also procedures for Greece and Italy, while several other EU Member States face a situation of excessive deficit.[2] Recent developments cannot be seen without taking into account past actions and trends in public finances.[3] We focus attention on the evolution of public finances since 1970 in the countries that initially 'sinned' against the Pact (France, Germany and Portugal).

We report in Figure 5.1 the general government balance, and its breakdown in revenue and expenditure ratios. A simple visual inspection shows that expenditure and revenue ratios have been following an increasing trend notably in France, Portugal and Spain. But with revenues lagging the expenditure rises; there has been a continuous deficit bias. There were some good reasons in 1991 to embark on consolidation by enshrining the 3 per cent deficit target in the criteria for EMU entry. The Maastricht rules have been effective in constraining further buoyant expenditure rises. Less than commensurate rises in revenue intake have led to persistent albeit gradually declining deficits. Since the start of EMU, fiscal positions have started to slip away again. As to the reasons for the breach of the Stability and Growth Pact, further expenditure rises in France and Portugal seem to blame, whereas in Germany large revenue reductions unmatched by expenditure cuts have pushed the deficit beyond the 3 per cent threshold. Spain, on the other hand, stands out for its balanced budget over recent years, which is the result of a sustained reduction in expenditures since 1993 that has levelled off in recent years. We consider Spain as an example of more prudent fiscal behaviour.

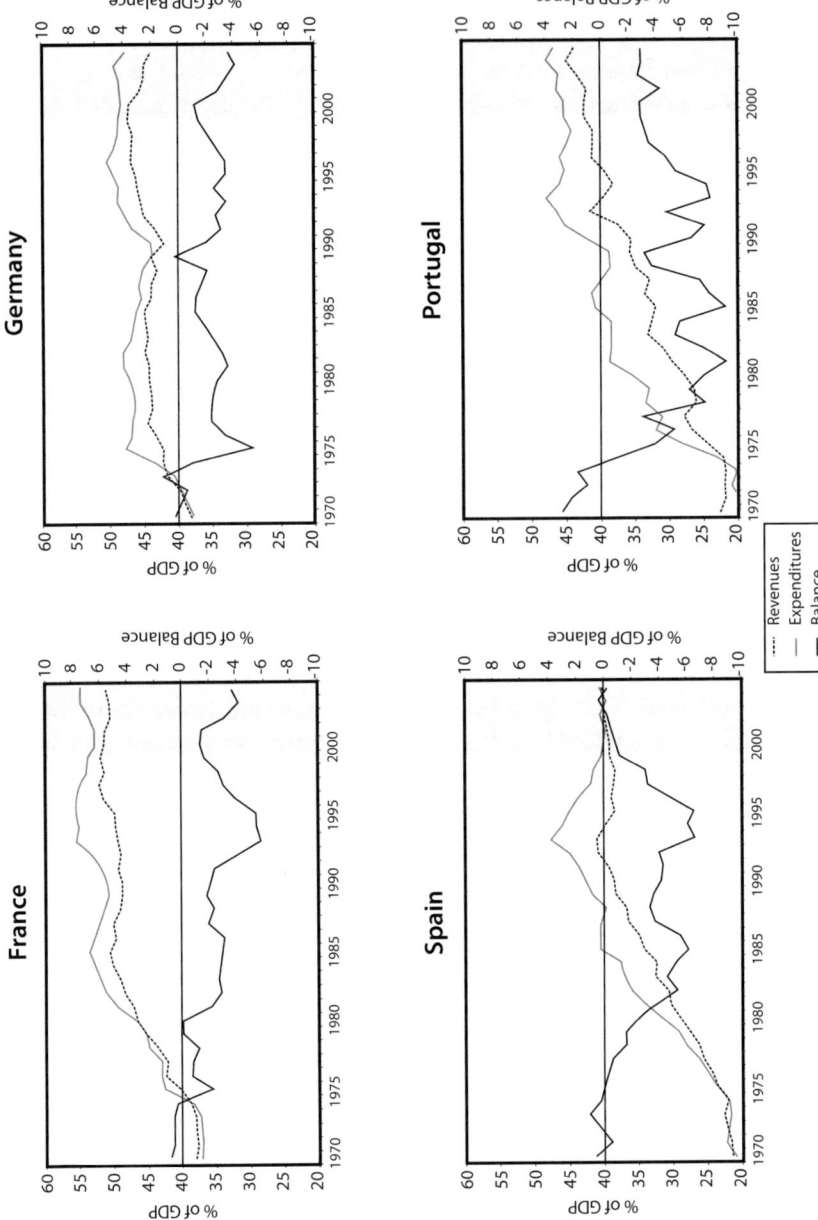

Figure 5.1 General government spending, revenue and deficit (percentage of GDP).
Source: AMECO database, updated on 4 April 2005. The shaded area indicates the start of EMU.

Note: Left-hand scale – revenue or spending / right-hand scale – deficit.

These budget developments cannot be separated from economic conditions. The balance can slip out of the control of fiscal authorities by higher than expected expenses on unemployment benefits and transfers, or less than budgeted revenues, owing to automatic stabilizers. Figure 5.2 compares some measures of the output gap and cyclically adjusted balances computed by the European Commission and the OECD, as well as a trend series retrieved from directly applying a Hodrick–Prescott filter on the raw series.[4]

The start-up of the EDPs to these countries seems justified on account of worsening structural balances. In all countries, economic conditions improved considerably at the onset of EMU and the overall deficit was notably reduced as a result. But the reversal of positive output gaps laid out the structural weakness of the balance in France, Germany and Portugal. Expenditures exceed average revenues over the cycle. In contrast, Spain presents an entirely different picture. The budget was brought close to balance, and was even in slight surplus. A constant spending share has been matched by gradually rising tax revenues.

5.3 An SVAR model for gauging fiscal indicators

There are a variety of reasons for which the cyclically adjusted balance does not properly reflect discretionary shifts under the control of the government. Its use in assessing fiscal balances is therefore debatable. Some problems are related to the properties of the econometric filters that are being used.[5] More importantly, we believe fiscal policy contributes to the size of economic fluctuations. And it does so by adjusting a variety of spending and revenue items. Recent general equilibrium theories of fiscal policies provide a rationale for real economic effects of fiscal policies, and stress the prevalence of its supply-side consequences over short-term demand effects. This is all the more important for the assessment of the new Stability and Growth Pact. We develop an indicator of discretionary fiscal policy stance that builds on the recent empirical literature on the effects of fiscal policy using structural VARs, and combine this with evidence on the cyclical behaviour of government budget. Next to its favourable properties, the indicator is best seen as a first step in verifying recent theories of fiscal policy as well as giving an instrument for assessing the quality of fiscal adjustments.

Fiscal indicators

The notion of structural balance is based on the premise that total output fluctuates around some unobserved trend that depends on the long-term potential growth path of the economy. In combination with some assumptions on the cyclical behaviour of fiscal policy, this allows deriving a cyclically adjusted balance. Common practice at the European Commission, IMF or OECD regards the determination of cyclical variation in output and the cyclicality of the budget as two distinct problems.

First, the output gap usually comes from some trend-extraction procedure with a statistical filter applied directly to real output. This decomposition in trending and cyclical components is usually done with a band-pass filter. Alternatively, the output gap is calculated as the distance from actual to potential output where the latter is based on a production function for the aggregate economy.[6] Second, a bottom-up approach is adopted for the derivation of the cyclical elasticities of the budget. The output elasticities of government revenues are based on the taxation structure of each main sub-item[7] – in some cases accounting for collection lags – and the elasticity of the tax bases to output. The spending elasticity is of relatively minor importance, as only the spending on unemployment benefits is adjusted for the cycle. Other budget components are assumed to be cyclically insensitive.

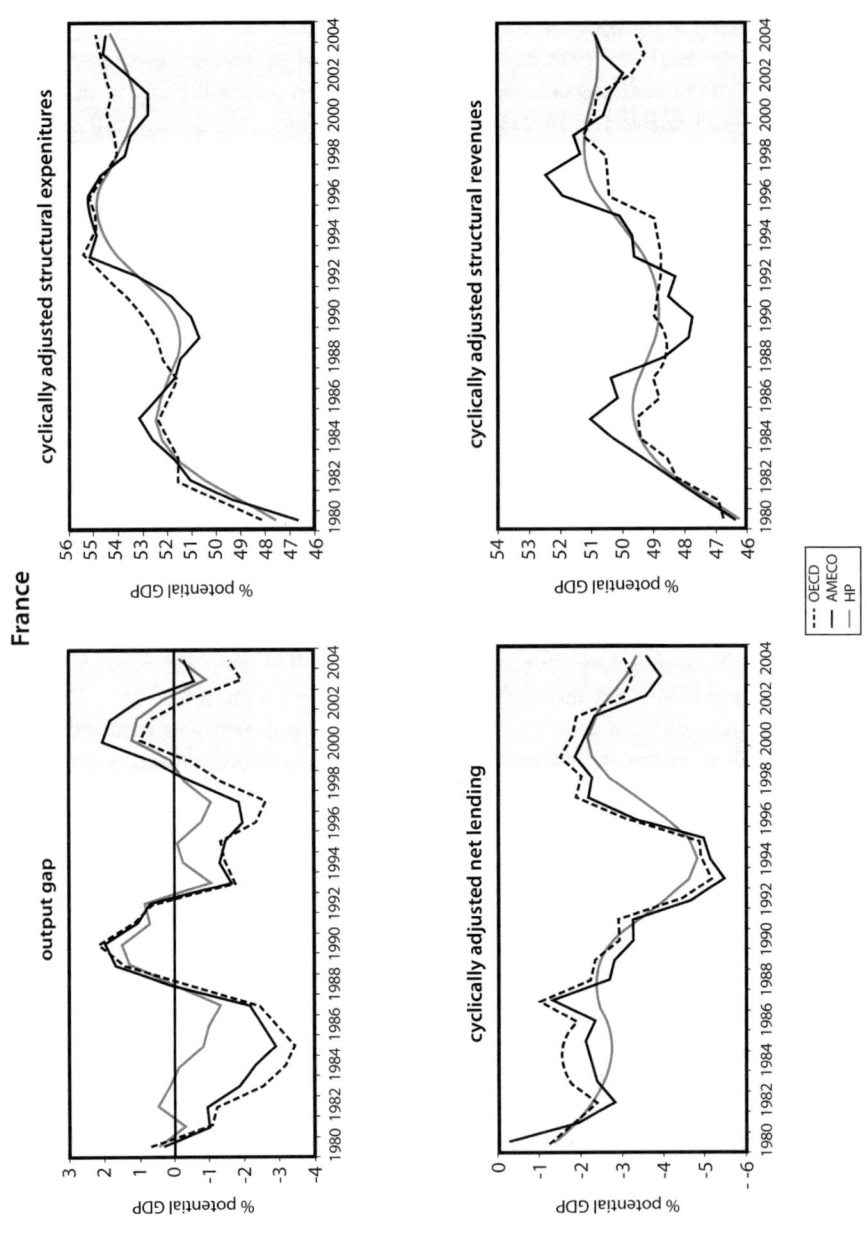

Figure 5.2a Output gap, cyclically adjusted net lending, spending and revenue (percentage of potential GDP)*: France.

Note: * indicated by arrows.

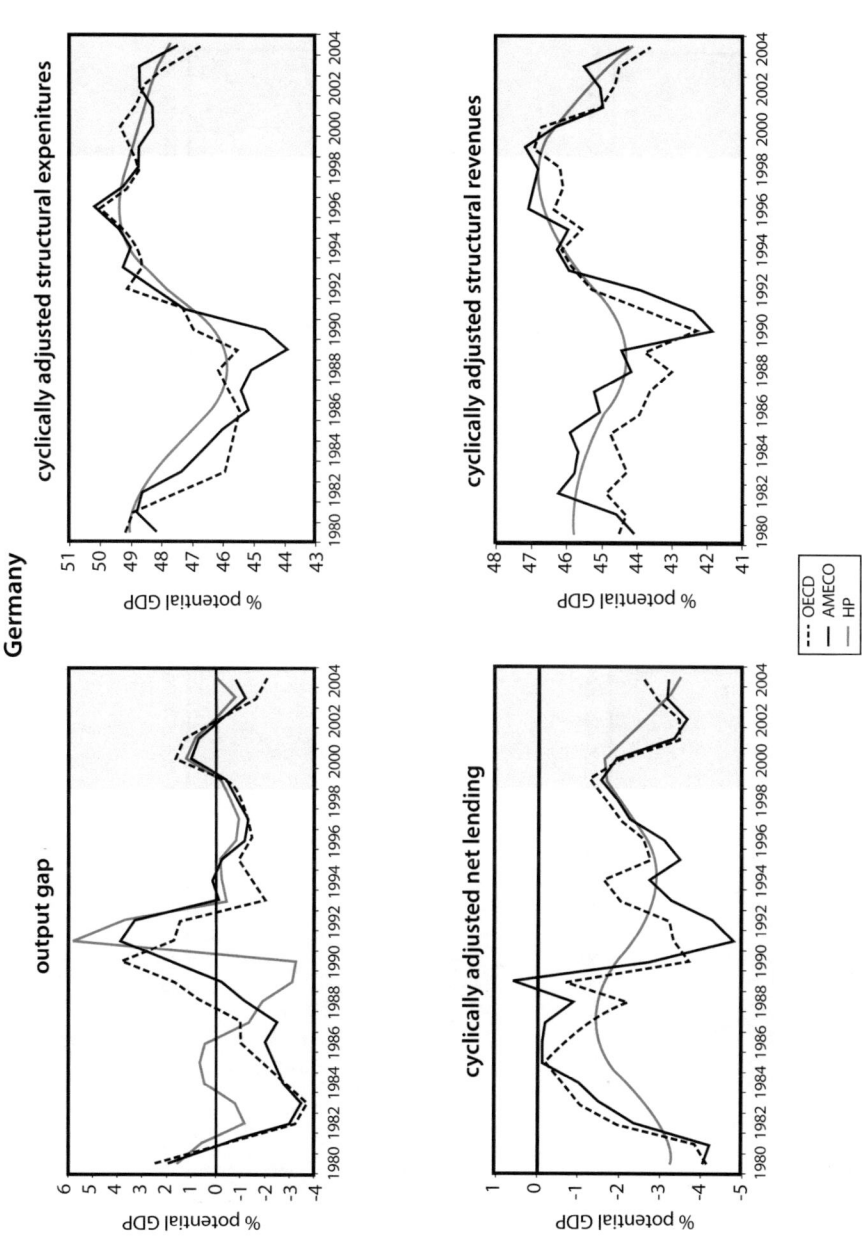

Figure 5.2b Output gap, cyclically adjusted net lending, spending and revenue (percentage of potential GDP)*: Germany.

Note: * indicated by arrows.

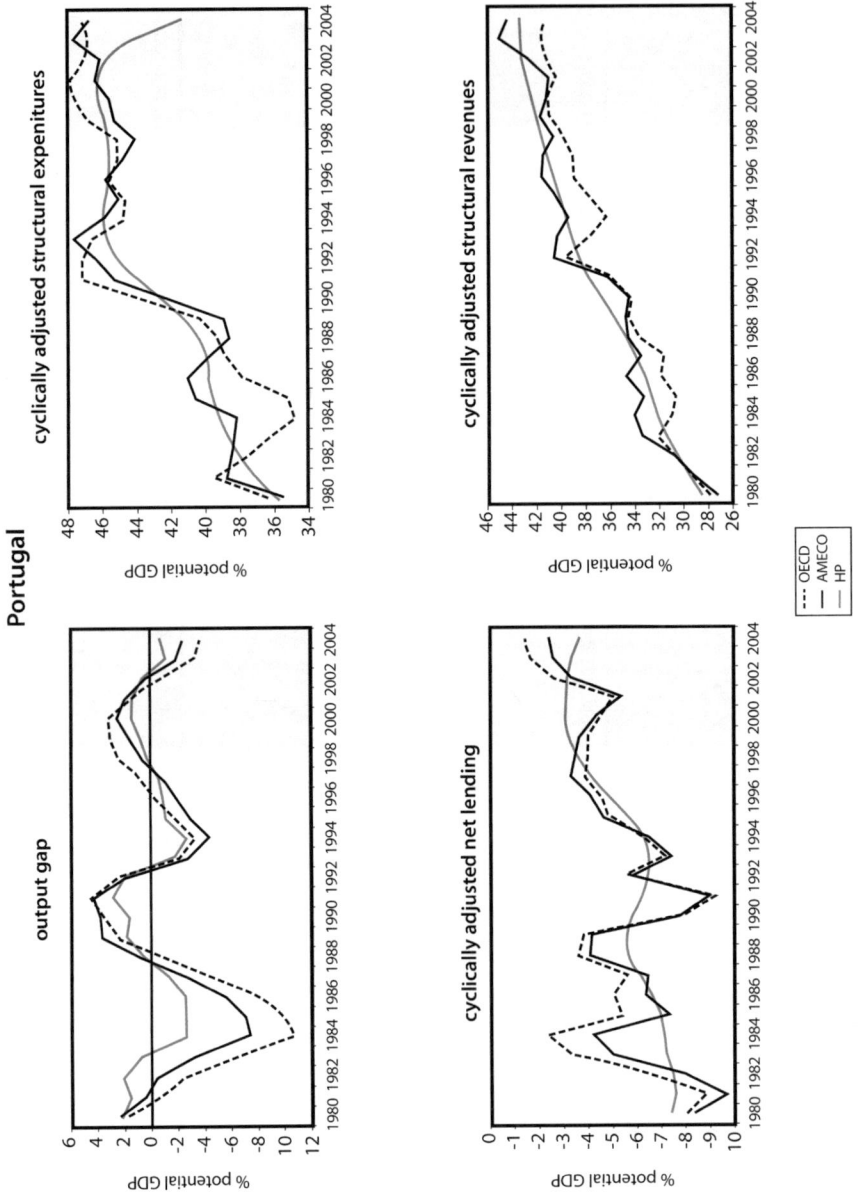

Figure 5.2c Output gap, cyclically adjusted net lending, spending and revenue (percentage of potential GDP)*: Portugal.

Note: * indicated by arrows.

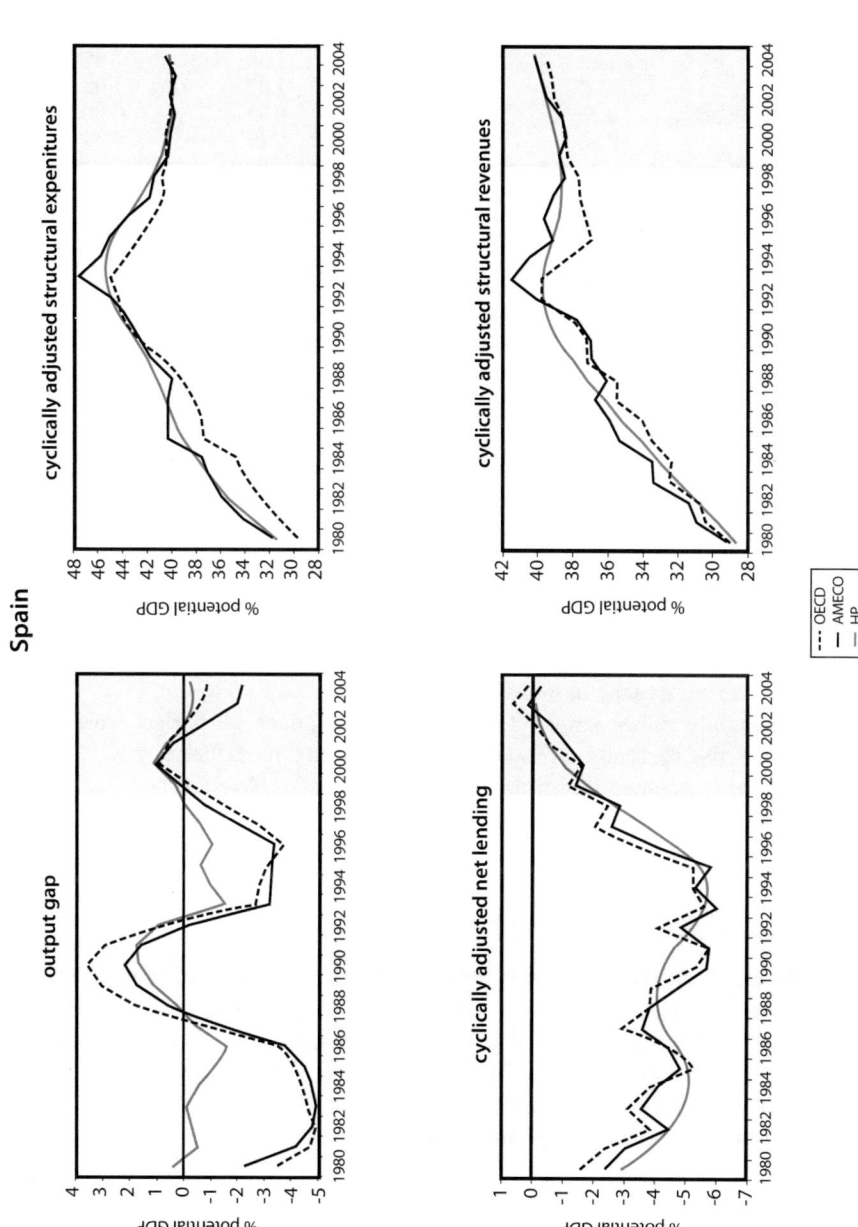

Figure 5.2d Output gap, cyclically adjusted net lending, spending and revenue (percentage of potential GDP)*: Spain.
Note: * indicated by arrows.

Table 5.1 OECD output elasticities of various budget items

	France	Germany	Portugal	Spain
Total spending	−0.11	−0.18	−0.05	−0.15
Corporate tax	1.59	1.53	1.17	1.15
Personal tax	1.18	1.61	1.53	1.92
Indirect tax	1.00	1.00	1.00	1.00
Social security contributions	0.79	0.57	0.92	0.68
Net lending	0.53	0.51	0.46	0.44

Source: Girouard and André (2005)

Table 5.1 gathers the elasticities from OECD for the major budget categories in the countries we study.[8] As in most other European countries, the cyclical elasticity of total net lending varies around 0.50. Most of the variation in the budget comes from pro-cyclical corporate and personal taxes.

Quite some uncertainty surrounds the computation of structural balances in this two-step procedure. Depending on the skewness of the distribution of the moving-average weights in the filter that is being applied and the phase of the economic cycle, trend output is biased towards actual values, especially towards the end of the sample. Another problem is posed by structural breaks. Windfall revenues or unexpected spending are entirely included in the structural balance if they have no economic effects. Filters distribute the effects of a break forward and backward on the trend. But this problem is not limited to statistical methods. Even if we use the production function or consider a deterministic trend a reasonable approximation to potential output, incorporating shifts remains a problematic issue. The production function approach, moreover, suffers from plenty of assumptions that make cumulative uncertainty rather large.[9] The various assumptions on budget elasticities are not as crucial for the cyclically adjusted balance, but are nevertheless not less problematic. Implicitly, it is assumed that average budget elasticities have a time-invariant linear relation to changes in the economy. We return to these difficulties in a sensitivity analysis in Section 5.4.

Towards an economic indicator of fiscal policy

The main difficulty in interpreting the structural balance is the absence of economic arguments to underpin the trend/cycle decomposition. There is an implicit assumption in the filtering methods on the frequency of the business cycle and hence on trend output under average economic conditions. And while the production function approach builds upon economic foundations, the dynamics are nonetheless driven solely by the longer-term effects of investment feeding back on changes in the capital stock.[10]

Macroeconomic models that allow for cyclical fluctuations around some steady-state trending growth path can be found in the growing class of Dynamic Stochastic General Equilibrium (DSGE) models with nominal rigidities. These models have by now been extended to include fiscal policy. In the initial Real Business Cycle models, there are only supply-side effects of fiscal policy that transmit through wealth effects and the labour/leisure choice (Baxter and King 1993). Micro-founded models based on sticky prices provide a rationale for stabilization policies, but even in the New Keynesian type of models of fiscal policy, the supply-side effects still tend to dominate demand-side effects of fiscal policy management (Linnemann and Schabert 2003). A larger role for demand-side effects of fiscal policy is only found in models that introduce some further imperfections via 'Rule of Thumb' consumers or a fraction of liquidity constrained consumers (Galí et al. 2005; Bilbiie et al. 2006). The latter models come also closer to replicating the results of the growing empirical literature on the effects of fiscal policy.

The main result of studies that use the VAR counterparts to DSGE models is that they can indeed recover significant effects of fiscal expansions on output. These are more in line with a positive 'Keynesian' effect on consumption, although the eventual multiplier is strongly reduced. The identification of fiscal policy is fraught with difficulties, however.[11] First, the implementation of announced changes in government policies is subject to lengthy and visible political negotiations that are anticipated in private agents' behaviour. As a consequence, fiscal shocks need not affect fiscal variables first. This is a problem of the shock being non-fundamental (Lippi and Reichlin 1994). Second, decisions on fiscal policy affect different groups in the public via a range of different spending and tax instruments. There exists no 'standard' fiscal shock: every political discussion considers the trade-off between a range of possible taxation and spending adjustments. The means of financing and the adjustment in expenditures and revenues wrap empirically relevant effects of different budget components in an aggregate fiscal shock without considering the path of public debt. Most studies focus on total spending or revenues, and find small and positive effects of government spending on consumption, but prolonged negative effects of higher taxation. Only a couple of studies consider the dynamic behaviour of some particular budget components.[12] Third, these identification problems are only exacerbated by the automatic reaction of fiscal aggregates to economic variables.

The seminal contribution of Blanchard and Perotti (2002) lies in using a semi-structural VAR that employs external institutional information on the elasticity of fiscal variables to output. Cleaning out the automatic cyclical reaction of the total fiscal balance leaves shifts to the cyclically adjusted balance as discretionary fiscal shocks. Blanchard and Perotti (2002) additionally impose some timing restrictions on the economic effects of discretionary policy. These timing assumptions avoid to some extent anticipation effects but would not capture these completely if implementation lags are important. Subsequent studies have mainly attempted to verify the original approach of Blanchard and Perotti (2002) with a variety of techniques and usually tend to confirm their findings.[13]

However, the empirical literature has hitherto ignored the supply and demand channels of fiscal policy that are at front-stage of the theoretical DSGE models. Such effects are only implicitly acknowledged in these VAR studies. Changes in tax revenues, for example, are usually found to have lasting effects on output. There are nevertheless two other strands of the empirical fiscal policy literature that attribute a role to supply-side variables. First, the literature on non-Keynesian effects of fiscal policy would argue that fiscal consolidation might have positive consequences on output. The composition of the fiscal adjustment thereby plays an important role (Alesina and Perotti 1995). The effects of consolidation on agents' expectations on the future economic outlook – measured by asset markets' reaction (Giavazzi and Pagano 1990) – suggests a role for permanent wealth and supply-side effects of fiscal policy. Second, most VAR studies have so far ignored the literature on the long-term growth effects of fiscal policies. The main message of the endogenous growth models that have been developed is that higher taxation unambiguously reduces output, but that these losses may be offset by using the proceeds for productive spending items (Barro 1990; King and Rebelo 1990). These seminal models have been made more realistic by allowing endogenous responses of labour (Turnovsky 2000). Typical tests of these growth models give empirical support to the role of spending and taxes to long-term growth (Kneller et al. 1999). It can be argued that additional government spending in catching-up countries such as Portugal and Spain had rather different effects than further expansions of the budget in France and Germany, for example. This provides an additional argument for including the former countries in our analysis.

The examination of the growth effects is also of substantial policy interest. In the assessment of EU Member States' policies under the revised Stability and Growth Pact, much attention is devoted to the quality of fiscal adjustments and the sustainability of public finances. The implementation of major structural reforms that raise potential growth – and hence have an impact on the long-term sustainability of public finances – can be considered grounds for temporary deviations of budget balance. There is thus need for a framework that assesses changes in fiscal instruments and distinguishes the short-term demand from the longer-run supply effects of such policies.

Methodology

We make a first step in setting up an empirical VAR model that allows for fiscal policy having distinct long- and short-term effects on output. The approach in this chapter rests on a combination of long-term restrictions and some assumptions on the short-run elasticities of budgetary items.[14] For the purpose of gauging a model-based fiscal indicator, we basically take shocks with permanent effects on output to drive long-term trends. Following Blanchard and Quah (1989), potential output is determined by so-called productivity or technology shocks that permanently affect output. This can then be complemented with further assumptions on the short-term behaviour of fiscal policies. Shocks with transitory output effects are classified as either cyclical or fiscal, following the elasticity approach of Blanchard and Perotti (2002).

We specify an empirical model of fiscal policy as a small-scale VAR in real output y_t and the expenditure g_t and revenue side t_t of the government budget. We can summarize the data properties in a VAR model (5.1), ignoring for ease of notation any deterministic terms:

$$B(L)X_t = \varepsilon_t \qquad (5.1)$$

where X_t refers to the vector of variables $[y_t \quad g_t \quad t_t]$, and ε_t contains the reduced form OLS-residuals. By rewriting the VAR into its Wold moving average form (5.2),

$$X_t = B(L)^{-1}\varepsilon_t \qquad \varepsilon'_t\varepsilon_t = \Omega \qquad (5.2)$$

and imposing some structure on the relation between reduced form residuals ε_t and structural shocks η_t via the transformation matrix A (such that $A\varepsilon_t = \eta_t$), we can write the model (5.2) as follows:

$$X_t = C(L)\eta_t = B(L)^{-1}A\varepsilon_t \qquad \eta'_t\eta_t = I \qquad (5.3)$$

Any SVAR analysis needs to impose at least as many restrictions as contained in the matrix A to identify the model. By imposing orthogonality of the structural shocks we have already six (i.e. the covariance matrix of OLS residuals $\Omega = AA'$). Hence, we need to choose at least three more restrictions. The ones we employ are a combination of long- and short-term restrictions. The latter shape the contemporaneous relations among the variables through a direct parameter choice on A. The former impose a long-term neutrality constraint on the effects of a structural shock j on some variable i. That is, the i,j-th element of the infinite horizon sum of coefficients, call it $C(1)_{ij}$, is assumed to be zero. This requires an indirect restriction in (5.3) on the product of the transformation matrix A and the inverted long-run coefficient matrix $B(1)^{-1}$. In other words,

$$[C(1)]_{ij} = [B(1)^{-1}A]_{ij} = 0 \tag{5.4}$$

For the system consisting of government expenditures, revenues and output, we assume three structural shocks to drive output and fiscal variables. The supply shock (η^q) drives the long-term trend rise in output and leads to the unit root behaviour of real output. This shock is isolated by assuming there are two further shocks in the model that both have temporary effects on output. I.e., we assume that $[C(1)]_{12} = 0$ and $[C(1)]_{13} = 0$ in (5.4). These shocks can be interpreted respectively as a generic business cycle shock (η^c) capturing short-term fluctuations around the moving steady state equilibrium for output, and a fiscal shock (η^f) with short-term 'demand' effects on output. In order to distinguish the business cycle shock from that to fiscal policy, we employ the elasticity approach advocated by Blanchard and Perotti (2002). We derive a shock to spending and/or revenues from which the cyclical effects have been removed. In other words, the shock with transitory effects on output – but unaffected by short-term variation in output – is the fiscal policy shock and reflects discretionary changes in the fiscal policy stance.[15] We take elasticities for government expenditures (γ) and revenues (α) with respect to output, and impose these values on the relation in A between the reduced form residuals for output (ε^y) and spending (ε^g) respectively revenues (ε^t).[16] The fiscal shock thus includes discretionary decisions unrelated to the cycle. Moreover, any government policy that interferes with the workings of automatic stabilizers on a systematic basis is considered as a fiscal intervention. Unlike other VAR studies, we split an overall change in fiscal policy into a part that has a short-term economic effect (the fiscal 'demand' shock), and into shocks that may have potentially long-term growth effects (the 'supply' shock).[17]

One important limitation of the current version of the model is that we cannot tell apart the growth effects coming from 'pure' technology shocks and those deriving from tax and spending decisions. Our supply shock is thus a combination of all shocks with long-term output effects. The negative effects of distortionary taxation or incentive-distorting spending show up in this shock, as well as the possibly positive effects of government investment. Instead, we isolate in the fiscal 'demand' shock only those changes in the discretionary budget stance that have temporary effects on output. A full-fledged analysis of the economic growth effects of fiscal policy would require additional restrictions.[18] The current identification is sufficient, though, for the purpose of deriving a fiscal indicator. We summarize our assumptions in (5.5) (see also Table 5.2):

$$C(1) = \begin{bmatrix} \bullet & 0 & 0 \\ \bullet & \bullet & \bullet \\ \bullet & \bullet & \bullet \end{bmatrix} \quad \text{and} \quad A = \begin{bmatrix} \bullet & \bullet & \bullet \\ \bullet & \gamma & \alpha \\ \bullet & \bullet & \bullet \end{bmatrix} \tag{5.5}$$

Table 5.2 Identification in the long and short term

Effect of shock on	Long-run restrictions		
	Supply shock η^q	Business cycle shock η^c	Fiscal shock η^f
Real GDP	•	0	0
Public spending	•	•	•
Public revenues	•	•	•
	Short-run restrictions		
	Supply shock η^q	Business cycle shock η^c	Fiscal shock η^f
ε^y	•	•	•
ε^g	•	•	γ
ε^t	•	•	α

Table 5.3 Parameters γ and α

	France	Germany	Portugal	Spain
Total spending, γ	−0.11	−0.18	−0.05	−0.15
Total revenues, α	0.58	0.59	0.47	0.49

Source: Authors' calculations.

We cannot simply set to zero the elasticity γ of government expenditures. Unemployment benefits move over the cycle in EU countries, even if their contribution to variation in total spending is not large. The parameter γ comes directly from the elasticities calculated by the OECD that we reported in Table 5.1. Instead of multiplying each revenue category by its cyclical elasticity and GDP share, we have subtracted the spending elasticity (row 2 in Table 5.1) – accounting for its share in GDP – from the elasticity of total net lending (row 7 in Table 5.1) so as to obtain the total elasticity of revenues α. The coefficients do not sum to zero as the budget is assumed to be countercyclical. Table 5.3 summarizes our parameter assumptions.

Gauging the fiscal indicator

The structural model then permits adopting a unified approach towards contemporaneously uncovering indicators of potential output y^* and the structural balance d^*. Basically, total output and government expenditures and revenues can be decomposed into the contribution of each of the structural shocks. We take the stance that only supply shocks determine potential output y_t^* in the long term. Both fiscal shocks and supply shocks determine structural expenditure g_t^* and revenues t_t^*.[19] Under this assumption, one can compute the structural deficit as in (5.6):

$$d_t^* = \frac{g_t^* - t_t^*}{y_t^*} \tag{5.6}$$

This fiscal indicator d^* can be interpreted as reflecting the discretionary stance of the fiscal authority. From the decomposition of the budget, we can then analyse whether such changes usually occur via spending or taxation measures.

This measure cannot directly be compared to the cyclically adjusted balances provided by the European Commission, the OECD or to those derived from some statistical filtering method. First, the output gap we derive need not correspond to the fluctuations around a smooth trend on some assumption on the frequency of the business cycle. The economic shocks that drive potential output reflect changes in productivity – that may derive from a variety of sources – and might vary over time. Our approach is best seen in the line of papers that investigate the role of nominal versus technology shocks in economic fluctuations (Nelson and Plosser 1982; King et al. 1991; Galí 1992).

Second, the variation in the structural balance is different from that in traditional two-step methods. This discrepancy owes to the definition of structural balance. This is perhaps best illustrated with an example. Consider a tax cut, for a given level of government spending and exogenous output. This would lead to a deficit, ceteris paribus. If fiscal policy indeed has real economic effects, as the empirical literature suggests, then the tax cut temporarily boosts output. As a consequence, tax revenues will increase and spending on unemployment benefits decrease, and the budget surplus will rise. The traditional measure for cyclical adjustment takes out all cyclical variation, also the one induced by fiscal policy, which leads to an overstatement of the structural balance. In our approach, we control for this economic effect of the tax cut. The SVAR model excludes that part of the variation in GDP due to discretionary fiscal measures whereas the conventional models take total output variation into account. But our approach even goes one step further. Imagine that the tax cut also raises potential output in the long term. This widens the gap between actual and potential output at the moment the fiscal shock occurs. Structural balance would be improved as the increased tax base (now, and in the future) makes the fiscal position more sustainable. Similar arguments can be made for the effects of spending. As a consequence, our indicator of structural balance does not necessarily display a smaller variation than traditional indicators. This will particularly be true if (a) the indicator is mainly driven by fiscal or supply shocks; or (b) if the underlying economic shocks we retrieve are more volatile than conventional output gap measures suggest.

Our model-based indicator has some favourable properties in comparison to more conventional measures. First, the long-term constraints hold the promise of imposing fewer contentious restrictions on the short-term effects of the fiscal shocks. Any anticipation effect and the contemporaneous reactions of fiscal balances to economic conditions are not constrained. Second, the simultaneous determination of a measure of cyclical output and fiscal balance is internally more coherent. While the method is definitely more complex, total uncertainty is quantified. We impose a minimal set of economic restrictions and the validity of these assumptions can be discussed. As the empirical model is also consistent with recent DSGE models of fiscal policy, these assumptions can be tested. Sensitivity analysis can make clear the weakness of the model in some specific direction. Moreover, progress in theoretical models of fiscal policy can lead to further refinements of the approach. Third, by adopting an economic – and not a statistical – method, the end-point problem of filters is eliminated. The indicator gives timely information on changes in the fiscal stance.[20] Finally, our indicator is also more relevant for the assessment of fiscal policy. Our measure indicates better the change in the stance of fiscal authorities, also with a view to growth effects and long-term sustainability.

At the same time, the econometric approach suffers from some weaknesses. First, extensions are difficult as the method is rather data-demanding – at least in the time series dimension.

The annual frequency of the data may lead to some difficulties in the identification of business cycle shocks, for example. Second, the gains of loosening the constraints of short-run effects of fiscal policy have to be offset against some additional complications (Sarte 1997). While both short- and long-term restrictions are sensitive to the exact parameter values imposed, substantially more uncertainty surrounds the estimates of the long-term inverted moving average representation in (5.2), especially in the short samples that we use (Christiano et al. 2006). The basic problem is that no asymptotically correct confidence intervals on $C(1)$ can be constructed. Faust and Leeper (1997) prove that there are no consistent tests for the significance of the long-term response. Specifying a priori the lag length of the VAR or choosing the horizon at which the long-run effect nullifies can solve this problem. One may also check the consistency of some short-term restrictions with the long-term behaviour of the model, as in King and Watson (1997). Third, there is a possibly large set of underlying shocks from which we extract only a few. As discussed above, we extract a generic supply and cyclical shock, as well as a fiscal shock. This necessarily involves a debatable linear aggregation over shocks. If each shock affects the economy in qualitatively the same way the shocks may be commingled. This is particularly acute for the analysis of fiscal policy, as different expenditure and revenue categories may indeed have different longer-run effects on output that are not distinguishable from technology shocks but, moreover, have similar short-term responses. Fourth, a problem may also occur of high frequency feedbacks. We observe fiscal policy only at an annual frequency. We assume the structural shocks to be orthogonal, but if there are mid-year revisions of the budget this may muddle both economic and fiscal shocks. This only stresses the problem of correctly identifying the timing of shifts in fiscal policies. Finally, a major assumption underlying the VAR model is parameter constancy. The conclusions of VARs are highly sensitive to the presence of structural breaks. Especially for fiscal policy, there is evidence of non-linear effects (see Giavazzi et al. 2000, for instance). We therefore run some stability tests on the VAR model.

5.4 Empirical analysis

Data

All data are annual and come from AMECO.[21] This database covers the longest available period at the time of writing, from 1970 up till 2004, for which fiscal data are available for France, Germany, Portugal and Spain. Fiscal data and output are deflated by the GDP-deflator and are defined in first differences of log-levels. In many studies, the fiscal data are scaled to GDP, but this clouds inference. As economic shocks affect both fiscal variables and GDP, this leads to a spurious negative correlation between the deficit and these shocks. Moreover, we are primarily interested in distilling a fiscal indicator on the basis of the historical decomposition of output. For the same reason, we do not concentrate on the effects of fiscal policy on private output but use total output instead. We also ignore possible co-integration between overall expenditures and revenues, which derives from the intertemporal budget constraint.[22] This implies that parameter estimates may no longer be efficient although still consistent. However, inference on the short-term results of the VAR would hardly be affected by non-stationarity of the data (Sims et al. 1990).

Data are defined following ESA-95 nomenclature. Definitions for the French budget changed in 1978. We linked the former series (going back to 1970) to the ESA-95 series and include an impulse dummy for this data break. We treat the effects of German Reunification in 1991 in a similar way. We further condition the models on these deterministic terms.

Table 5.4 VAR break date test

France		Germany		Portugal		Spain	
1992***	[1989, 1996]	1976***	[1974, 1978]	1997***	[1995, 2001]	1998***	[1996, 2003]

Source: Bai et al. 1998

Notes:
*** Denotes significance of the break date at 1%; break date is sup-Quandt break date;
Years in brackets are the confidence interval at 33% (Bai 1997).

Before estimating the structural model, we want to check for other possible breaks in the VAR. We follow the method of Bai et al. (1998) and apply the sequential sup Quandt–Andrews likelihood ratio test on the VAR model. Sample size forces us to consider a single break date only, as the optimal search concentrates on the central 70 per cent of the sample and consequently leaves too few degrees of freedom for examining multiple breaks. We correct for a possible change in volatility before and after the break date. As in Stock and Watson (2003), we weigh each period's residuals by their average volatility. The lag length in the VAR is henceforth set to one year (following the Bayesian Information Criterion).

Table 5.4 reports the results. For Germany, we could detect a further break in the data in 1976, related to the large increase in social spending under the Brandt government. For France, Portugal and Spain in contrast, we find a significant break date that is seemingly related to the Maastricht consolidations, albeit the confidence bounds are rather large and span nearly the entire 1990s. It is nevertheless suggestive of the change in the conduct of fiscal policy under the effect of the Maastricht rules. Because of this imprecision, we refrained from explicitly modelling these shifts with additional dummy variables.

The transmission channels of fiscal policy

We first discuss some general results of our small-scale model, and assess the properties of output and fiscal series, and the role of the various structural shocks. The following paragraphs discuss the fit of the model in terms of impulse response functions and the forecast error variance decomposition.[23] We have summarized all results in Figures 5.3 and 5.4. This prepares the ground for an analysis of the fiscal indicator in Section 5.4.

The effect of productivity shocks is to lift up real output permanently (Figure 5.3). The speed of accumulation is rather fast: after five years, the major part of the shock has worked out. In Germany, this happens even faster. The sampling uncertainty around the effect is large, but given the large bounds we have used, the significance of most impulse responses after some years is actually surprising. To what extent are these supply shocks driven by fiscal developments? In France and Portugal, these shocks go hand in hand with positive long-term effects on total expenditures and revenues as well. This effect is also strongly significant.[24] The difference between revenues and spending responses is not significant, hence it is not obvious that this leads to a build-up of public debt. In Germany and Spain, on the contrary, revenues do not change significantly, but government expenditures shrink considerably, leading to large accumulated surpluses at a horizon of ten years.

But whether the causality runs from fiscal policy to productivity growth, or vice versa, is not obvious. Recall that the supply shock contains productivity shocks that may emanate from the private as well as the public sector. The significant co-movement of spending and revenues suggests that fiscal 'supply' shocks are an important source of the overall

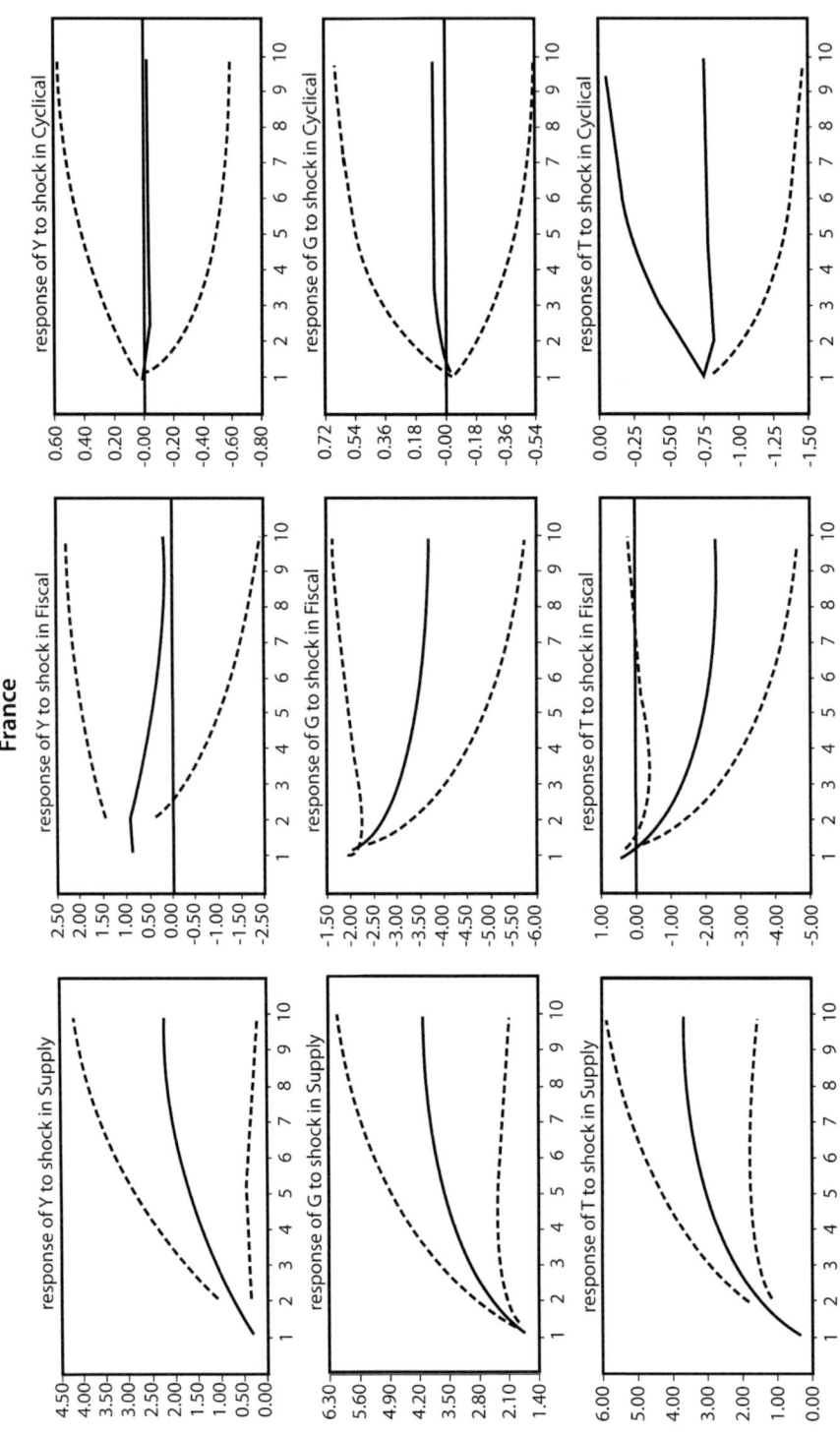

Figure 5.3a Impulse responses (response to a one standard deviation shock): France.

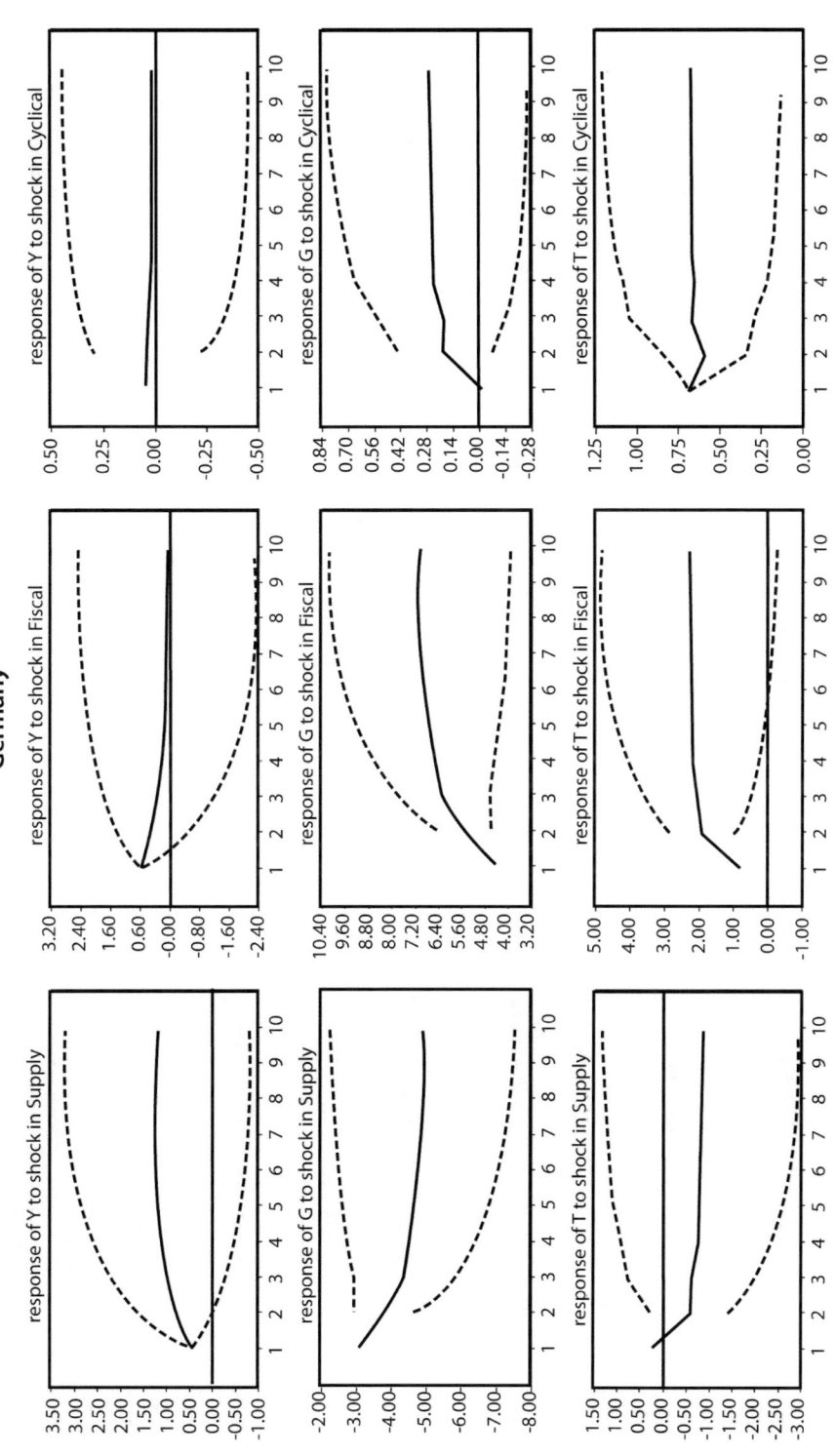

Figure 5.3b Impulse responses (response to a one standard deviation shock): Germany.

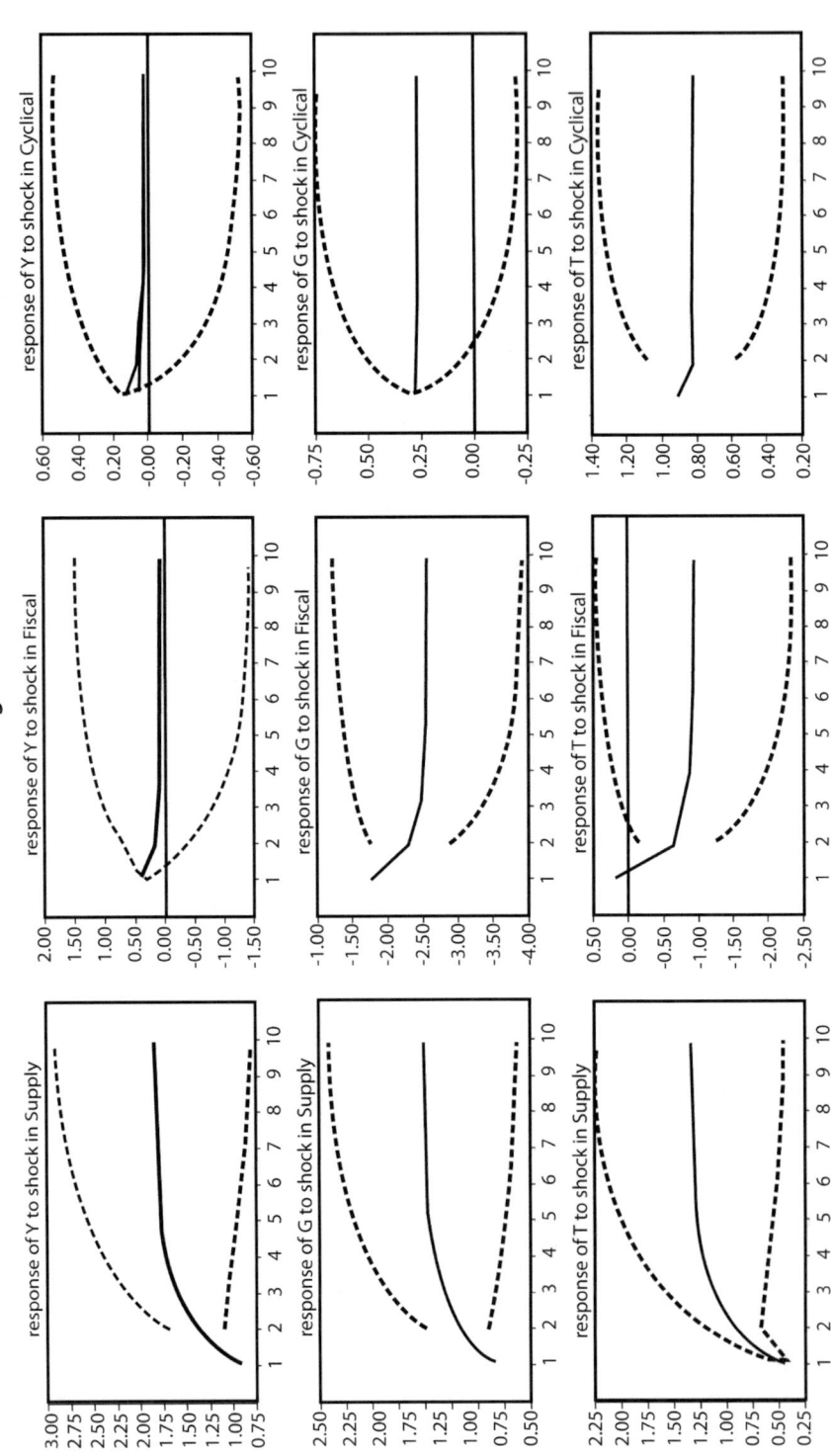

Figure 5.3c Impulse responses (response to a one standard deviation shock): Portugal.

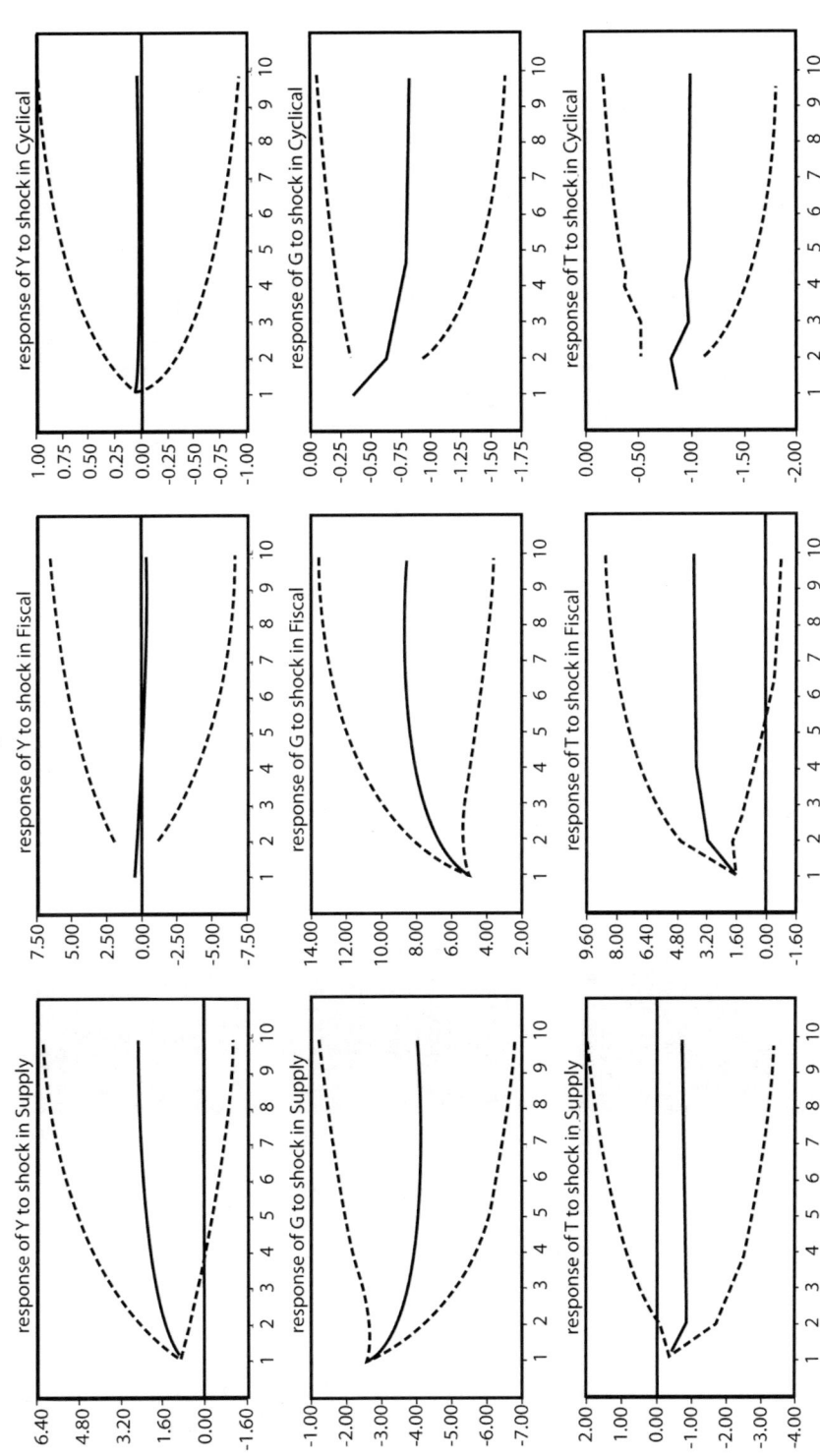

Figure 5.3d Impulse responses (response to a one standard deviation shock): Spain.

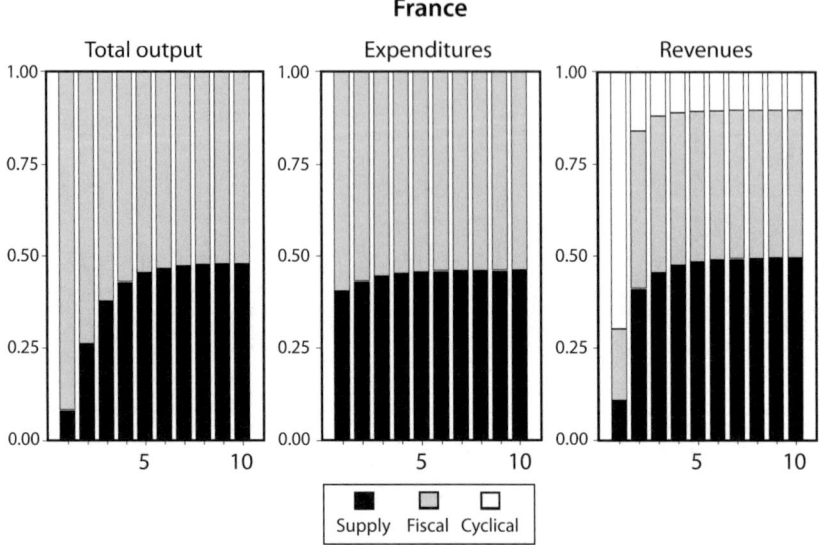

Figure 5.4a Forecast error variance decomposition: France.

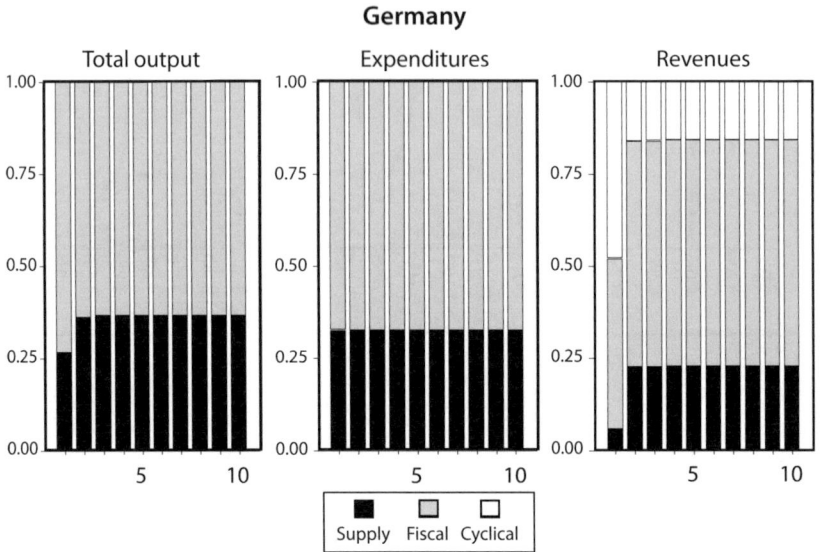

Figure 5.4b Forecast error variance decomposition: Germany.

productivity shock.[25] If these relations are positive (the case of France and Portugal), this implies higher spending or that tax revenues have contributed to economic growth. In the opposite case (Germany or Spain), a reduction of spending – and less so a lower tax burden – would trigger higher potential output growth. But there are a few alternative explanations. Positive economic shocks that enlarge the tax base would – for a given tax rate – automatically lead to a larger revenue intake owing to automatic stabilizers. For reasons of political

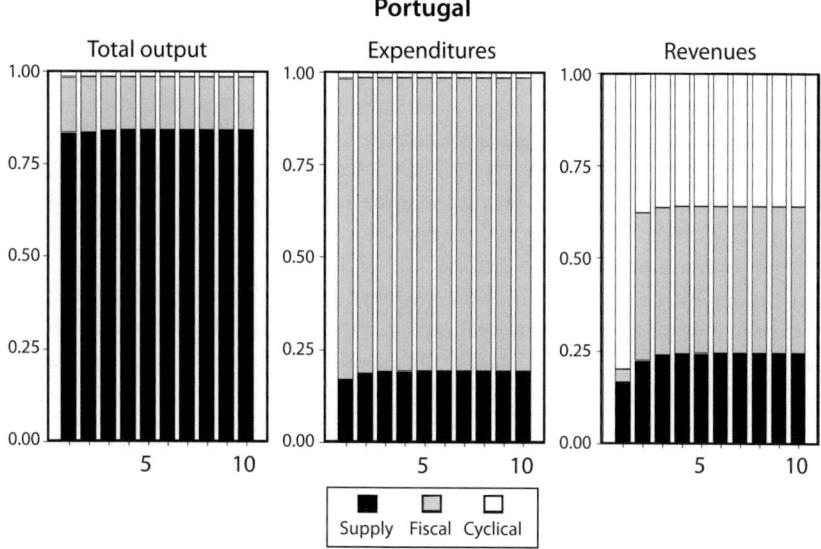

Figure 5.4c Forecast error variance decomposition: Portugal.

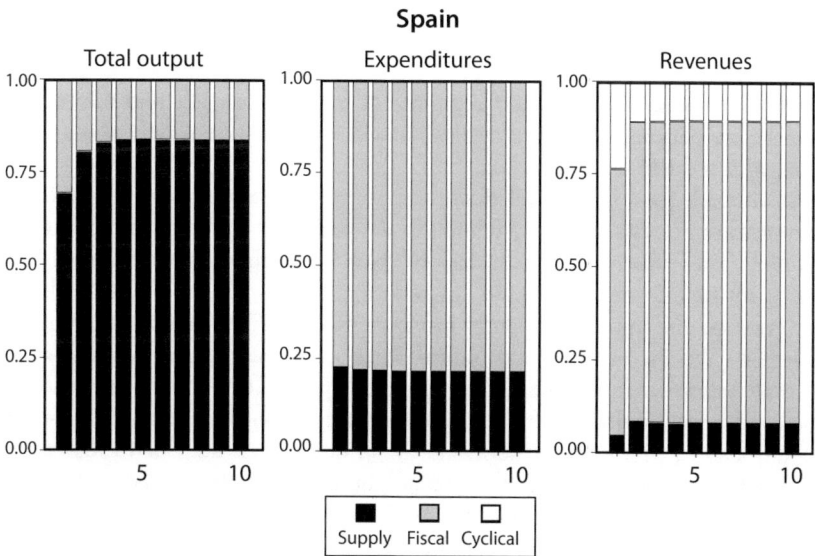

Figure 5.4d Forecast error variance decomposition: Spain.

economy, this could lead the government to directly spend the proceeds of the treasury. This expansion of the budget could consequently get locked in and lead to a permanent rise in government expenditure. This mechanism would work for both permanent and cyclical shocks, if we assume that the government does not systematically react in different ways to permanent or transitory economic shocks. This allows us to gain some insight into the importance of the private versus public productivity shocks. The fiscal responses to cyclical shocks, which include business cycle shocks with transitory output effects that are not related to fiscal policy, can give some indication. Surprisingly, the effects of cyclical shocks on output are hardly significant and indicate the small size of temporary economic fluctuations.[26] As a consequence, there is not always an obvious simultaneous rise in tax revenues. In Germany and Portugal, government revenues do rise in response to a positive output gap, and this effect remains permanent. Moreover, in both countries government expenditures tend to rise as well. This gives some support for the 'ratcheting up' effect on spending. In France or Spain, instead, government spending does not react in a significant way and tax revenues even tend to decline.

If we consider in some more detail the two countries in which catching-up phenomena may be expected to be important, we cannot clearly distinguish between the two alternative explanations. In both Spain and Portugal the reaction of fiscal variables to temporary and permanent shocks is similar. This downplays the importance of productive fiscal policy contributing to economic growth. A comparison of the impulse responses shows that only a minor effect would be left in the case of Portugal. Evidence on Spanish public finances presents a slightly different picture. Positive supply shocks are accompanied by a strong decrease in total spending, and this effect is much more pronounced than the reduction in spending after a cyclical shock.

In France and Germany, instead, the reaction of fiscal variables to permanent shocks is opposite to the reaction to business cycle shocks and supports the view that fiscal variables drive long-term growth in both countries. That spending and revenues go up after a positive supply shock, whereas there is a non-significant response or a decline following cyclical shocks, would suggest a larger role for productive public spending in France instead. Evidence for Germany rather seems to indicate a too-large size of government. We find that revenues and spending go up permanently after cyclical shocks, but positive supply shocks tend to be associated with reductions in spending.

The fiscal shock then regards all discretionary policy interventions on spending and/or revenues that are not systematically related to the cycle and have only temporary effects on the economy. These discretionary fiscal shocks have somewhat prolonged effects on output. There is a lot of uncertainty around this effect and none of the responses is really significant. We scale the impulse responses in Figure 5.3 such that they always display positive output effects. We do not find the typical result of small positive Keynesian effects on output in all countries. In Germany and Spain, a typical Keynesian response would follow upon demand-boosting deficits. In France and Portugal, on the other hand, fiscal contractions would lead to positive short-term effects on output instead. Such different responses likely depend on the composition of the fiscal adjustment or other structural parameters in the respective economies, but cannot be further examined in the current model.

The different responses of spending and revenues to both economic shocks might indicate a delicate issue in the identification of policy. If fiscal policy reacts in a systematic way to economic shocks by changing its discretionary use of spending and/or revenues, this simultaneity blurs the distinction between the economic and the fiscal shock. This might be the case in France and Spain where tax revenues decrease after positive temporary output shocks, for example. But another indication is given by the rise in spending in economic booms in Germany or Portugal. It indicates policies that react in a discretionary way so as to repeal the use of automatic stabilizers. The fiscal indicator captures these policy biases. Our discussion will show how important this policy bias is for understanding fiscal trends in EU countries.

What does this imply for the contribution of fiscal policies to output variation (Figure 5.4)? Supply shocks account for at least 50 per cent of total variance in output at all horizons, and this goes up to 90 per cent in Portugal and Spain. For the latter countries, this was perhaps to be expected given their strong economic growth over the last two decades. Most of the variation in output is thus caused by productivity shocks even at short horizons. As we do not separately identify private and public supply shocks, we cannot really quantify the relative magnitude of both channels. But as pointed out above, we think that productive spending or revenues has contributed to some extent to the variance of output. The demand effects of fiscal policy in France and Germany are at least as large as those of supply effects. In Portugal or Spain, instead, only a minor role is played by discretionary fiscal policy. The contribution of cyclical fluctuations to variations in output is negligible, as was to be expected from the results on the impulse responses.

What factors can account for these results? The large role played by fiscal policy in explaining output variation is not inconsistent with previous findings in the literature for large EU countries (De Arcangelis and Lamartina 2004), but seems on the higher side of the range usually found. If we take the result at face value, it would suggest that the temporary demand effects of fiscal policy are probably much larger than the supply effects in the long term. This would imply that both RBC and New Keynesian models are missing some aspects of fiscal transmission. But as we cannot precisely quantify the importance of the latter shocks, we would not want to claim validation of any of the theoretical models with our approach. This result nevertheless reveals that models of fiscal policy need to attribute important roles to both demand- and supply-side effects.

We think that the reason for the large contribution of fiscal policy is to be found elsewhere. To the extent that automatic stabilizers reduce the volatility of economic fluctuations, the tendency of governments to reduce taxation and/or raise spending in a pro-cyclical way only adds to short-term output fluctuations and brings about aggregate macroeconomic instability. This policy volatility can moreover have negative effects on the long-term growth prospects of the economy.[27] The unwinding of previous taxation decisions goes against the principle of 'tax smoothing'. The pro-cyclicality of budgets implies negative supply-side effects. This explains the surprisingly low contribution of cyclical fluctuations.

Before going deeper into the past trends in fiscal policy, we want to check our model on some other aspects too. We compute the output gap based on the historical decomposition of the output series as actual minus potential output $(y - y^*)$. In Figure 5.5 (top left panel),[28] we have repeated for comparison the output gaps of the European Commission, OECD and the one obtained by applying a Hodrick–Prescott filter. There is a rather close correspondence between these measures and our supply shock based gap for France and Germany. Given that we have used the OECD elasticities only for distinguishing shocks with transitory effects on output, this is all the more remarkable. The smooth gaps for Portugal and Spain shows us the importance of supply relative to demand shocks in both countries. This might indeed be expected given the strong economic catch-up that both countries have experienced. We believe that potential output tracked much closer actual output developments in these countries. The usual statistical filtering methods are not adequate to capture this trend behaviour over small samples. Cyclical fluctuations are therefore rather minor. We provide some further robustness checks in Appendix 5.B.[29]

Overall, in all countries, there definitely was an improvement in economic conditions at the start of EMU. We find that economic conditions have worsened in both France and Germany in recent years. We nevertheless find the crisis in Germany to have set in somewhat earlier and to be more prolonged. As cyclical fluctuations are not large, we do not find much economic slack in recent years in Spain or Portugal.

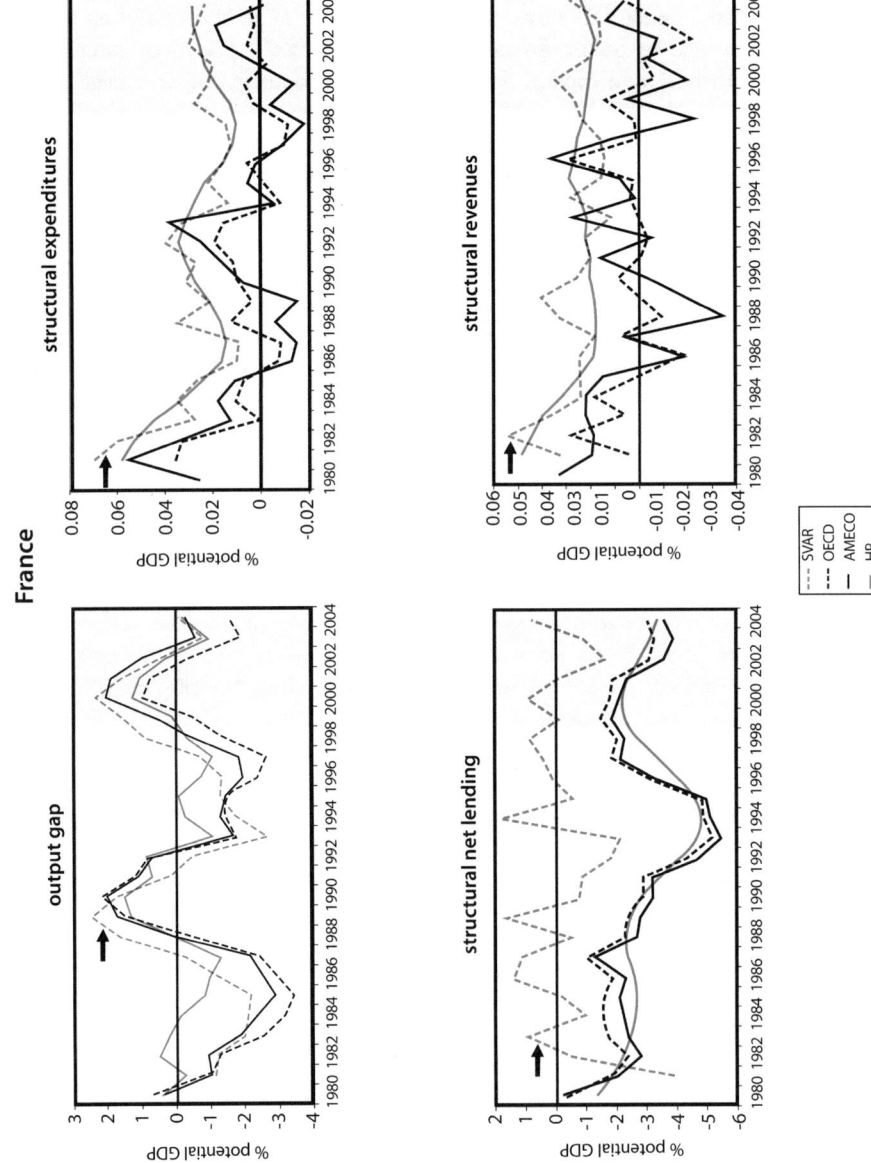

Figure 5.5a SVAR indicator of output gap, structural net lending, expenditure and revenues (percentage of potential GDP): France.

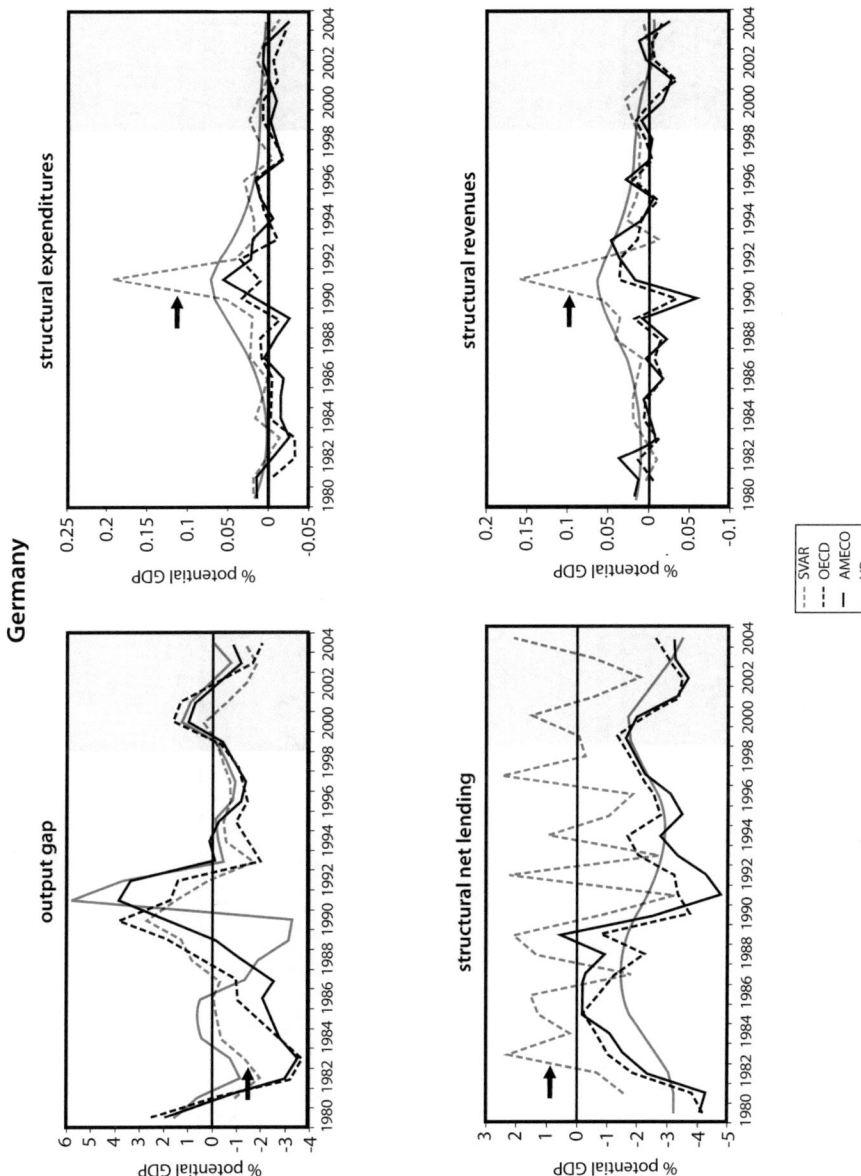

Figure 5.5b SVAR indicator of output gap, structural net lending, expenditure and revenues (percentage of potential GDP): Germany.

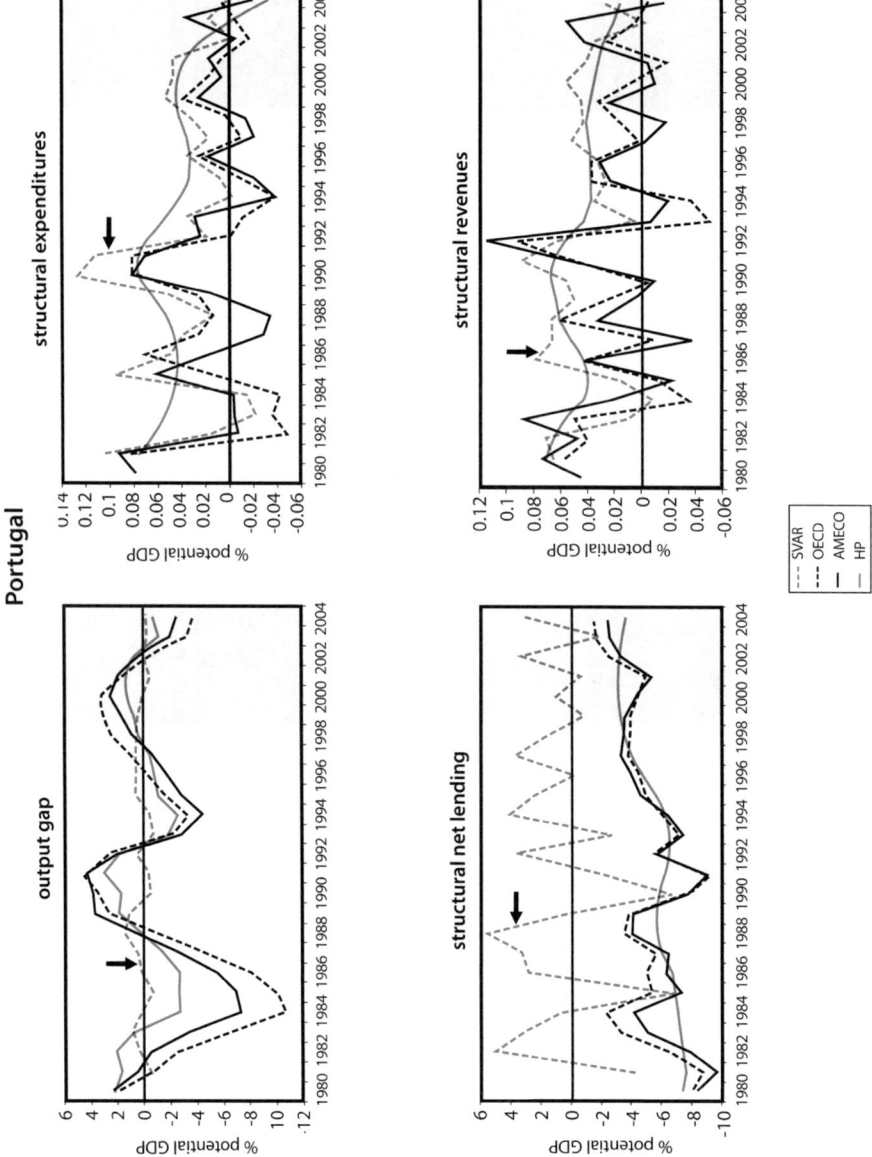

Figure 5.5c SVAR indicator of output gap, structural net lending, expenditure and revenues (percentage of potential GDP): Portugal.

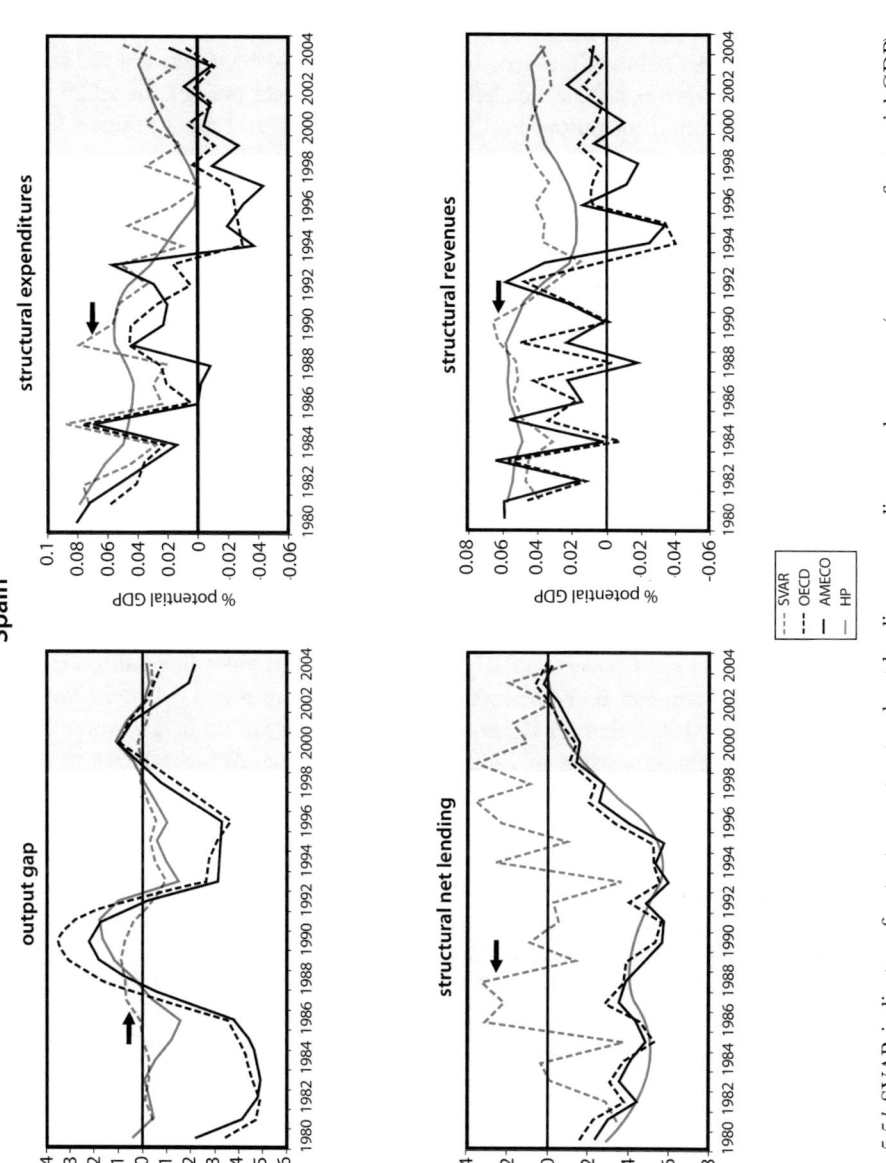

Figure 5.5d SVAR indicator of output gap, structural net lending, expenditure and revenues (percentage of potential GDP): Spain.

The fiscal indicator

We are now ready to discuss the indicator of discretionary fiscal stance. In general, the measure is more volatile than the measures derived with conventional methods (see Figure 5.5, bottom left panel). In many instances, our measure leads the smoothed measures in the direction of change. The fiscal indicator is usually smaller than the cyclically adjusted deficit. This reflects the definition of the structural balance, by which we take out the automatic stabilizers and the induced stabilization effects caused by fiscal policies. In addition, fiscal policy also affects permanent output and therefore the structural fiscal position fluctuates around balance.

The indicator is also much more volatile. This follows from the major contribution of supply and fiscal shocks to the variation in output, spending and revenues (Figure 5.4). As we discuss below, one of the causes of this strong volatility – apart from the dominant supply-side shocks – is the pro-cyclical bias that characterizes fiscal policy making that induces extra variation, especially so in government revenues.

We may then expect our fiscal measure to coincide with some episodes of fiscal laxness or retrenchment. We consider the budget to undergo a strong expansion (contraction) when the cyclically adjusted primary balance falls (increases) by at least two percentage points of GDP in one year, or at least 1.5 percentage points on average in the last two years. This is the measure proposed by Alesina and Ardagna (1998). In Table 5.5, we gather those fiscal years in which a strong expansion or adjustment has occurred in our dataset (see Afonso 2006).

At first sight, the correspondence is rather close. Comparing the changes in Figure 5.5 (bottom left panel) to the years in Table 5.5, we detect all events that the Alesina–Ardagna measure also suggests. For example, we find the budgetary cost of Reunification on German public finances to have been large. The Maastricht rules have also led to considerable fiscal retrenchment in France and Spain. There are a few events in Portuguese fiscal policy over the 1980s that we do not date exactly. But we do find a switch between contraction and expansion starting in 1982–1983. The Alesina–Ardagna measure does not pick up all expansions and contractions that we find, however. Some of these episodes correspond to well-known changes in the fiscal stance (e.g. the 'Mitterrand' budgets in France in 1981). Another major expansion in France in 1992 follows upon a string of expansionary budgets. Spain equally undergoes major expansions in the early 1980s and 1990s (1981 and 1993 respectively). Fiscal policy is also lax in Portugal (1990). Prolonged contractions occur over the 1980s in France, Germany and Spain too.

Concentrating on the period just before EMU, we can see a substantial shift in discretionary policies towards structurally positive net lending ratios. This is perhaps least visible in Germany, but the initial conditions were probably not such as to urge a strong and prolonged

Table 5.5 Large fiscal expansions and contractions

	Expansions	Contractions
France	–	1995–96
Germany	1990–91	1982–83
Portugal	1980–81	1982–83, 1986, 1992
Spain	–	1995–96

Source: Adapted from Afonso (2006), following the measure used by Alesina and Ardagna (1998)

consolidation for reaching the Maastricht deficit limit. A substantial consolidation had already taken place at the end of the 1980s. In the other countries, the structural effort was more drawn out. France had already started consolidation in 1993, while it gathered pace in Portugal and Spain only in 1995. This also confirms evidence in Fatás and Mihov (2003a).

How has this consolidation been achieved? The right-hand-side panels of Figure 5.5 plot the growth rates of structural expenditures and revenues. These reveal that structural consolidations in the 1990s have been based on a mixture of expenditure and revenue measures. But the combination of adjustments in the policy instruments has changed over time in a remarkably similar fashion in all countries. Initially, we see relatively moderate expenditure growth and in some cases even relevant spending cuts (Germany and Portugal). This strategy is reversed closer to the deadline of EMU. Tax increases start to bear the largest burden for bringing down deficits. Given the urgency of qualifying for the EMU criteria, taxes have seemingly been the easiest instrument to adjust. Notice the rather close match between the VAR measure of structural spending and revenues and the (difference log of the) HP-trend on unadjusted total expenditure and revenues. The measures of OECD and AMECO display slightly lower growth rates. This owes again to our definition of the structural series. The efforts in reaching EMU led to the levelling off or even moderate declines in debt ratios. A plot of the structural fiscal indicator to the debt ratio shows how well the indicator captures these consolidations in debt (Appendix 5.B).

What went wrong, then, with the application of the Stability and Growth Pact in France, Germany and Portugal upon entry to EMU? The causes are again rather similar across countries. The increased tax revenues in the years prior to EMU led to a starting point of structural surplus. The persistence in these tax rises improved actual balances thanks to the favourable economic conditions at the time. But this has been exploited to increase expenditures in a commensurate way. Especially in Portugal, the expansion in expenditures seems to have held back an improvement in the structural position. The only exception here is Spain, which further brought down expenditure, even in the presence of strong revenue increases. Simultaneously, the tax revenues that stream in during economic boom seem to have been undone by decisions to bring down tax rates in most countries. This considerably worsened the structural balance. As economic boom turned into bust again, the decline in revenues led to a substantial worsening of actual balances, pushing the deficit beyond the 3 per cent threshold. However, the revenue declines have hardly ever been matched by sufficient cutbacks in government spending in the following years. Corrective measures in 2004 have improved the structural deficit. But the measures are mainly taken on the revenue side again, by once more undoing previous decisions to cut tax rates. To avoid further infringement of the budget rules, the adjustment in Germany and France has taken place via the route of tax rises during economic slack. This has once more reinforced the pro-cyclical bias in fiscal policy making. This also highlights the mechanism by which spending gets locked in, and causes a 'ratcheting up' in the size of government.

The overall situation seems less dramatic in Portugal, as revenue changes have been supported by equivalent spending decisions.[30] For Spain, the moderate decline in tax revenues in 2001 and 2002 was not entirely matched with spending cuts, leading to a slight deterioration of the structural indicator. The expansionary measures taken in 2004 have led to a breach of a balanced structural budget for the first time since 1995. Unsurprisingly, the expansion of fiscal policies in all countries reflects itself in rising debt ratios in recent years (see Appendix 5.B).

How useful is our indicator for assessing budgetary reform? We have argued above that aggregate spending or revenue measures contribute to long-term growth. Its contribution may perhaps be small relative to productivity rises in the private sector, and part of the effect could be swamped due to pro-cyclical policies that induce macroeconomic fluctuations (and its consequent negative effects on growth). We do not believe this is the final word on the contribution of fiscal policy. A more detailed analysis of different spending/tax items could shed light on their specific growth-enhancing effects.

Some sensitivity analysis

The results might be influenced by some particular parameter value that we have drawn from the OECD (Girouard and André 2005) in order to distinguish business cycle and fiscal demand shocks. There are various reasons for considering these aggregate elasticities with some caution.

First, elasticities are assumed to be time-invariant. These are not representative of the tax and spending structures that have prevailed in historical samples, however. In some countries, the expansion of the welfare state has led to gradually larger tax bases and dramatic changes in tax systems (Portugal and Spain). But even in France and Germany, time-variation cannot be neglected. Budget elasticities tend to move over the business cycle as well (Bouthevillain et al. 2001). Changes in elasticities also throw up a more subtle difficulty in the interpretation of the fiscal shocks that we have already discussed in Section 5.4. On the revenue side, discrete policy changes involve decisions on the ratio of average to marginal tax rates and the breadth of tax bases rather than on total amounts.[31] Only if changes in total revenue amounts coincide with these decisions do we correctly identify shocks on the revenue side of the budget. Second, given the difficulties in identifying all channels through which changes in interest rates and inflation may impinge on various revenues and spending categories, the OECD simply abstains from adjusting interest payments for cyclical variation and assumes the net effect of inflation to be zero.[32] This only reinforces the argument in favour of our economic approach in which we specify a role for long-term and business cycle fluctuations. However, our use of the OECD numbers can be argued to be inconsistent as these have been derived under these methods. Finally, auxiliary assumptions on the various parts of the calculation of budget elasticities may cumulate into quite some uncertainty in the final estimates of elasticity.

Our first robustness check on the elasticity parameters illustrates the effects of this uncertainty. We conduct a grid search on different values for γ and α that Girouard and André (2005) provide. Table 5.6 shows the wide range of net lending elasticity that is obtained by varying only the elasticity of wages to output two standard errors below and above its point estimate.[33] For all possible combinations of this revenue elasticity α and for a given spending elasticity γ, we impose the identification scheme as in (5.5) on the VAR. For any of the parameter values in Table 5.6, we always find convergence to a result identical to that obtained with the point estimate of the elasticity.[34] The uncertainty about the elasticity

Table 5.6 Net lending elasticity and parameters γ and α

	France	Germany	Portugal	Spain
Net lending	0.53	0.51	0.46	0.44
	[0.46. 0.61]	[0.39. 0.61]	[0.42. 0.50]	[0.38. 0.49]
Total spending, γ	−0.11	−0.18	−0.05	−0.15
Total revenues, α	[0.51. 0.66]	[0.46. 0.68]	[0.44. 0.52]	[0.43. 0.53]

Source: Girouard and André (2005)

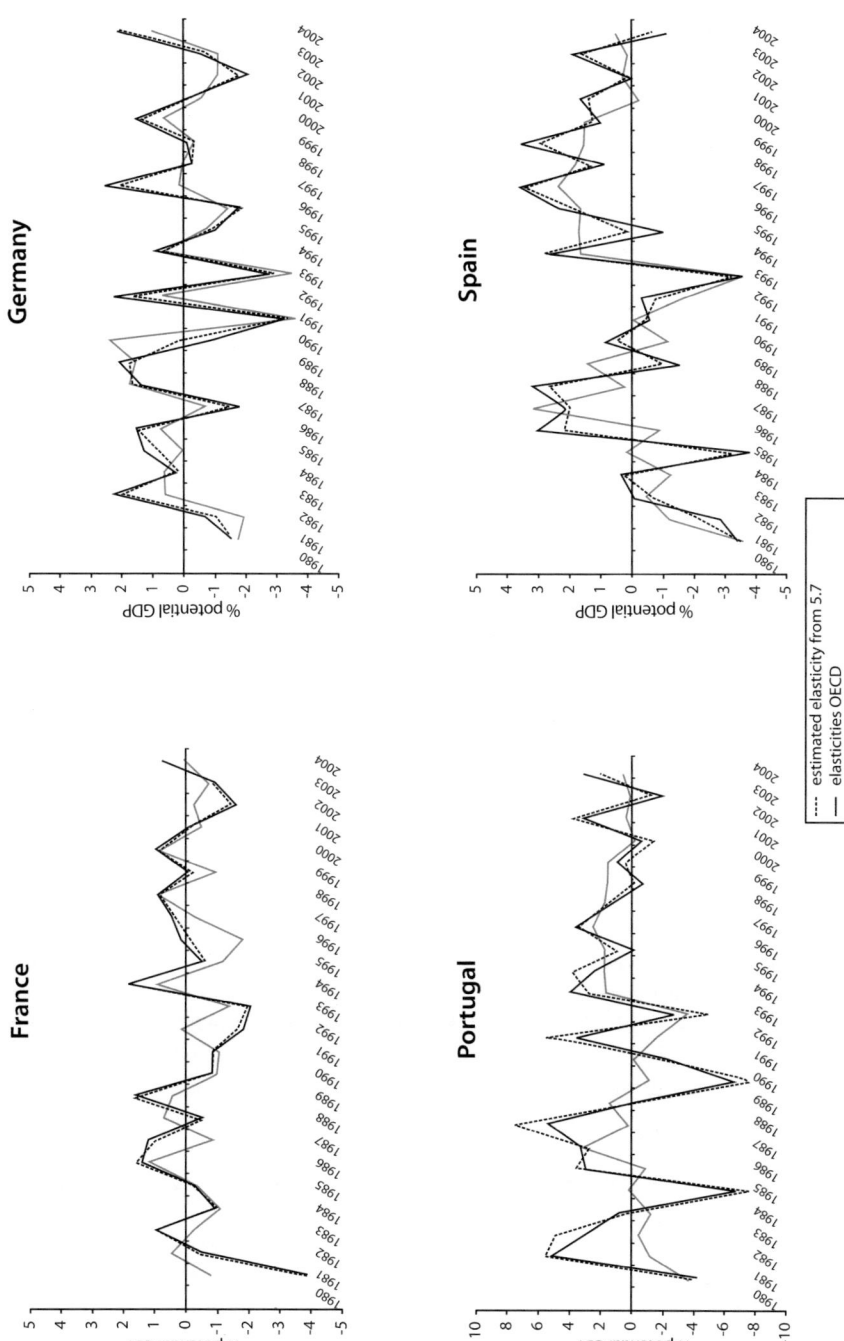

Figure 5.6 Sensitivity analysis: SVAR indicators of structural net lending (percentage of potential GDP): France, Germany, Portugal and Spain.

does not seem to play a major role, then, and this confirms the findings of Blanchard and Perotti (2002) or Marcellino (2002).

One of the other interesting scenarios is the one in which we switch off the elasticities. By setting γ and α equal to zero, we assume that neither spending nor revenues react to the cycle. This consequently attributes a larger role to discretionary fiscal policies. The effect on the structural indicator depends, however, on the relative contribution of changes in taxes or spending to fiscal shocks. Figure 5.6 contrasts the structural indicator obtained with the OECD elasticities against the one with zero elasticities. The effect is only marginal. In most periods, the results are rather similar. This reflects again the prevalence of the supply relative to the temporary economic shocks. Oftentimes, there are more prolonged periods of moderate deviations.

Fiscal policy might be more seriously biased against automatic stabilizers than our 'zero-elasticity' scenario suggests. There is quite some evidence that in European countries, governments have been systematically overturning the working of automatic stabilizers (Galí and Perotti 2003; Lane 2003). The true expenditure and revenue elasticities may therefore be biased upward in comparison to observed elasticities. As a consequence, we would attribute too much of the variation in fiscal policies to the economic cycle and too little to the offsetting systematic discretionary adjustments.

To illustrate this phenomenon for Germany, France, Portugal and Spain, we follow Lane (2003) in estimating the output elasticity of the main budgetary items: i.e. we regress in (5.7) the main budget items on economic growth for the sample period 1970–2004,

$$d \log X_{i,t} = \omega_i + \gamma_i d \log Y_t + \mu_{i,t} \tag{5.7}$$

where X is total spending, government investment, current spending (consumption and wage spending), or interest payments, and Y_t is real output. Likewise, we estimate model (5.7) where X contains either total revenues, current revenues or (in)direct tax revenues. The estimates are also repeated for the decades 1970–1980, 1981–1990, and 1991–2004, as we have reasons to expect quite some time variation. Table 5.7 reports the results of an OLS estimation of (5.7), with a correction for first-order autocorrelation.

The switch from small negative spending elasticities in OECD (Girouard and André 2005) to a strongly positive elasticity is very strong in Germany and Portugal, where it is significant for all budget items. Government investment is the most pro-cyclical budget component. But the main category driving this result is – in absolute terms – government consumption. In Germany, a large role is also played by wage spending in the last decade. Fiscal spending expansions under positive economic growth are strongly concentrated in increased wage spending in Portugal. In contrast, Spain and, in particular, France have not been subject to a similar bias. No expenditure item – except for interest payments – shows significant signs of pro-cyclicality.

We have argued before that the pro-cyclical bias in fiscal policy is mainly due to reversals in taxes. We indeed confirm the pro-cyclicality of revenues as in all countries, elasticities are significantly larger than the corresponding elasticities from OECD (see also Table 5.1).[35] This is especially pronounced in the 1990s in all countries, with the exception of Germany. The changes over decades are quite marked and hide significant adjustments in tax systems. Only in Germany is the response of revenues pro-cyclical in all sub-samples. For France, Portugal and Spain, the elasticities in the 1970s are not significant. This must be related to the development of tax systems in the latter two countries; the result for France seems more puzzling.[36]

Table 5.7 Budget elasticities from OLS on equation 5.7

	France				Germany			
	1970–2004	1970–80	1980–90	1990–2004	1970–2004	1970–80	1980–90	1990–2004
Total spending	0.32	−0.47	0.38	−0.09	1.04***	−0.06	1.28***	1.22***
Investment	1.46	−4.09	6.52*	6.13*	3.55**	−1.84	5.06*	4.39*
Current spending	−0.15	−0.07	0.34	−0.55*	0.73***	−0.21	1.00**	0.88***
Consumption spending	0.19	−0.26	0.63	−0.53*	0.98***	−0.24	0.53	1.30***
Wage spending	−0.16	−0.45	0.50	−0.08	1.04***	0.03	0.40**	1.37***
Interest payments	−3.94***	−8.12***	−5.20**	−0.41	0.68**	0.26	−0.49	0.92**
Total revenues	1.73***	1.18	0.56	1.48***	1.47***	2.94***	1.52***	1.24***
Current revenues	1.86***	1.16	0.81	1.97***	1.46***	3.31***	1.48***	1.19***
Total tax revenues	1.18***	0.83	−0.08	1.47**	1.15***	1.87***	1.40***	1.09***
Direct tax revenues	2.07***	1.61	−0.14	3.12**	1.30***	2.50**	1.17***	1.28***
Indirect tax revenues	0.61**	0.81	0.02	0.54	0.94***	1.08***	1.57***	0.87***
	Portugal				Spain			
	1970–2004	1970–80	1980–90	1990–2004	1970–2004	1970–80	1980–90	1990–2004
Total spending	0.67**	−0.37	1.23**	1.46***	0.03	−0.15	−0.45	0.33
Investment	0.76	−1.39	5.35***	2.67	−0.37	2.60	−4.09	2.83
Current spending	0.76***	−0.16	0.96**	1.14***	0.22	−0.27	0.22	−0.07
Consumption spending	0.77***	0.10	1.40***	1.39***	0.22	−0.10	0.29	0.26
Wage spending	0.60**	−0.39	1.53***	1.54***	0.63	0.00	0.83*	0.33
Interest payments	−1.39	−2.67	−2.35	0.48	−1.31	−0.17	−2.71	−4.56***
Total revenues	1.58***	1.31	2.27**	2.59***	1.36***	0.71	1.36***	2.95***
Current revenues	1.62***	1.30	2.30**	2.90***	1.42***	0.71	1.36***	3.05***
Total tax revenues	1.24***	0.82	1.07	1.70***	0.99**	0.35	0.78	1.81***
Direct tax revenues	1.36***	0.96*	1.31	2.87***	1.08*	−0.26	2.35***	1.43***
Indirect tax revenues	1.02***	0.65	0.74*	1.04***	0.91*	0.99	−0.87	2.15***

Note:
*/**/*** denotes significance at the 10/5/1% significance levels, respectively

These results show that latent policy pressures on spending or revenue bring about adjustments that usually reverse the effects of automatic stabilizers. The 'actual' elasticities incorporate all cyclical reactions, coming from the automatic adjustments via the underlying tax and spending structure and systematic interventions of fiscal policy makers. If we choose to impose the 'actual' elasticity in the VAR model (5.5), the interpretation of the fiscal shock is one that includes all discretionary interventions. The drawback of the approach is that our 'cyclical' shock is a mongrel reaction to economic conditions, in which we cannot tell apart the importance of systematic policy and the economic cycle. The difference in the structural indicator – obtained with the OECD elasticities – can then be attributed to the pro-cyclical bias in fiscal policy.

Table 5.8 summarizes the elasticities that we have taken from Table 5.7 for the entire sample period for re-estimating the VAR. Figure 5.6 compares the structural indicator. We find convergence to the same solution as in the basic case: there are only some marginal differences for the case of Portugal.

What does the insensitivity of the results to assumptions on the budget elasticities tell us? The forecast error variance decomposition reveals nearly equivalent roles for demand

Table 5.8 Elasticities imposed on equation 5.5

	France	Germany	Portugal	Spain
Total expenditure, γ	0.32	1.04	0.67	0.03
Total revenue, α	1.73	1.47	1.58	1.36

Source: Authors' calculations

effects of fiscal policies and supply shocks in Germany and France, whereas supply shocks tend to dominate in Spain and Portugal. If we recover nearly similar fiscal policy shocks whether correcting for automatic stabilizers, setting them to zero or taking the systematic variation in fiscal policy into account, this is due to the little importance of cyclical economic shocks. This does not mean that the automatic stabilizers are irrelevant. The stabilizing effects of the structure of the spending and taxation system will still work their way to economic variables via the longer-term supply-side effects. It does not necessarily mean that 'letting the automatic stabilizers work' will lead to superior economic outcomes as such. Fiscal policy that refrains from manipulating spending or taxes at every economic turn shields the economy from further shocks. Fiscal policies ought to focus attention on the longer-term effects of fiscal policy, rather than destabilizing it.

5.5 Conclusion

Recent years have seen the launch of excessive deficit procedures to Portugal, France and Germany, and later for several other EU Member States. The reasons for the breach of the deficit rules in recent years are still open to discussion. A variety of political and economic factors probably underlie the increase in public deficit and debt ratios. The revised Pact loosens the numerical limits and leaves more room for a country-specific interpretation of the medium-term budgetary objective. First, it allows for a gradual adjustment effort under unfavourable economic conditions, as long as consolidation continues in good economic times. Second, the revised Pact also attributes more importance to the quality of the budget adjustment. The revised Pact provides for the implementation of structural reforms that carry temporary budgetary costs, but which through positive supply-side effects enhance the structural balance and thus the long-term sustainability of public finances.

This chapter takes a first step in developing an economic indicator of discretionary fiscal stance that takes into account both the cyclical short-term and the long-term supply-side aspects of fiscal policy. We analyse the budgetary outlook for France, Germany, Portugal and Spain by uncovering underlying past trends in revenue and expenditure. Our approach combines insights from the growing empirical literature on the effects of fiscal policy modelled via structural VARs with statistical methods for cyclically adjusting fiscal balances. Our approach innovates on existing evidence in using a mixture of short- and long-term restrictions to identify economic and fiscal shocks in a small-scale empirical model in output and fiscal variables. This allows for permanent shocks to determine trending behaviour of output and fiscal variables à la Blanchard–Quah. Discretionary fiscal adjustments are captured by filtering out the fiscal balance for cyclical reactions of budget items following Blanchard and Perotti (2002).

The model-based indicator we develop shows that pre-EMU consolidations have in the last instance been based mainly on revenues. The slippages of recent years owe to the unwinding of these measures without accompanying spending cuts. This showed up in larger deficits when economic conditions worsened, and a 'ratcheting up' in the size of government in economic booms. Recent corrective measures seem to rely mainly on increasing revenues again. The pro-cyclical bias in fiscal policies has not been eliminated. Governments implement bad policies in good times. Fiscal policy induces additional economic fluctuations and contributes to aggregate macroeconomic instability. As a consequence, the short-term effects of fiscal policy outweigh supply-side effects in the longer term. A Pact that counters these policy reversals can lead to more sensible policies that also focus on the long-term quality of public finances.

The analysis in this chapter is consistent with a growing theoretical literature on the effects of fiscal policy. DSGE models with nominal rigidities offer a rationale for fiscal stabilization policies. At the same time, these New Keynesian models consider both supply- and demand-side effects of fiscal policy, and find the former to dominate. We find that both the supply and demand effects of fiscal policy are important. The current version of the model does not allow us to quantify the contribution of supply shocks. The results suggest that the government budget can have long-term growth effects, but mostly so in catching-up countries such as Portugal or Spain. More elaborate empirical models could incorporate refinements in the compositional adjustment of budget balance. This would allow for an explicit assessment of the channels through which fiscal policy transmits its effects. Allowing for a different reaction of various budget items to demand and supply shocks can be a first step in that direction. We think in particular of spending categories that are considered productive (like government investment). This can verify some endogenous growth theories of fiscal policy (Turnovsky 2000). A major channel through which fiscal policy acts is also the labour market, either directly – via wage spending or public employment – or indirectly. Finally, instead of specifying a model in output and fiscal policies only, the inclusion of prices and/or interest rates can lead to a more accurate description of the economic shocks.

Appendix 5.A Data sources

	Definition		*Source*
g_t	Total expenditure		AMECO
t_t	Total revenues		AMECO
y_t	GDP		AMECO
Other	GDP deflator		AMECO
	Potential GDP		AMECO/OECD
	Output gap		
	Cyclically adjusted expenditure (categories)		
	Cyclically adjusted revenue (categories)		
	Cyclically adjusted net lending		
Other	Chronology of cycle[a]	Growth rate cycle peak and through dates' chronology are determined by two consecutive quarters of negative growth in smoothed industrial production.	Economic Cycle Research Institute (ECRI) at www.businesscycle.com, algorithm updated in September 2005

Appendix 5.B The fiscal indicator: some additional results

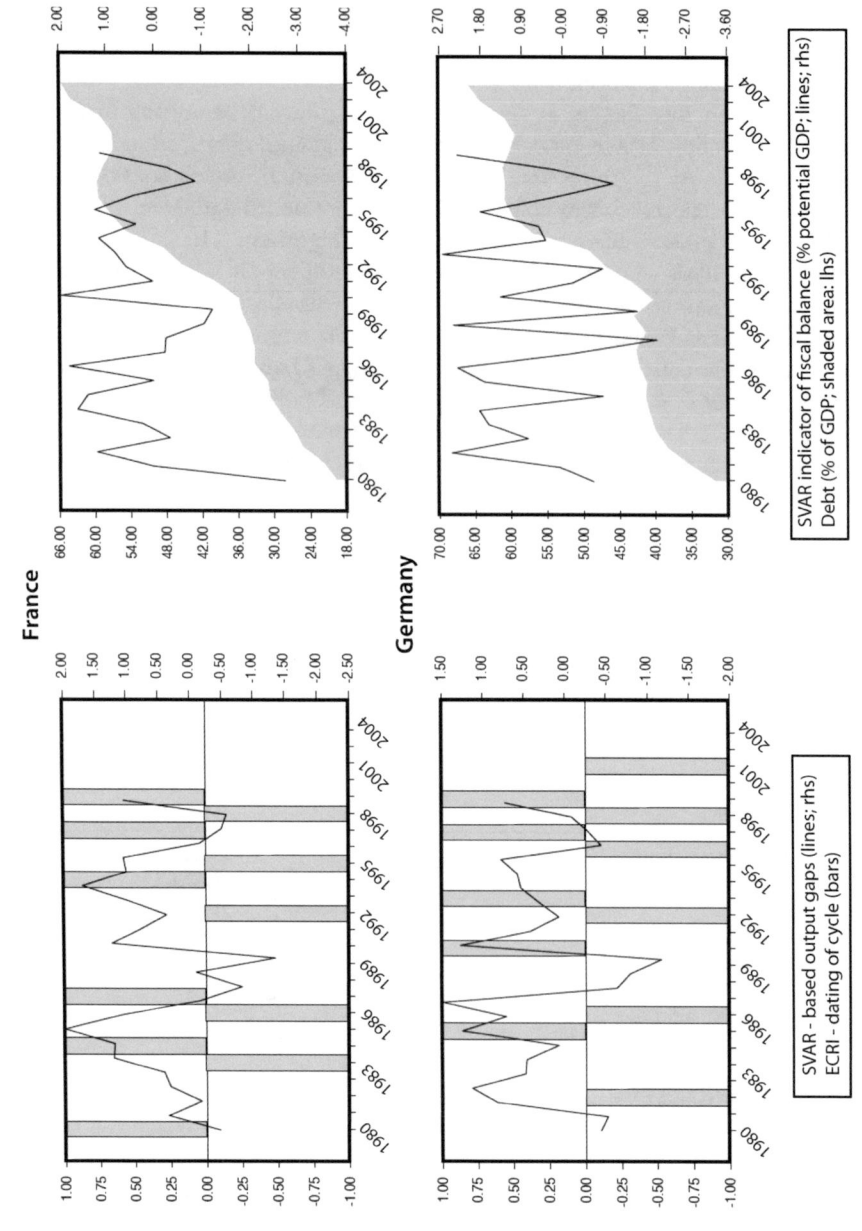

France and Germany.

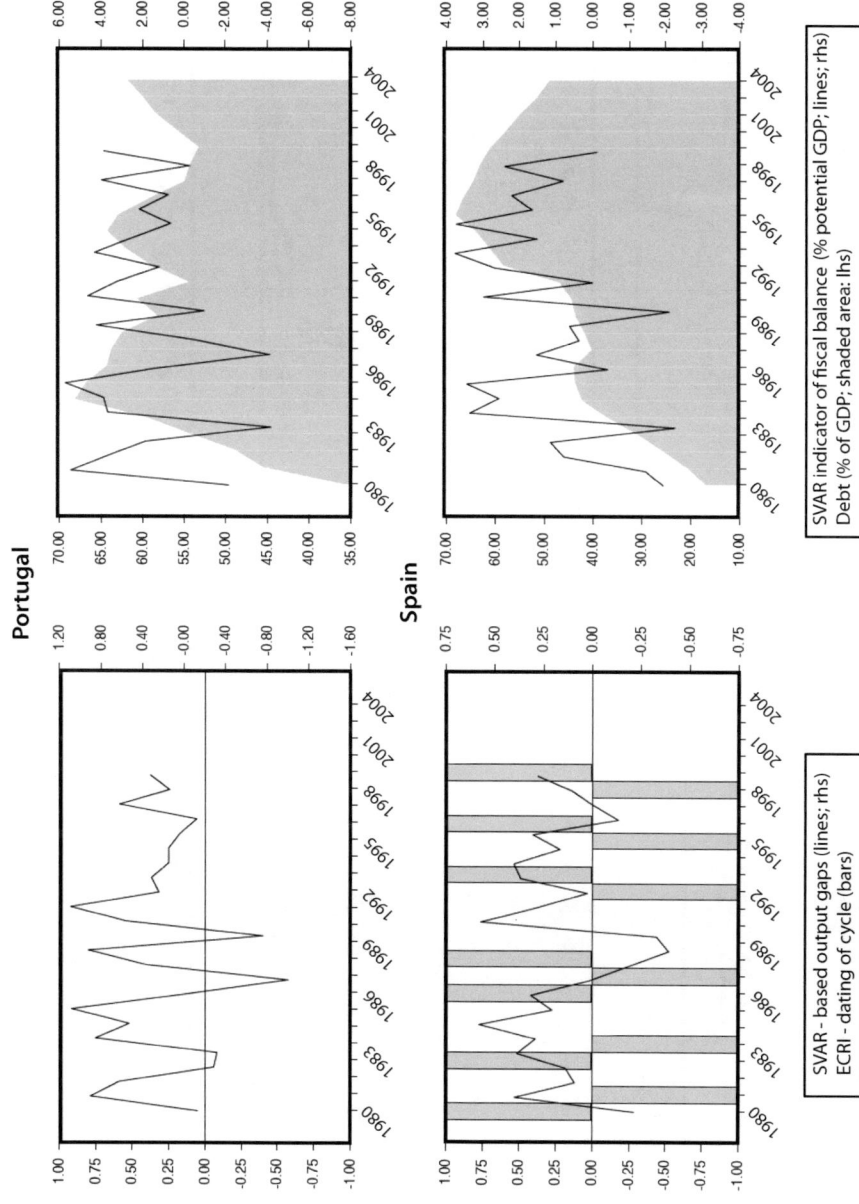

Portugal and Spain.

Appendix 5.C Recursive estimates of budget elasticities

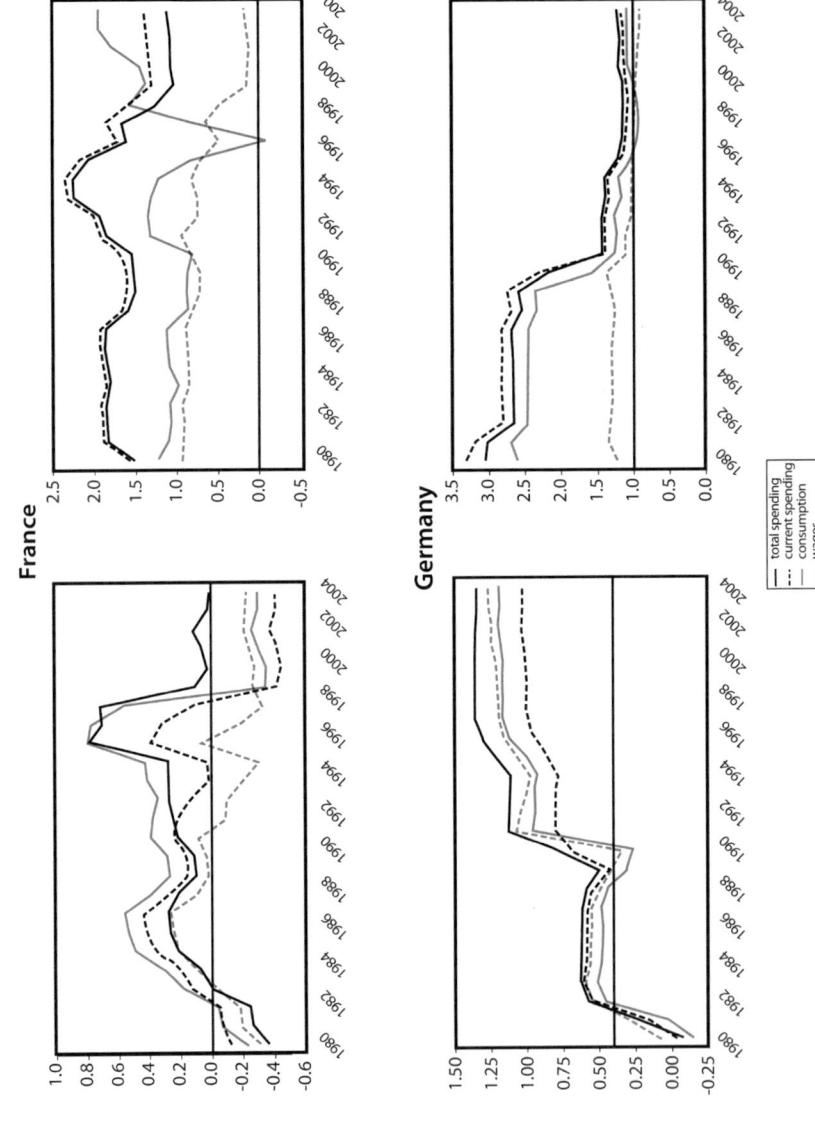

France and Germany.

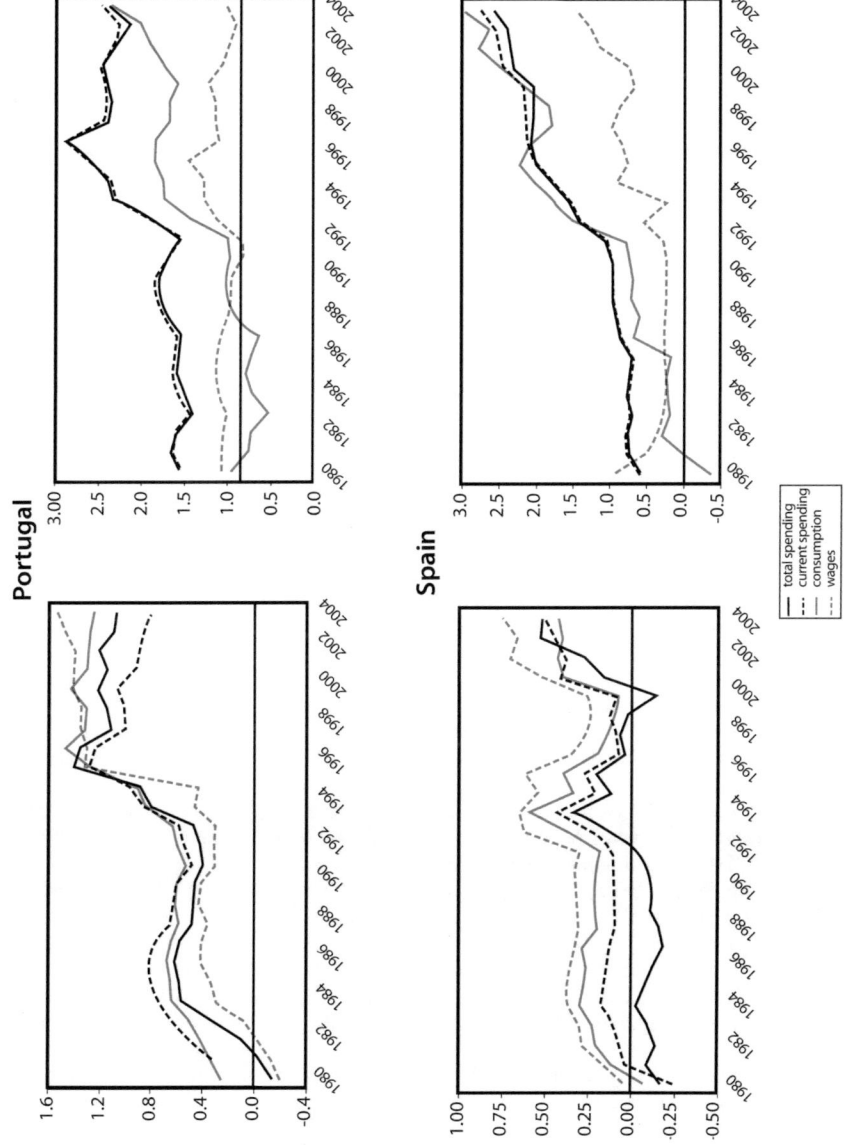

Portugal and Spain.

Notes

1 We are grateful to Luís Costa, Arne Gieseck, Michael Thöne, Jürgen von Hagen, Jan in 't Veld, seminar participants at the ECB (Frankfurt), at ISEG/UTL (Lisbon), at the 61st European Meeting of the Econometric Society (Vienna), and at the DG ECFIN workshop on Fiscal Indicators for EU Budgetary Surveillance (Brussels) for helpful comments and discussions. Valuable assistance of Renate Dreiskena with the data is highly appreciated. The opinions expressed herein are those of the authors and do not necessarily reflect those of the ECB or the Eurosystem. Peter Claeys thanks the Fiscal Policies Division of the ECB for its hospitality. This research was supported by a Marie Curie Intra-European Fellowship within the 6th European Community Framework Programme. UECE is supported by FCT (Fundação para a Ciência e a Tecnologia, Portugal), financed by ERDF and Portuguese funds.
2 The other countries that faced an EDP are the Netherlands, Slovakia, Poland, Malta, Hungary, Cyprus and the Czech Republic. For further details see the EC website at: http://europa.eu.int/comm/economy_finance/about/activities/sgp/procedures_en.htm
3 Afonso (2005) questions the sustainability of public finances in most EU countries.
4 The smoothing parameter has been set at 6.25, adjusting with the fourth power of the observation frequency to the annual frequency of the data (Ravn and Uhlig 2002).
5 Figure 5.2 has already illustrated that differences between the various methods are certainly not minor.
6 The European Commission backs up a Hodrick–Prescott-based decomposition with results from the production function approach (European Commission 1995). The OECD uses only the production function method (Giorno et al., 1995). The IMF has no uniform strategy but the production function method prevails for industrialized countries (IMF 1993). Many other approaches abound. Methods that use a Beveridge–Nelson decomposition or track output developments with unobserved components are less common. Blanchard (1993) asks what the primary surplus would have been had the unemployment rate remained the same as the previous year. Chouraqui et al. (1992) compare different moving benchmarks. Cohen and Follette (2000) use spectral analysis to isolate low frequency changes in fiscal policy.
7 The OECD adjusts only social contributions, corporate, personal and indirect taxes.
8 Girouard and André (2005) update the elasticities in a previous OECD study by van den Noord (2002).
9 These assumptions relate to its functional form, the presence of returns to scale, technological progress, the utilization rates of production factors and the use of auxiliary estimates.
10 Potential output is nevertheless assumed exogenous in the production function approach.
11 A full discussion of the problems in identifying the effects of fiscal policy is provided in Perotti (2005).
12 Ramey and Shapiro (1998) look into the sectoral reallocation effects following shocks. A particular role in the transmission of fiscal policy shocks is also played by the labour market. A couple of papers compare the effects of consumptive government purchases to increases in public employment (Finn, 1998; Pappa, 2005; Cavallo, 2005). Perotti (2004) and Kamps (2004) examine the output and labour market effects of government investment.
13 Mountford and Uhlig (2002) retrieve different types of fiscal shocks among those that conform to some a priori sign restrictions on the entire impulse response or variance decomposition of fiscal variables. Canova and Pappa (2002) select only those shocks that satisfy formal sign restrictions on the conditional cross-correlation of the responses to the orthogonalized shocks of the variables in the model.
14 There are a few applications of fiscal VARs that use similar restrictions and are mostly inspired by a practical interest in determining structural balances. See Bouthevillain and Quinet (1999), Dalsgaard and de Serres (2001) or Bruneau and De Bandt (2003), who all specify an SVAR model in output and the deficit ratio. They recover structural deficits from the contribution of fiscal shocks to the variance of deficits. Likewise, a measure of the gap is constructed from the contribution of supply shocks to output variations. Hjelm (2003) is closer to our model as he is interested in simultaneously determining potential GDP and the cyclically adjusted balance. He uses Cholesky-ordered long-term restrictions in a model with output, employment and the budget balance to identify economic and labour market shocks. The cyclically adjusted balance then is that fraction of the budget balance that is not explained by business cycle shocks. This leaves only

the supply and labour market shocks in determining structural balance, but no separate role for the government is stipulated.
15 This is not a replication of the results in Blanchard and Perotti (2002) as they require additional short-term constraints on the timing of the effects whereas we consider long-term constraints.
16 We therefore need to impose two different coefficients γ and α which results in one over-identifying restriction. Blanchard and Perotti (2002) instead net out the cyclically sensitive transfers from spending, and assume a zero elasticity on other spending categories. As the sensitivity analysis in Section 5.4 demonstrates, this does not seem to affect our results.
17 For this reason, we do not expect responses to our fiscal shock to be similar to those documented in the empirical literature. Our distinction is more consistent with the theoretical models of fiscal policy.
18 We make some suggestions in the concluding section. We considered the effect of loosening the long-term constraint on either government spending or revenues. We could not reject longer-term effects of fiscal shocks, endorsing the hypothesis that supply-side effects of fiscal policy decisions affect the 'supply' shock.
19 Ultimately, the sustainability of fiscal policy is determined by the overall fiscal balance as well as potential output growth. Alternatively, one may view structural fiscal policy as depending on the decisions of fiscal policy makers only (Bruneau and De Bandt 2003).
20 The inclusion of structural breaks remains problematic, however. But in contrast to statistical methods, the economic consequences of one-off fiscal events are modelled in our approach.
21 Details are in Appendix 5.A. A program containing the RATS code for the SVAR model is available from the authors upon request.
22 For such an analysis, see Claeys (2004).
23 Impulse responses follow a one standard shock, and are plotted over a ten-year horizon with 90 per cent confidence intervals, based on a bootstrap with 5,000 draws.
24 As the long-term elasticity of both spending and revenues is larger than unity, this looks like a 'Wagner' style government expansion owing to economic growth.
25 We considered the effect of loosening the long-term constraint on either government expenditures or revenues in extensions of the structural VAR model in 5.3. We could not reject longer-term effects of fiscal shocks, endorsing the hypothesis that supply-side effects of fiscal policy decisions are part of the 'supply' shock.
26 This is a likely consequence of the annual frequency of the fiscal data.
27 We are certainly not the first study to document that European countries have not left automatic stabilizers to work, but instead have overturned these in a pro-cyclical way. We do show, however, the macroeconomic instability that results as a consequence. With other models, Alesina and Bayoumi (1996) showed how fiscal policy at the US state level rather contributes to macro-economic instability, and how fiscal rules have been useful in constraining discretion. Similar cross-country evidence is provided by Fatás and Mihov (2003b).
28 We plot all series over the period 1980–2004 only.
29 A rough indication on the robustness of our output gap measure can also be given by the dates of peaks and troughs in the business cycle. We plot in Appendix 5.B the first difference of the output gap against the chronology of peak to trough turning points of the growth cycle provided by the Economic Cycle Research Institute (ECRI). These calculations are based on monthly industrial production series. Our measure matches the changes in the output gap in all countries.
30 One should notice that several one-off measures mask the true deterioration in the Portuguese or the Spanish budget in recent years. Under the revised Pact, the deficit net of one-off and temporary measures is considered. Our procedure does not necessarily consider the effects of such measures to be nil.
31 Similar arguments can be put forward for various expenditure items.
32 Eschenbach and Schuknecht (2004) argue that government revenues and expenditures are also affected by asset price changes in ways not accounted for by standard cyclical-adjustment methods.
33 The wage elasticity is used for calculating the elasticity of the income tax. See Girouard and André (2005) for an extensive discussion and a quantification of this uncertainty.
34 The results of the impulse response analysis are largely unchanged. Effects are estimated slightly less precisely, and the effects of the business cycle shock in Portugal are not clear.
35 If the government decides to raise tax rates in economic crises, this leads to a stronger than expected reaction of revenues in the following economic boom.

36 The time variation in elasticities is also apparent from a recursive regression of (5.7). Coefficient plots are summarized in Appendix 5.C, which further documents some of the problems with constant elasticities. We have not reported the elasticities of interest payments and investment, as these coefficients are much more volatile than those of other budget items. There are relevant breaks associated with major shifts in fiscal policy (e.g. German Reunification, democracy in Portugal and Spain). For most spending categories, we remark a modest decline over time in Germany and a more outspoken one in France, while changes are minor for most revenue categories. Portugal and Spain have seen a large rise in elasticities of all items, owing to the expansion of their welfare states. This rise has pushed elasticities even above those in Germany and France.

Discussion

Jan in 't Veld

The chapter by António Afonso and Peter Claeys provides a new method of calculating indicators of fiscal policy. The objective is to uncover any underlying past trends behind developments in public finances that may explain the current budgetary outlook. The authors propose their fiscal indicator as an alternative to the standard method of cyclically adjusting budget balances (CABs), which according to them does not properly reflect discretionary shifts under control of government. They interpret their results in great depth and conclude that a pro-cyclical bias in fiscal policy has resulted in a ratcheting-up in the size of governments. I do not disagree with the general thrust of their analysis of what has gone wrong with fiscal policy in EMU in recent years. Rather than commenting on the specific aspects of the four countries considered, I would like to give here a more general discussion of the method and the resulting indicator with a view to its usefulness for policy evaluation.

The strength of the chapter is in my view that the approach based on structural VARs allows for a simultaneous determination of a measure of cyclical output and fiscal balance. According to the authors their fiscal indicator has an advantage over standard CABs that it captures the so-called supply-side effects of fiscal policy. It should be pointed out that the criticism the authors put forward to justify their alternative approach, i.e. the difficulties in interpreting the structural balance in the absence of economic arguments to underpin the trend-cycle decomposition, applies chiefly to statistical trend extraction procedures and less to the production function approach adopted by the European Commission. Having said that, the proposed VAR-based indicators provide an interesting alternative to the CABs. The production function approach does not take into account the growth effects of fiscal policy due to taxation and productive spending, while this indicator in principle could include this. As the authors point out, it is therefore more consistent with the distinction between supply- and demand-side effects of fiscal policy adjustments found in recent DSGE models, which unlike earlier RBC models not only incorporate supply-side effects through wealth effects and labour/leisure choice but also give a larger role to demand-side effects by including financial frictions such as liquidity constraints. (Results from these models suggest fiscal policy has a significant demand-side effect and counter-cyclical fiscal policy has reduced output volatility.)

A second advantage of the VAR-based indicators that the authors propose is that they allow identification of confidence bands. The standard CABs have large cumulative uncertainty due to the various assumptions made in calculating output gaps but this is never shown explicitly. Just like Bayesian-estimated DSGE models (which have a proper structural identification), the SVAR method applied by the authors allows for an explicit assessment of uncertainty.

SVARs are useful tools. However, it is important to be aware of their shortcomings in properly identifying short- and long-run effects. It has been shown to be difficult to estimate precisely the long-run effects of shocks using a short data sample. Faust and Leeper (1997) show that SVARs that achieve identification through long-run restrictions may perform poorly when estimated over sample periods typically utilized, and various other papers have illustrated this. The authors do not describe the estimation of the SVAR model in great detail, and many of the problems surrounding SVAR identification may not apply to their model, but judging on some of their results the proper identification of cyclical and supply shocks seems problematic.

The authors use a mixture of short- and long-term restrictions to identify economic and fiscal shocks. They identify three structural shocks: (i) 'supply' shocks that drive long-term trend rise in output (also including fiscal policy, i.e. a combination of shocks); (ii) 'cyclical' shocks that capture short-term fluctuations around steady state equilibrium (transitory); (iii) 'fiscal' demand shocks distinguished by the elasticity approach (the discretionary policy stance, but excluding those policies that have long-term growth effect, like productive spending and tax policies). When this identification scheme is applied to the data, the resulting IRFs and forecast error variance decomposition seem at first sight somewhat puzzling. The chapter would benefit from further explanation of some of the results: e.g. the negligible contribution of 'cyclical' shocks to the variation in output, the persistent contribution of discretionary 'fiscal' shocks (although these are restricted to have no long-run output effect) to the total variance in output even at longer horizons, and various other features in country-specific IRFs, like the non-Keynesian effects of fiscal shocks in France and the relation between positive supply shocks and a decline in expenditure in Germany.

I suspect part of the problem of not correctly identifying cyclical, discretionary fiscal and supply shocks is due to the use of annual data by the authors and the estimation of the model with a one-year lag structure. The question is whether this allows for the proper identification of cyclical shocks and their distinction from supply shocks and fiscal shocks. It would be interesting to see the results when quarterly data are used instead (like Blanchard and Perotti 2002 and Perotti 2005).

Another problem is that the authors do not distinguish compositional detail. Different revenue measures have different long-term supply effects, and the same applies for different expenditure measures. Looking at total revenues and total expenditure is not very revealing in this context. This is regrettable, as the authors rightly argue that it is highly desirable that an economic indicator of fiscal policy takes into account supply-side effects. In its current form, though, without disaggregating expenditure and revenues, it remains something of a black box and one cannot distinguish long-term fiscal policy effects from other long-term shocks that are included in the 'supply' shock.

The resulting structural deficit is defined as structural expenditure minus structural revenues (both driven by discretionary fiscal shocks and supply shocks). The fiscal indicator is smaller than standard CABs and much more volatile. The volatility makes it difficult to interpret the authors' results in any depth and hampers a comparison with the cyclically adjusted balances calculated by the Commission and the OECD. As it appears that the indicator is surprisingly insensitive to assumptions on newly estimated budget elasticities, it seems likely that this volatility is related to the problems in correctly identifying cyclical shocks, as so much is attributed to discretionary fiscal policy shocks. I suspect that if the shock identification problems can be overcome, this method could deliver some very useful insights into the underlying past trends behind developments in public finances. I look forward to seeing future extensions of the authors' approach.

Part III
Reliability of fiscal indicators

6 The reliability of EMU fiscal indicators: risks and safeguards

Fabrizio Balassone, Daniele Franco and Stefania Zotteri[1]

6.1 Introduction

The effectiveness of any fiscal rule crucially depends on the indicators to which it is geared. The indicators should be resilient to manipulation and opportunistic exploitation. EMU fiscal rules rely on yearly targets set in terms of traditional indicators of deficit and debt. Continued compliance with these targets is expected to ensure long-term fiscal sustainability. Arguably, reference to forward-looking indicators would have been more appropriate. However, such indicators require complex computations, often relying on strong assumptions, and do not lend themselves to being adopted for the enforcement of formal rules, especially in a multinational context where moral hazard issues gain prominence (Balassone and Franco 2000).

Having dismissed sophisticated indicators for the sake of effective monitoring, the expectation is that EMU fiscal indicators should score high in terms of reliability. However, recent episodes of large upward deficit revisions suggest that this is not always the case. The chapter acknowledges that all fiscal indicators can be manipulated. Therefore, replacing current indicators with new ones would not solve the problem. By highlighting the weak spots of EMU fiscal indicators, the chapter aims at identifying ways to improve monitoring.

The chapter points out that EMU's deficit indicator is particularly fragile in two respects.[2] First, since it measures *net* borrowing, it draws a line between transactions in financial and non-financial assets, with the latter alone being considered in the computation of deficits. But the distinction between financial and non-financial transactions is not clear-cut, and the available margins of interpretation can be used opportunistically.[3] Second, EMU's deficit indicator is measured on an *accrual* basis, relying on estimates which are by their nature subject to an element of subjective evaluation.[4]

Partly reflecting concerns over these fragilities, since 1994 EU Member States have been required to provide the European Commission with a reconciliation account between deficit figures and the corresponding change in debt, the latter being a good proxy of the *cash gross borrowing* (Balassone et al. 2006). Moreover, when reliance on accrual accounting within the European System of Accounts (ESA) increased (with the switch from the 1979 to the 1995 version of the system), Eurostat specified that revenue computed in accrual terms should include only those items that are likely to be actually cashed in and that over the medium term accrual and cash data should converge.[5]

However, in the implementation of the excessive deficit procedure relatively little effort was put into the analysis of consistency between deficit and debt data, thus failing to exploit synergies arising in the joint monitoring of EMU fiscal rules. The problem is witnessed by the tolerance exerted by European institutions towards Member States submitting incomplete reconciliation accounts. It is probably a consequence of the failure to give operational content to the debt rule, and the subsequent focus on the deficit rule.[6]

The chapter argues that even simply comparing deficits with changes in debt can help the early detection of inconsistencies in fiscal data. Indeed, changes in general government debt were much larger than initial deficit figures in Greece, Italy and Portugal before the large upward deficit revisions experienced in recent years.

Nevertheless, the chapter points out that consistency checks between deficits and changes in debt must go deeper than the overall difference between the two indicators. Since different items in the reconciliation account (henceforth, SFA for stock-flow adjustment) can offset each other, an underestimated deficit does not necessarily imply a large discrepancy between deficit and change in debt.

The chapter presents a simple model of the incentives to resort to window dressing under EMU deficit and debt rules, based on the partition of SFA into two groups.[7] One group includes items that can be used to affect the Maastricht deficit but leave the change in debt unaltered (a 'deficit-specific' SFA), the other includes items that can be used to reduce the change in debt but leave the Maastricht deficit unaffected (a 'debt-specific' SFA). Econometric estimates based on such models provide evidence that deficit-specific SFA tend to increase with the underlying deficit, and debt-specific SFA tend to offset the impact of such an increase on total SFA. This suggests not only that opportunistic accounting may have taken place to ensure formal compliance with the deficit rule, but also that debt-specific SFA may have been used to make the ensuing deficit–debt discrepancy less visible.

Attention to the quality of statistics has increased in recent years, also in the context of the reform of the Stability and Growth Pact (SGP). Based on case studies and econometric evidence, the chapter welcomes this development and argues that detailed analysis of SFA components is crucial to the full exploitation of the monitoring synergies arising from the presence of two fiscal indicators.

The remainder of the chapter is organized as follows. Section 6.2 briefly reviews the reconciliation account between EMU's deficit and debt indicators. It discusses how the headline deficit can be kept low through increases in some SFA components and how other SFA components can partly offset the ensuing negative effects on debt dynamics. Section 6.3 analyses large deficit revisions in Greece, Italy and Portugal. Section 6.4 discusses a simple model of fiscal gimmickry and provides econometric evidence suggesting that, indeed, different SFA components have been selectively used to reduce both reported net borrowing and the visibility of deficit-specific fiscal gimmickry. Section 6.5 concludes the chapter.

6.2 The reconciliation account (SFA)

For the purpose of EMU fiscal rules, deficit is defined as the general government *net* borrowing computed on an *accrual* basis in accordance with ESA95, and debt is defined as general government *gross* financial liabilities at *face value*.[8] A simplified reconciliation account between the change in Maastricht debt (Δb) and the Maastricht deficit (d^m) can therefore be written as:

$$\Delta b \equiv d^m + CA + FA_a - FA_s - VE \tag{6.1}$$

where:

(a) *CA* is the difference between cash and accrual valuations (the latter is used to compute the Maastricht deficit d^m, the former determines the actual financing needs and therefore is reflected in changes in liabilities as measured by Δb);
(b) FA_a and FA_s are, respectively, acquisitions and sales of financial assets (which must be added to *net* borrowing – d^m – to obtain a measure of *gross* borrowing, consistent with the change in gross liabilities – Δb);
(c) *VE* (i.e. valuation effects) is a summary measure of SFA arising from changes in the face value of outstanding liabilities[9] and from differences between the face value of a bond and its issue price.[10]

Identity (6.1) suggests three observations concerning the scope for 'opportunistic' accounting:

(a) underestimation (overestimation) of accrued expenditure (revenue) allows reporting a lower Maastricht deficit (d^m) but leaves the change in debt (Δb) unaffected as it is offset by an increase in cash-accrual differences (*CA*);
(b) similarly, the adoption of loose standards in the identification of payments/receipts reflecting acquisition/sales of financial assets, reduces the reported d^m but leaves Δb unaffected due to the corresponding increase/decrease in FA_a/FA_s;
(c) sales of financial assets (FA_s) and debt restructuring operations (a component of *VE*) can be used to reduce the change in debt but have no effect on the Maastricht deficit.[11]

Therefore:

(a) a large difference between Δb and d^m should alert towards the possibility that d^m is underestimated;
(b) a small difference between Δb and d^m cannot be taken to exclude an underestimation of d^m since sales of assets and debt restructuring can be used to offset inflated cash-accrual differences and net acquisition of financial assets.

This suggests rewriting (6.1) in order to partition total SFA into two groups. One group includes items that can be used to affect the Maastricht deficit but leave the change in debt unaltered (a 'deficit-specific' SFA, x), the other includes items that can be used to reduce the change in debt but leave the Maastricht deficit unaffected (a 'debt-specific' SFA, z):[12]

$$\Delta b \equiv d^m + x - z \qquad (6.2)$$

Mapping identity (6.1) into identity (6.2), however, is not a straightforward exercise. First, there are items in the reconciliation account that do not belong to either x or z (this is the case of valuation effects arising from fluctuations in the value of foreign currency-denominated debt and because of bonds issued above/below par).[13] Second, some of the individual items in identity (6.1) may be affected by attempts at reducing d^m as well as Δb (this is the case of asset sales, FA_s, whose total can be lowered by an opportunistic classification of transactions aimed at lowering d^m, and can be increased by privatization programmes undertaken to reduce Δb).

For the purpose of this chapter, we use the following definitions:

$$z = PRIV + VE \qquad (6.3)$$
$$x = CA + FA_a - OFA_s$$

where *PRIV* indicates revenues from the sale of assets arising in the context of privatization programmes and OFA_s indicates other revenue from the sale of financial assets.

The proposed treatment of *VE* and FA_s reflects data availability constraints and carries some costs. First, based on these definitions, z includes all valuation effects (*VE*), irrespective of whether they can or cannot be controlled by the fiscal authorities. This is likely to introduce considerable noise in z and may impede the detection of any systematic pattern in 'debt-specific' SFA. Second, it is implicitly assumed that sales of financial assets different from privatization do not reflect debt reduction motives. This may somewhat blur the distinction between 'deficit-specific' and 'debt-specific' SFA components, making it more difficult to detect a systematically selective use of SFA items.

Table 6.1 reports the average values of total, deficit-specific, and debt-specific SFA, according to the definitions in (6.3) for the countries which were EU members over 1994–2004 (excluding Luxembourg). The table shows that the discrepancy between changes in debt and deficits has been by no means negligible over the period considered (the average for the EU as a whole amounts to 0.6 per cent of GDP). The table also highlights a much higher value for the deficit-specific SFA component (1.0 per cent of GDP), and the offsetting role of debt-specific SFA (averaging at 0.3 per cent of GDP).

Table 6.2 reports similar information, but it is based on the original data releases by Greece, Italy and Portugal (i.e. before the revisions which have occurred since 2002). The overall SFA averages at 0.9 per cent of GDP for the EU countries considered. This is the net result of a deficit-specific component of 1.2 per cent of GDP, partly offset by the debt-specific component (0.3 per cent of GDP on average).

Table 6.1 Total SFA and its components (percentage of GDP) after revisions

	Deficit-specific SFA (x)	Debt-specific SFA (z)	Total SFA
Belgium	−0.3	0.3	−0.6
Denmark	0.8	0.7	0.1
Germany	0.7	0.0	0.7
Greece	3.2	0.0	3.2
Spain	0.3	−0.3	0.7
France	0.5	0.0	0.5
Ireland	2.0	0.5	1.5
Italy	1.1	0.9	0.2
Netherlands	−0.1	0.3	−0.5
Austria	1.2	0.5	0.7
Portugal	0.9	1.3	−0.3
Finland	1.4	−0.9	2.3
Sweden	1.5	1.0	0.5
United Kingdom	0.4	0.4	0.1
EU average	1.0	0.3	0.6

Note: Average values over 1994–2004, data after revisions occurred since 2002

Table 6.2 Total SFA and its components (percentage of GDP) before revisions

	Deficit-specific SFA (x)	Debt-specific SFA (z)	Total SFA
Belgium	−0.3	0.3	−0.6
Denmark	0.8	0.7	0.1
Germany	0.7	0.0	0.7
Greece	5.0	−0.9	5.9
Spain	0.3	−0.3	0.7
France	0.5	0.0	0.5
Ireland	2.0	0.5	1.5
Italy	1.4	0.7	0.7
Netherlands	−0.1	0.3	−0.5
Austria	1.2	0.5	0.7
Portugal	1.5	1.3	0.1
Finland	1.4	−0.9	2.3
Sweden	1.5	1.0	0.5
United Kingdom	0.4	0.4	0.1
EU average	1.2	0.3	0.9

Note: Average values over 1994–2004, data before revisions occurred since 2002

6.3 Deficit revisions in Italy, Portugal and Greece

Evidence supporting the usefulness of cross-checking fiscal data is provided by three case studies of significant deficit data revisions. These revisions concerned the 2001 deficit outcome in Italy and Portugal and the 2003 deficit outturn in Greece. In all three cases, the initial deficit figure was consistent with the forecasts by international organizations. This seems to indicate that by looking at the ESA95 deficit in isolation all parties involved can get a biased view of fiscal trends.[14]

Italy: the 2001 deficit outturn

In March 2002, the Italian Statistical Office (Istat) released the first statistics concerning the 2001 net borrowing. Back then, the deficit was estimated to be 1.4 per cent of GDP. The outcome was very close to the range of forecasts published by international organizations. After several revisions, the 2001 deficit is currently estimated to be 3.1 per cent of GDP.

Changes to the 2001 net borrowing figures took place between June 2002 and March 2006. In particular, in June 2002 Istat raised its estimate from 1.4 to 1.6 per cent of GDP, primarily on account of higher health care expenditure. One month later, Eurostat announced its decision on the accounting treatment for the purposes of the excessive deficit procedure of securitizations carried out by governmental authorities. This implied an upward revision of Italy's deficit to 2.2 per cent of GDP. In February 2003, Istat again published a higher figure for the 2001 deficit: 2.6 per cent of GDP. This new estimate was due to the availability of more complete information on the different government tiers' economic accounts. Two years later, in March 2005, Istat once more revised upwards the 2001 deficit, to 3.0 per cent of GDP, because of the reclassification of capital transfers from the general government to the Ferrovie dello Stato (the state-owned railway company) from financial to real transactions. Two months later, in May 2005, the 2001 deficit was estimated to be 3.2 per cent of GDP mainly because of the upward revision of transfers to firms. Finally, in March 2006, due to a GDP upward revision, the 2001 deficit was indicated to be 3.1 per cent of GDP.

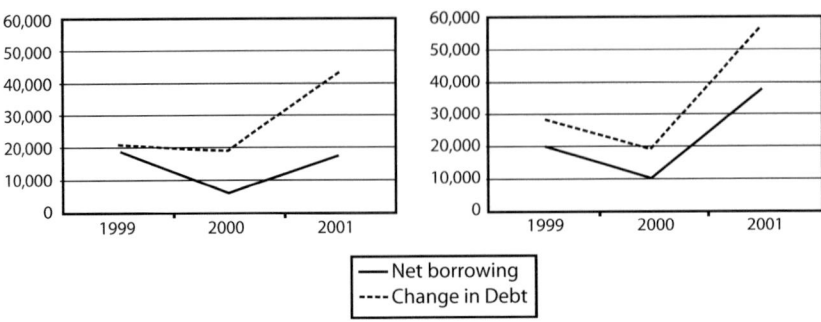

Figure 6.1 Italy: net borrowing and change in debt (millions of €; March 2002 data (left panel) and March 2006 data (right panel)).

The overall revision can be interpreted in terms of the deficit-specific SFA component (x) considered in the previous section: x was initially overestimated. More specifically, the deficit revision reflects a reduction of the cash-accrual adjustment by 0.6 percentage points of GDP, an increase in the sale of assets by 0.6 points (the reclassification of securitization), and a reduction in acquisitions of financial assets by 0.5 points (mainly, the reclassification of capital injections in the railway company).

The decline initially reported for the deficit between 2000 and 2001 (from 1.7 percent to 1.4 per cent of GDP) was in sharp contrast with the dynamics of the change in debt. According to the data available in March 2002, the latter rose from 1.6 per cent of GDP in 2000 to 3.5 per cent in 2001. This indicator turned out to be more stable than ESA95 net borrowing: overall, it was revised upwards by 0.7 percentage points of GDP; moreover, revisions took place only up to March 2003.

Figure 6.1 shows the divergence between the ESA95 deficit and the change in debt as it first appeared in March 2002 (left panel) and as it appears now (right panel). After the revisions, the dynamics of the ESA95 deficit are clearly closer to that of the change in debt. The joint examination of the indicators could have provided an early warning of the likely forthcoming revisions. Banca d'Italia in its annual report released in May 2002 in fact carried out this comparative exercise.[15]

Portugal: the 2001 deficit outturn

In March 2002 – in its first notification about the 2001 fiscal outcomes – Portugal estimated the general government deficit to be 2.2 per cent of GDP as against 1.5 per cent in 2000. At that time, the most up-to-date deficit forecasts by international institutions were somewhat more favourable.

Eurostat stated that it was not in a position to certify the Portuguese figures because, among other reasons, of the lack of information on capital injections to public corporations – which had been treated as acquisition of shares and other equities with no effect on the government deficit. Moreover, Eurostat stressed that – as some of these capital injections might be reclassified as transfers – the notified deficit was to be considered as provisional and likely to be increased.

In the spring of 2002 a commission headed by the Banco de Portugal and also composed of representatives of the Ministry of Finance and the National Statistical Institute was set up with the mandate of analysing and updating the government accounts. In September, the

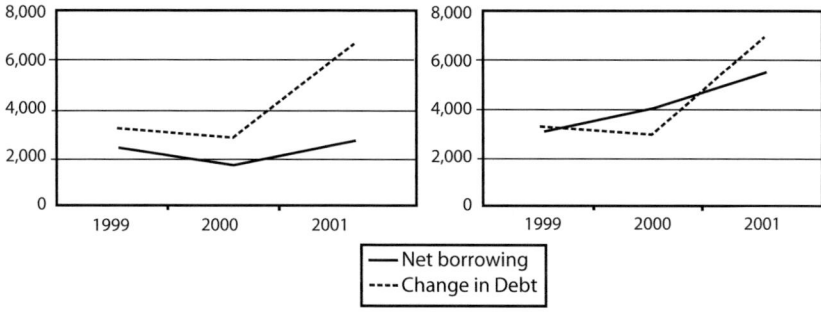

Figure 6.2 Portugal: net borrowing and change in debt (millions of €; March 2002 data (left panel) and April 2006 data (right panel)).

figure for the 2001 deficit was revised upwards to 4.1 per cent of GDP. This revision was due to a number of factors: new data on the accounts of the local authorities; the inclusion in the budget accounts of some injections of capital into publicly owned companies; changes to the methods used to account for expenditure carryovers and revenue connected with the EU structural funds; and the expiration of a derogation regarding the methods of recording tax and social contribution receipts accruing in the year.

Between September 2002 and September 2004 the deficit was slightly revised upwards twice, to 4.4 per cent of GDP. In September 2004, Eurostat stressed that there were still ongoing discussions with the Portuguese authorities concerning the consistency between accrual and cash data for the period 2001–2004. One year later, the 2001 deficit-to-GDP ratio was revised downwards to 4.2 because of an upward revision of GDP. At that time, Eurostat said that it intended to clarify reported cases of capital injections undertaken between 2001 and 2004 by various governments, including Portugal. At present, according to the European Commission 2006 spring forecasts, the Portuguese 2001 deficit is estimated to be 4.3 per cent of GDP. Therefore, the overall revision with respect to the original data release amounts to 2.1 per cent of GDP.

The initially reported increase in the deficit between 2000 and 2001 (from 1.5 to 2.2 per cent of GDP) was markedly smaller than the one observed for the change in debt. The latter rose from 2.5 per cent of GDP in 2000 to 5.5 per cent in 2001. Over time, the 2001 change in debt was revised only slightly and mostly because of GDP revisions. According to the most recent European Commission data – the change in debt increased from 2.4 in 2000 to 5.3 in 2001. The left panel of Figure 6.2 shows the initial divergence between ESA95 deficit and the change in debt; the right panel shows the same variables after the revisions.

Greece: the 2003 deficit outturn

At the beginning of March 2004, in its first notification of the 2003 fiscal outcome, Greece estimated the general government deficit at 1.7 per cent of GDP, as against 1.4 per cent in 2002. At that time, the most up-to-date forecasts by international institutions were broadly in line with the data notified by Greece. After several revisions, the 2003 deficit is currently estimated to be 5.8 per cent of GDP.

Revisions occurred between March 2004 and March 2006. Indeed, already by the end of March 2004 Greece sent updated data to the European Commission, revising upwards the 2003 deficit to 3.0 per cent of GDP. In April, in publishing the spring forecasts, the

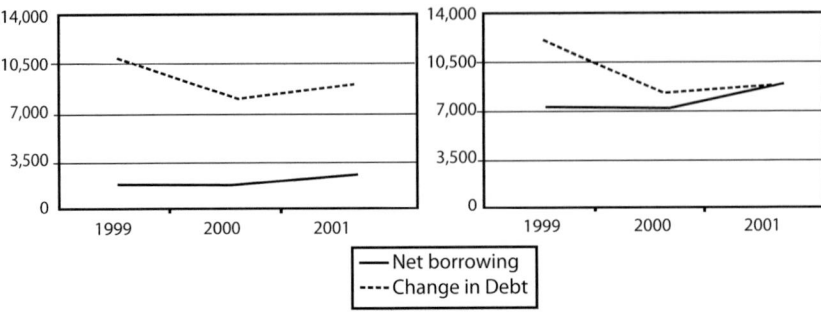

Figure 6.3 Greece: net borrowing and change in debt (millions of €; March 2004 data (left panel) and April 2006 data (right panel)).

Commission took into account the latter notification. It stressed that 'the data for 2003 are not yet validated by Eurostat and do not therefore provide a reliable basis for assessing the budgetary situation at this stage'. The Commission also noted that '[a] fact-finding mission is being prepared for the end of April in order to have more information about the budgetary situation in this country and decide on steps to be taken'.

At the beginning of May, following an additional notification, Eurostat verified that in 2003 the general government deficit was 3.2 per cent of GDP. In September, the deficit and debt figures for the years 2000–2003 were significantly revised. In particular, the 2003 deficit was estimated at 4.6 per cent of GDP and the 2003 debt was indicated at 109.9 per cent of GDP.

Both in the March 2005 notification and in that of September 2005, Greece revised the 2003 deficit upwards by more than half a percentage point of GDP (to 5.2 and 5.7 per cent of GDP, respectively). In March 2006 the 2003 deficit was estimated to be 5.8 per cent of GDP.

As to the deficit, the overall revisions were essentially due to: lower tax revenue (mainly VAT); lower payments received from EU institutions in the context of structural funds programmes; the reclassification, as a financial transaction, of a payment from the Saving Postal Bank to government; upward revisions of military expenditure and of interest payments; lower than expected surpluses of social security funds; and incorrect recording of hospitals' expenditure.

With reference to the debt, the revisions were due to the previous underestimation of bonds with capitalized interests and to the overestimation of consolidating assets of social security.

The initially reported increase in deficit between 2002 and 2003 (from 1.4 per cent to 1.7 per cent of GDP) was in line with that observed for the change in debt, the latter rising from 5.6 per cent of GDP in 2002 to 5.9 per cent in 2003. However, the level of the two indicators was markedly different (left panel of Figure 6.3). The right panel of Figure 6.3 shows how revisions have completely cancelled the 2003 discrepancy and significantly reduced those for previous years.

6.4 Fiscal rules and window dressing: a simple model

An econometric analysis of SFA in EU member countries was first provided by von Hagen and Wolff (2005). Their paper refers to the theoretical framework developed in von Hagen and Harden (1995, 1996) and Milesi-Ferretti (2003), where governments have an incentive to circumvent fiscal rules by hiding the budgetary implications of fiscal policies in less visible accounting items (that is, in the SFA). The likelihood of this type of window-dressing decreases with the costs associated with detection. The authors argue that binding deficit rules were introduced only with the start-up of EMU – i.e. the SGP – and therefore focus their analysis on differences in the correlation between reported deficits and SFA before and after EMU. They find no such correlation before 1998, but a negative one (large and significant) thereafter, suggesting that SFA were in fact substituting for other transactions which would have had an impact on deficits.

Buti et al. (2007) develop a model where total SFA is split into two components (one that can be used to reduce reported deficits and the other to impact debt figures). In this way they can separately analyse the interaction between each of the Maastricht fiscal rules and fiscal gimmickry. They assume that governments minimize a quadratic loss function whose arguments are the deviation of output from its optimal level (influenced by the 'true' deficit), deviations of reported deficit and debt from the respective fiscal rule, and the size of accounting gimmicks. The model suggests that both the deficit-specific and the debt-specific components of SFA are positively related to the 'true deficit', and that only the debt-specific component also depends on the debt level (though the sign of the relation is ambiguous *ex ante*). The empirical results are partly in line with the theoretical predictions of the model.[16] Notably, the authors find that the introduction of the SGP had an (increasing) impact on the deficit-specific component of the SFA, but none on the debt-specific component.

In this section, following Buti et al. (2007) we provide separate econometric analysis of deficit-specific and debt-specific SFA components. However, we refer to a different model as the basis for our estimating equations. We assume that governments derive utility (U) from running primary deficits (p): $U = U(p)$. This can be justified either by assuming that governments are short-sighted and only care about the short-term output gains that can be attained through higher deficits, or by reference to the political gain directly attainable by increasing transfers targeted to specific groups. In either case, the assumption is consistent with the rationale for having a fiscal rule specifying a maximum threshold for the deficit, suggesting the need to counteract an asymmetric deficit bias.[17]

Governments' utility maximization is constrained by compliance with Maastricht's debt and deficit rules. The debt rule mandates that the debt-to-GDP ratio (b) must be lower than 60 per cent and, if higher than such threshold to begin with, it must be declining towards 60 per cent at a satisfactory pace. As we have noted earlier, the 'satisfactory pace' has never been defined, therefore we model this rule as requiring:

$$\Delta b = p + rb - yb - z \leq W \qquad (6.4)$$

where $W = 0$ if $b > 60$, $W = 60 - b$ if $b < 60$

i.e. the change in the ratio of debt to GDP (Δb) – as determined by the 'true deficit' ($d = p + rb$ where rb indicates interest payments), the reducing effect of output growth (yb) and the debt-specific SFA (z) – must be negative if b is above 60 per cent to start with.[18] The change in the debt ratio can be positive if $b < 60$ to start with, but it cannot bring b above 60 per cent of GDP.[19]

The deficit rule requires that reported deficits (d^m) be lower than 3 per cent of GDP. Similarly to what happens for the debt ratio, if the reported deficit ratio is above 3 per cent to start with, a gradual reduction is expected. Without loss of generality, and by analogy with the debt rule, we assume that in this case the reported deficit, as a minimum, must not increase further. The deficit rule is therefore modelled as:

$$d^m = p + rb - x \leq H \tag{6.5}$$

where $H = 3$ if $d^m < 3$, $H = d^m$ if $d^m > 3$

where x denotes the deficit-specific SFA component.[20]

We assume that x and z only arise because of opportunistic accounting aimed at ensuing formal compliance with the rules. Therefore we also impose non-negativity conditions on x and z ($x \geq 0$ and $z \geq 0$).

Finally, we assume that primary deficits (P) and the opportunistic use of deficit and debt-specific SFA (x and z, respectively) carry a cost $C = C(p, x, z)$. Following Buti et al. (2007) the costs can be thought of as deriving from the risk of being caught (higher x and z are more visible) as well as from suboptimal allocation of resources.

In sum, the maximization problem facing the authorities can be described as follows:

$$Max_{p,x,z} \quad U(p) - C(p, x, z) \tag{6.6}$$

s.t. $\quad p + rb - yb - z \leq W \quad$ where $W = 0$ if $b > 60$, $W = 60 - b$, if $b < 60$

$\quad\quad\; p + rb - x \leq H \quad$ where $H = 3$ if $d^m < 3$, $H = d^m$ if $d^m > 3$

$\quad\quad\; x, z \geq 0$

whose Lagrangean is:

$$U(p) - C(p, x, z) - \lambda_1[p + rb - yb - z - W] - \lambda_2[p + rb - x - H] + \lambda_3 x + \lambda_4 z \tag{6.7}$$

with first order conditions:

$$U' - C_p - \lambda_1 - \lambda_2 = 0 \tag{6.8a}$$

$$-C_x + \lambda_2 + \lambda_3 = 0 \tag{6.8b}$$

$$-C_z + \lambda_1 + \lambda_4 = 0 \tag{6.8c}$$

$\lambda_1 \geq 0 \quad\quad p + rb - yb - z - W \leq 0 \quad \lambda_1[p + rb - yb - z - W] = 0 \quad (6.8d)$

$\lambda_2 \geq 0 \quad\quad p + rb - x - H \leq 0 \quad\quad\quad \lambda_2[p + rb - x - H] = 0 \quad\quad (6.8e)$

$\lambda_3 \geq 0 \quad\quad x \geq 0 \quad\quad\quad\quad\quad\quad\quad\quad\quad \lambda_3 x = 0 \quad\quad\quad\quad\quad\quad\quad\quad (6.8f)$

$\lambda_4 \geq 0 \quad\quad z \geq 0 \quad\quad\quad\quad\quad\quad\quad\quad\quad \lambda_4 z = 0 \quad\quad\quad\quad\quad\quad\quad\quad (6.8g)$

When Maastricht's deficit and debt rules are not binding (i.e. $\lambda_1, \lambda_2 = 0$), x and z are equal to zero. But when rules are binding we have

$$z = p + rb - yb - W \tag{6.9}$$

$$x = p + rb - H \tag{6.10}$$

We use these equations as the basis for our econometric analysis and estimate the following two regressions:

$$z_t = \alpha_0 + \alpha_1 d_t + \alpha_2 y_t b_{t-1} + \alpha_3 W_t + \varepsilon_a \tag{6.11}$$

$$x_t = \beta_0 + \beta_1 d_t + \beta_2 H_t + \varepsilon_b \tag{6.12}$$

where $d = p + rb$ is the 'true deficit'; $W_t = 0$ if $b_{t-1} > 60$, $W_t = 60 - b_{t-1}$, if $b_{t-1} < 60$; and $H_t = 3$ if $d^m_{t-1} < 3$, $H_t = d^m_{t-1}$ if $d^m_{t-1} > 3$.

From the signs in (6.9) and (6.10), we expect:

(a) $\alpha_1 > 0$; α_2, $\alpha_3 < 0$
(b) $\beta_1 > 0$; $\beta_2 < 0$

We expect both types of SFA to be positively related to the level of the 'true deficit' ($\alpha_1, \beta_1 > 0$): the higher the 'true deficit', the higher the x and z values required for formal compliance with the rules (see also Buti et al. 2007).

The debt level plays no direct role, and it only affects the debt-specific SFA through the 'growth effect' (i.e. the reduction of the debt ratio determined by GDP growth, which is larger the larger the debt). The use of z to keep debt dynamics under control becomes less necessary when the growth impact is higher, hence the negative sign expected for α_2.

The constraints determined by the deficit and debt fiscal rules enter directly the corresponding estimating equations. We expect the levels of z and x to be negatively correlated with, respectively, the maximum allowed change in debt and the maximum allowed deficit ($\alpha_3, \beta_2 < 0$). In other words, the more binding the fiscal rule the higher the incentives to resort to fiscal gimmickry.

Since x, z, and p (and therefore d) are simultaneously determined, we report results obtained using two stage least squares. We present two sets of estimates: one uses the most recent data releases, the other one considers the values first reported by Greece, Italy and Portugal over the period 1998–2004 (that is, data published before the statistical revisions discussed in Section 6.3). We also introduce a dummy variable to test for structural breaks after 1998.

The sample includes data for 15 countries over 1994–2004. We also run regressions on the sub-sample of euro-area members. Deficit-specific SFA are obtained from the Buti et al. (2007) dataset as the sum of cash-accrual differences and of net acquisitions of financial assets, excluding privatization, following the discussion in Section 6.2. The 'true deficit' is obtained by summing the deficit-specific SFA to deficit data used in the context of the excessive deficit procedure as reported in the AMECO database. The 'growth effect' is computed using data from the AMECO database. Finally, and again in line with the discussion in Section 6.2, debt-specific SFA are obtained residually by subtracting from total SFA the deficit-specific SFA component and the growth effect.

Tables 6.3 and 6.4 report the estimation results, which are in line with expectations from the model. All coefficients are correctly signed, statistically significant and exerting quantitatively large effects on the dependent variables. There is no significant difference between results for the EU15 and those for the euro area. Using the original data releases for Greece, Italy and Portugal induces an improvement in the regression fit for the deficit-specific equation, but not for the debt-specific one, possibly reflecting the limited extent of revisions to changes in debt compared to revisions in deficits.

Table 6.3 Determinants of deficit- and debt-specific SFA – EU15

Dependent variable	Deficit SFA (x)		Debt SFA (z)	
Data set	Current values (2)	Original values (3)	Current values (2)	Original values (3)
Constant	0.5	1.28*	1.63**	1.39*
	0.94	2.32	2.62	2.04
Dummy 1999	0.97**	1.09**	0.38	0.19
	3.29	3.54	1.25	0.57
'True deficit'	0.31**	0.33**	0.33**	0.31**
	5.97	6.11	5.62	4.94
Growth effect			−0.34**	−0.29*
			2.89	2.19
Deficit rule (H)	−0.27*	−0.45**		
	2.43	3.97		
Debt rule (W)			−0.2**	−0.18**
			5.72	4.76
Number of observations	134	134	129	129
R^2: within	0.276	0.339	0.385	0.329
between	0.353	0.398	0.446	0.348
overall	0.299	0.346	0.203	0.159

Notes:
(1) Adjusted T-statistics in italics. *, ** indicate coefficient significance at the 95% and 99% level, respectively. 'True deficit' and 'H' are instrumented by their lagged values
(2) Data as in the latest releases available
(3) 1998–2004 data for Greece, Italy and Portugal are those from first official releases

Table 6.4 Determinants of deficit- and debt-specific SFA – euro area

Dependent variable	Deficit SFA (x)		Debt SFA (z)	
Data set	Current values (2)	Original values (3)	Current values (2)	Original values (3)
Constant	0.27	1.5*	1.65**	1.39*
	0.46	2.27	2.13	1.62
Dummy 1999	0.87**	0.98**	1.71	−0.05
	2.8	2.91	0.5	0.13
'True deficit'	0.29**	0.32**	0.30**	0.28**
	4.78	4.83	3.97	3.38
Growth effect			−0.35**	−0.29*
			2.68	1.99
Deficit rule (H)	−0.21	−0.48**		
	1.68	3.67		
Debt rule (W)			−0.2**	−0.18**
			4.69	3.83
Number of observations	101	101	99	99
R^2: within	0.258	0.349	0.330	0.269
between	0.451	0.408	0.467	0.378
overall	0.345	0.340	0.195	0.151

Notes:
(1) Adjusted T-statistics in italics. *, ** indicate coefficient significance at the 95% and 99% level, respectively. 'True deficit' and 'H' are instrumented by their lagged values
(2) Data as in the latest releases available
(3) 1998–2004 data for Greece, Italy and Portugal are those from first official releases

The deficit-specific SFA is positively correlated with the 'true deficit'. For each one per cent of GDP increase in the 'true deficit' there is an estimated 0.3 per cent of GDP increase in deficit-specific SFA. The deficit-specific SFA is also negatively correlated with the maximum allowed deficit (H). The increase in deficit-specific SFA associated with a 1 per cent of GDP increase in the allowed maximum deficit is estimated at 0.2–0.25 per cent of GDP, using the data set which includes recent revisions to data for Greece, Italy and Portugal, and to almost 0.5 per cent of GDP, excluding such revisions.

The debt-specific SFA is positively correlated with the 'true deficit'. For each 1 per cent of GDP increase in the 'true deficit', there is an increase by about 0.3 per cent of GDP in debt-specific SFA, enough to offset the corresponding estimated increase in deficit-specific SFA. The debt-specific SFA is negatively correlated with the 'growth effect'. For each 1 per cent of GDP increase in the growth effect, there is a 0.30–0.35 per cent of GDP decrease in debt-specific SFA. Finally, the debt-specific SFA is also negatively correlated with the maximum allowed change in debt (W). For each 1 per cent of GDP increase in the allowed maximum change in debt, there is an estimated 0.2 per cent of GDP decrease in debt-specific SFA.

Similar to von Hagen and Wolff (2005) and to Buti et al. (2007) we find a structural break around 1998. In line with the result in Buti et al. (2007), the break appears to affect only the equation for deficit-specific SFA. There are two possible explanations for this. One is the usual argument that the introduction of the SGP has made the deficit rule more stringent and increased the incentive to use SFA. The other is that with the switch to the accrual-based ESA95 in 1999, a further channel of deficit-specific SFA opened, namely cash/accrual differences, which was previously not available. However, the interpretation of this result should be postponed to a thorough analysis of time-specific common shocks.

6.5 Conclusions

The reliability of EMU's fiscal indicators has been questioned by recent episodes of large upward deficit revisions. This chapter points out that EMU's deficit indicator is particularly fragile in two respects: the identification of transactions in financial assets and the assessment of accrued revenue and expenditure. It argues that margins for opportunistic accounting mainly arise from these two weak spots.

Even the simple comparison between deficit and change in debt can help early detection of inconsistencies in fiscal data. Evidence from three case studies of significant deficit data revision suggests the usefulness of cross-checks between deficit and changes in gross debt to reduce the scope for fiscal gimmickry.

Changes in general government debt were much larger than initial deficit figures in Greece, Italy and Portugal, before the large upward deficit revisions experienced in recent years. In Italy, the revision process was gradual and lasted four years. Although the initial discrepancy between the change in debt and the deficit was more than 2 per cent of GDP, the highest annual revision amounted to only 0.8 points. In Greece, a large discrepancy between the two indicators was present for several years before the process of statistical revisions abruptly started in 2004.

Nevertheless, since different items in the reconciliation account between deficit and change in debt can offset each other, consistency checks must go deeper than the overall difference between the two indicators. Italy provides an interesting example. In 2001 total SFA amounted to 4.3 per cent of GDP, as against 'only' 1.2 per cent in 2000. However, deficit-specific SFA were higher in 2000 than in 2001 (3.4 vs 3.0 per cent of GDP), and the increase in total SFA in 2001 reflected the decline in the offsetting debt-specific SFA.

Table 6.5 General government net borrowing/lending, 2000–2004*

	2000				2001				2002				2003			2004	
	Spring of 2001	2002	2003	2004	Spring of 2002	2003	2004	2005	Spring of 2003	2004	2005	2006	Spring of 2004	2005	2006	Spring of 2005	2006
Belgium	0.0	0.1	0.1	0.2	0.2	0.4	0.5	0.6	0.0	0.1	0.1	0.0	0.2	0.4	0.1	0.1	0.0
Denmark	2.5	2.5	2.6	2.6	2.7	3.1	3.1	3.2	1.9	1.7	1.7	1.2	1.5	1.2	1.0	2.8	2.7
Germany	1.3	1.2	1.1	1.3	−2.7	−2.8	−2.8	−2.8	−3.6	−3.5	−3.7	−3.7	−3.9	−3.8	−4.0	−3.7	−3.7
Greece	−0.9	−0.8	−1.9	−2.0	0.1	−1.4	−1.4	−3.6	−1.2	−1.4	−4.1	−4.9	−1.7	−5.2	−5.8	−6.1	−6.9
Spain	−0.3	−0.3	−0.8	−0.9	0.0	−0.1	−0.4	−0.5	−0.1	0.0	−0.3	−0.3	0.3	0.3	0.0	−0.3	−0.1
France	−1.3	−1.3	−1.4	−1.4	−1.4	−1.5	−1.5	−1.5	−3.1	−3.2	−3.2	−3.2	−4.1	−4.2	−4.2	−3.7	−3.7
Ireland	4.5	4.5	4.3	4.4	1.7	1.1	1.1	0.9	−0.1	−0.2	−0.4	−0.4	0.2	0.2	0.2	1.3	1.5
Italy	−0.3	−0.5	−0.6	−0.6	−1.4	−2.6	−2.6	−3.0	−2.3	−2.3	−2.6	−2.9	−2.4	−2.9	−3.4	−3.0	−3.4
Luxembourg	5.3	5.8	6.1	6.3	5.0	6.4	6.3	6.2	2.6	2.7	2.3	2.0	−0.1	0.5	0.2	−1.1	−1.1
Netherlands	2.0	2.2	2.2	2.2	0.2	0.1	0.0	−0.1	−1.1	−1.9	−1.9	−2.0	−3.0	−3.2	−3.1	−2.5	−1.9
Austria	−1.1	−1.5	−1.5	−1.5	0.1	0.3	0.2	0.3	−0.6	−0.2	−0.2	−0.5	−1.1	−1.1	−1.5	−1.3	−1.1
Portugal	−1.4	−1.5	−2.8	−2.8	−2.2	−4.2	−4.4	−4.4	−2.7	−2.7	−2.7	−2.9	−2.8	−2.9	−2.9	−2.9	−3.2
Finland	6.7	7.0	6.9	7.1	4.9	5.1	5.2	5.2	4.7	4.3	4.3	4.1	2.3	2.5	2.5	2.1	2.3
Sweden	4.0	3.7	3.4	5.1	4.7	4.5	2.8	2.5	1.2	0.0	−0.3	−0.2	0.7	0.2	0.1	1.4	1.8
UK	2.1	1.8	3.9	3.8	1.0	0.8	0.7	0.7	−1.4	−1.6	−1.7	−1.6	−3.2	−3.4	−3.3	−3.2	−3.3
Euro area **	0.3	0.2	0.1	0.1	−1.3	−1.6	−1.6	−1.7	−2.3	−2.3	−2.4	−2.6	−2.7	−2.8	−3.1	−2.8	−2.9

Notes:
* Spring notifications' initial estimates and subsequent revisions (as a percentage of GDP). A negative sign indicates a deficit; a positive sign indicates a surplus. UMTS proceeds are included
** Excluding Greece in 2000

Table 6.6 General government debt, 2000–2004*

	2000				2001				2002				2003				2004		
	Spring of 2001	2002	2003	2004	Spring of 2002	2003	2004	2005	Spring of 2003	2004	2005	2006	Spring of 2004	2005	2006	Spring of 2005	2006
Belgium	110.9	109.3	109.6	109.1	107.5	108.5	108.1	108.0	105.4	105.8	105.4	103.2	100.5	100.0	98.5	95.6	94.7
Denmark	47.3	46.8	47.4	50.1	44.4	45.4	47.8	47.8	45.2	47.2	47.2	46.8	45.0	44.7	44.4	42.7	42.6
Germany	60.2	60.3	60.2	60.2	59.8	59.5	59.4	59.4	60.8	60.8	60.9	60.3	64.2	64.2	63.8	66.0	65.5
Greece	103.9	102.8	106.2	106.2	99.7	107.0	106.9	114.8	104.9	104.7	112.2	110.7	102.4	109.3	107.8	110.5	108.5
Spain	60.6	60.4	60.5	61.2	57.2	56.9	57.5	57.8	54.0	54.6	55.0	52.5	50.8	51.4	48.9	48.9	46.4
France	58.0	57.4	57.2	57.2	57.2	56.8	56.8	57.0	59.1	58.6	59.0	58.2	63.0	63.9	62.4	65.6	64.4
Ireland	39.1	38.9	39.3	38.4	36.6	36.8	36.1	35.8	34.0	32.3	32.6	32.1	32.0	32.0	31.1	29.9	29.4
Italy	110.2	110.6	110.6	111.2	109.4	109.5	110.6	110.7	106.7	108.0	108.0	105.5	106.2	106.3	104.2	105.8	103.8
Luxembourg	5.3	5.6	5.6	5.5	5.5	5.6	5.5	7.2	5.7	5.7	7.5	6.5	4.9	7.1	6.3	7.5	6.6
Netherlands	56.3	56.0	55.8	55.9	53.2	52.8	52.9	52.9	52.6	52.6	52.6	50.5	54.8	54.3	51.9	55.7	52.6
Austria	62.8	63.6	66.8	67.0	61.7	67.3	67.1	67.1	67.9	66.6	66.7	66.0	65.0	65.4	64.4	65.2	63.6
Portugal	53.8	53.4	53.3	53.3	55.6	55.6	55.6	55.9	58.0	58.1	58.5	55.5	59.4	60.1	57.0	61.9	58.7
Finland	44.0	44.0	44.5	44.6	43.6	43.8	43.9	43.8	42.7	42.6	42.5	41.3	45.3	45.3	44.3	45.1	44.3
Sweden	55.6	55.3	52.8	52.8	56.0	54.4	54.4	54.3	52.4	52.6	52.4	52.0	51.8	52.0	51.8	51.2	50.5
UK	42.9	42.4	42.1	42.1	39.0	39.0	38.9	38.8	38.6	38.5	38.3	37.6	39.8	39.7	39.0	41.6	40.8
Euro area **	70.0	70.0	70.2	70.4	71.6	69.2	69.4	69.6	71.3	69.2	69.5	69.8	70.4	70.9	71.2	74.1	74.5

Notes:
* Spring notifications' initial estimates and subsequent revisions (as a percentage of GDP)
** Excluding Greece in 2000

Table 6.7 General government change in debt, 2000–2004*

	2000			2001			2002			2003			2004	
	Spring of 2001	2001	2003	Spring of 2002	2003	2004	Spring of 2003	2004	2005	Spring of 2004	2005	2006	Spring of 2005	2006
Belgium	0.3	0.4	0.2	2.0	1.9	1.6	−0.1	0.3	0.3	−2.1	−2.1	−2.0	0.5	0.8
Denmark	−2.5	−2.6	−2.6	−0.5	−0.4	−0.6	1.0	0.7	0.7	−1.2	−1.3	−1.3	−0.4	0.0
Germany	0.8	0.6	0.6	0.5	0.5	0.5	2.4	2.4	2.4	3.9	3.9	4.1	3.3	3.2
Greece	6.4	6.3	8.7	4.0	8.3	8.3	5.7	5.6	5.8	5.9	5.8	5.7	9.1	8.9
Spain	1.8	1.8	2.0	0.7	0.3	0.4	0.5	0.6	0.8	−0.3	−0.2	−0.2	1.0	0.8
France	1.4	1.4	1.4	1.8	1.8	1.8	3.8	3.7	4.0	5.5	6.0	5.8	4.3	4.5
Ireland	−3.8	−3.8	−3.6	1.6	1.4	1.7	0.5	0.3	0.3	1.1	1.0	1.0	0.4	0.3
Italy	1.5	1.6	1.5	3.5	3.8	4.2	0.5	1.0	1.1	1.6	1.6	1.9	3.5	3.6
Luxembourg	0.1	0.3	0.2	0.2	0.1	0.2	0.2	0.3	0.5	−0.6	0.0	0.2	0.9	0.6
Netherlands	−2.7	−2.8	−2.9	0.2	0.5	0.5	1.6	1.6	1.6	3.3	2.7	2.6	2.7	2.0
Austria	1.0	1.3	2.6	0.0	2.0	2.0	1.8	1.2	1.2	0.1	0.4	0.2	2.0	1.9
Portugal	2.2	2.5	2.5	5.5	5.5	5.5	5.2	5.2	5.2	2.5	2.5	2.3	3.8	3.7
Finland	0.9	1.0	1.2	0.9	1.1	1.1	0.2	0.1	0.2	3.7	3.8	3.6	1.7	1.7
Sweden	−6.8	−6.8	−6.5	2.4	3.2	3.2	−0.2	0.1	0.1	1.3	1.4	1.7	1.3	1.0
UK	−0.7	−0.8	−0.8	−1.4	−1.4	−1.4	1.4	1.4	1.4	3.4	3.4	3.4	3.8	3.7
Euro area **	0.9	0.9	1.0	1.6	1.7	1.8	2.1	2.1	2.2	2.9	3.1	3.2	3.3	3.3

Notes:
* Spring notifications' initial estimates and subsequent revisions (as a percentage of GDP)
** Excluding Greece in 2000

Econometric estimates discussed in Section 6.4 provide evidence that deficit-specific SFA tend to increase with the underlying deficit and debt-specific SFA tend to offset the impact on total SFA of such an increase. This suggests not only that opportunistic accounting may have taken place to ensure formal compliance with the deficit rule, but also that debt-specific SFA may have been used to make the ensuing deficit-debt discrepancy less visible.

Attention to the quality of statistics has increased in recent years also in the context of the reform of the SGP. Since 2004, notifications include more detailed information, and now refer to the various sub-sectors of the general government. In addition, some steps have recently been taken to improve statistical governance at the EU and national level.

The regulation concerning the statistics used for the excessive deficit procedure has been amended. The role of Eurostat as the statistical authority in the context of the excessive deficit procedure has been reinforced by introducing formal requirements of completeness and internal consistency of fiscal data reported to the Commission and by disciplining Eurostat's interaction with Member States through 'dialogue' and 'methodological' visits. In order to improve transparency and accountability of national statistical authorities, the Regulation mandates the public availability of data reported by Member States as well as of inventories describing the methods, procedures and sources used by Member States, and requires the publication by Eurostat of regular reports on the quality of data. To bolster the operational capacity of the Commission, Eurostat has conducted an internal redeployment of staff in order to reinforce the activities linked to the validation of economic and fiscal accounts and created a dedicated unit. Finally, the directors of national statistical institutes and Eurostat adopted a European Statistics Code of Practice, defining standards for the independence of the national and community statistical authorities. The Code lists a set of indicators to be used to review the implementation of the Code itself. The Commission is setting up a reporting system to monitor adherence to the Code of Practice by the national statistical authorities and Eurostat.

The analysis of SFA along the breakdown suggested here may enhance the effectiveness of these reform efforts. To this end, the reconciliation account between deficit and change in debt reported in the notifications should identify all financial assets and therefore there should be no residual item labelled as 'other assets'. Moreover, national authorities should routinely provide justification for cash-accrual differences in annual data for individual accounting items. In due time Member States should also be requested to provide a full set of government accounts covering both deficit formation and its financing. Such a set of accounts should include both cash and accrual figures.

Given the unavoidable information asymmetry between the community and Member States, ensuring the independence of the national statistical institutions is crucial. This is not just an issue of enforcement of fiscal rules; it is an issue of accountability to the public and of good management of public resources. (See Tables 6.5, 6.6 and 6.7.)

Notes

1 The views expressed in this paper are those of the authors and do not commit Banca d'Italia. We thank Marco Buti, João Nogueira Martins and Alessandro Turrini for kindly making available to us the dataset used for the article. We thank João Nogueira Martins also for his valuable discussion and the participants to the European Commission Workshop on fiscal indicators in the EU Budgetary Surveillance for useful suggestions.
2 There is also an issue concerning the definition of the public sector whose deficit and debt have to be considered (see Balassone et al. 2006).

3 This problem is similar to the one arising in the application of the 'golden rule', where the deficit measure should only take into account current transactions and exclude capital ones (see Balassone and Franco 2001).
4 Cash-based deficit measures are by no means exempt from the risk of manipulation. However, contrary to what happens with accrual estimates, manipulation of cash figures obtained by postponing payments and/or demanding anticipated payments finds a natural limit in the voice of the interested counterparts.
5 The Treaty and annexed protocols rely on the ESA for the definition of deficit. When the Treaty was signed in 1992, and until 1999, the ESA79 version of the system was in place, which allowed government accounts to be computed mostly on a cash basis. ESA95 was first implemented in 2000, in the release of fiscal data for 1999. See Eurostat (2000) and Regulations (EC) N° 2516/2000 and 995/2001.
6 The debt rule demands that, if the debt-to-GDP ratio is above 60 per cent, it must be declining at a 'satisfactory' pace. However, the meaning of 'satisfactory' is yet to be defined.
7 The model is similar in spirit to Buti et al. (2007), but differs in several significant respects.
8 This is not the debt definition provided by ESA95, but the relevant financial instruments and the reference sectors are those specified within that framework.
9 For example, those due to debt restructuring operations or to fluctuations in the exchange rate affecting the value in domestic currency of foreign currency denominated debt.
10 The face value of a bond is used to compute Δb while its issue price measures the financing actually received by the government and therefore reflects the financing needs measured by the cash gross borrowing requirement, i.e. by $d^m + CA + FA_a - FA_s$.
11 Importantly, such operations may leave the government's net asset position unaffected or even worsen it. In this respect, one should also control the extent of one-off measures affecting directly d^m (Milesi-Ferretti 2003). There is, of course, no implication here that privatizations are by definition bad policy. However, if they are undertaken with the sole purpose of reducing gross debt – regardless of the economics underlying the transaction – then the operations can be questioned.
12 See also Buti et al. (2007).
13 Note, however, that by issuing bonds above par, a government could reduce the change in debt associated with a given deficit.
14 This section is a summary and update of the analysis conducted in two earlier papers (Balassone, Franco and Zotteri 2004 and 2006).
15 The report also included an analysis of the composition of total SFA.
16 The authors find no statistically significant relationship between the two components of SFA and 'true deficits'. They find evidence of a positive relationship between reported deficits and deficit-specific SFA and of a negative relationship between reported deficits and debt-specific SFA. Only debt-specific SFA are found to be affected (negatively) by the debt level.
17 The quadratic loss function adopted in Buti et al. (2007) is symmetric in deviations from the optimal real output growth where real output growth depends linearly on the 'true deficit'.
18 With respect to the analysis in Section 6.2, scaling the variables by GDP requires the consideration of the reducing effect exerted by output growth on the debt ratio.
19 In this way we explicitly model the constraint also for countries where $b < 60$ (Buti et al. 2007, assume $z = 0$ for $b < 60$).
20 This formulation allows differentiating the constraints applying to countries with reported deficits above and below 3 per cent of GDP, rather than using dummy variables at the estimation stage.

Discussion

João Nogueira Martins[1]

The fiscal convergence criteria of the Maastricht Treaty and the Stability and Growth Pact have stimulated a large strand of economic literature. Most of this literature is on how to interpret the available data, how to perform cyclical adjustments, how to identify the underlying budgetary position and the discretionary behaviour of government, etc. The infrastructure of indicators (how the deficit is defined; how it is compiled; how reliable and accurate it is; should it be compiled on a cash or on an accrual basis; should it cover a narrowly defined government or a wider public sector) has received much less attention. Balassone, Franco and Zotteri are among the rare authors to have devoted attention to these issues. And they have done it with quite a provocative spirit, even daring to consider that the indicators that are relevant for fiscal surveillance in the EU have been a 'misleading compass', as they put it in previous and related papers (Balassone, Franco and Zotteri 2006).

The effectiveness of fiscal rules depends crucially on the quality of the fiscal indicators. The quality of statistical indicators can be generically defined as 'fitness for use'. It is, in fact, a complex multidimensional concept; it covers relevance, timeliness, coherence, completeness, comparability across time and space, accuracy, reliability, transparency, etc. The topic of the chapter is on reliability; in technical terms, reliability refers to the closeness of the initial values to the subsequently revised figures. The authors note that the EU fiscal indicators do not score high in terms of reliability. This is worrying for two reasons: First, in the implementation of the EU fiscal framework, the most relevant decisions – such as deciding whether an excessive deficit exists or has been corrected, if a given country is complying with Council recommendations, or even if a country has fulfilled the criteria to enter the euro area, or ultimately whether the Council will have to impose sanctions – are taken on the basis of the first outcomes. The subsequently revised data – though of better quality – appear too late to have any decisive impact on the policy decisions. So if the first outcomes are subject to large revisions afterwards, important decisions will be taken on the basis of wrong data. A second reason to be worried is that, as the authors point out, given that the fiscal rule is based on a rather simple indicator, one would expect it to be reliable. Presumably, other more complex fiscal indicators were rejected (implicitly if not explicitly) because the government deficit would be simple, easy to compile and reliable.

Balassone et al. establish a link between lack of reliability and opportunistic manipulation, i.e. political pressure to get data that are rosier than the reality, at least the first outcomes even if these are revised afterwards. If the lack of reliability is directly connected with opportunistic manipulation, then the solutions the authors propose seem to be quite appropriate: (i) increase the scrutiny of the government accounts and (ii) strengthen the status of the data compilers, by giving more independence and accountability to the national statistical institutes. In the last two or three years, the Commission has taken several steps in this direction, including all the suggestions by the authors. Obviously, it is very early to say how fruitful such steps are.

But are political pressures and opportunistic behaviour the main cause of the lack of reliability of fiscal data in the EU? Or are there other causes? If the lack of reliability of government accounts was directly and decisively connected with political pressures, one would expect the countries with less reliable data to be those that have had more problems with the respect of the EU fiscal reference values, and vice versa. The three countries that the authors use in their case studies (Greece, Italy and Portugal) would confirm the conjecture. Yet we could also expect similar problems with the French and German figures. Now, if we consider data reported by Member States since 1994, France and Germany have the most reliable deficit data in the EU.[2] So the question is: what do the French and Germans have that prevents them having to resort to the same gimmickries as Greece, Italy and Portugal? (Or, do they resort to other tricks?) If I now apply the model proposed in the chapter, I am led to conclude that France and Germany bear larger costs (C_x) for entering in data manipulations with the purpose of hiding their deficits. Why? Is this because of institutional reasons? Are the French and German statistical institutes more independent than in other Member States? It would be interesting to research what can be done to increase the reputation costs for producing unreliable data in Greece, Italy and Portugal.

If we try identifying which are the EU Member States with the less reliable accounts we get some surprising results. Among the countries that have reported the less reliable data we find not only Greece, Portugal and Italy, but also Sweden, Luxembourg and Denmark. Now, these are among the countries that have had less trouble in complying with the EU fiscal framework. Of course, the data revisions in Sweden and Denmark did not catch public opinion, as did the ones in Italy and Portugal, not to say Greece, but the magnitudes are not dissimilar. My point here is that the opportunistic manipulation of data certainly has an implication of the reliability of data, but there are other factors at play. It may be the reputation of the data compilers, irrespective of their status of independence, or the resources, competence or expertise available to each statistical institute, or even the more or less complex institutional arrangements in each country, or because some countries enter into more complex transactions than others. Or perhaps the reliability difficulties would simply reflect the fact that our accounting rules are excessively complex and unreliability is somewhat inevitable, or very costly to avoid. We do not know. We also need more research on this.

The authors identify two fragilities of the deficit indicator: (i) the fact that it is measured in an accrual basis and (ii) the fact that it is measured net of financial transactions. Do the authors believe that these two fragilities are such that the deficit definition should be changed? Would a cash deficit including some financial transactions be a better, and more reliable, definition? My understanding is that the authors believe that the current deficit definition is still preferable to any other, and they simply want to pinpoint the areas that need to be closely scrutinized by Eurostat.

Notes

1 The views expressed in this chapter are those of the author and are not attributable to the European Commission.
2 For an analysis of the reliability of government deficit and debt statistics in most EU countries, see Gordo Mora and Nogueira Martins (2007).

7 Uncertainty bounds for cyclically adjusted budget balances

Ray Barrell, Ian Hurst and James Mitchell

7.1 Introduction

This chapter addresses issues concerning the uncertainty surrounding estimates of the output gap and, in turn, the cyclically adjusted budget deficit. Uncertainty about the size of the output gap is likely to be reflected in uncertainty about the size of the cyclical adjustment to be applied to the budget deficit. Our main objective in this chapter is to evaluate the uncertainty associated with a commonly used estimate of the output gap and to demonstrate how this should be reflected in uncertainty about the cyclically adjusted budget deficit. The degree of uncertainty associated with the estimate of the output gap for a period in the past, when computed now, is noticeably less than that associated with the estimate of the current (or real-time) gap. Since typically policy makers are concerned about the current gap, we focus on evaluation of real-time estimates and their uncertainty. Uncertainty about the cyclically adjusted budget deficit is further compounded by uncertainty over the link between the output gap and the budget deficit. If the gap were to be caused by tax rich elements of demand, such as consumption, then the impact of a given gap on the deficit would be larger than when the gap is caused by changes in a tax poor component of demand, such as exports. We therefore undertake a further analysis of the sources of shocks and study their impact on the uncertainty surrounding the budget deficit.

In the second section of the chapter we discuss methods of estimating the output gap and the associated uncertainty. We focus on the Harvey–Trimbur (Harvey and Trimbur 2003) estimator, which approximates a parametric version of the ideal band pass filter discussed in Baxter and King (1999). We utilize this estimator in part because it allows an analytical derivation of its standard deviation, which we present in this section. We then present and evaluate real-time estimates of the output gap and the associated uncertainty for the UK, Germany, France, Italy, Spain, the Netherlands and Belgium. In the third section we calculate the cyclically adjusted budget deficits from the real-time output gap data and present uncertainty bands around these estimates. The fourth section looks at the sensitivity of our results, by applying different coefficients from a model-based analysis of multipliers to the output gap in the calculation of the cyclically adjusted deficit. The final section draws conclusions about the difficulties associated with producing reliable estimates of the cyclically adjusted budget deficit.

7.2 Estimating the output gap and its uncertainty

Model uncertainty

The output gap, the difference between actual and potential output, has an importance in the popular debate which can tend to run ahead of the problems in measuring it; the output gap is not observable. The choice of what measure, or estimator, of the output gap to use is more than a dry academic issue. As the analysis of Canova (1998) showed, for example, inference can be sensitive to measurement. In this chapter we largely abstract from issues concerning model uncertainty and consider just one leading output gap estimator – the Harvey–Trimbur cycle. This is sufficient to make our point that use of the output gap in real time can be problematic since it is often measured imprecisely. The Harvey–Trimbur cycle is a model-based estimator based on unobserved components (UC). It is a generalization of the class of Butterworth filters that have the attractive property of allowing smooth cycles to be extracted from economic time series – indeed, ideal band pass filters emerge as a limiting case; see Harvey and Trimbur (2003).

Statistical and parameter uncertainty: estimation in real time

An additional source of uncertainty associated with output gap estimates derives from the fact that policy makers do not have the luxury of being able to wait before deciding whether the economy is currently lying above or below its trend level. They have to decide, without the benefit of hindsight, whether a given change to output in the current period is temporary or permanent: that is, whether it is a cyclical or trend movement. As discussed by Mitchell (2003) their problem can be interpreted as a forecasting one, since these real-time output gap estimates are forecasts, in the sense that they are expectations of the output gap conditional on incomplete information. Only with the arrival of additional information, such as revised historical data and data not available at the time, do the output gap estimates eventually settle down at their 'final' values.[1] These real-time or end-of-sample output gap (point) estimates have been found to be unreliable, in the sense that there is a large and significant revision or forecasting error; see Orphanides and van Norden's (2002) application to the US economy and Mitchell's (2003) to the euro area.

Since, in the absence of data revisions, revisions to real-time output gap estimates are explained by forecasting errors, it is important when de-trending in real time to produce good forecasts of the (log) level of the underlying series. Application of an UC model can be seen implicitly to forecast future values optimally. This follows from the fact that for a correctly specified model, application of the one-sided Kalman filter is equivalent to application of the two-sided filter (smoother) to the underlying series extended infinitely into the future with optimal forecasts. These optimal, minimum mean square error, forecasts are derived via the Kalman filter, exploiting the state–space representation for a given output gap estimator. There is therefore no need for forecast extensions.

We note that when computing the cyclically adjusted budget deficit the European Commission in fact relies on a production function approach to measuring the output gap; see Denis et al. (2006). But since TFP is de-trended with a Hodrick–Prescott filter there remains an end-of-sample problem. Future values of TFP are therefore forecast prior to application of the de-trending filter in an attempt to improve the reliability of the real-time estimates. But, as mentioned above, reliability will only be improved if 'good' forecasts are produced. Indeed, since the Hodrick–Prescott filter implicitly assumes the data are generated by an IMA(2,2) model, if future values are forecast using an alternative model, this then raises concerns about why the Hodrick–Prescott filter is itself used if an IMA(2,2) model is not believed to be the 'true' model. In any case, given that the European Commission must be uncertain about the accuracy of its measure and also still expects revisions to its real-time output gap estimates it should, as we consider below, produce a measure of uncertainty associated with it and in turn the cyclically adjusted budget deficit. Even if the estimates are not revised, they are not known with certainty, and hence must have a sampling distribution. As the Hodrick–Prescott filter is a mechanical device it is possible that the uncertainty of the estimates would have to be bootstrapped from the data, but it is still possible to estimate uncertainty measures.

Real-time and 'final' estimates of the output gap in the euro area

To investigate the unreliability of real-time output gap point estimates for euro area economies the following experiment is undertaken. Full sample or final estimates of the output gap are derived using data available over the (full) sample-period using data up to 2006q1. Real-time output gap estimates are computed recursively from 1980q1. We use data from the 1960s to 1980q1 to provide a real-time estimate of the output gap for 1980q1.[2] Then data up to 1980q2 are used to re-estimate the output gap (that involves re-estimation of the parameters of the models used to measure the output gap) and obtain real-time estimates for 1980q2.[3] This recursive exercise, designed to mimic real-time measurement of the output gap, is carried on until data for the period up to 2006q1 are used to estimate the real-time output gap for 2006q1. These last estimates are the 'final' values, where real-time and full sample estimates converge.

Throughout we use only the latest vintage of GDP data. What we call the real-time estimate is strictly the quasi-real estimate of Orphanides and van Norden (2002). If we considered real-time data we should expect to find an even greater degree of unreliability associated with the real-time estimates. Nevertheless revisions to published GDP data were found by Orphanides and van Norden (2002) to be less important than so-called statistical revisions. Statistical revisions are explained by the arrival of new data helping macroeconomists, with the advantage of hindsight, better to understand the position of the business cycle, and also perhaps revising what model they use to identify and estimate it.

Table 7.1 gives an indication of what the real-time and final output gap estimates look like. It lists the average real-time and final output gaps over a calendar year. Consistent with previous research, these figures indicate how unreliable real-time output gap estimates can be. They often paint a different picture to the final estimate, and clearly illustrate how one can misjudge the position of the business cycle in real time. In general the full sample estimates are more 'long period' volatile than are the real-time estimates. The latter tend to track actual output more closely, suggesting that perhaps too much signal is read into the current data.

We can draw out further relevant differences between the real-time and final estimates shown in Table 7.1. The German output gap estimates suggest that it was difficult to estimate the degree of excess capacity in the period after German unification and that data at the time may have been interpreted as suggesting trend growth had risen, when it probably had not. The same could be said of the mini-boom around 2000, when perceptions of the subsequent period of slow growth were absent.

The lack of cyclicality in the real-time output gap estimator is also apparent in the outturns for France and Italy, but in both cases the 'short period' volatility of the real-time estimator is apparent. The strength of the early 2000s boom in France is only really apparent with hindsight, and the same is true in Italy, although subsequent below capacity growth may be apparent there. The correlation of the real-time and final estimates is stronger in Italy than for the other countries.

The Spanish output gap, measured either in real time or over the full sample, appears to be much less 'long term' volatile than the other estimates presented here. This may reflect too little quarterly noise in the data, or the generally smooth evolution of actual output.

Table 7.1 Real-time and final output gaps as yearly averages

	Germany		UK		France		Italy		Spain		Netherlands		Belgium	
	Final	Real-time	Final	Real-time	Final	Real-time	Final	Real-time	Final	Real-time	Final	Real-time	Final	Real-time
1990	2.47	1.41	2.70	0.62	2.38	0.43	2.15	0.44	-0.21	-0.58	1.80	0.36	1.44	0.05
1991	3.16	1.50	-0.86	-0.07	1.92	0.55	1.71	-0.62	0.56	-0.31	1.71	-0.03	1.10	-0.39
1992	1.80	-0.03	-3.02	-1.43	1.30	0.17	0.59	-1.01	0.14	-0.33	0.40	-0.37	0.41	-0.58
1993	-0.48	-1.50	-3.15	-0.91	-0.88	0.13	-1.93	-2.12	-0.86	-0.73	-1.26	-0.64	-2.07	-0.90
1994	-0.34	-1.91	-1.54	-0.52	-1.41	-0.96	-1.28	-1.45	0.41	0.34	-1.56	-0.39	-0.94	0.08
1995	-0.31	-1.10	-0.92	0.58	-1.47	-0.72	-0.02	-0.27	0.14	0.50	-1.41	0.01	0.81	0.71
1996	-0.94	-1.14	-0.85	0.50	-2.29	-0.53	-1.00	-0.30	-0.11	0.14	-1.21	0.14	-0.76	-0.03
1997	-0.72	-1.01	-0.37	0.61	-2.12	-0.74	-0.66	-0.33	-0.04	0.17	-0.39	0.29	0.24	0.35
1998	-0.74	-0.62	0.20	0.81	-1.06	-0.41	-0.88	0.07	-0.12	0.27	0.76	0.48	-0.38	0.08
1999	-0.30	-0.69	0.73	0.83	0.11	-0.02	-0.59	-0.05	-0.04	0.03	1.94	0.39	0.06	0.12
2000	1.48	0.01	1.66	1.03	1.83	0.30	1.63	0.95	0.28	0.16	2.80	0.30	1.33	0.42
2001	1.52	0.19	1.28	0.91	1.81	0.99	1.94	0.88	0.07	-0.32	2.19	-0.04	0.47	-0.28
2002	0.46	-0.37	0.55	0.28	0.93	0.54	1.03	-0.22	-0.15	-0.26	0.64	-0.53	0.05	-0.54
2003	-0.58	-0.95	0.49	-0.04	0.37	0.13	0.00	-0.81	-0.09	-0.09	-0.70	-0.87	-0.72	-0.54
2004	-0.75	-0.93	0.76	0.16	0.35	-0.15	-0.22	-0.86	-0.03	0.09	-0.93	-1.09	-0.12	-0.02
2005	-0.63	-0.68	-0.13	-0.09	-0.09	-0.08	-1.12	-1.08	0.07	0.13	-0.91	-0.79	-0.35	-0.09

Notes: Output gaps as a percentage of trend GDP; real time estimates based on a sample from the start of data to the date where the gap is recorded; full sample uses all data. German GDP data was 'spliced' at unification so that the GDP of united Germany moved in line with West Germany before unification and with total Germany thereafter

Conversely the Netherlands shows long and large cycles which evolve in a smooth way whichever technique is used, while Belgian data show much more 'short period' volatility in the estimates of the cycle.

The real-time unreliability of output gap (point) estimates is summarized more fully in Table 7.2, for both full sample and real-time estimates. The table also examines the filtered estimates or the quasi-final estimates in the parlance of Orphanides and van Norden (2002). UC models use the data in two ways in the sense that first they estimate the parameters of the model, denoted by the vector Θ, and second, they use these estimates to obtain the filtered and smoothed estimates of the output gap, namely the quasi-final and final estimates of the output gap, respectively. The filtered and smoothed estimates are the expected value of the output gap conditional on information available at time $t (t = 1, 2, ..., T)$ and T, where $T \geq t$, respectively. Let us denote the real-time estimates, based on recursively updated estimates of the parameters of a given UC model Θ, by $y_{t|t}$; let $y_{t|T}$ denote the final estimates of the output gap at time t, that use full-sample information T to estimate Θ, and then let $y_{t|t}(\hat{\Theta}_T)$ denote the filtered estimates of the output gap at time t using these full-sample based parameter estimates.

Table 7.2 indicates that as the future becomes the present output gap estimates are revised. Real-time point estimates of the output gap in the euro area are unreliable, in the sense that there is a large and important revision error. This is reflected by the correlation coefficients against the final estimates being on average only 0.44. Reflecting the importance of *ex post* information in redefining the parameter values, the filtered estimates are

Table 7.2 The unreliability of real-time output gap point estimates

		Mean	Min.	Max.	SD	Correlation vs 'final'	RMSE
Belgium	'final'	−0.042	−2.353	2.117	0.958	1	0
	filtered	−0.025	−1.526	1.029	0.555	0.51	0.827
	real time	−0.016	−1.265	0.975	0.492	0.391	0.89
France	'final'	−0.15	−2.516	2.496	1.44	1	0
	filtered	−0.405	−1.541	1.165	0.691	0.773	1.038
	real time	−0.231	−1.768	1.161	0.555	0.59	1.203
Germany	'final'	−0.083	−2.399	3.533	1.423	1	0
	filtered	−0.212	−2.187	2.432	1.033	0.644	1.103
	real time	−0.299	−2.402	1.852	1.064	0.485	1.317
Italy	'final'	−0.048	−3.732	3.659	1.597	1	0
	filtered	−0.388	−2.661	1.455	1.029	0.726	1.156
	real time	−0.316	−2.499	1.67	1.064	0.614	1.291
Netherlands	'final'	−0.158	−3.275	2.877	1.491	1	0
	filtered	−0.124	−1.718	0.954	0.647	0.687	1.148
	real time	−0.079	−1.227	0.716	0.536	0.232	1.465
Spain	'final'	0.001	−1.139	0.842	0.337	1	0
	filtered	0.021	−0.86	0.743	0.285	0.467	0.325
	real time	0.039	−1.005	1.228	0.371	0.385	0.396
UK	'final'	−0.438	−4.998	4.868	2.461	1	0
	filtered	0.481	−2.181	3.136	1.207	0.84	1.835
	real time	0.317	−2.9	2.474	1.071	0.405	2.375

Notes: SD is the standard deviation of the output gap; correlation vs 'final' is the correlation of the filtered or real-time output gap estimate against the full-sample estimate; RMSE is the root mean squared error of the filtered or real-time estimate against the 'final' estimate

more reliable than the real-time estimates: correlation is higher averaging 0.66. Parameter uncertainty appears to be a dominant source of the unreliability of real-time estimates. We note that while one might consider an output gap estimator for which there is no parameter uncertainty (such as the Hodrick–Prescott filter), so that the filtered and real-time estimates are equivalent, our experience suggests that there remains a significant difference between the real-time and 'final' output gap estimates; e.g. see Mitchell (2003).

Uncertainty associated with output gap estimates

It is not simply a question of this output gap forecast proving to be right and another forecast proving to be wrong. Point forecasts are better seen as the central points of ranges of uncertainty. A forecast of 2 per cent must mean that people should not be surprised if the output gap turns out to be a little larger than that. Moreover, perhaps they should not be very surprised if it turns out to be much larger or indeed nothing at all. Therefore, consistent with recent developments in the forecasting literature, it is important to provide a description of the uncertainty associated with real-time output gap estimates via interval or density forecasts. Indeed, the 'optimal' real-time estimate of the output gap need not equal the mean or conditional expectation. It can be 'rational' to use biased real-time estimates. Furthermore, measures of uncertainty are useful in their own right if interested in analysing and communicating, for example, risk and volatility, or the probability of a downturn. Our concern in this chapter is with producing measures of uncertainty associated with the cyclically adjusted budget deficit estimate, as measured in real time.

Measuring the uncertainty associated with the output gap

We consider a simple approach to measure uncertainty that relies on a state–space representation for the output gap estimator. Conditional on Gaussianity (of the disturbances driving the components of the state vector) and knowledge of the covariance matrix of the estimated state vector, confidence intervals around the output gap can be presented, and density estimates derived.[4] Other distributions could be considered, although we confine attention to the Gaussian case since this both has the advantage of simplicity/familiarity and is sufficient to illustrate the role of forecasting uncertainty.

Let $P_{t|t}$ denote the Kalman filter based variance of the output gap at time t, $y_{t|t}$, using information available up to time t; the output gap is one of the elements of the state vector in the UC model. Then conditional on Gaussianity, the density is $N(y_{t|t}, P_{t|t})$, from which the 95 per cent confidence interval around the point estimate, for example, can be extracted. Note that we are considering filter uncertainty only and ignoring parameter uncertainty. Accounting for parameter uncertainty should be expected to increase the width of the confidence bands around the point estimates.

With known and constant parameters, uncertainty is greater around the real-time (strictly the 'filtered' estimate) than the 'final' estimate. This is seen as follows. Denote the revision between the real-time and final estimates by $R_{t|T} = y_{t|T} - y_{t|t}$. With known and constant parameters (i.e. for the filtered rather than real-time estimates of Table 7.1), this variance $P_{t|t'}$ decreases as t' increases; $P_{t|t} = P_{t|T} + Var(R^*_{t|T})$. The variance of the filtered (or one-sided) estimate is therefore greater than that of the smoothed (or two-sided) estimate, $P_{t|T}$, by a positive scalar equal to the variance of the revisions between the filtered and smoothed estimates $R^*_{t|T}$ where $R^*_{t|T} = y_{t|T} - y_{t|t}(\hat{\Theta}_T)$. This is the familiar result that the variance of the filtered (forecasted) estimate is equal to the variance of the outturn, $P_{t|T}$, plus the

Table 7.3 Standard deviations of output gap estimates in selected years – full sample and recursive compared

		1990	1995	2000	2005
Belgium	Full-sample	0.881	0.881	0.887	1.069
	Recursive	1.145	1.380	1.283	1.261
France	Full-sample	2.169	2.184	2.192	2.686
	Recursive	3.956	2.996	3.057	2.822
Germany	Full-sample	1.018	1.021	1.043	1.448
	Recursive	1.309	1.605	1.976	1.557
Italy	Full-sample	1.067	1.071	1.089	1.472
	Recursive	1.645	1.800	1.691	1.680
Netherlands	Full-sample	1.718	1.722	1.738	2.043
	Recursive	1.164	1.373	1.422	2.078
Spain	Full-sample	0.430	0.430	0.431	0.522
	Recursive	0.799	0.503	0.649	0.625
UK	Full-sample	1.393	1.431	1.470	2.226
	Recursive	2.526	2.740	2.521	2.363

square of the bias, $Var(R^*_{t|T})$. This assumes the revision process has mean zero so that $Var(R^*_{t|T}) = E(R^*_{t|T})^2$.

Just as point estimates of the output gap forecast in real-time can be evaluated *ex post* against the final estimates (as in Tables 7.1 and 7.2), the accuracy of real-time measures of uncertainty can and should be evaluated *ex post*; see Mitchell (2003) for further details. This is possible since a 'good' interval forecast, as defined by Christoffersen (1998), should both have correct *unconditional* coverage (in the sense that on average observations fall in the interval to the predicted degree) and second be such that observations fall inside the interval in a random manner which is not clustered. Below we focus on how the uncertainty estimates associated with the output gap can be used to produce a measure of uncertainty associated with the cyclically adjusted budget deficit.

We detail the uncertainty concerning output gap estimates for selected years in Table 7.3. Although recursive, real-time, estimates give less 'long-term' volatility, they are in general noticeably less certain than full sample estimates. Hence even if we think, in real time, that the economy has an output gap of around zero, we cannot be at all certain about that. In 1990 six out of seven countries have real-time estimates that were 30 to 100 per cent less certain than the full sample estimate. A similar pattern is clear in 1995 as well, with only the Netherlands having a real-time estimate that is more certain than the full sample estimate. Full sample uncertainty rises over the time period and approaches that of the real-time estimate. Only in Spain are both estimates of the uncertainty in the gap low and stable.

7.3 Cyclically adjusting the budget deficit

The patterns of evolving uncertainty detailed above should be reflected in our uncertainty about the scale of the cyclically adjusted budget deficit. The relationship between the deficit as a percent of GDP (BUD) and the cyclically adjusted deficit as a percentage of GDP (CABUD) depends on the sensitivity of revenues and expenditure to the cycle. The links between output and the budget deficit are discussed, for instance in Mélitz (2000), Blanchard and Perotti (2002) and Wyplosz (2002). It is common to assume that an increase in the output gap of 1.0 per cent of GDP (more use of capacity) reduces the deficit by 0.5 per cent of GDP; we discuss this assumption further in Section 7.4 below. We may write the cyclically adjusted budget deficit (CABUD) for the UK, for example, as dependent on the observed deficit (BUD) and the output gap (OG)

$$\text{UKCABUD} = \text{UKBUD} - 0.5 * \text{UKOG} \tag{7.1}$$

Given the uncertainty in the output gap, and on the assumption that the budget deficit and the cyclical coefficient are known, then we may write the standard deviation SD of the CABUD as a function of the standard deviation of the output gap:

$$\text{SD(UKCABUD)} = 0.5 * \text{SD(UKOG)} \tag{7.2}$$

We apply this formula across seven European countries, applying the time varying estimates of the standard deviation of the output gap to produce bounds of uncertainty around budget deficits. The SD of the full sample estimate has generally settled down by 1990, but the real-time estimates of the SD vary noticeably over time.

We focus here on estimating the real-time cyclically adjusted deficits. These are of concern to policy makers, who have to make decisions in real time. In Barrell et al. (2006) we also plotted the cyclically adjusted deficits, based on final estimates of the output gap and its uncertainty (SD). Unsurprisingly these indicate less uncertainty about the central estimate than the real-time estimates. In any case, Figures 7.1–7.7 below plot, alongside the real-time cyclically adjusted budget deficit and the predicted degree of uncertainty, the final (point) estimate for the cyclically adjusted budget deficit. Differences between this and the real-time estimates indicate further the potential for making policy mistakes in real time. In each chart we also plot the outturn for the deficit denoted ** GBR.

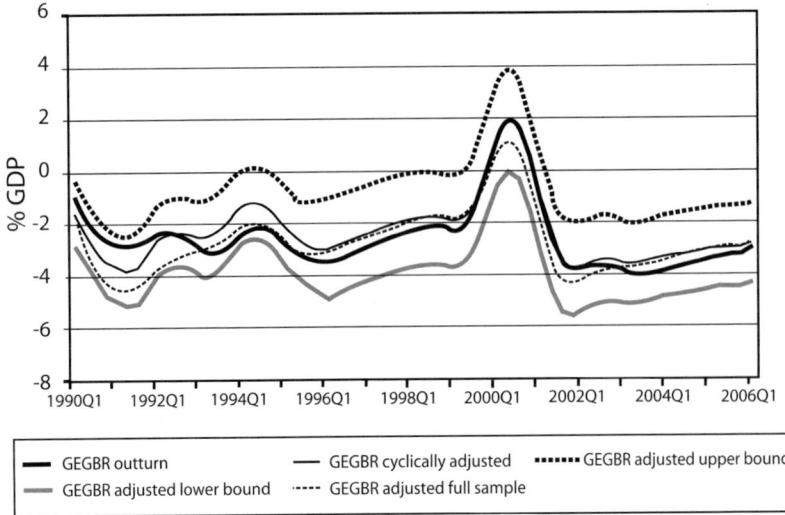

Figure 7.1 Germany: budget deficit cyclical adjustment – real time.

Our budget deficit data have not been adjusted for any of the myriad of one-off measures we have seen in the last decade in Europe; hence we include mobile phone receipts in the deficit. This explains why most countries go into surplus around 2000. After 2002, when these receipts fade away, Germany and Italy show cyclically adjusted deficits that are more than two standard deviations away from zero, suggesting it is very unlikely that they could ever be judged to have been 'in balance or surplus'. France, on the other hand, has a cyclically adjusted deficit that just about includes zero within its 95 per cent confidence bounds; but this reflects the noticeably greater uncertainty about the French output gap than that in the other countries. The Netherlands, Belgium and Spain are all close to balance or in

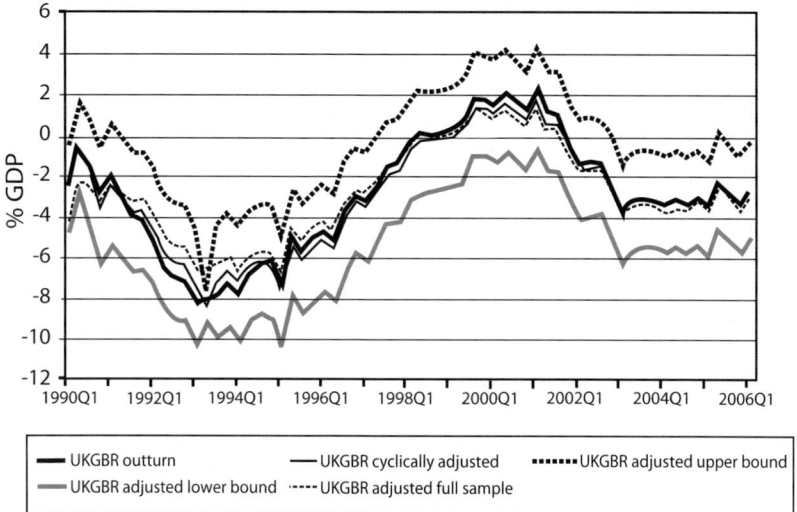

Figure 7.2 UK: budget deficit cyclical adjustment – real time.

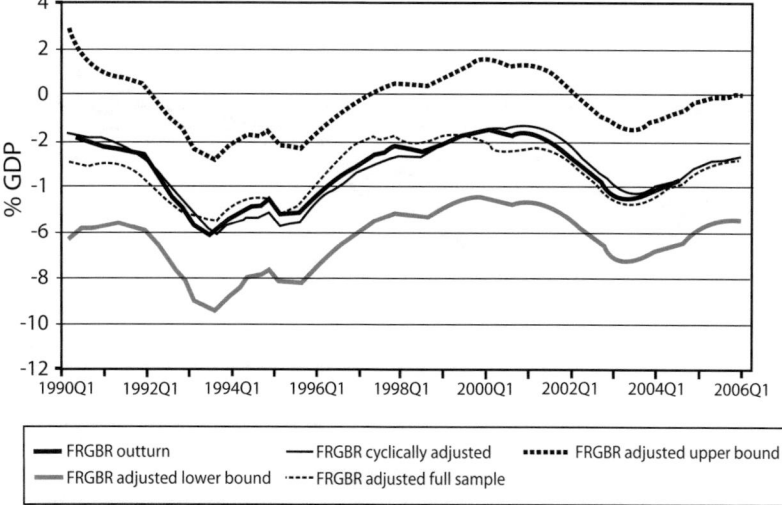

Figure 7.3 France: budget deficit cyclical adjustment – real time.

surplus in a cyclically adjusted way in the last few years. The UK has been in a statistically significant deficit position for some years, but this judgement is both marginal, and less pressing than for France, for instance, because the UK is not a member of EMU (Figures 7.1, 7.2, 7.3).

Inspection of Figures 7.1 to 7.7 also shows that the actual deficit falls within the confidence bands, which could have been computed in real time, around the cyclical adjusted budget deficit. This is not surprising, and perhaps not a source of great relief, given how wide the degree of uncertainty associated with the real-time estimates is.

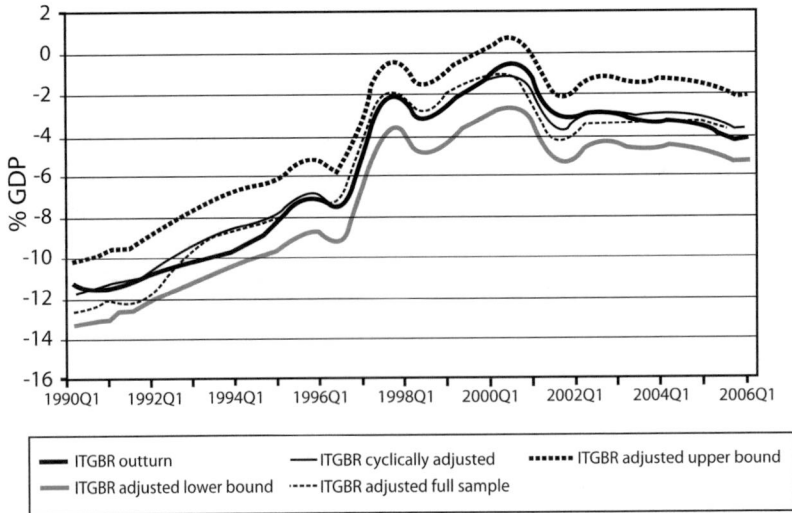

Figure 7.4 Italy: budget deficit cyclical adjustment – real time.

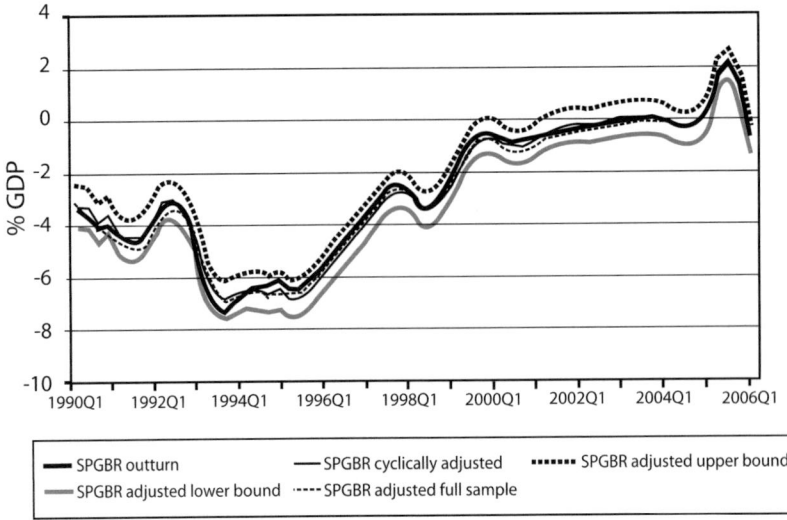

Figure 7.5 Spain: budget deficit cyclical adjustment – real time.

The real-time estimates of the CAB for France suggest that the country was in sustained deficit with little chance of achieving its commitments. However, there was a sustained improvement in the run-up to EMU, with zero being well inside the uncertainty bounds for some years. After the formation of EMU, fiscal discipline appears to have been reduced, and zero drops out of the bounds.

The Italian budget position improved markedly between 1990 and 1996, and by 1997 the target of zero appears to be temporarily at least within the bounds of probability. Special measures between 1997 and 2001 gave a plausible looking outturn, but the central estimates and the bounds have recently moved away from zero (Figure 7.4).

The low level of uncertainty around the Spanish budget deficit reflects the low uncertainty around the output gap estimates using our estimator of the output gap. However, these narrow bands leave the budget well within the bounds of close to zero over the last three years. The bounds using this estimate still suggest that the underlying position is strong, but the estimator is not the only one available, and an alternative estimator would help shed light on the position (Figure 7.5).

The Netherlands is the only country to include both zero and 3 per cent within the real-time 95 per cent confidence interval in the last five years of our sample. It is hence the only country where we are statistically unable to see whether or not it is likely to meet one or both of its Treaty and Council commitments. However, even given the uncertainty about the current cyclical position, which is greater here than in most other countries (except perhaps France) we can be reasonably sure that the surplus we currently see has some structural component and is unlikely, at the 95 per cent confidence level, to involve an underlying deficit position in breach of the 3 per cent floor. However, in 2003 for a period the budget deficit was sufficiently large that it is unlikely that it could be explained by cyclical factors, in that the bounds did not include zero (Figure 7.6).

The uncertainty surrounding the output gap estimate in Belgium is noticeably lower than in the Netherlands, and we can be relatively sure, at the 95 per cent level, that the current position represents a structurally adjusted budget deficit of somewhere between -1.5 and +1.5 per cent of GDP (Figure 7.7).

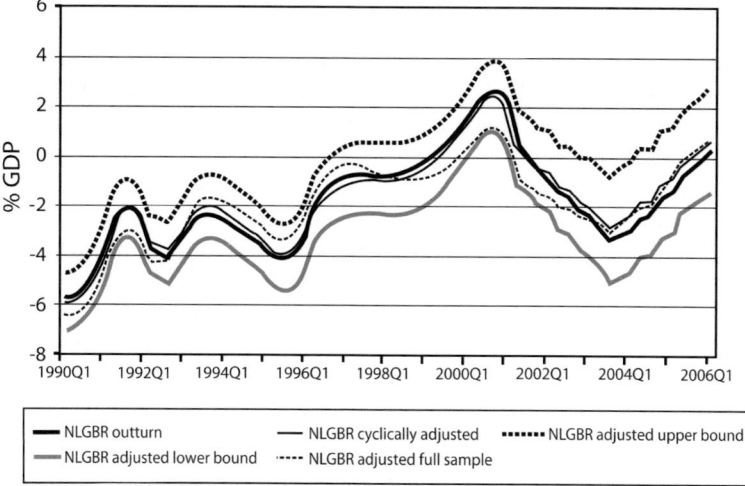

Figure 7.6 Netherlands: budget deficit cyclical adjustment – real time.

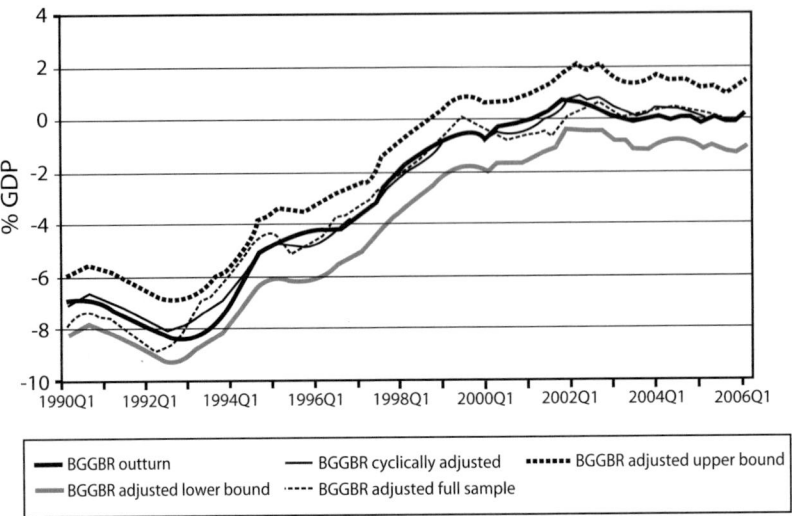

Figure 7.7 Belgium: budget deficit cyclical adjustment – real time.

7.4 Uncertainty in the adjustment

The cyclical adjustment of the budget deficit is not just subject to uncertainty over the output gap, but also to uncertainty over the impact of the output gap on revenues and on spending, and we should take account of both of these at the same time.[5] Tax revenues tend to fall with the cycle and at least some items of expenditure can be regarded as cyclically sensitive.[6] Transfers to individuals in relation to their employment state are clearly cyclically sensitive, and this sensitivity varies across countries. In our sample it is low in Italy and high in Germany, for instance, and hence we would expect the German budget deficit to be more cyclically sensitive than that of Italy. Expenditure and taxes generally move less than one for one with the level of spending, although in some countries, such as Germany, tax rates are higher on cyclically sensitive variables. A slowdown in activity in Germany driven by weak consumption would reduce tax revenues rather more than it would in the UK, for instance. Income taxes also fall less than in proportion to the output gap because of the existence of thresholds and higher rates. As we can see, the details of individual countries benefit and tax systems should affect the relationship between budgets and cycles.

There has been considerable debate about the scale of changes in revenues and spending in relation to the cycle. It is widely thought that a 1 per cent deviation in GDP from its trend might cause a 0.5 per cent of GDP change in the budget deficit. This figure is perhaps a little high and it should differ noticeably between countries and will also depend on the causes of the cyclical movement. A slowdown in activity driven by falling export demand is likely to have noticeably less impact on revenues than one driven by weak consumer spending, as the latter is more tax rich than the former. It is clear from this that producing a single gross measure of the sensitivity of the budget to the cycle is at best misleading. Although a single measure is simple and transparent, the trade-off with information about the causes of the shift in the budget may be too great.

Discerning discretionary fiscal policy moves is difficult, as it involves the detailed analysis of budgets and their impacts. Changes in tax rates and the definition of tax bases must be seen as discretionary movements in the government position, as must changes in plans for expenditure on goods services and transfers. In general an improvement in the budgetary position made by a conscious discretionary policy might be expected to have a contractionary impact on the economy in the short term, although it might lead to lower long-term real interest rates, and these might offset the contractionary impact of the policy.

It is important not to assume that any non-cyclical movement in the budget represents discretionary policy. Random variations in tax receipts or in spending may push the budget outturn well away from its predicted level without there being a cyclical explanation or a discretionary policy driving the change. Economic models cannot encompass all of the factors driving the economy, and models explaining tax receipts are bound to be incomplete descriptions. Tax receipts may change even when both the tax base and the tax rate do not move. A change in tax paying behaviour after the introduction of self-assessment in the UK in the 1990s could not have been picked up by any model. A shift in the pattern of consumption away from taxed to untaxed goods may not be picked up in equations for indirect tax receipts unless we have very detailed models. Both of these events will look like random (but explicable) elements in our analysis of taxes.

Modelling the economy

We use the National Institute Global Model, NiGEM, to scale the relationship between output gaps and the budget deficit. It is an estimated world model, which uses a 'New Keynesian' framework in that agents are presumed to be forward-looking but nominal rigidities slow the process of adjustment to external events.[7] Economies are linked through the effects of trade and competitiveness and are fully simultaneous. There are also links between countries in their financial markets as we model the structure and composition of wealth, emphasizing the role and origin of foreign assets and liabilities. We have forward-looking wages, forward-looking consumption, forward-looking exchange rates, and long-term interest rates are the forward convolution of short-term interest rates.

Each country has a description of its domestic economy that can be broken up into sectors: the government, the labour market, consumption behaviour, the supply side of the economy and financial markets. We need to ensure that interest rates, r_t, are set to stabilize the economy. We use a policy of nominal aggregate targeting and inflation rate targeting, or the two-pillar strategy advocated by the European Central Bank

$$r_t = \gamma_1(P_t Y_t - (P_t Y_t)^*) + \gamma_2(\Delta P_t - \Delta P_t^*) \tag{7.3}$$

All variables are in logs, PY is (the log of) nominal GDP, P is (the log of) the Consumer Price Index (CPI) inflation rate, and a * denotes a target.

We have models of direct and indirect taxes, and of government spending. We consider the financing of the government deficit (BUD), and we allow either money (M) or bond finance (DEBT).

$$\text{BUD} = \Delta M + \Delta \text{DEBT} \tag{7.4}$$

Current fiscal revenues can be disaggregated. Personal taxes (TAX, which includes both personal income tax and social security contributions) depend on personal incomes. Corporate taxes (CTAX) depend on longer term profitability. Indirect taxes (MTAX) depend on consumer expenditure. Transfers to individuals (TRAN) depend upon prices and on unemployment, and hence these vary with the economic cycle. Government consumption and investment (GC and GI) which are assumed to be on plan except for random fluctuations, and they are not influenced by the cycle. As GC and GI are in constant prices, we convert them to nominal terms using the private consumption CED deflator. Government interest payments (GIP) are modelled as the income on a perpetual inventory, the change in the debt stock each period paying the long interest rate in the issue period until it is replaced.[8] The budget balance thus reads:

$$\text{BUD} = \text{TAX} + \text{MTAX} + \text{CTAX} - \text{TRAN} - \text{GIP} - \text{GC} * \text{CED} - \text{GI} * \text{CED} \quad (7.5)$$

We normally assume budget deficits are kept within bounds in the longer term, and taxes rise to do this. We can describe the simple fiscal rule as

$$\text{Tax}_t = \text{Tax}_{t-1} + \phi[\text{GBRT} - \text{GBR}] \quad (7.6)$$

where Tax is the direct tax rate, GBRT and GBR are the government surplus target and actual surplus. The feedback parameter ϕ is designed to remove an excess deficit in less than five years. If fiscal solvency is 'off', it is turned back on again after our experiment.

Brunila et al. (2002) use the Commission model QUEST to quantify the impacts of output on the budget deficit, and we can evaluate the properties of our model similarly. In general, output effects on the budget increase with the size of the government sector and the share of cyclically sensitive components of taxation and spending, and hence we would expect them to vary across countries. Country-specific factors such as the degree of openness and the flexibility of the labour market will also matter. Blanchard (2000) and Barrell and Hurst (2003) suggest that supply shocks are different from demand shocks in their impacts, and hence we only analyse the relation between output and the deficit in response to shocks to demand. In order to do this we evaluate the impact of demand changes on the economy and on tax revenues, and then look at the effects of tax changes on output.

We may write the shock multiplier as (where tax is direct taxes, itax is indirect taxes, ctax is corporation tax, tran is transfers, C is consumption, I is investment, X is exports and Y is GDP):

$$\frac{dy}{dS} = \frac{dy}{d\text{tax}} * \frac{d\text{tax}}{dS} + \frac{dy}{d\text{itax}} * \frac{d\text{itax}}{dS} + \frac{dy}{d\text{ctax}} * \frac{d\text{ctax}}{S}$$
$$+ \frac{dy}{d\text{tran}} * \frac{d\text{tran}}{dS} \quad (7.7)$$
$$+ \frac{dy}{dC} * \frac{dC}{dS} + \frac{dy}{dI} * \frac{dI}{dS} + \frac{dy}{dX} * \frac{dX}{dS}$$

The left hand side of this expression is the shock multiplier, which we evaluate for consumption, investment and exports, and the last three terms represent the shock multipliers if there were no automatic stabilizers. If we have a consumption shock then dI/dS and dX/dS are set to zero by definition, and similarly for investment and export shocks. In order to evaluate the impacts of shocks on the deficit we need to evaluate the first four terms of the right-hand side of this expression. This requires that we calculate the impact of each shock on tax revenues and on transfer spending, and that we calibrate the effect of an unanticipated change in tax revenues on output.

Table 7.4 Multiplier effects of a 1 per cent of GDP impulse for one year

	Consumption	Investment	Exports	Average
France	0.70	0.62	0.67	0.68
Germany	0.89	0.77	0.89	0.89
Italy	0.60	0.53	0.58	0.59
UK	0.64	0.60	0.64	0.64
Spain	0.80	0.73	0.85	0.83
Euro area	0.72	0.65	0.73	0.72

Notes: UK in EMU. Interest rates fixed for the first year. No fiscal feedbacks for the first year. The ECB uses a two-pillar strategy. The exchange rate and the long rate are forward-looking. Average uses the variance of the errors on the structural equations weighted by the share of GDP for the component

We first look at the impact of 1 per cent of GDP changes in consumption, investment and export volumes sustained for one year, when they return to baseline for one quarter and subsequently the dynamics of the model are allowed to work (Table 7.4). We assume that there is no interest rate response in this year, but after the year the monetary authorities respond. The fiscal authorities are assumed to leave tax rates unchanged for the year and then adjust direct taxes to achieve their budget target. The model is run with forward-looking financial markets, and exchange rates and long rates jump in the first period.[9] These multipliers are generally below those for discretionary changes in government spending on goods and services, but these multipliers are also likely to be below 1.0. Barrell et al. (2004) discuss standard fiscal simulations on NiGEM and suggest reasons why Germany has the largest multipliers on this table. The average of these three demand shocks is taken by evaluating the estimation variance of the equations, reflecting the uncertainty in our understanding of them, and weighting the multipliers by these variances, multiplied by the shares each has in GDP, and rescaled so that the weights add to one. Hence a larger component (consumption) may have a more similar weight to a more uncertain component (investment) than GDP shares would suggest.

The impact of the shocks on the public finances will depend upon the importance of the three types of tax we model (direct, indirect and corporate) as well as the significance of transfers in the economy. We would expect shocks to consumption to have a much more significant impact on the budget as consumers' expenditure is a significant part of the indirect tax base. However, the significance of indirect taxes varies between countries, and hence the impacts of the consumption shock also vary. Investment and export shocks are likely to be less tax rich.

The impact of any shock on the economy affects the government budget directly and indirectly through either spending or tax receipts. If the output effect of the shock is small then the impact on income and corporate tax revenues will be smaller, as will the impact on transfer payments. Output effects will be smaller the more open the economy and the more consumption smoothing, or rather the smaller are liquidity constraints. The generosity of transfer payments differs significantly between countries, and is probably least important in Italy, for instance. Hence small open financially liberalized economies with low multipliers will have lesser effects from shocks on the budget, and large countries with generous social security systems will have larger effects. In addition the impacts of a shock on the budget depend on whether the item being shocked is taxed heavily. We can see from Table 7.5 that the impact of consumption shocks on the budget is markedly higher than investment or export shocks, as we would expect, and in general export shocks have slightly more budgetary impacts than do investment shocks.

Table 7.5 Effects on budget as a percentage of GDP of a 1 per cent of GDP impulse for one year

	Consumption	Investment	Exports	Average
France	0.46	0.14	0.15	0.31
Germany	0.58	0.27	0.31	0.45
Italy	0.47	0.18	0.20	0.28
UK	0.36	0.18	0.20	0.27
Spain	0.59	0.24	0.28	0.42
Euro area	0.51	0.19	0.22	0.34

Notes: UK in EMU. Interest rates fixed for the first year. No fiscal feedbacks for the first year. The ECB uses a two-pillar strategy. The exchange rate and the long rate are forward-looking. Budget effects from shocks are rescaled to give the impacts of a 1 per cent change in GDP

Table 7.6 Effects on budget as a percentage of GDP when GDP changes by 1 per cent as a result of shocks

	Consumption	Investment	Exports	Average
France	0.67	0.23	0.22	0.45
Germany	0.66	0.35	0.35	0.51
Italy	0.79	0.35	0.34	0.48
UK	0.57	0.30	0.30	0.42
Spain	0.74	0.33	0.32	0.52
Euro area	0.73	0.29	0.29	0.46

Notes: UK in EMU. Interest rates fixed for the first year. No fiscal feedbacks for the first year. The ECB uses a two-pillar strategy. The exchange rate and the long rate are forward looking.

Table 7.6 records the rescaled impact of the shocks on budget deficits, so that we can see the tax richness of each shock when GDP changes by 1 per cent as a result. We utilize these estimates in the analysis of uncertainty over the budget deficit, and we attribute the probabilities from Barrell and Hurst (2003) to each source of shocks in order to produce an average effect. Our analysis suggests that the impact of the cycle on the budget should be closer to 0.45 than the 0.50 used above and in other studies. But if we are clear on the source of the shocks that have driven the output gap then we can be more accurate in our assessment of the cyclically adjusted budget position.

If receipts have different sensitivities to the output gap, then the nature of the shock facing the economy will determine whether the downturn is budget rich or not. Given the frequency of different types of shocks in the 1990s to the five economies we look at, we can say that the average adjustment for demand shocks should be 0.52 for Spain, 0.51 for Germany, 0.48 for Italy, 0.45 for France and 0.42 for the small government UK. We can see that if shocks are from exports or from investment then the impacts on the deficit are noticeably smaller than the multipliers associated with consumption shocks, with an average impact of 0.33 for investment shocks in the large euro area countries and 0.32 for export shocks in the same group. Consumption shocks have more impact on tax revenues, and the average impact is 0.66 for France and Germany, and 0.75 for Italy and Spain. Hence we need to look at the source of demand shocks in order to evaluate the cyclical adjustment that would be appropriate in a given situation. This parameter uncertainty increases the uncertainty bounds involved in evaluating deficits, but it may not be an insurmountable problem to decide whether a downturn in demand is driven by domestic or by foreign factors.

Table 7.7 Cyclically adjusted budget deficits*

		GBR	Full sample			Real time		
			Cyclically adjusted	Upper bound	Lower bound	Cyclically adjusted	Upper bound	Lower bound
UK	1992	−6.433	−4.923	−3.538	−6.308	−5.720	−2.871	−8.570
b=0.5	2004	−3.211	−3.590	−1.680	−5.501	−3.289	−0.956	−5.623
UK	1992	−6.433	−5.436	−4.522	−6.351	−5.963	−4.082	−7.843
b=0.33	2004	−3.211	−3.462	−2.201	−4.723	−3.263	−1.723	−4.803
UK	1992	−6.433	−5.074	−3.828	−6.321	−5.792	−3.227	−8.356
b=0.45	2004	−3.211	−3.552	−1.833	−5.272	−3.282	−1.181	−5.382
UK	1992	−6.433	−4.440	−2.612	−6.268	−5.492	−1.731	−9.254
b=0.66	2004	−3.211	−3.712	−1.190	−6.234	−3.314	−0.234	−6.395
Germany	1992	−2.474	−3.376	−2.378	−4.374	−2.457	−1.131	−3.783
b=0.5	2004	−3.679	−3.305	−2.130	−4.480	−3.216	−1.684	−4.747
Germany	1992	−2.474	−3.069	−2.411	−3.728	−2.463	−1.587	−3.338
b=0.33	2004	−3.679	−3.432	−2.657	−4.208	−3.373	−2.363	−4.384
Germany	1992	−2.474	−3.286	−2.388	−4.184	−2.459	−1.265	−3.652
b=0.45	2004	−3.679	−3.343	−2.285	−4.400	−3.262	−1.884	−4.640
Germany	1992	−2.474	−3.665	−2.348	−4.982	−2.452	−0.701	−4.202
b=0.66	2004	−3.679	−3.186	−1.635	−4.737	−3.068	−1.046	−5.089
France	1992	−3.945	−4.595	−2.465	−6.726	−4.032	−0.908	−7.155
b=0.5	2004	−3.710	−3.887	−1.480	−6.295	−3.633	−0.859	−6.407
France	1992	−3.945	−4.374	−2.968	−5.780	−4.002	−1.941	−6.064
b=0.33	2004	−3.710	−3.827	−2.238	−5.416	−3.659	−1.829	−5.490
France	1992	−3.945	−4.530	−2.613	−6.448	−4.023	−1.212	−6.834
b=0.45	2004	−3.710	−3.870	−1.703	−6.036	−3.641	−1.144	−6.137
France	1992	−3.945	−4.803	−1.991	−7.616	−4.059	0.064	−8.183
b=0.66	2004	−3.710	−3.944	−0.766	−7.122	−3.608	0.053	−7.270

Notes:
GBR denotes the deficit as percentage of GDP.
* Changing the effect (b) of OG on CABUD

In Table 7.7 we set out the upper and lower bounds for budget deficits in both real time and over the full sample for 1992 and for 2004 for the UK, France and Germany using estimates of the impacts of the gap on the deficit. We use 0.33 to represent the impact of external shocks on deficits, 0.66 to estimate the impact of domestic demand shocks. We also include estimates based on a sensitivity of 0.45, which is the shocks weighted average from Barrell and Hurst (2003).

We are particularly interested in whether or not a set of bounds around a cyclically adjusted deficit might for instance include a possibility that the country was close to balance or in surplus in a cyclically adjusted sense. We can see from the table that only France saw itself in this position, and then only in 2004 if shocks were predominantly from consumption and the real-time estimate was to be used. In this table no country and coefficient pair, either in real time or over the full sample, could be said to be clearly in line with a Treaty commitment not to breach a deficit floor of 3 per cent of GDP, even in a probabilistic sense of being 95 per cent certain that this is not the case. This suggests that even if we include all the one-off measures in the last five years it is very unlikely that the UK, France and Germany have been running a structural surplus. Thus it is very likely that they have breached a reasonable level of borrowing of 3 per cent of GDP.[10]

7.5 Implications and conclusions

Monetary Union requires some form of fiscal pact, and although it is in the interests of all to follow that pact, it is in the interests of each country to find special reasons why the pact constraints may not apply to it in a particular year. The pact was designed to set limits to borrowing, with penalties available for sustained breaches of the targets. These penalties are supposed to take account of the impacts of the cycle on the deficit, but these impacts are uncertain. We have investigated one representative estimator of the output gap and derived its distribution, giving us a simple way of evaluating its uncertainty. This in turn allows us to put uncertainty bounds around the budget deficit given an estimate of the output gap on the deficit. We then discuss the uncertainties involved in the relationship between the output gap and the deficit, showing that the source of shocks impacts on the uncertainty surrounding a deficit projection.

All estimates of the output gap are uncertain, and ours is probably no worse than others. Even those that are not revised are not known with certainty at the point when they are made. There is a strong case for using production function based estimates of the output gap, as in Denis et al. (2006), but these are more difficult to calculate than our measure, and it is more complex, but not impossible, to evaluate the associated uncertainty. Even if we know with certainty the parameters of the production function we still have to estimate trend hours, trend productivity and the equilibrium level of employment. If these are estimated using a filter, which is common, then it is possible to evaluate directly their uncertainty and feed this into the gap. If they are the result of reduced form calculations, then a more complicated process of looking at the error variance on the reduced form has to be gone through.

It is our contention that the error bounds around any estimate of the output gap are wide. Given these uncertainties it will always be possible to put bounds around the cyclically adjusted deficit. We strongly advocate that this should be done by all official bodies involved with the evaluation of deficits in Europe as well as by the scientific community. It would be more prudent to accept that we are ignorant rather than argue about point estimates of gaps; hence we should evaluate budget deficits in probabilistic terms. This would involve asking whether a budget target is within the 95 per cent (or 64 per cent) bounds around the cyclically adjusted deficit. In undertaking this analysis it is also useful to discuss the source of weak demand that has caused the output gap and then use an appropriate coefficient (perhaps not 0.5) in the adjustment. In all cases humility over our ignorance and strength about the obvious, such as the scale of recent deficits in France and Germany, are important characteristics of sensible debate.

Notes

1. Values are never truly final because data revisions and the arrival of new data are a continuous process.
2. We ignore the fact that GDP data are published with, at least, a one-quarter lag.
3. In the notation of Harvey and Trimbur (2003) we set $m = n = 2$ in each recursive sample, although for the UK we consider also increasing n to $n = 3$. The models are not subjected to standard goodness-of-fit tests to help identify potential weaknesses/model mis-specification. Future work should consider this.
4. The Kalman filter recursions automatically return estimates of the covariance matrix of the state vector. The diagonal elements of these matrices then can be used to construct the confidence intervals and density estimates. This approach has also been followed, for example, by Orphanides and van Norden (2002).
5. More formally, if $CABUD = ADJ * OG$ and the adjustment factor and the output gap were independent then $var(CABUD) = var(ADJ) * var(OG) + mean(ADJ)^2 * var(OG) + mean(OG)^2 * var(ADJ)$. It would be possible for us to utilize this formula, but OG and adj may not be independent, and hence it would be misleading. Calculating the joint distribution of OG and adj is possible, but would be time-consuming, and we leave it to a later project.
6. Although we may be able to find a statistical relation between other items of expenditure and the cycle, we regard such movements as discretionary, and we would not include them in our adjustments.
7. The structure and the simulation properties of NiGEM are described in, Barrell et al. (2004).
8. The perpetual inventory attempts to take account of countries like Italy and Belgium where there are large proportions of short-term public debt.
9. Multipliers are always less than one in these models, and are generally less than those given in unstructured VAR analyses such as that of Blanchard and Perotti (2002).
10. The UK uses a different set of guidelines, and sets its borrowing to be no greater than the level of public investment over a cycle. Given this has not exceeded 2 per cent of GDP we could make a simple adjustment to our figures of this magnitude; hence we can say that the balance of probabilities is that it has not been meeting its target over the last four years; e.g. see Kirby and Mitchell (2006).

Discussion

György Kopits[1]

The chapter by Barrell, Hurst and Mitchell constitutes an excellent analytical exercise. It was a pleasure to read it. The chapter is a rigorous attempt at gauging the degree of uncertainty associated with the measurement of the cyclically adjusted budget (CAB) balance (and of the underlying output gap) in major EU member economies. Apart from the solution of analytical and computational challenges, my interest in this work is primarily from the standpoint of the policy maker.

When reading the chapter I was reminded of the book by former US Treasury Secretary Rubin (Rubin and Weisberg 2003) about his approach to decision making during his years in government and in investment banking. The essential point was that he took policy decisions or business decisions always with a view to assessing and weighing in real time the uncertainties surrounding those decisions – without the benefit of any formal gauge. In particular, the conduct of fiscal policy for stabilization purposes presupposes real-time estimates of the output gap. At the supranational EU level, output gap estimates are necessary for surveillance to ascertain whether a member country's underlying fiscal position is in line with the requirements of the Stability and Growth Pact. Beyond the realm of fiscal policy, reliable output gap estimates are also a key ingredient in the formulation of monetary policy, not only by central banks that follow a Taylor rule, but even by those that target inflation alone. Yet the reliability of such estimates is viewed with widespread scepticism – as expressed for example recently by Rogoff (2006, p. 320). Therefore, in this broad context, the experiment reported in this chapter is most welcome from the perspective of multiple users.

The chapter contributes to a clearer understanding of the cyclically adjusted budgetary position in real time. It makes a quantitative assessment of the uncertainty surrounding point estimates of the output gaps, by comparing real-time estimates with full-sample measures of the gap. It applies a model-based approach, drawing on unobserved components. The resulting output gap measures and the respective uncertainty bands are then translated into CAB measures on the basis of stylized budgetary sensitivity parameters. By this measure, the authors find that in Italy, France, Germany and to a lesser extent the UK, the general government accounts have not been close to balance or in surplus position in recent years. On the other hand, for Spain, the Netherlands and Belgium fiscal balance is obtained. These results can be examined on the basis of four criteria: robustness, sensitivity, versatility and usefulness.

On *robustness*, in principle, the calculations seem reasonable, although it is surprising that the uncertainty bands are rather wide for most countries. Less surprising is that the real-time bands are larger than the full-sample bands. However, on this criterion, the jury is still out until further testing with alternative methodologies (as done to some extent for the

United Kingdom). Furthermore, the capacity of this approach to capture structural shifts is questionable, and more important, there remains an end-point problem. A possible solution of this problem may lie in the application of the trend-cycle filter developed by Mohr (2005) that combines an HP filter with an unobserved-components model-based approach.

A closely related criterion is the *sensitivity* to alternative budgetary parameters. Obviously, the entire computational chain cannot be stronger than the weakest link. In this regard, the sensitivity test conducted on the budgetary impact of various GDP components is persuasive. And, of course, future application of this approach could be fine-tuned to specific countries and specific periods.

As regards *versatility*, the results for Spain and the Netherlands give rise to some scepticism. It would be worth probing deeper whether the narrow uncertainty bands for Spain are attributable to some peculiar structural characteristic, model specification or virtual absence of statistical error. In the case of the Netherlands the estimates are counter-intuitive in that the real-time bands are somewhat narrower than the full-sample bands. Perhaps this is due to unusually large revisions of the underlying data.

Research on the uncertainty of real-time estimates of the output gap should be *useful* for policy-making purposes. A retrospective assessment of the cyclically adjusted budgetary position has considerable value added for fiscal policy analysis.[2] Specifically, this should provide more reliable information for national policy decisions, as well as for surveillance by EU authorities under the Pact, especially in assessing performance under the excessive deficit procedure.

However, a pending question, to be tackled by future researchers, concerns the forward-looking application of the estimated uncertainty around real-time output gaps. In other words, this would involve inquiring into the extent to and manner in which past estimates of uncertainty bands can be extrapolated to the period ahead with a view to better capturing, and possibly to counteracting, the impact of cyclical fluctuations around trend output. Beyond fiscal policy, as anticipated in my opening remarks, this line of research is potentially useful for monetary policy as well. Estimates of the uncertainty in real-time measures of the output gap should be helpful for the preparation of increasingly accurate growth forecasts, including through fan charts that presuppose a reliable point estimate for the current time period.[3]

Finally, estimates of the uncertainty around real-time output gaps underscore the importance of exercising caution and transparency in actual policy formulation. Indeed, by and large, these findings should discourage governments from relying on optimistic macroeconomic projections, and EU entities from accepting them. In this respect, my favourite is Canada's rule-of-thumb approach, whereby the government builds fiscal forecasts on macroeconomic projections generated by private sector (mostly think-tanks) consensus, subject to a small conservative safety margin.

Notes

1 The views expressed in this chapter are those of the author and are not attributable to the National Bank of Hungary.
2 In a way, this is analogous to the analysis in Chapter 2, regarding the reaction of fiscal policy for restoring sustainability
3 At present relatively few central banks prepare fan charts for growth along with the usual fan charts for inflation. Among the exceptions, the Bank of England and the National Bank of Hungary publish them in their periodic inflation reports.

Bibliography

Abel, A. B., N. G. Mankiw, L. H. Summers and R. J. Zeckhauser (1989), 'Assessing Dynamic Efficiency: Theory and Evidence', *Review of Economic Studies*, 56: 1–20.
Afonso, A. (2005), 'Fiscal Sustainability: The Unpleasant European Case', *FinanzArchiv*, 61(1): 19–44.
——(2006), 'Expansionary Fiscal Consolidations in Europe: New Evidence', *ECB Working Paper*, 675.
Alberola, E., J. M. González Mínguez, P. Hernández de Cos and J. M. Marqués (2003), 'How Cyclical Do Cyclically-adjusted Balances Remain?', *Hacienda Pública Española/Revista de Economía Pública*, 166: 151–181.
Alesina, A. and S. Ardagna (1998), 'Tales of Fiscal Contractions', *Economic Policy*, 27: 487–545.
Alesina, A. and T. Bayoumi (1996), 'The Costs and Benefits of Fiscal Rules: Evidence from US States', *NBER Working Paper*, 5614.
Alesina, A. and R. Perotti (1995), 'Fiscal Expansions and Adjustments in OECD Countries', *Economic Policy*, 21: 205–248.
Auerbach, A. J. and L. J. Kotlikoff (1987), *Dynamic Fiscal Policy*, Cambridge: Cambridge University Press.
Auerbach, A. J., J. Gokhale and L. J. Kotlikoff (1991), 'Generational Accounting: A Meaningful Alternative to Deficit Accounting', in D. Bradford (ed.), *Tax Policy and the Economy*, vol. 5, Cambridge, Mass.: MIT Press.
——(1994), 'Generational Accounting: A Meaningful Way to Evaluate Fiscal Policy', *Journal of Economic Perspectives*, 8(1): 73–94.
Auerbach, A. J., L. J. Kotlikoff and W. Leibfritz (1999), *Generational Accounting around the World*, Chicago: University of Chicago Press.
Bai, J. (1997), 'Estimation of a Change Point in Multiple Regression Models', *Review of Economics and Statistics*, 79(4): 551–563.
Bai, J., R. Lumsdaine and J. Stock (1998), 'Testing for and Dating Common Breaks in Multivariate Time Series', *Review of Economic Studies*, 65: 395–432.
Balassone, F. and M. Francese (2004), 'Cyclical Asymmetry in Fiscal Policy, Debt Accumulation and the Treaty of Maastricht', *Banca d'Italia Temi di Discussione*, 531.
Balassone, F. and D. Franco (2000), 'Assessing Fiscal Sustainability: A Review of Methods with a View to EMU', Banca d'Italia, *Fiscal Sustainability*, 22–60, Rome.
——(2001), 'EMU Fiscal Rules: A New Answer to an Old Question?', Banca d'Italia, *Fiscal Rules*: 33–58, Rome.
Balassone, F., D. Franco and R. Giordano (2004), 'Market Induced Fiscal Discipline: Is There a Fall Back Solution for Rule Failure?', in Banca d'Italia, *Public Debt*, Rome.
Balassone F., D. Franco and S. Zotteri (2004), 'EMU Fiscal Indicators: a Misleading Compass?', paper presented at the *XVI Villa Mondragone International Seminar*, June.
——(2006), 'EMU Fiscal Indicators: A Misleading Compass?', *Empirica*, 33(2): 63–87.
Ballabriga, F. (1997), 'Bayesian Vector Autoregressions', *ESADE Working Paper*, 155.
Ballabriga, F. and C. Martinez-Mongay (2003), 'Has EMU Shifted Monetary and Fiscal Policies?', in M. Buti (ed.), *Monetary and Fiscal Policies in EMU. Interactions and Coordination*, Cambridge: Cambridge University Press.

——(2005), 'Sustainability of EU Public Finances', *European Economy – Economic Papers*, 225.

Barrell, R. and A. I. Hurst (2003), 'Benchmarks and Targets under the SGP – Evaluating Safe Deficit Targets Using NiGEM', *National Institute Economic Review*, 185: 54–63.

Barrell, R., B. Becker, J. Byrne, S. Gottschalk, A. I. Hurst and D. van Welsum (2004), 'Macroeconomic Policy in Europe: Experiments with Monetary Responses and Fiscal Impulses', *Economic Modelling*, 21(5): 877–931.

Barrell, R., A. I. Hurst and J. Mitchell (2006) 'Uncertainty Bounds for Cyclically Adjusted Budget Balances', paper presented at the European Commission Workshop on Fiscal Indicators for Budgetary Surveillance (Brussels, 22 September).

Barro, R. (1990), 'Government Spending in a Simple Model of Endogenous Growth', *Journal of Political Economy*, 98: 103–125.

Baxter, M. and R. G. King (1993), 'Fiscal Policy in General Equilibrium', *American Economic Review*, 83(3): 315–334.

——(1999), 'Measuring Business Cycles: Approximate Band-pass Filters for Economic Time Series', *Review of Economics and Statistics*, 81: 575–93.

Bilbiie, F., A. Meier and G. Müller (2006), 'What Accounts for the Change in US Fiscal Policy Transmission?', *ECB Working Paper*, 582.

Blanchard, O. (1993), 'Suggestions for a New Set of Fiscal Indicators', in H. Verbon and F. Van Winden (eds), *The Political Economy of Government Debt*, North-Holland Elsevier Science: 307–325.

——(2000), 'Commentary', *Federal Reserve Bank of New York Economic Policy Review*, 6 (1): 69–74.

Blanchard, O. and R. Perotti (2002), 'An Empirical Characterisation of the Dynamic Effects of Changes in Government Spending and Taxes on Output', *Quarterly Journal of Economics*, 117(4): 1329–1368.

Blanchard, O. and D. Quah (1989), 'The Dynamic Effects of Aggregate Demand and Supply Disturbances', *American Economic Review*, 79(4): 655–673.

Bohn, H. (1995), 'The Sustainability of Budget Deficits in a Stochastic Economy', *Journal of Money, Credit and Banking*, 27: 257–271.

——(1998), 'The Behavior of US Debt and Deficits', *Quarterly Journal of Economics*, 113: 949–963.

——(2005a), 'The Sustainability of Fiscal Policy in the United States', *CESifo Working Paper*, 1446.

——(2005b), 'An Absurdly Weak Unit Root Condition for Intertemporal Budget Constraints', mimeo, UCSB.

Boije, R. (2004), 'The General Government Structural Budget Balance', *Sveriges Riksbank Economic Review*, 1: 5-33.

Boije, R. and J. Fischer (2006), 'Fiscal Indicators in a Rule-based Framework', in Banca d'Italia, *Fiscal Indicators*, Rome.

Bouthevillain, C. and A. Quinet (1999), 'The Relevance of Cyclically-adjusted Public Balance Indicators – The French Case in Indicators of Structural Budget Balances', in Banca d'Italia, *Indicators of Structural Budget Balances*, Rome.

Bouthevillain, C., P. Cour-Thimann, G. Van den Dool, P. Hernández de Cos, G. Langenus, M. Mohr, S. Momigliano and M. Tujula (2001), 'Cyclically Adjusted Budget Balances: An Alternative Approach', *ECB Working Paper*, 77.

Braconier, H. and T. Forsfält (2004), 'A New Method for Constructing a Cyclically Adjusted Budget Balance: the Case of Sweden', *NIESR Working Paper*, 90.

Brandner, P. and L. Diebalek (2000), 'Zerlegung von Budgetsalden in strukturelle, konjunkturelle und diskretionäre Komponenten', Studie des Österreichischen Instituts für Wirtschaftsforschung im Auftrag der Oesterreichischen Nationalbank (unpublished).

Brandner, P., L. Diebalek and H. Schuberth (1998), 'Structural Budget Deficits and Sustainability of Fiscal Positions in the European Union', *Oesterreichische Nationalbank Working Paper*, 26.

Bruneau, C. and O. De Bandt (2003), 'Monetary and Fiscal Policy in the Transition to EMU: What do SVAR Models Tell Us?', *Economic Modelling*, 20: 959–985.

Brunila, A. and C. Martinez-Mongay (2002), 'Fiscal Policy in the Early Years of EMU', in M. Buti and A. Sapir (eds), *EMU and Economic Policy in Europe. The Challenge of the Early Years*, Cheltenham: Edward Elgar.

Brunila, A., M. Buti, and J. W. in 't Veld (2002), 'Fiscal Policy in Europe: How Effective Are the Automatic Stabilisers?', *European Economy – Economic Papers*, 177.

Buiter, W. H. and C. Grafe (2003), 'Reforming EMU's Fiscal Policy Rules: Some Suggestions for Enhancing Fiscal Sustainability and Macroeconomic Stability in an Enlarged European Union', in M. Buti (ed.), *Monetary and Fiscal Policies in EMU. Interactions and Coordination*, Cambridge: Cambridge University Press.

Buti, M. (2007), 'Will the New Stability and Growth Pact Succeed? An Economic and Political Perspective', in F. Breuss (ed.), *The Stability and Growth Pact: Experiences and Future Aspects*, Wien: Springer-Verlag.

Buti, M., D. Franco and H. Ongena (1997), 'Budgetary Policies during Recessions – Retrospective Application of the "Stability and Growth Pact" to the Post War Period', *European Economy – Economic Papers*, 121.

Buti, M., S. Eijffinger and D. Franco (2003), 'Revisiting the Stability and Growth Pact: Grand Design or Internal Adjustment', *European Economy – Economic Papers*, 180 (also available as *CEPR Discussion Paper*, 3692).

——(2005), 'The Stability Pact Pains: A Forward-looking Assessment of the Reform Debate', *CEPR Discussion Paper*, 5216.

Buti, M., J. Nogueira Martins and A. Turrini (2007), 'From Deficits to Debt and Back: Political Incentives under Numerical Fiscal Rules', *CESifo Economic Studies*, 53(1): 115–152.

Canova, F. (1998), 'Detrending and Business Cycle Facts', *Journal of Monetary Economics*, 41: 475–512.

Canova, F. and E. Pappa (2002), 'Price Dispersions in Monetary Unions: The Role of Fiscal Shocks', *CEPR Discussion Paper*, 3746.

Canzoneri, M., R. Cumby and B. Diba (2001), 'Is the Price Level Determined by the Needs of Fiscal Solvency?', *American Economic Review*, 91: 1221–1238.

Cavallo, M. (2005), 'Government Employment and the Dynamic Effects of Fiscal Policy Shocks', *Federal Reserve Bank of San Francisco Working Papers in Applied Economic Theory*, 16.

Chouraqui, J., R. Hagemann and N. Sartor (1992), 'Indicators of Fiscal Policy: a Reassessment', *OECD Economics Department Working Paper*, 78.

Christiano L., M. Eichenbaum and E. Vigfusson (2006), 'Assessing Structural VARs', *NBER Working Paper*, 12353.

Christoffersen, P. F. (1998), 'Evaluating Interval Forecasts', *International Economic Review*, 39, 841–862.

Claeys, P. (2004), 'An SVAR Analysis of Stabilisation Policies in EMU', *European University Institute Working Paper*, 22.

Coeuré, B. and J. Pisani-Ferry (2003), 'A Sustainability Pact for the Eurozone', mimeo, École Politechnique, Paris.

Cohen, D. and G. Follette (2000), 'The Automatic Stabilisers: Quietly Doing Their Thing', *Federal Reserve Bank of New York Economic Policy Review*, 6: 35–67.

Council of the European Union (2005), *Improving the Implementation of the Stability and Growth Pact*, 7423/05.

Cutler, D. M. (1993), 'Review of Generational Accounting: Knowing Who Pays, and When, for What We Spend by Laurence J. Kotlikoff', *National Tax Journal*, 46(1): 61–67.

Dalsgaard, T. and A. de Serres (2001), 'Estimating Prudent Budgetary Margins', in Brunila, A., M. Buti and D. Franco (eds), *The Stability and Growth Pact – The Architecture of Fiscal Policy in EMU*, Basingstoke, Palgrave: 123–154.

Danmarks Nationalbank (2005), *Annual Report of the Board of Governors*.

De Arcangelis, G. and S. Lamartina (2004), 'Fiscal Shocks and Policy Regimes in Some OECD Countries', in R. Beetsma, C. Favero, C. Missale, V. A. Muscatelli and P. Natale (eds), *Fiscal Policies, Monetary Policies and Labour Markets – Key Aspects of European Macroeconomic Policies after Monetary Unification*, Cambridge: Cambridge University Press: 224–255.

Denis, C., D. Grenouilleau, K. McMorrow and W. Röger (2006), 'Calculating Potential Growth Rates and Output Gaps – A Revised Production Function Approach', *European Economy – Economic Papers*, 247.

Diamond, P. (1996), 'Generational Accounting and Generational Balance: An Assessment', *National Tax Journal*, 49: 597–607.

Diebalek, L., W. Köhler-Töglhofer and D. Prammer (2005), 'The Austrian Stability Pact 2001–2004 – Design, Objectives and Effectiveness', *Wirtschaftspolitische Blätter*, 2: 291–305.

Doan, T., R. Litterman and C. Sims (1984), 'Forecasting and Conditional Projections Using Realistic Prior Distributions', *Econometric Reviews*, 3(1): 1–100.

Domar, E. D. (1944), 'The Burden of the Debt and the National Income', *American Economic Review*, 34: 798–827.

Economic Policy Committee (2001), *Budgetary Challenges Posed by Ageing Populations and Impact on Public Spending on Pensions, Health, and Long-term Care for the Elderly and Possible Indicators of Long-term Sustainability of Public Finances*, EPC/ECFIN/655/01-EN.

Eschenbach, F. and L. Schuknecht (2004), 'Budgetary Risks from Real Estate and Stock Markets', *Economic Policy*, 39: 313–346.

European Commission (1995), 'The Commission Services' Method for the Cyclical Adjustment of Government Budget Balances (Technical Note)', *European Economy*, 60: 35–56.

——(2001), 'Public Finances in EMU – 2001', *European Economy*, 3.

——(2004), *Strengthening Economic Governance and Clarifying the Implementation of the Stability and Growth Pact*, COM(2004) 581.

——(2005), 'Public Finances in EMU – 2005', *European Economy*, 3.

——(2006), 'The Long-term Sustainability of Public Finances in the European Union', *European Economy*, 4.

Eurostat (2000), *ESA Manual on Deficit and Debt*, Luxembourg: Eurostat.

——(2006), *Structures of the Taxation Systems of the European Union*, Luxembourg: Eurostat.

Fatás, A. and I. Mihov (2001), 'Fiscal Policy and Business Cycles: An Empirical Investigation', paper presented at the *XIII Symposium of Moneda y Crédito*, Madrid, November 2000 (published Spanish version: 'Politica Fiscal y Ciclos Económicos: una Investigación Empirica', *Moneda y Crédito*, 212: 167–210).

——(2003a), 'On Constraining Fiscal Policy Discretion in EMU', *Oxford Review of Economic Policy*, 19(1): 112–131.

——(2003b), 'The Case for Restricting Fiscal Policy Discretion', *Quarterly Journal of Economics*, 118(4): 1419–1447.

Faust, J. and E. M. Leeper (1997), 'When Do Long-run Identifying Restrictions Give Reliable Results?', *Journal of Business and Economic Statistics*, 15(3): 334–353.

Federal Accounting Standards Advisory Board (2004), 'Discussion Memorandum' by Richard Fontenrose, October.

Feldstein, M. (2005), 'The Euro and the Stability Pact', *NBER Working Paper*, 11249.

Finn, M. (1998), 'Cyclical Effects of Government's Employment and Goods Purchases', *International Economic Review*, 39: 635–657.

Forni, L. and S. Momigliano (2004), 'Cyclical Sensitivity of Fiscal Policies Based on Real-Time Data', *Applied Economics Quarterly*, 50(3): 299–326.

Galí, J. (1992), 'How Well Does the IS-LM Fit Postwar US Data?', *Quarterly Journal of Economics*, 107(2): 709–738.

Galí, J. and R. Perotti (2003), 'Fiscal Policy and Monetary Integration in Europe', *Economic Policy*, 37: 535–572.

Galí, J., D. Lopez-Salido and J. Valles (2005), 'Understanding the Effects of Government Spending on Consumption', *NBER Working Paper*, 11578.

Gavin, M. and R. Perotti (1997), 'Fiscal Policy in Latin America', *NBER Macroeconomics Annual*: 11–61.

General Administration of the Treasury, Kingdom of Belgium (2005), 'Federal Government Debt', Annual Report.

Giavazzi, F. and M. Pagano (1990), 'Can Severe Fiscal Contractions Be Expansionary? Tales of Two Small European Countries', in S. Fischer (ed.), *NBER Macroeconomic Annuals*, 5: 75–122.

Giavazzi, F., T. Jappelli and M. Pagano (2000), 'Searching for Non-linear Effects of Fiscal Policy: Evidence from Industrial and Developing Countries', *European Economic Review*, 44: 1259–1289.

Giorno, C., J. Richardson, D. Rosevaere and P. van den Noord (1995), 'Estimating Potential Output, Output Gaps and Structural Budget Deficits', *OECD Economic Studies*, 24: 167–209.

Girouard, N. and C. André (2005), 'Measuring Cyclically-Adjusted Budget Balances for OECD Countries', *OECD Economics Department Working Paper*, 434.

Gokhale, J. (2004), 'Comments on Public Debt, Ageing, and Fiscal Sustainability', in Banca d'Italia, *Public Debt*, Rome.

Gokhale, J. and K. A. Smetters (2003), *Fiscal and Generational Imbalances: New Budget Measures for New Budget Priorities*, American Enterprise Institute Monograph, Washington, DC: AEI Press.

——(2006), 'Fiscal and Generational Imbalances: An Update', in J. Poterba (ed.), *Tax Policy and the Economy*, 20, Cambridge, Mass.: MIT Press.

Gokhale, J., B. Page and J. R. Sturrock (1997), 'Generational Accounts for the United States: An Update', *Federal Reserve Bank of Cleveland Economic Review*, 33(4): 2–23.

Gordo Mora, L. and J. Nogueira Martins (2007), 'How Reliable are the Statistics for the Stability and Growth Pact?', *European Economy – Economic Papers*, 273.

Hallerberg, M. and R. Strauch (2002), 'On the Cyclicality of Public Finances in Europe', *Empirica*, 29: 183–207.

Hamilton, J. D. and M. Flavin (1986), 'On the Limitations of Government Borrowing: A Framework for Empirical Testing', *American Economic Review*, 76: 808–819.

Harvey, A. C. and T. Trimbur (2003), 'General Model-Based Filters for Extracting Trends and Cycles in Economic Time Series', *Review of Economics and Statistics*, 85: 244–255.

Haveman, R. (1994), 'Should Generational Accounts Replace Public Budgets and Deficits?', *Journal of Economic Perspectives*, 8(1): 95–111.

Hercowitz, Z. and M. Strawczynski (2004), 'Cyclical Ratcheting in Government Spending: Evidence from the OECD', *Review of Economics and Statistics*, 86(1): 353–361.

Hillier, D. R. (1996), 'From Cash to Accrual: The Canadian Experience', in 'Perspectives on Accrual Accounting', *International Federation of Accountants Occasional Paper*, 3, New York.

Hjelm, G. (2003), 'Simultaneous Determination of NAIRU, Output Gaps and Structural Budget Balances: Swedish Evidence', *NIER Working Paper*, 81.

HM Treasury (2003), *Fiscal Stabilisation and EMU*, London: HM Treasury.

——(2006), *The Financial Statement and Budget Report*, London: HM Treasury.

IMF (1993), *World Economic Outlook*, Washington, DC: IMF.

——(2004), *World Economic Outlook*, Washington, DC: IMF.

Indicateurs de progrès de l'économie française (2006, revised), Finances Publiques.

International Federation of Accountants (IFAC) (1995), 'Resource Accounting: Framework of Accounting Standard Setting in the United Kingdom Central Government Sector', *Public Sector Committee Occasional Paper*, 5, New York.

Jaeger, A. (1990), 'The Measurement and Interpretation of Structural Budget Balances', *Empirica*, 17(2): 155–169.

——(1993), 'Structural Budget Indicators for the Major Industrial Countries', *World Economic Outlook*, Washington, DC: IMF.

——(1998), 'Fiscal Stabilization Policy under EMU', in G. R. Kincaid, W. Lee, B. Drees, A. Jaeger, K. Krajnyák and C. Purfield, 'Germany. Selected Issues and Statistical Appendix', *IMF Staff Country Report*, No. 98/111, Ch. I: 8–39.

Kamps, C. (2004), 'The Dynamic Effects of Public Capital: VAR Evidence for 22 OECD Countries', *Kiel Institute Working Paper*, 1224.

Katterl, A. and W. Köhler-Töglhofer (2005), 'The Impact of EU Accession on Austria's Budget Policy', Oesterreichische Nationalbank, *Monetary Policy & The Economy*, Q2/05: 101–116.

King, G., C. Plosser, J. Stock and M. Watson (1991), 'Stochastic Trends and Economic Fluctuations', *American Economic Review*, 81(2): 819–840.

King, R. and S. Rebelo (1990), 'Public Policy and Economic Growth: Developing Neoclassical Implications', *Journal of Political Economy*, 98: 126–150.

King, R. and M. Watson (1997), 'Testing Long-run Neutrality', *Federal Reserve Bank Richmond Quarterly Review*, 83(3): 69–101.

Kirby, S. and J. Mitchell (2006), 'Prudence and UK Trend Growth', *National Institute Economic Review*, 197: 58-64.

Kneller, R., M. Bleany and N. Gemmell (1999), 'Fiscal Policy and Growth: Evidence from OECD Countries', *Journal of Public Economics*, 74: 171–190.

Kotlikoff, L. J. (1989), 'From Deficit Delusion to the Fiscal Balance Rule', *NBER Working Paper*, 2841.

Kwiatkowski, D., P. C. B. Phillips, P. Schmidt and Y. Shin (1992), 'Testing the Null Hypothesis of Stationarity Against the Alternative of a Unit Root', *Journal of Econometrics*, 54: 159–178.

Lane, P. R. (2003), 'The Cyclical Behaviour of Fiscal Policy: Evidence from the OECD', *Journal of Public Economics*, 87: 2661–2675.

Larch, M. and M. Salto (2005), 'Fiscal Rules, Inertia and Discretionary Fiscal Policy', *Applied Economics*, 37: 1135–1146.

Linnemann, L. and A. Schabert (2003), 'Fiscal Policy in the New Neoclassical Synthesis', *Journal of Money, Credit and Banking*, 35(6): 911–929.

Lippi, M. and L. Reichlin (1994), 'VAR Analysis, Non-Fundamental Representation, Blaschke Matrices', *Journal of Econometrics*, 63: 307–325.

Lüder, K. (2002), 'Government Budgeting and Accounting Reform in Germany', *OECD Journal on Budgeting*, 2, Supplement 1.

McCallum, B.T. (1984), 'Are Bond-financed Deficits Inflationary? A Ricardian Analysis,' *Journal of Political Economy*, 92: 123–135.

Marcellino, M. (2002), 'Some Stylised Facts on Non-Systematic Fiscal Policy in the Euro-Area', *CEPR Discussion Paper*, 3635.

Mayes, D. and M. Virén (2004), 'Pressures on the Stability and Growth Pact from Asymmetry in Policy', *Journal of European Public Policy*, 11(5): 781–797.

Mélitz, J. (2000), 'Some Cross-Country Evidence about Fiscal Policy Behaviour and the Consequences for EMU', *European Economy – Reports and Studies*, 2: 3–21.

Milesi-Ferretti, G. (2003), 'Good, Bad, or Ugly? On the Effects of Fiscal Rules with Creative Accounting', *Journal of Public Economics*, 88: 377–394.

Ministry of Finance of Sweden (2005), *Budget Statement, Economic and Budget Policy Guidelines*, Stockholm: Ministry of Finance.

Mitchell, J. (2003), 'Should We Be Surprised by the Unreliability of Real-time Output Gap Estimates? Density Estimates for the Eurozone', *NIESR Discussion Paper*, 225.

Mohr, M. (2005), 'A Trend-cycle (-season) Filter', *ECB Working Paper*, 499.

Mountford, A. and H. Uhlig (2002), 'What Are the Effects of Fiscal Policy Shocks?', *CEPR Discussion Paper*, 3338.

Musgrave, R. A. and P. B. Musgrave (1984), *Public Finance in Theory and Practice*, Singapore: McGraw-Hill.

Nelson, C. and C. Plosser (1982), 'Trends and Random Walks in Macroeconomic Time Series: Some Evidence and Implications', *Journal of Monetary Economics*, 10: 139–162.

OECD (2003), *Economic Outlook*, 74(2), Paris: OECD.

Office of Management and Budget (2006), *The Budget of the United States Government, Fiscal Year 2007*, Washington, DC: United States Government Printing Office.

Orphanides, A. and S. van Norden (2002), 'The Unreliability of Output-gap Estimates in Real Time', *Review of Economics and Statistics*, 84: 569–583.

Pappa, E. (2005), 'New Keynesian or RBC Transmission? The Effects of Fiscal Policy in Labour Markets', *CEPR Discussion Paper*, 5313.

Perotti, R. (2004), 'Public Investment: Another (Different) Look', *IGIER Working Paper*, 277.

——(2005), 'Estimating the Effects of Fiscal Policy in OECD Countries', *CEPR Working Paper*, 4842.

Quintos, C. E. (1995), 'Sustainability of the Deficit Process with Structural Shifts', *Journal of Business and Economic Statistics*, 13: 409–417.

Ramey, V. and M. Shapiro (1998), 'Costly Capital Reallocation and the Effects of Government Spending', *Carnegie Rochester Conference on Public Policy*, 48: 145–194.

Ravn, M. and H. Uhlig (2002), 'On Adjusting the HP-Filter for the Frequency of Observations', *Review of Economics and Statistics*, 84: 371–380.

Reynolds, A. (2004), 'Deficits, Interest Rates, and Taxes: Myths and Realities', *Cato Institute Policy Analysis*, 517.

Richardson, R. (1996), 'Opening and Balancing the Books: The New Zealand Experience', in 'Perspectives on Accrual Accounting', *International Federation of Accountants Occasional Paper*, 3, New York.

Rogoff, K. (2006), 'Impact of Globalization on Monetary Policy', in Federal Reserve Bank of Kansas City, *The New Economic Geography: Effects and Policy Implications*, Jackson Hole, Wyoming: Federal Reserve Bank of Kansas City.

Rubin, R. and J. Weisberg (2003), *In an Uncertain World: Tough Choices from Wall Street to Washington*, New York: Random House.

Samuelson, P. A. (1954), 'The Pure Theory of Public Expenditure', *Review of Economics and Statistics*, 36(4): 387–389.

Sarte, P. (1997), 'On the Identification of Structural Vector Autoregressions', *Federal Reserve Bank of Richmond Economic Review*, 83(3): 45–67.

Sims, C., J. Stock and M. Watson (1990), 'Inference in Time Series Models with Some Unit Roots', *Econometrica*, 58: 113–144.

Stock, J. and M. Watson (2003), 'Has the Business Cycle Changed and Why?', in M. Gertler and K. Rogoff (eds), *NBER Macroeconomics Annual*, 17, Cambridge, Mass.: MIT Press: 159–218.

Swedish National Financial Authority (Ekonomistyrningsverket) (2001), *Accrual Accounting in Swedish Central Government*, Stockholm: National Financial Authority.

Talvi, E. and C. Vegh (2000), 'Tax Base Variability and Procyclical Fiscal Policy', *NBER Working Paper*, 7499.

Tornell, A. and P. R. Lane (1999), 'The Voracity Effect', *American Economic Review*, 89: 22–46.

Trehan, B. and C. E. Walsh (1988), 'Common Trends, the Government's Budget Constraint and Revenue Smoothing', *Journal of Economic Dynamics and Control*, 12: 425–444.

——(1991), 'Testing Intertemporal Budget Constraints: Theory and Applications to US Federal Budget and Current Account Deficits', *Journal of Money, Credit and Banking*, 23: 206–223.

Tujula, M. and G. Wolswijk (2004), 'What Determines Fiscal Balances? An Empirical Investigation in Determinants of Changes in OECD Budget Balances', *ECB Working Paper*, 422.

Turnovsky, S. (2000), 'Fiscal Policy, Elastic Labour Supply and Endogenous Growth', *Journal of Monetary Economics*, 45: 185–210.

Van den Noord, P. (2000), 'The Size and Role of Automatic Fiscal Stabilizers in the 1990s and Beyond', *OECD Working Paper*, 230.

——(2002), 'Automatic Stabilisers in the 1990s and Beyond', in M. Buti, J. Von Hagen and C. Martinez-Mongay (eds), *The Behavior of Fiscal Authorities: Stabilisation, Growth and Institutions*, London: Palgrave: 130–148.

Von Hagen, J. and I. J. Harden (1995), 'Budget Processes and Commitment to Fiscal Discipline', *European Economic Review*, 39: 771–779.

——(1996), 'Budget Processes and Commitment to Fiscal Discipline', *IMF Working Paper*, 78.

Von Hagen, J. and G. Wolff (2005), 'What Do Deficits Tell Us about Debts? Empirical Evidence on Creative Accounting with Fiscal Rules', *Journal of Banking and Finance*, 30: 3259–3279.

Wierts, P., S. Deroose, E. Flores and A. Turrini (eds) (2006), *Fiscal Policy Surveillance in Europe*, Basingstoke: Palgrave Macmillan.

Wyplosz, C. (1999), 'Economic Policy Coordination in EMU: Strategies and Institutions', paper presented at the *German–French Economic Forum* in Bonn, 12 January 1999.

——(2002), 'Fiscal Policy: Institutions vs Rules', *CEPR Discussion Papers*, 3238.

Index

Abel et al. 76
accrual accounting 46–47, 54, 75, 153; evaluation of 53
Afonso 134, 146
ageing population 45
Alberola et al. 84, 87, 101–102
Alesina and Ardagna 134
Alesina and Bayoumi 147
Alesina and Perotti 47, 115
AMECO database 89, 163
ARIMA model 174
Auerbach and Kotlikoff 53, 75
Auerbach et al. 48, 54
Austria; consolidation packages 95; federal structure of government 92; fiscal policy in 89
automatic stabilizers 83, 117, 186; revenue intake 126; undermining of 84

Bai et al. 121
Balassone and Francese 44, 86–87, 95
Balassone and Franco 71, 153, 170
Balassone et al. 153, 169–171
Ballabriga 42
Ballabriga and Martinez-Mongay 8, 22
Banca d'Italia 158
Banco de Portugal 158
Barrell and Hurst 186, 188, 190
Barrell et al. 180, 187, 191
Barro 115
Baxter and King 114, 173
Bayesian Vector Autoregressive (BVAR) methodology 27
Belgium, output gap estimates 177
Bilbiie et al. 115
Blanchard 146, 186
Blanchard and Perotti 106, 115–117, 138, 140, 147, 150, 179, 191
Blanchard and Quah 106, 116, 140
Bohn 8, 10–11, 22
Boije 83, 105
Boije and Fischer 105
Bouthevillain and Quinet 146
Bouthevillain et al. 136

Braconier and Forsfält 87, 105
Brandner and Diebalek 84
Brandner et al. 87
Bruneau and De Bandt 146–147
Brunila and Martinez-Mongay 7
Brunila et al. 186
budget balance 47; adjustment for demand shocks 188; asymmetric cyclical behaviour 95; automatic stabilizer component 83; core balance 83; cyclical component of 87; cyclically adjusted 83, 103, 149; decomposing of 88, 103; levels of 12; structural 1, 87
budget deficit 7, 11, 180, 183; cyclically adjusted 173–174; impacts of output 186; relation to output gap 184; uncertainty bounds 190; uncertainty of cyclical adjustment 179, 184
budget elasticities, time variation of 136
budget measures, the information provision role of 48
Buiter and Grafe 8
business cycle shock 117
Buti et al. 7–8, 85, 161–163, 165, 170
Butterworth filters 174

Canova 174
Canova and Pappa 146
Canzoneri et al. 8, 11
cash-accrual differences 169
Cavallo 146
Chouraqui et al. 146
Christiano et al. 120
Christoffersen 179
Claeys 147
Coeuré and Pisani-Ferry 8
Cohen and Follette 146
Consumer Price Index (CPI) 185
covariance matrix 117
Cutler 75
cyclical conditions 1, 44; fiscal response to 16

Dalsgaard and de Serres 146
De Arcangelis and Lamartina 129

debt, definition of 154
debt accounting in EU15 11, 15, 34–35
debt accumulation, response of the primary surplus to 13, 27
debt developments, in EU15 11
debt levels 8, 11, 41–42; reduction of 14
debt stocks, reaction of the primary balance to 21
debt sustainability pact 8
debt-to-GDP ratio 16, 36, 43, 45, 74, 161; changes in 14
deficit, definition of 154
deficit-to-GDP ratio 86
Denis et al. 174, 190
Denmark, reliability of fiscal data 172
Diamond 75
Diebalek et al. 102
Doan et al. 42
Domar 43
Dynamic Stochastic General Equilibrium (DSGE) models 106, 114

ECOFIN Council 8
Economic and Monetary Union (EMU) 7, 45, 109; compliance with requirements 71; fiscal framework of 107; fiscal indicators 153, 165; fiscal pact 190; fiscal rules 153; second stage of 13
economic cycle 83
economic integration, effects on fiscal behaviour of 24
Economic Policy Committee 71
employment, equilibrium level of 190
EU benchmark 58
euro, purchasing power of 45
European Central Bank (ECB) 45, 185
European Commission 3, 7, 14, 41–42, 78, 85, 87, 89, 109, 119, 146, 149, 153, 159, 174; output gaps 129; reporting of fiscal data to 169
European Statistics Code of Practice 169
European System of Accounts (ESA) 153
Eurostat 58, 60, 65, 74, 77, 153, 157–160, 169–170
Excessive Deficit Procedure (EDP) 7, 106–107; implementation of 153; regulation of statistics 169
expenditures, non-indexation of 105

Fatás and Mihov 87, 135, 147
Faust and Leeper 120, 150
Federal Accounting Standards Advisory Board 75
Feldstein 46
financial assets, identification of transactions 165
Finn 146
fiscal adjustment 65

fiscal convergence criteria 171
fiscal data, times series properties of 10
fiscal developments 11
fiscal discipline 7, 85; deterioration of 31
fiscal framework, European 85; implementation of 171
fiscal gimmickry 154; incentives 163; reducing 165
fiscal imbalance 49; accruals 65; estimates of 60; evaluation of 54; infinite-horizon calculation of 55
fiscal imbalance (FI), budget allocation component of 63–64; demographic component of 62–63; EU countries (percent of GDP) 61–62; indicator 79
fiscal impulse 47
fiscal indicators 1, 79; quality of 171
fiscal policy, automatic stabilization through 86; behaviour over time 84; contribution to output variation 128; degree of neutralizing automatic stabilizers 138; discretionary 46, 83; economic indicator of 114; endogenous growth theory of 141; non-Keynesian effects of 115; productivity growth and 121; stabilization role of 7; sustainable 31; transmission channels 121
fiscal reaction functions 8, 11, 31, 43–44
fiscal rules, effectiveness of 171
fiscal shocks 88, 115; short-term vs long-term 117
fiscal surveillance, in the EU 1, 171
Forni and Momigliano 86–87, 95, 102
France, fiscal expansions and contractions 134; fiscal policy responses 126; general government balance of 107; output gap 109; output gap estimates 175; reliability of fiscal data 172; spending elasticities 138

Galí 119
Galí and Perotti 47, 84–85, 87, 92, 101, 138
Galí et al. 115
Gaussianity 178
Gavin and Perotti 85
generational accounting 48; evaluation of 54
generational imbalance 49; evaluation of 56
Germany, fiscal expansions and contractions 134; fiscal policy responses 126; general government balance of 107; output gap 109; output gap estimates 175; reliability of fiscal data 172; spending elasticities 138
Giavazzi and Pagano 115
Giavazzi et al. 115, 120
Giorno et al. 146
Girouard and André 86, 114, 136, 138, 146–147
Gokhale 75–77
Gokhale and Smetters 56–57, 65, 75–77

Gokhale et al. 75
Gordo Mora and Nogueira Martins 105
government balance; in EU15 32–33
government debt 9, 11, 27, 41, 76; accounting of 11; accumulation of 11; changes in 154, 165; development in 13; expected return on 10; interest rate on 16
government investment 86
Greece; deficit revisions in 159; reliability of fiscal data 172
gross government debt; implicit interest rates of 34
growth dividend 13–14, 42

Hallerberg and Strauch 84
Hamilton and Flavin 10
Harvey and Trimbur 174, 191
Harvey–Trimbur cycle 174
Haveman 75
Hercowitz and Strawczynski 86
Hillier 75
Hjelm 146
HM Treasury 47
Hodrick–Prescott filter 109, 129, 174

IMF 85, 146
Indicateurs de progrès de l'économie française 77
information asymmetry 169
Institute of Economic Research (WIFO) 102
interest expenditure 12, 41; ratio to GDP of 13
interest payment; in EU15 32–33
intertemporal budget balance 53
intertemporal budget constraint (IBC) 9
intertemporal marginal rate of substitution 10
Italy, deficit revisions in 157; output gap estimates 175; reliability of fiscal data 172

Jaeger 84
Japan, debt development in 11

Kalman filter 88, 174, 178
Kamps 146
Katterl and Köhler-Töglhofer 92
King and Rebelo 115
King and Watson 120
King et al. 119
Kneller et al. 116
Kotlikoff 75
Kwiatkowski et al. 36

Lane 86–87, 138
Latin America, fiscal policy in 85
life-cycle stages 51
lifetime net payments 49
lifetime net tax rate 49
Linnemann and Schabert 115
Lippi and Reichlin 115

Lisbon Strategy 106
long-term budgetary conditions, reporting of 65
long-term fiscal indicator 46
long-term sustainability 1, 7, 48, 51, 71, 73, 78, 119
Lüder 75
Luxembourg, reliability of fiscal data 172

Maastricht criteria 13, 42
Maastricht rules 107, 121, 134
Maastricht Treaty 9, 11, 24, 45, 83, 106, 171
Marcellino 138
Mayes and Virén 86–87
McCallum 43
medium-term objectives (MTOs) 1, 8
Mélitz 86–87, 179
Milesi-Ferretti 160, 170
Mitchell 174, 178–179
monetary union, objective of 45
Mountford and Uhlig 146
Musgrave and Musgrave 43

National Institute Global Model 185
Nelson and Plosser 119
Netherlands, output gap estimates 177

OECD 22, 86–87, 89, 95, 109, 114, 118–119, 135–136, 138, 146; fiscal policies in 86; output gaps 129
old-age dependency ratio 78
Orphanides and van Norden 174–175, 177, 191
output gap, error bounds 190; estimates of 173; measuring the uncertainty of 178; production function approach 174; reaction of the primary surplus to 21; real-time estimation of 174; uncertainty 178

Pappa 146
permanent balance rule 8
Perotti 146, 150
policy actions, non-systematic discretionary 16
Ponzi financing schemes 9
Portugal, deficit revisions in 158; fiscal expansions and contractions 134; fiscal policy responses 126; general government balance of 107; output gap 109; reliability of fiscal data 172; spending elasticities 138
potential growth 116; productivity shocks 116
primary surplus, in EU15 32–33; posterior distribution of 28
primary surplus lag 16
privatizations proceeds 16
production function, parameters of 190
public debt 7
public finance, long-term sustainability 116, 140; sustainability of 106

Quandt–Andrews likelihood ratio test 121
QUEST 186
Quintos 10

Ramey and Shapiro 146
random walk 88
Ravn and Uhlig 146
Real Business Cycle models 114
real discount rate 60
Richardson 75

S2 sustainability gap indicator 78
Sarte 120
semi-structural VAR 115
shock multiplier 186
short-horizon fiscal measure 47
Sims et al. 120
simultaneity bias 22
skewness 114
Spain; fiscal expansions and contractions 134; fiscal policy responses 126; general government balance of 107; output gap 109; output gap estimates 175; spending elasticities 138
Stability and Growth Pact (SGP) 1, 7, 45, 78, 83, 106, 109, 171; application of 135; preventive arm 1; revised 1, 45, 103, 106, 116, 140, 154
Stock and Watson 121
stock-flow adjustment (SFA) 13, 161; debt-specific 154; deficit-specific 154
structural balance, variation in 119
structural breaks 120
structural deficit 118, 150
structural shocks 150
structural VAR model 109, 149

sustainability; ad hoc vs model-based 8; definition of 9
sustainability condition 16, 24
Sweden, reliability of fiscal data 172
Swedish National Financial Authority 75

Talvi and Vegh 85
tax and expenditure rules 104
tax poor elements of demand 173
tax rates, changes in 184
tax receipts, random variations 185
tax rich elements of demand 173
Tornell and Lane 85
total factor productivity 174
transversality condition (TC) 9
Trehan and Walsh 10
trend-cycle decomposition 149
Tujula and Wolswijk 86–87
Turnovsky 115, 141

unemployment benefits 118
unfunded obligation measure 46
unit root tests 10–11, 36
United Kingdom, budget deficits in 182
US Congressional Budget Office (CBO) 79
USA, debt development in 11

van den Noord 86, 146
von Hagen and Wolff 165

white noise 22
Wierts et al. 46
Working Group on Ageing Populations (AWG) 71
Wyplosz 86, 101, 179

eBooks – at www.eBookstore.tandf.co.uk

A library at your fingertips!

eBooks are electronic versions of printed books. You can store them on your PC/laptop or browse them online.

They have advantages for anyone needing rapid access to a wide variety of published, copyright information.

eBooks can help your research by enabling you to bookmark chapters, annotate text and use instant searches to find specific words or phrases. Several eBook files would fit on even a small laptop or PDA.

NEW: Save money by eSubscribing: cheap, online access to any eBook for as long as you need it.

Annual subscription packages

We now offer special low-cost bulk subscriptions to packages of eBooks in certain subject areas. These are available to libraries or to individuals.

For more information please contact webmaster.ebooks@tandf.co.uk

We're continually developing the eBook concept, so keep up to date by visiting the website.

www.eBookstore.tandf.co.uk